AgriSelling

W. DAVID DOWNEY

MARILYN HOLSCHUH

MICHAEL A. JACKSON

Edited by Kathleen Erickson

Library of Congress Card Number 82-73827

ISBN 0-932250-34-3

Published by Doane Agricutural Services Company
11701 Borman Drive, Suite 100
St. Louis, Missouri 63146
800-535-2342

AgriSelling

W. David Downey
Professor
Purdue University
West Lafayette, IN

Marilyn Holschuh
Vice President
Agri Business Group, Inc.
Indianapolis, IN

Michael A. Jackson
President
Agri Business Group, Inc.
Indianapolis, IN

Edited by Kathleen Erickson

The authors acknowledge the significant contributions of colleagues, co-workers and clients who shared their ideas and experiences - many of which are woven into the fabric of this book.

We especially thank those on the Agri Business Group staff for their diligent and commitment in the design, layout and preparation of the manuscript, for printing.

We dedicate this book to the professional salespeople from whom we have learned so much over the years and to our families for their selfless support and understanding during the completion of the book.

Preface

Agriculture is undergoing radical change. Consumers are demanding more assurance that their food is safe and healthy; that the environment is preserved; and that animals are treated humanely. Increasingly complex regulations impact nearly all farm production decisions. The reduction of farm subsidies around the world has increased the volatility of markets - and increased risks for farmers and agricultural businesses alike. Sweeping new technologies force farmers to make complex and costly decisions. Farms are rapidly consolidating into fewer, larger, and more sophisticated business units that are far more demanding of their suppliers and those through whom they market their products. Competition among those serving farmers has become fierce.

All of this brings new importance to the role of the agricultural salesperson. Farmers need solutions to difficult production and marketing problems - often utilizing complex products, new technologies and new communication methods. Traditionally, it was enough to have a good product, a pleasant personality, and to work hard. But today's highly competitive market has thrust agricultural suppliers and marketers into intense battles for fewer, larger customers. And the ag salesperson is on the front lines of the battle.

Salespeople are more important to farmers, too. Recent research makes it clear that today's commercial farmers are depending more and more on salespeople to bring them solutions to problems - often involving complex technology and business principles. Agricultural salespeople must possess a wide range of technical, business, and communication skills to be successful in this highly competitive environment.

The ability to effectively serve today's increasingly sophisticated and demanding commercial producer's demands highly effective communication and problem - solving skills. Professional agricultural salespeople must be well grounded in the fundamentals of identifying customer needs and effectively communicating solutions to problems utilizing complex agricultural technologies and business tools. That is what this book is about. It provides a solid base of highly effective selling tools that have been proven to be very useful in finding and communicating solutions to farmers' and agribusinesses' problems.

The selling profession is also rapidly gaining stature on the campuses of agricultural colleges and universities. Many schools are recognizing that a majority of today's agricultural graduates, regardless of their major, find their career entry point to be agricultural sales. Farm input industries and agricultural marketing firms are aggressively searching for agricultural graduates who have an understanding of an appreciation for the selling profession. The response has been the development of sales and marketing courses at many colleges and universities.

Agribusinesses also have recognized the growing importance of the sales function in marketing their products and services to their customers. Many agribusinesses routinely focus extensive resources on recruiting, training, and developing sophisticated field marketers who can more effectively communicate their increasingly complex technology to farmers. Today, field sales people are often "empowered" with far greater authority to tailor a unique "value bundle" for individual customers. And customers expect to do business with someone who knows how to get to the root of their problems and find solutions.

This book is intended for the student in the classroom who is interested in learning the tools necessary to enter the agricultural selling profession; for the new ag salesperson who is looking for ways to become more effective; and for the experienced salesperson who wants to refresh their basic selling skills. It offers selling techniques and methods that are proven effective with farmers and agribusinesses - and demonstrates the effectiveness of the methods with examples from many current agriselling professionals.

There are many good books and articles on selling and their concepts certainly apply to agriculture. But there are few that deal with the uniquenesses of the agricultural marketplace. This book addresses these uniquenesses by providing numerous examples of salespeople and situations from many facets of agriculture across North America. Real life illustrations from highly successful agricultural salespeople from many different ag industries are woven into the fabric of this book for the purpose of helping the reader understand ideas more easily and to demonstrate the true value of the concepts.

This book is written by those who know and understand agriculture - and who have worked closely with field salespeople for many years in virtually every agricultural industry and at every level. You will not only see agricultural examples throughout this book. You will also recognize the important nuances that are so important in dealing with the agricultural sector. And you will learn directly from a wide variety of highly successful agrisalespeople who share their experiences, beliefs, and techniques with you.

This book is not intended to be a model for the "right way" to sell. Indeed, its underlying premise is that there is no one "right way" to do it. Each company, each person, and each situation are greatly different. The concepts and methods in this book are intended to provide the fundamentals on which each individual can adapt to their own unique personality, style, and situation.

Finally, the underlying philosophy of this book is that agriselling is, and always must be, problem solving - for mutual benefit of both the customer and the agribusiness. Professional agriselling involves a combination of technical solutions to complex problems using sales and marketing tools. This is an approach that can generate an ethical and profitable result for both the buyer and the seller.

If you have experiences you would like to share or questions you would like to ask, feel free to contact the authors of this book directly. We are anxious to continue to learn from professionals.

TABLE OF CONTENTS

Part One

What is Selling and How People Buy

Do you remember when you were in the third grade and the teacher asked what everyone wanted to become? Very few people said they wanted to become a salesperson. Yet in agricultural selling, your job is one of the most important in the industry. Agriculture is a business where technology and innovation happen quickly. The business today is significantly different than twenty years ago. And in another twenty years, it will have changed again. Agriculture is an industry in a constant state of evolution. Some of the most exciting new products *in any industry* can be found in agriculture-and they are being adopted by thousands of small and large independent business owners, across a worldwide geography. What does selling have to do with all this progress?

Until somebody sells something, nothing happens.

Chapter One

What is Agri Selling?

Learning Objectives:
Upon completion of this chapter, you will be able to:
1. describe some of the rewards of being an agricultural salesperson;
2. list several key skills that contribute to success as a salesperson;
3. explain the role of planning in a successful sales effort;
4. give one example of a "best practice" for at least two of the selling process steps.

Agri Selling

Imagine a career where your primary responsibility is to bring people the solutions they need to their business problems...where you are paid to help people fulfill their potential...where you are rewarded when you help businesses prosper...and where you get to set your own schedule most of the time.

Sound too good to be true? Are you a fast-track consultant, dashing through airports with a cell phone glued to your ear, nicely off-setting that distinguished streak of gray at your temples? Maybe. But you could just as easily be a bright, young, committed agricultural salesperson, with only one year on the job.

It sounds like a great career...and it is. The keys to success in agricultural selling are there for anyone with enough persistence and commitment to their customers' success. They are there for you, too – if you are willing to learn how to use them and to use them consistently.

This book approaches agri selling from three perspectives:

- Part I: What is Selling and How People Buy
- Part II: Customer Value and Your Role
- Part III: Effective Selling Skills

The best people to explain what selling means are salespeople. In this chapter, we have gathered a "panel" of successful salespeople from across the industry. They are male and female, younger and older. Some have many years of experience; others have only a few. They sell everything from swine antibiotics to sod. And yet, despite all of their differences, they have a very consistent understanding of agricultural selling. Throughout this book, they'll share their experiences, challenges and "tips" with you. Let's begin by introducing you to them, and then asking them to define "agri selling."

The Panel

Larry Barmann
American Cyanamid
Marketing Specialist, IMI-Corn
Red Oak, Iowa
Education: B.S., Industrial Arts Education,
Northwest Missouri State University, 1976
Selling Since 1984

Larry was raised on a farm in Northwest
Missouri. He started his career experience
teaching high school industrial arts. In 1983, he joined American Cyanamid as a
sales representative in Red Oak, Iowa, and in 1996 began his current job as
Marketing Specialist, IMI-corn. Larry is very dedicated to continuing education,
saying, "There's always more to learn—more to know. Keeping up on continuing
education efforts really benefits me, my customers and my company." Larry is
CCA-certified and a member of several Iowa corn, soybean and agribusiness
organizations.

Earl Bell
ELANCO Animal Health, Eli Lilly & Company
Sales Representative
Rocky Mount, North Carolina
Education: B.S.A., General Agriculture,
University of Arkansas, 1970
Selling since 1970

Earl lived on a family farm in Montrose,
Arkansas, raising row crops, cattle, hogs and
chickens. Earl earned a Bachelor of Science in agriculture from the University of
Arkansas. He took his elective courses in psychology because he hoped for an
agricultural sales career. Following college, Earl went to work for Elanco Animal
Health Company in Memphis, Tennessee, as a sales representative. In 1971 he
moved to Charlotte, North Carolina, as a sales rep detailing Elanco products in
the veterinary industry. In 1973 Earl created a swine and veterinary sales territory
in Eastern North Carolina where he worked for ten years. He moved to
Indianapolis, Indiana for two years as an Elanco package products marketing
manager. From 1984 to the present, Earl has again called North Carolina home as
an ELANCO sales representative.

Earl says, "Most urban people don't understand how technological innovations are used to increase productivity at the farm level. This makes agriculture an exciting and challenging industry to be in. Globally, the U.S. farming industry is one of the most efficient because of technology utilization. This is why we enjoy the greatest variety and lowest food prices in the world." Earl believes in working within one's industry to enhance its productivity. He holds leadership positions in the North Carolina Pork Council and was 1998 Council President.

Bill Brockett
Virginia Beef Corporation
Owner and President
Haymarket, Virginia
Education: B.S., Animal Science,
Oklahoma State University, 1965
Selling Since 1965

Bill comes from a family farm in Atlantic County, New Jersey. They raised 400 acres of vegetables and 50 head of beef cattle. His professional career began with Virginia Beef Corporation, right out of college. He started as a general farm manager, became a vice president in 1968 and became president in 1972. In 1978, Bill became VBC owner and remains so today. Bill says, "Commodities markets are a fascinating reality. Virginia Beef Corporation is a totally hedged operation so we must be on top of the market on a daily basis. With the ever-changing global economy and markets, the salesperson's challenge will become even more demanding in this area. Learn as much as you can about global economies, markets, monetary systems and politics because they will directly affect your business." Bill is involved with the National Cattlemen's Beef Association and is a national policy committee member.

Stacy Dunn
AgrEvo USA Company
Sales Representative
Indianapolis, Indiana
Education: B.S., Agriculture,
Purdue University, 1996
Selling Since 1996

Stacy grew up on a small farm, raising horses
and dairy feeder calves. She believes that her ag
sales internships for two summers were highly beneficial...especially in
competing for jobs among peers. She was hired as the first AgrEvo sales rep in
Indiana. She says, "It has been great to see my company be accepted and grow. I
now have a 12-county territory and about 45 regular retailers and seed
companies as customers." Stacy plans to acquire CCA certification and is a
member of state seed trade and plant food associations.

Tom Giese
Cenex/Land O' Lakes
Livestock Production Specialist
Canby, Minnesota
Education: B.S., Agricultural Economics,
Minor in Business Administration,
North Dakota State University, 1988
Selling Since 1988

Tom was raised on a Minnesota hay and grain, dairy, hog and horse operation. He
joined Land O' Lakes right out of NDSU, had some company-based training
courses, and then "hit the field." Tom really enjoys selling. He strives to help
develop the customer's business through innovative ideas and by educating them
about opportunities. Tom says, "That's kind of my whole background – just taking
care of people. I try to find out what they do best and work with them." He's an
active member of several livestock associations.

Martin Harry
BASF Canada, Inc.
Technical Sales Representative
Ingersoll, Ontario, Canada
Education: B.S., Agricultural Economics,
University of Guelph, 1982
Selling Since 1982

Martin was raised on a Trenton, Ontario grain and livestock farm. His selling career includes three years with Elanco selling ag chemicals in Saskatchewan; one year with Syntex selling animal health products; and then ten years with Sandoz. He is currently with BASF, selling crop protection. Martin says, "Agri selling is my career. I would not know what else to do. I came from a farm and wanted to stay in agriculture. Practicality and being from the farm have all been key in helping me relate to people." His active leadership roles in Ontario crop protection and agronomy organizations help him stay current on issues and technology impacting his customers.

Donna Berry Hines
Pfizer Animal Health
Swine Industry Specialist
Quincy, Michigan
Education: B.S., Agricultural Sales and
Marketing, Purdue University, 1991
Selling Since 1991

Donna grew up on a 120 sow farrow-to-finish operation. Her family also raised 1500 acres of corn and soybeans, near Greencastle, Indiana. She worked throughout high school and college at a 600 sow farrow-to-finish operation. Her sales career with Pfizer began right out of college as a sales associate for 6 months. For a year and a half, she was an associate sales representative before moving into her current status as a swine industry specialist. Donna says, "In that first seven years, I lived in four different cities and states in order to accept promotions. I started in Kansas City, Missouri, then took positions in Lincoln, Nebraska; Minneapolis, Minnesota; and now, Quincy, Michigan. To be promoted, you need to be mobile." Donna is an associate member of the state pork organization.

Jim Jackson
Land O'Lakes, Inc.
Swine Program Manager
Indianapolis, Indiana
Education: B.S., Animal Science,
Ohio State University; 1980
Selling Since 1980

Before, during, and after graduating from
college, Jim worked on grain and livestock
operations, with heavy involvement in care and management of swine and
cattle. He spent six years as a multi-county feed sales specialist; two years as a
regional representative, managing a number of feed specialists; and ten years as
a swine program manager before his current role managing swine programs for
two regional cooperatives. Jim says, "My approach to ag sales and my customers
has always focused on professionalism. Since starting in sales, I wanted to make
my emphasis very technical and focus on being very objective. Ag selling is a
business attitude and professional acumen by which you can live." Jim stays
active in Ohio and Indiana pork organizations.

Wesley McCoy
Dow AgroSciences
Senior Account Manager, Retired
Edina, Minnesota
Education: B.S., Animal Science,
North Dakota State University, 1948
Selling Since 1953

A North Dakota small grain farm was home to
Wes in early years. As a 4-H'er he received a Sears Roebuck scholarship to attend
NDSU. After two years as an ag instructor, Wes became the County Agriculture
Agent for Swift County in Benson, Minnesota. After four years there, he joined
the (then) Dow Chemical Company, where he had an active career spanning 37
years. Wes says, "The bottom line is - you have got to help people – got to want to
and enjoy helping people. You help your dealer, that helps the farmer. That's
what's important. That's why we do this." Wes has been very active in state crop
production retailer organizations, including holding several leadership roles.

Ray McLaughlin
Blue SEAL Feeds
Dairy Product Manager
Dairy Manager at Bow, New Hampshire Facility
Londonderry, New Hampshire
Education: A.S., Animal Husbandry, State
University of New York, Canton Agricultural
and Technical College, 1981
Selling Since 1981

Ray's small dairy farm background helped him learn what he needed to know to get jobs on neighboring, large dairy operations. Those jobs helped pay his way through college, and helped him realize how much he wanted to stay involved in agriculture. Ray says, "I always had the goal of farming, and when I had an offer from Blue SEAL Feeds, I found that feed sales seemed to be a good niche for me. I like it for the challenges, and that's what still drives me. It drives me because you are always on the cutting edge with industry leaders." Ray spent five years as a direct feed sales rep, and then 18 months as an assistant area manager, feed sales. For six years he was a dairy feed sales rep, and for two and a half years, he was a dairy nutritionist and sales rep before becoming Dairy Products Manager as well as Dairy Manager at Blue SEAL's Bow, New Hampshire Facility. Ray reads sales and dairy industry periodicals at least six hours per week.

Aaron McWhorter
Sports Turf Company, Inc. and
North Georgia Turf, Inc.
Owner and President
Whitesburg, Georgia
Education: B.A., History, State
University of West Georgia, 1970;
M.Ed, State University of West Georgia, 1989
Selling Since 1986

Aaron was raised on the family dairy farm in Franklin, Georgia. After two years as a high school coach and teacher, he spent several years in farming, first as owner and operator of a dairy farm, and then as a row crop farmer. He owned and operated a Ford Tractor dealership for three years before becoming owner and president of a sod farm and eventually his own company, focusing on production of sod for construction of athletic fields. Education was important to good selling is good educating. But before you can effectively bring a solution to a customer, you have to be well-educated yourself. Then, being able to organize that information and using it for the customer is effective education." Aaron is a member of several sod and turf grass associations, as well as sports contracting associations.

Ron Pettet
ProAgCo
Sales - Petroleum and General Feed
Logansport, Indiana
Education: B.S., Vocational Agriculture,
Purdue University; 1971
M.S., Animal Science, Purdue University
Selling Since 1972

Ron grew up on a grain and livestock farm near Remington, Indiana. He began his professional career as a Vo-Ag teacher in Bedford, Indiana for two years, followed by another two years teaching in Tipton, Indiana. He began agri selling as a swine production specialist for two years. He then became a district feed specialist for four years, and spent fifteen years as a regional sales manager. Currently, Ron is a sales representative in petroleum and general feed. "I think some really important essential items about successful selling that have influenced my career are these: first, everything is selling; second, when you are with customers, or even those in the community who associate you with your role, there is a professionalism in how you act that helps build relationships and trust. Building those relationships and trust is what helps me get the essential information I need to better serve that person's needs." Ron has maintained a herd of Simmental beef cattle at his home for the last twenty two years.

Dan Puck
Dow AgroSciences
Sales Representative
Madison, Wisconsin
Education: B.S., Agronomy,
Iowa State University, 1986
Selling Since 1987

Dan is the fifth -generation Puck to grow up on the family farm in Eastern Iowa. After selling for Dow for three years in Appleton, Wisconsin, he moved to Madison where he's been for the last eight years as a sales rep. Dan says, "You have to have the kind of disposition and personality for agri selling—you easily warm up to people, you enjoy new people, you are not intimidated by that. Good salespeople may even consider it somewhat of a challenge to go out and endear yourself to people who may be two or three times your senior. If you've got the fundamental people skills, you can sell and continue to learn how to sell better and better all the time." Dan has been a Certified Crop Advisor since 1994 and is a member of his state fertilizer and chemical association.

Debbie Stiles
BASF Canada, Inc.
Senior Marketing Associate, Soybean Products
Guelph, Ontario
Education: B.S.C., Agricultural Business,
University of Guelph; 1989
Selling Since 1990

Debbie grew up on the family dairy farm in Marmora, Ontario. Following college, she joined Sandoz as a technical sales representative. She attended a French Immersion program and sold in a territory in Eastern Ontario and Southwestern Quebec for three years. With BASF, Debbie was a technical sales representative before becoming a Senior Marketing Associate in Soybean Products. Debbie says, "Customers look for one main thing in their salesperson—professionalism. My customers look for a salesperson who is organized, very professional, who understands their business, while at same time can empathize and relate with them on the personal level." Debbie maintains CCPC certification and makes a dedicated effort to maintain technical competencies through reading appropriate trade literature.

Bill Stuever
Consolidated Nutrition, L.C.
Regional Director of Operations
Springfield, Missouri
Education: B.S., Animal Science,
Oklahoma State University, 1970
Selling Since 1973

Bill's family dairy farm in Virginia was a good background for a career involvement with livestock. Following college, he owned and managed beef livestock operations, merchandising purebred cattle in Norman, Oklahoma. Bill then spent five years as a district sales manager, six years as a regional sales manager for feed, six years as a marketing manager for beef feed and is currently director of operations for feed manufacturing. Bill says, "When I began selling, I knew how to spell the word salesperson, but that's about it. That's the way I began to make my living. Companies, schools, and universities need to prepare people to be good salespeople. It is extremely important to understand the basics of sound agri selling. Selling is a big opportunity for any individual who wants to stay involved in agriculture, especially considering the income and opportunity for growth in the sales and sales management areas." Bill is active in new business development for his company and is a board member for the local Victims of Violent Crimes Center.

David Suttle
WorldCom Advanced Networks
Director, Network Channel Sales
Hilliard, Ohio
Education: B.S., Business Administration,
Ohio State University, 1979
Selling Since 1981

Growing up, David spent his summers working alongside his cousins at the family cattle farms in Northwest Indiana and near Ashland, Ohio. He was a sales engineer for two years with Toledo Scale; a salesperson for four years involved in sports promotion and event marketing, and since 1985 has worked for CompuServe (which in 1998 became WorldCom Advanced Networks) selling value-added data communications services from Hilliard, Ohio. David says, "Selling is a lot of hard work. It is the preparation of understanding who your prospects are, why they're good prospects and how you're going to be able to put a credible business case in front of them. Selling shouldn't be viewed as something you learn once. It's a constant evolution. Industry changes, product changes, competition changes, regulations changes—they all affect your ability to sell and the way in which you will sell. Continuing education is critical. That feeds your creativity. Creativity is critical no matter what type of sales you are in or where." David is a voracious reader of trade, industry and business periodicals.

Donald Upton
United Cooperative Farmers, Inc.
General Manager
Fitchburg, Massachusetts
Education: B.S., Poultry Science,
University of Massachusetts, 1963
Selling Since 1962

Donald was an active 4-H'er with poultry and gardening projects. He continued as a 4-H leader for five years. He began his professional selling career as a sales rep for a major agricultural pharmaceutical company, remaining for seven years. For the next six years he was vice president for sales and marketing for a major egg production operation. Currently and for over twenty three years, Donald has been general manager responsible for all sales of the animal feed manufacturer United Cooperative Farmers. Donald says, "I guess I get the most satisfaction out of watching people grow in the organization. We've had so many good people and it is so much fun to put the team together and watch them work and watch them come up with the ideas. There's a lot of joy and pleasure in trying to hire the right person, train the right person, and let them have the responsibility. I think in selling, it's great to see personal growth in employees." Donald is involved in numerous Northeast associations and organizations.

Rob Vincent
American Cyanamid
Sales Representative
Iowa City, Iowa
Education: B.S., Animal Science,
Iowa State University, 1990
Selling Since 1992

Rob grew up on a Carlisle, Iowa farm, raising sheep as 4-H projects and working for neighboring farmers. Out of college, Rob joined American Cyanamid in the Crop Protection Products department. He says, "When I first started, selling was not at all what I thought it would be. Selling to me was walking into a clothing store, and a retailer asking you what you were looking for. It's a lot more involved. The planning, the knowledge you have to have of yourself, your products, your customers, your competitors, is critical. Know your products backward and forward so you can know how to fit the customer's need. Also, instead of a walking encyclopedia, be a walking ear...the more you listen, the more successful you'll be." Rob is active in Cyanamid's Agriculture Legislative Affairs Committee and internal technical training programs such as Cyanamid Technical Certification, which provides continuing education in all aspects of the agronomic industry. He is a member of numerous agricultural crop and business associations.

Debra Warman
American Cyanamid
Master Sales Representative
Minnesota Lake, Minnesota
Education: B.S., Entomology,
University of Minnesota, 1979
Selling Since 1979

Raised in a rural community, Deb had a strong interest in entomology, a field in which she pursued a degree at the University of Minnesota. Following graduation, she was hired by Cyanamid, whose main products at that time were insecticides. Selling became her passion and after sixteen years with the company, a career choice of sales, and an exemplary sales record, Deb became a Master Sales Representative, a position viewed by American Cyanamid as a leadership and mentoring position. "I really enjoy fostering growth in other salespeople. It is a very satisfying part of what I do," says Deb. She maintains CCA certification and is an avid reader of industry and trade publications. Deb says, "You cannot be an informed sales rep without reading. Agriculture is always changing. You need to use as many sources of information as you can. Continuing education not only keeps you abreast of developments in the field, but increases your overall professionalism."

Bob Woods
Penn Jersey Products, Inc.
New Holland, Pennsylvania
Sales Supervisor
Education: B.S., Agricultural Education,
Pennsylvania State University, 1972;
M.S.Ed, Temple University, 1975
Selling Since 1979

Bob was born and raised on a 50-60 cow dairy farm in Franklin County, Pennsylvania. The family also raised corn and alfalfa. He began his professional career teaching Vocational Agriculture, Farm Management and Agribusiness in the state's top agriculture program at Garden Spot High School. He also was director of cooperative education for the vo-ag program which placed high school seniors in the ag industry. In 1979, Bob joined Penn Jersey as a sales supervisor. Bob says, "I sell Harvestores. It is a big investment for the long term. They last. Sometimes it's hard to understand that this silo is more expensive than their whole farm was way back when. You've got to understand what the customer might be *thinking and feeling* about purchasing an item like this. It is here you have to do your job well as the seller who has the customer's best interest at heart. I really love selling."

Selling in agriculture means solving problems and uncovering opportunities, by helping your customer select and use products and services that meet business goals. Over the years, the definition of selling has changed. And with this change, the type of person who enjoys selling, and is successful selling, has changed also.

In the past, product selling was predominant. The salesperson had a quota and a good pitch and needed little else. The salesperson sold products *whether or not* they were the best choice for the customer. In fact, the less the product was needed, the more aggressively it was sold. That type of salesperson was never very popular in agriculture, and today there are (thankfully) very few of them left.

The next type of seller we saw was a relationship seller. This person stressed the tie between salesperson and buyer—and in agriculture, it often was a close community or family tie. Relationships *are* important to successful selling...but they are no longer enough alone. A salesperson who is great at building relationships, but doesn't have the business or technical knowledge to help customers increase profits, will have a tough time today.

Today's <u>professional agri seller</u> focuses on meeting the needs of customers. By meeting needs through products, services and technical knowledge, the seller earns the right to return to each customer and sell again. Over time, the knowledge of the customer as a person and as a business owner or manager creates the relationship of a trusted consultant—and a lot of personal loyalty.

Selling is important to the customer, because new products, services, ideas and solutions come to the customer through the efforts of salespeople. Selling is important to the business, because sales provide a consistent source of income for your business. This income makes everything possible—from a regular paycheck for you to the investment in products and technologies for the future.

The Rewards of Selling

What does it feel like to be an agricultural salesperson? What are the rewards? Why do people choose that profession in the first place? Let's hear what top salespeople have to say.

Bob Woods

In 1979, I started selling Harvestores. I found it was probably as much work as being a teacher—if you wanted to be good. I have been doing it from that time on and I've loved every minute of it. I've always said, "If you don't enjoy what you are doing, you better get out of it!" I tell the people I work with, "I don't have to sell Harvestores to make a living; I just really like it, and it's been very, very good to me. I have been offered a lot of other jobs. But, I like what I do. And I don't have to go to the city to do it. In life you can be anything you want to be, as long as you put your best foot forward and go get it. I would like to sell Harvestores as long as I can.

Bill Stuever

I enjoy working with people. I enjoy satisfying people's needs...what I can provide for them with a product or service. It's fun for me to say "You know, I have this product or service and I can provide it to you at a reasonable price." Then, I enjoy the follow up on what I said I was going to do. So I see myself as a service person and a provider of goods and services."

Larry Barmann

I see selling as a real calling...a vocation. It has been for me. I enjoyed the teaching that I did, but I found myself on a treadmill being in the same building, doing the same things. The sales career offers a great deal of freedom, flexibility and interaction. No year is the same. There are always new challenges and problems.

Donald Upton

> *I absolutely believe that selling experience is really good for an individual as far as their advancement into other areas. The first reason is probably that these individuals have such a variety of experience. They're in the field; they know the customers; they know the products. They have to be on the cutting edge of what's necessary to keep moving the company ahead. So they have a whole different concept from financial people, the marketing people, the engineering department, or technology researchers, who don't have that exposure. But I think it is the customer contact that is the key difference. Salespeople see what's necessary in the field and it makes them better people—people who ask a lot of the right questions and give creative direction once they get inside a customer's head.*

Martin Harry

> *I like the satisfaction of really helping people, having a product they want or need that really fits their needs. Another big reward I get is when the dealer does something for you. In this business, they're my customers. Sometimes they surprise you—buy your lunch, or do something for you, or ask you to help them set pricing. That's really satisfying because then you know it is a true relationship.*

Rob Vincent

> *To me, there's something unique about agri selling. Small things you learn about when someone has a baby, a death—it's really good to keep track of those things...to make notes beyond what "buyer type" they are. It's a little more involved. Ag people take the time to do those things and mean them.*

What Skills Are Needed to Succeed?

Agricultural salespeople are professionals. They are smart, knowledgeable about products and services, understand the customer's business and understand how to "fit" products and services into different situations. If you traveled with top salespeople, this is what you would see, as they work with customers. What you would <u>not</u> see is the "other half" of their professional skills—their planning, strategizing, preparation, and follow-up. Successful selling demands good skills in a sales call - but *professional* selling demands planning and persistence.

Ray McLaughlin

> *We work with people straight out of college to veterans who have been selling for a number of years. I think selling in agriculture is different than selling insurance or cars...so I would probably choose somebody with some experience selling in agriculture. That person would of course have to have a high level of intelligence, but I think more important is what I would term "fire in the belly." If I had somebody that has all the ability in the world but lacks a little bit in desire, versus somebody with lots of desire who may not possess all the talents and all the*

ability, generally the second one will excel long-term over and above the first one. And it's just because of the fire in the belly, if you will, and work ethic.

Ron Pettet

One of the most pervasive impressions I have of selling, looking back at these years of experience, is that everything is selling. Everyone sells in some way or another, even the minister at church on Sunday, in a way is selling to you. Sales is not what you'd imagine when you picture the fast-talking car salesman on TV. But selling is effectively communicating...listening, questioning, responding to people's needs and wants. There is a definite attitude of professionalism that has to accompany you at all times and in all situations. When you are with people, you are selling!

Dan Puck

This sales thing is kind of unique. There are a lot of different ways to describe all the things that make up sales and how to do them, but it all comes down to the art of relationships. Do that well, really care about people, show them you're interested in them and it all pays off in better relationships.

Stacy Dunn

Well, I have at this point only been selling a couple of years. I think it is different than I thought it would be. All the way through sales you're told that it is a flexible job and takes a lot of patience and time management and motivation. That is all true. It can also be really hard. Self-discipline is the most critical element—the single biggest responsibility I can identify. If you do not have self-discipline, you do not want to be in this job.

Debbie Stiles

My customers look for a salesperson who is organized, very professional, who understands their business, while at the same time can empathize/relate with them on a personal level as well. Selling in agriculture is not a "good ol' boy" system today. It is all about individuals in business together—customer and salesperson alike who can be business colleagues—professionals.

Earl Bell

You must enjoy what you do to be successful. If you don't have a passion for your work, you will not be successful. To me, the only way to have that passion is to really understand what your industry is trying to get accomplished—understand where it is going—and become an industry leader. I have been fortunate to work with Elanco because we believe in getting involved within our industry. In most facets of life you tend to get back what you give out. Generally speaking you will be rewarded for the work that you do within your industry. Within my company's sales group, there are four fundamental skills we work hard to develop.

1.   *We have to be able to assess complex situations on our feet.*
2.   *We have to be problem-solvers.*
3.   *We have to be able to make decisions.*
4.   *We have to be able to anticipate potential opportunities.*

David Suttle

> *Selling shouldn't be viewed as something you learn once. It's a constant evolution. Industry changes, product changes, competition changes, regulations changes – they all affect your ability to sell and the way in which you will sell. Just because you finish college doesn't mean your education is finished. I read 6-7 periodicals a week, from The Wall Street Journal to trade magazines and selling newsletters. It requires sacrifices. You don't do all that reading "8 to 5," you do it outside the "8 to 5" window. Continuing education and creativity are critical, no matter what type of sales you are in.*

How Customers Buy

In order to use the selling skills just described, the professional salesperson has to understand what customers need and above all how they buy. It isn't necessary to be a psychologist—but it is necessary to be a good listener, and to understand decision-making processes within each customer's business.

Donna Hines

> *I work with 18 accounts. My producers all have 3000 sows or more. On top of that, I work with key influencers —vets, nutritionists, feed sales reps, etc. So, it is a job in itself keeping individuals within large organizations and their specific roles and reporting relationships straight. When you are working with a producer that has 15,000 sows, there are a lot of people that are involved. You have to call on many of these people —Purchasing Agents, Owner, Production Managers, etc. Occasionally, in these types of operations, the right hand isn't always sure what the left hand is doing. So you have to work with all the different levels of people and get them to come up with the same solution.*

Bill Stuever

> *I don't believe in being a born salesperson, I wasn't! I believe you can be trained. It is the skill of recognizing not only the personalities you are dealing with, but being able to recognize where those personalities are within a given conversational forum. Then being able to address those needs and issues as they come up. That's all done by training, people observation, understanding body language and listening to what people want.*

Tom Giese

> *Each farm, each operation, each individual in an operation is different... You've got to do your research and planning and you've really got to know the farm.*

You've got to know their buying styles, know what they like and dislike, find their hot button... Find out what they want to do; ask a lot of questions. I want to fill those needs and wants.

<u>Earl Bell</u>

In sales you need to understand who within an organization needs to be detailed before they can make product decisions. A customer may purchase millions of dollars from their supplier. Consequently they need to have confidence in their supplier and specifically the sales representative. Regardless of the order size, customers need to have trust in the supplier company and its representatives. Every customer deserves that you respect his time and that you work hard to understand his needs so that you can help solve his problems. With all accounts, you should build good relationships with as many of the key people as possible.

In animal production, you have nutritionists and veterinarians that you assume would have the most influence as to what antibiotics are going into their rations. In some large production companies, decisions are made by a group of managers. This can complicate your selling process. When companies get together and buy cooperatively, they multiply their volume seeking to get reduced prices. Purchasing agents get involved in the product buying and bidding process. The job of a good sales representative is to keep the customers focused on the specific benefits of your product versus generic commodity type products. If the salesperson does not successfully articulate his product's unique properties then his customers may not use products that make them the most money. Sometimes this can be a difficult process in trying to use the correct tools to illustrate the full value of your products.

Part Two: Customer Value and Your Role

In order to sell, your product or service must be "worth something" to the customer. The value your customer perceives, for your specific products and services, is the result of their past experiences, their current goals, and their hopes for the future. (It is also a function of what your competitor is offering!)

As a salesperson, you are part of a larger effort to identify customer needs and develop the products and services that will satisfy those needs. The planning process that analyses the market and identifies opportunities is called a *market strategy* or *market plan*. Not every company has a formal plan, although most larger companies do. However, every company makes choices about the type of products they will sell, the prices they will charge, how they will distribute products to their customers, how they will promote and advertise them and how they want their people to interface with customers. These decisions guide the efforts of all salespeople in a company. By working consistently, the company's salespeople can help it achieve its financial objectives as well as the competitive success it desires.

Salespeople play a critical role in delivering value—but they need to understand it from two aspects. First, they need to understand the larger concepts of value their company is trying to communicate through its products, services, pricing, etc. The salesperson will find that life is much easier if he/she can get aligned with this strategy and use the marketing tools that have been prepared. Second, the salesperson must understand value as the customer defines it. The heart of the salesperson's job is to put the potential value of the company's products and services to work in a customer business—and in the process, to create real value for that customer.

Ray McLaughlin

Selling at its most basic level is almost this basic: exchanging a product that someone needs for a price. Without that "need" in that statement, there's no incentive to buy or sell. Then the next step is to determine what that need means. Dairymen at two different farms in a row may tell me they want the same thing...but it will mean something totally different when the older dairyman tells you he wants "good conversion" vs when the 35-year old progressive dairyman tells you he wants "good conversion." You really have to pay close attention to the personal characteristics of the individual as well as the intended meaning of what they say they want.

Wes McCoy

Once, while we were sitting in on a product management team, I told this group of company leaders, "Which one of you at the table here has stood in the field with the sprayer all plugged up because your product failed and had the stuff running down your arm while you try to unplug the nozzles?" Well, none of them had done that. I had. I had been in the field. I had worked side by side with my customers. Now I had their attention. They went back to the drawing board and came back with an improved product. The development research said "Now I have a good —no a better—product, but it's going to cost more than the other product. But we are going to offer this as an alternative, with a money-back guarantee." It became the number one seller. We didn't want to sell cheap stuff, we wanted to sell what worked for the customer. I was the valuable, intricate link from the customer to the company. The result was a product that was of greater value to the customer even though it had a higher price tag. It sold.

Bill Brockett

Value for most of our customers is quality. We look at sod; sod's supposed to be green. That's pretty simple. They say, "Green side up, stupid." But on sod, you've actually got a whole lot of quality factors there...density, color, etc. We've gone a step further than the normal sod producer has. We carry a national research plot right here on the farm; we have the government, USDA heavily involved. We have about 100 varieties of sod there and we make our selection for the varieties we are going to plant based on the test plot grown right here. Anybody can come see it—it's open to the public. We can take a customer out there and say, "Here's why we planted this variety, because two years, five years out, ten years out, we'll be long gone, but you might still be owning that grass. You could plant a lot cheaper variety that would look good on the very first day you put it down and then two years later, might not be as good."

Debbie Stiles

You have to do your part in the marketing mix. I think it is very important for new people to understand what the company's needs are and what approach it's taking, what the marketing procedures and goals are. It is important they understand it so they don't over-promise—don't take a direction the company is not headed. It is important for the salesperson to communicate to the customer where we're going, up front, and what the limitations are and what the expectations are. Knowing those up front eliminates surprises.

Ray McLaughlin

We initially introduce salespeople to what our company is all about —our products, what we can do with them, pricing, customer segments, what kind of marketing programs we have, etc. ...(after a year) most of the segmenting, targeting and prioritizing of accounts on a customer basis is done by the salesmen themselves. They do a lot of asking and finding out. We provide them with data sheets. After a couple calls and retrieving information, they should be able to have a real good base of what that dairyman's needs and wants are. We can incorporate that into our territory management program and then be able to selectively target customers or prospects, where our products fit their needs, and/or they have holes in their program that make them vulnerable to breaking with their current supplier, given some proper direction. Selectively prioritizing these segments is a real advantage to the company, the salesperson and the customer. It's the plan – the strategy – that makes selling work for all parties involved.

Jim Jackson

An area that few salespeople are prepared for is in building comprehensive business plans for prospects or customers. While attempting to write these plans the salespeople also struggle with incorporating our company's strategies and goals. These areas are difficult for new salespeople to master but are very important to the customer and the company... The starting point for new salespeople is a clear understanding and buy-in of the overall company strategy, direction and tactics used to meet our goals. Salespeople should be involved with the development of these items...Once over this hurdle, new salespeople can begin to help the customer and our company grow their businesses. Successful salespeople know their customer's business and business goals. Incorporating these with our company's goals is sometimes difficult but important. New salespeople and/or new people out of college usually take some time to develop these skills and insight.

Part Three: Effective Selling Skills

There are a series of steps and associated skills in the selling process:
- prioritizing and prospecting;
- selling strategy and call plans for top accounts;
- building a relationship with selected accounts;
- uncovering account needs, opportunities and values;
- presenting a solution or "value bundle" that meets account needs;
- answering questions and overcoming objections;
- closing the sale;
- following up to ensure satisfaction.

Prioritizing and Prospecting

An efficient and effective selling effort begins with identifying key groups of customers, focusing on their needs, and prioritizing or "targeting" those accounts where your products or services will likely be needed and their value understood and appreciated. Everyone has heard the old saying, "You can't sell snow to an Eskimo." Well, by segmenting all potential customers and choosing the high-potential segments or groups for your resources, you can avoid "selling snow to an Eskimo" and make sure you approach customers who need and value what you bring.

Martin Harry

We get a dollar goal each year. We have to figure out who we want to get what dollars from. I have a database of large to small farmers I can use. Where is your potential? Start there. Look at their product mix—corn and beans. Find out what weeds are problems here. Identify the customer's problems with those weeds. Overall, you have to have a database of information, then make appointments. This day and age, that's what works.

Rob Vincent

The very first year, my boss gave me my budget, and I was overwhelmed. I saw those numbers and thought to myself, "How are you ever going to meet the numbers!" And the first year, I didn't quite make my goal. I would get so nervous and wrapped up on if my plan and pitch were just right, that I didn' get the sale...

Debbie Stiles

> *One thing I find in working with new salespeople we are training is that they are doing what I did when I started. They think you have to be on the road every day of the month...working every Saturday, etc. I found that I was so disorganized, I was doing well for the dealers from a "shoot from the hip" perspective, but I really wasn't strategically planning. And, I wasn't satisfying my superiors from the paperwork aspects of it. And, in order for them to plan well, they need my data, my paperwork to be accurate...it's a trap you get into as an aggressive new salesperson. You want to go, go, go, but it's so important to plan, it's not even funny.*

Dan Puck

> *Planning and organizing for me means time on the computer. It also helps me manage my resources. Like everybody, we have budgets. By knowing where my sales are, and by figuring it out based on a percentage of total business from one particular customer, I can automatically figure out—back-calculate—on my spreadsheets how much support is their fair share of my total dollar goal amount. This helps me know the total amount of money I can justify spending on a trip or meeting, etc. It helps me explain to customers that there is a reason why we have certain limits, so it really helps me with my customers. There are facts and numbers behind what you can commit to them, and the resources that go along with that.*

Ray McLaughlin

> *I think it's real important that, right out of the gate, they understand that prospecting is the way for them to be successful. The biggest mistake people make in prospecting is not doing it! One of the pitfalls of veteran salespeople is that they stop doing it, or they put blinders on—why they can't call on this particular account, or that particular account. Pretty soon, an area with a lot of potential is cut down by themselves. We put a lot of emphasis on helping salespeople know where they're putting their efforts and how those efforts will pay off for them in the form of sales results.*

Bill Stuever

> *If they're cold calling, they'll be surprised at what they can dig out just by cold calling to uncover new opportunities. It may be that the person you're talking to on a cold call has an uncle who might turn out to be the prospect. Or, the prospect you are talking to is a better prospect than you originally thought. There are a lot of opportunities out there that just won't show themselves to you. You have to uncover them by prospecting and cold calling.*

Selling Strategy and Call Plans

Planning for your territory as a whole is critical to making the best use of your time. Planning carefully for each account and for each call to that account is critical to making the best use of customer time. Both are important. There are three elements that successful agricultural salespeople plan:

- a selling strategy or "game plan" for getting the account's business;
- a specific, often written, objective stating what you want to achieve on each call within the overall strategy;
- a formal or informal plan for each sales call.

Debra Warman

I have a strategy for each account and a plan for each sales call—and for the interaction with the customer. The two strategies work together in the selling cycle. The salesperson gets opportunities to execute both as the season goes on. In the winter time, we will focus more on getting new business with customers as well as keeping the repeat business. In the springtime, you follow up on the commitments you actually made in the winter. If things don't work, you fix them. The thing about the account strategy and the call strategy is, you may build them or develop them somewhat independently. Still, it is essential that you have that big picture of how the account strategy and the call plans interact with one another to accomplish your overall objectives.

Whenever I make a call, I must have a purpose in mind. I will ask myself what my key objectives are and what I want to accomplish in this call. I have to have a reason and be prepared. I also like to evaluate what happened in the call when I leave. If you don't plan the call, you are basically going in without a path to follow.

Bill Stuever

In order to know where in the sale you are at any moment, you have to have a plan and know what your objectives are. I think one of the best ways is to ask yourself "What's the reason I am talking to this person today?" It takes some thought before you go to the appointment. The easy answer is, "Oh, it's to sell him everything I've got." That's not always the case. If it's a first call, or even a second call, your objective may be altogether different than what a third or fourth call would be. Before you go into that call—whichever time it is - you need to have analyzed who the prospect is, what's gone on before, if anything, and then have an objective in your mind. It's a heck of a lot better to write it down and say "This is what I want to accomplish."

Donald Upton

Of course the first thing today is that we require all the sales force to make appointments. No one calls on a customer anymore unless they have a bonafide appointment. Then, when we get done with each call, the salesperson has to stop for five minutes and input the computer as to what they did on that call, who they talked to, what objectives they accomplished and what follow-up will be, etc. We do this if it's a regular customer or a potential account. It helps all of us work as a team to track customers and prospects and best address their needs in a timely manner.

<u>Stacy Dunn</u>

I have a 12-county territory and about 45 regular retailers and seed companies. When I was taught about preparing for visits with these customers in college, I didn't realize the importance of it. There are too many people, too many different intricacies to keep track of if you don't have a specific plan for each individual before you dive in.

Building a Relationship with Selected Accounts

A sound customer relationship is still necessary for long-term customer sales and satisfaction. The relationship with some customers can be quite personal—a friendship. With other customers, the relationship remains somewhat more distant and professional, although still cordial. Perhaps the hallmark of a sound customer relationship is that the customer knows he/she can be honest with you—about needs, problems, concerns, budgets, etc. And you, in turn, know you must be completely honest with the customer, about product performance features, benefits, and comparative value. How does a salesperson go about building this type of close relationship?

<u>Aaron McWhorter</u>

I think most salespeople—I sure do—enjoy being able to take a potential customer and build a relationship, by educating them, them building some dependence and respect for what we can do...reliance on us...in other words, building a trust. We went into a new architect's office and spent two hours with him and when we left, we had a relationship that they trusted us and went way, way, way out of their way to see that we got the work. To be real honest about it, that comes from two things. I have been real hands-on for a long time. The skills I use in selling are based on the fact that most of what we are doing, I have been doing hands-on at some point. Second, you can't take a salesperson and give him the verbiage. You really have to know the material. You know how it is, when you take a test in school, and you walk in that door, and you have no doubt in your mind whatsoever that you are going to ace that test. It doesn't matter what he could ask, you know you can answer the question. When I sit down with somebody to talk about building a sports field, I have reached that level.

Dan Puck

> *A lot of guys will just launch into their sales presentation...what they want to accomplish. That's jumping the gun. I think that this part of selling is called the "open" as much referring to getting people to open up, as much or more than opening your presentation. When you are with someone and they ask where you live, where you are from, etc., you tend to open up. They tend to become comfortable with that and open up as well. You both tend to start volunteering information and become involved and learn about each other through sharing about yourselves. In the sales call, you want to let people know that you are interested in them. That is the ultimate in rapport-building. Then, if you can get into the business by reaching them—in helping them through the business you both want to accomplish, you've opened up the customer...you've opened the door to a good relationship. You've opened the call.*

Uncovering Account Needs, Opportunities and Values

Your job as a salesperson is to meet the needs and wants of the customer. To meet those needs, you must uncover them. Experienced salespeople have learned that what they think the customer needs is immaterial. It's what the customer thinks he/she needs that counts. Many salespeople are able to provide a valuable service for their customers by helping them focus on their needs, instead of customers feeling a general sense of dissatisfaction or wondering if "things could be better." The key is to understand what the customer wants, before making a recommendation or presenting benefits of your product or service.

Bill Brockett

> *To determine what the customer wants, just plain listen. Be in constant communication with him. Don't have a closed mind on what is or isn't possible on your end. In other words, it is possible to give him what he wants instead of taking the reverse attitude: "That's an impossible question." Work on it with him and see if you can't accommodate what he wants. Lots of times, there's just a communication gap there. What he's asking for and what you have might be the same thing, but you just might not realize it without further investigation and further massage of the whole thing. By listening well, sometimes you as a salesperson can help the customer figure out what he wants. Sometimes, the customer talks around what he wants, or hasn't really had to put it into words before. Communication is essential for determining the customer's needs each and every time.*

Bill Stuever

> *Probing—asking open-ended or closed-ended questions, probing to uncover hidden needs, you really have to do those kind of things. But don't get hung up on doing it so much that you forget to listen—I really stress the conversational side of probing.*

Presenting a Solution or "Value Bundle" That Meets Account Needs

Once a salesperson has uncovered the customer's needs and opportunities to improve, it's time to develop a recommendation and present it to the customer. It's not unusual, in some of today's complex agribusinesses, to ask for several days to complete your analysis before presenting your ideas. Some customers might even ask you for a formal written bid or proposal. Whether you are presenting a complex analysis or are sharing the benefits of continuing the same simple program, the keys to an effective presentation are similar. Stay focused on the customer at all times; be honest about product strengths and limitations at all times; and adjust the way you present to the way the customer likes to do business.

Larry Barmann

Overall, in selling, I think it is most important to be honest to yourself and to your customers. Certainly, don't be so overzealous as to misrepresent yourself or your product as far as what it will or won't do. Establish that sense of trust with your customers at all levels. Do what you say you are going to do. Be accessible. Strive to be THE person so that, if someone is sitting there with a question, that person will say "I think I'll give Larry a call." Be organized.

Debbie Stiles

Sometimes, new salespeople try to use one style or sales presentation on all people. Altering your sales presentation thoroughly...this kind of planning truly sets apart one's success record from the random approaches of newer people. New or old salespeople try to give the same program or sales presentation to all customers across the board. If you present the same presentation, but approach it tuned to their personality and potential, then you can make a difference.

Answering Questions and Overcoming Objections

Objections and questions are a part of selling. It would be the rare salesperson who could judge exactly what the customer needed and explain it in exactly the right way, first time out, every time. When questions come up, they need to be answered right away. The only exception is price—many salespeople like to "hold" on that question until they've had a chance to talk to the customer about value. When you hear an objection, listen carefully—your customer is telling you what it would take before he/she will buy from you. It's much easier to remove roadblocks of misunderstanding, misinformation or lack of knowledge when you know where they are!

Wes McCoy

You gotta be snoopy, I guess. Maybe that's better put like this—when you meet with an objection, you simply have got to be persistent, innovative and creative. I remember one time, I got to a farm down around Stephen's Point, Wisconsin. There were lots of vegetable farms around there, and I just stopped in cold at one place and got talking to the guy. He was telling me about a problem he had with one of his vegetable crops. I said to him, "You know, sounds to me like you got nematodes." And the guy says, "I knew you'd say that." So I convinced him to let me take a soil sample to be analyzed. I split the sample and sent half of it to the University of Wisconsin and half to Dow for analysis. When I called him to tell him that the results showed a serious nematode problem, he said, "Yeah, I knew you'd say that. You want to sell me some chemical." But I told him, "And I knew that's what you'd say, so I split the sample and had results from both Dow and the University!" I took the results over so he could look at them himself. He could no longer object. He no longer thought I was out just for myself. That convinced him and I got a truck load order right away.

Closing the Sale and Following Up to Ensure

The final step in a sales call is to "close the call" —to ask for commitment on some level—and to set the steps that will occur next. You might be closing the sale, and setting up delivery and after-sale service. Or, you might simply be getting the commitment of the customer that you may call again, or that they will gather some information on the business before your next visit. In selling, you can create loyalty only through consistent performance—your performance as well as your product's performance. You want a customer to depend on you. You want to be able to deliver everything you have promised. For these reasons, closing and follow-up are critical to your next sale. You must set expectations you can achieve, and then achieve them and surpass them. It's also wise to plan a cycle of calls with each customer, according to their preference, that allows you to continue to follow up and plan with them throughout the year.

Rob Vincent

I think one of the most obvious things I learned in the first year or so was that you can plan and execute, but if you don't ask: "Will you buy the product," you don't or maybe won't know the answer to that question. More or less, that's your end objective...to close the sale...so ask for it.

Bill Stuever

Every sales call deserves to be brought to a conclusion. The prospect is waiting for it, believe it or not. Prospects want to be asked. Prospects probably aren't going to do anything unless they are asked. There are many ways to close – like the alternative choice close, the Ben Franklin close – the important thing is to find the one that works for you. Also, there's something that happens after the close that's critical—shut up. As soon as you ask for the person's business, shut your mouth. So many salespeople young and old, will ask for the close and start talking before the prospect can...they'll talk themselves right out of it. Then, the most important thing...once you get the order, you thank them very much and you leave. You don't stand around to let them take it back. Those are old time basic things, but they work.

<u>Dan Puck</u>

We are really big on business planning sessions with customers....Go in and have a session to probe about what worked well...Do you plan to grow? Expand? Hire more people? Then get more specific with the customer. Ask them what worked well and what didn't, of your products and others' products. Ask if they are thinking about changing things. Then leave it at that. Afterward, try to jot down some notes...figure out where the seams or holes are where you could bring some service, meet some needs. Through business planning and partnering together, you really can find better ways to service your people.

Summary

Agricultural selling can be a wonderful career. As a salesperson, your expertise is essential, and you will always be encouraged to build it. Your creativity is essential to helping customers "think outside the box" and discover new solutions. Your business skills can go to work for your customers, and as they prosper so will you.

Excellent selling performance requires knowledge and skill in several areas, as well as an attitude of persistence and an honest desire to help customers. Before you can sell successfully, you need to understand how customers buy: what types of information each considers; what logical process is used; and why it is so important to treat each one as an individual.

The second major focus of knowledge and skill concerns your "fit" into your company's strategies. These strategies include the specific "value" that your company can bring to customers, through products, programs and above all through you as a salesperson. It's also extremely helpful for salespeople to understand strategy. Then they can uncover, understand and use marketing communications and customer service tools in ways that help customers <u>and</u> help move the company closer to its objectives.

The third area of skills and knowledge focus for salespeople is on their individual skills. Effective salespeople are always looking for ways to improve. Even a slight adjustment can make a big difference. As one salesperson likes to put it, "One more hit for each ten times at bat is the difference between a .300 and a .400 hitter – and that's a difference worth paying for!"

Review Questions

1. In this chapter, an evolution of selling is discussed. It begins with product selling, moves to relationship selling, and concludes with professional agri selling. Give a description of each of these types of selling and distinguish the differences between them.

2. List and discuss at least three skills the salesperson needs to succeed.

3. Give an example from one of the panelists that describes why it is important to understand how people buy.

4. Besides the product itself, salespeople are part of the value they bring the customer. Cite at least two examples from the panel of sales experts that show how a salesperson helped bring value to the customer.

5. Planning is a critical element in developing selling strategies and call plans. What are three elements that successful agri salespeople plan?

Chapter Two

The Sales Profession

Learning Objectives:

Upon completion of this chapter, you should be able to:

1. define agricultural selling as the creation and delivery of solutions that bring value to the customer;
2. identify the five building blocks of agricultural selling;
3. describe three key activities of agricultural salespeople;
4. differentiate between direct and indirect selling responsibilities;
5. describe the different types of agricultural selling by channel level;
6. understand the role of the salesperson in creating customer satisfaction.

What is Selling?

Selling is the process of helping people access the information, products and services they need to meet their personal and business goals. Selling, in its most general sense, could therefore happen through any access channel - an industry magazine advertisement, a self-service parts store, or even the Internet. However, most selling in agriculture still depends on the person-to-person interaction between a salesperson and a customer. This interaction is key to the selling process. The salesperson's information about products and services is important

to the customer making the best possible decision. Knowledge of the customer's business - whether it is a distributor/wholesale supplier, a retail business, or a production business such as farming, ranching, horticulture, aquaculture or floriculture - is also critical to helping make a good decision.

Creating Value for the Customer

As a salesperson, you play the key role in delivering value to the customer. You do this not only through your knowledge. Your ability to discuss business situations, identify needs, use your knowledge to create solutions, and follow-up to make sure solutions are working are perhaps more critical than your knowledge. Most products—especially tangible products such as fertilizer, equipment, feed and crop protection—have inherent value. This value comes from the use of the product. It can be expressed in concrete terms: in dollars and cents saved or earned through improved output, in time saved, etc. This quantitative value is measurable and fairly obvious, if the salesperson has done a good job of matching products and services to needs.

There are other types of value delivered through the salesperson, however. These types of value are less tangible and less measurable, but no less important. Through you, the customer can not only access good products, but products and corresponding business solutions that are easier to use, more convenient, more reliable, readily serviced, more dependable, and that come with technical support needed to ensure a good "fit" with current business practices. The salesperson not only represents products—he or she must also bring education, direct service support, and must facilitate expert technical support.

There are many good product solutions available to farmers, ranchers, greenhouse managers, breeders and the retail and wholesale businesses that supply them. Some products have clear advantages over others, especially in specific situations. However, many products could be characterized as *commodities*. They are available through many suppliers and seem almost interchangeable. Yet customers continue to prefer to do business with some companies and brands rather than others. Why? To these customers, even though the product solutions may seem largely the same as everyone else's, the *total solution* is different - worth their loyalty. That difference begins with the salesperson.

Creating Unique Value Bundles

Most agricultural selling is business-to-business selling. Most companies provide their salespeople with a variety of services and support, geared toward meeting the business needs of customers. The job of the salesperson is to trim, tuck and fit those products and services to give each customer the highest possible value for a fair price. Let's look at two examples.

Jim recently made a visit to Elm Hill Farms, a medium-sized farrow-to-finish swine operation, to check on the performance of his company's feed and to see whether the owner, Bob Harking, might be interested in upgrading his line of nursery feeds. Bob and Jim talked about the operation, and about Bob's progress toward some production goals he and the family had set about a year ago. It seems that the current feeds were performing about as well as could be expected, given the fact that there had been some intestinal problems with the baby pigs the last month or so. The pigs had been immunized against TGE, and Bob's veterinarian thought the cause of the problem was probably bacterial. Bob was about to begin putting an antibiotic in the watering system, when Jim realized that he could offer Bob the antibacterial protection the baby pigs needed through a feed additive. This additive wasn't an ingredient in the nursery feeds Jim has been buying, but it seemed like a good idea to add it to a new nursery feed – one designed to be even easier on the baby pig's digestive processes. Bob decided to try it, and within a few weeks, most of the problem cleared up and his production goals were back on track.

Jesse Rodriguez worked for a company that provided computer hardware and software business solutions. Since she had grown up on a large citrus operation in Southern California, she was asked to take over a sales territory that included several large fertilizer/chemical retail businesses that served fruit and vegetable growers south of Fresno. Jesse's company offered a full range of business software and a variety of work station and network PCs. In talking with retail managers in her new territory, she learned that each of them had a unique way of doing business. Some used the computer for as much as possible – even Emailing between locations. Others used it only for accounting. With her knowledge of their type of business and her knowledge of computers, she was able to "custom-build" computer business solutions for several large retailers, upgrading their current capacity and speed and allowing them to accomplish what they wanted their computers to accomplish. Today, Jesse has a strong customer base among retailers – one she is careful to maintain by learning about each business before making a recommendation or proposal.

In both of these examples, the sales representatives understood a lot about their products and services. In both cases, the products were very good – but not the only good products available. In both cases, however, the salespeople were able to use their knowledge of products, services and the customer's business to create a unique solution. And in both cases, the customer wouldn't have discovered this "better" solution without the help of a competent salesperson.

A variety of additional services is often available to "add value" and create a unique value bundle for each customer. Some salespeople may have flexibility in billing customers, in making special arrangements for delivery, in sending out a financial expert, veterinarian or agronomist to "trouble-shoot" especially difficult situations, or in offering special product/price packages to lock in the sale. These types of services enrich the value bundle even more. The key element to any value bundle is the product/service match made by the salesperson, working collaboratively with a customer. Of course, not all businesses can meet every customer's demands for special services. Salespeople need to have clear direction from a manager regarding the "ingredients" they can freely choose from in building a value bundle, and the cost to the company of any special services.

Dan Puck
Dow AgroSciences
Sales Representative
Madison, Wisconsin

I consider selling a profession. Number one you have to have self-starters who don't need supervision to accomplish their goals. If you look at the workforce, you have workers who support people, they take care of the manufacturing, hands-on type work, who need some type of supervision. People who enter a profession are people who don't need that type of direction. They become a veterinarian, a computer scientist, you don't have a lot of supervision or anyone looking over you. You are responsible for your own choices and decisions on a higher plane. To be a salesperson, you have to do that. You don't have supervision directly, you have to be a self-starter, you choose how you want to accomplish goals and what steps you want to take to get there.

The second reason I think sales is a profession is because I think dealing with people is kind of an art form itself. I look at people I've known over the years that aren't in sales, and salespeople tend to get smooth, or polish the art of meeting, working with people that tends to help others open up and talk their background, themselves. You can stand back and tell that these salespeople are skilled at the art of making people feel comfortable, and getting people to talk about things—anything they may want to talk about. That just comes from practice, from being in the business, from using the skill you have inside you of trying to establish relationships with people for the purpose of establishing or conducting business. So, it is subtle, and hard to define, but being focused, able to pick up on non-verbal signals, all you take for granted is part of that.

Learning how to negotiate is another real skill that differentiates salespeople from some other professions, and it's something that they tend to pick up over time. In other scientific or research endeavors, you don't necessarily have to hone those skills. In sales you really have to learn how to gather information, how to overcome objections, then how to negotiate and once again that comes down to extracting information from people and positioning things with them to hopefully help them understand the value of what you are trying to sell.

Selling is a Profession

What is a "profession" - and what are the characteristics of a "professional?" Webster[1] defines a profession as a "specific, identifiable craft for and about a specific group of people, products and services." Agricultural selling is the specific "craft" of creating and delivering business solutions for people who manage businesses involved in food and fiber production and marketing.

The profession of selling rests on a foundation that contains these building blocks (Figure 2.1).

Figure 2.1
Building Blocks of Professional Selling

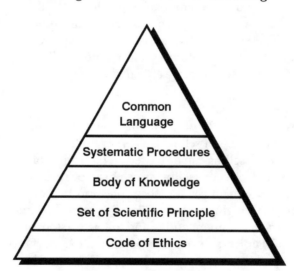

Code of Ethics

One hallmark of any profession is its adherence to a strict code of ethics[2]—a code that governs member behavior. Doctors, lawyers and other professionals have review boards to ensure that each member of the profession is an ethical practitioner. For agricultural salespeople, this "review board" is their customer base. While there is considerable interest in certifying specific areas of knowledge for professional agricultural salespeople (such as the Certified Crop Advisor certification process administered through the American Society of Agronomy),

---

[1] Steinmeitz, Sol (Editor) Random House Webster's Dictionary (Second Edition). Ballantine Books. New York, New York: 1996

[2] For a sample of Code of ethics, see Appendix A.

the customer and his or her peers will always be the most powerful review board for a salesperson. Regardless of what certification processes exist for technical knowledge, the most successful and highly-regarded members of the agricultural selling profession in any community are also the most ethical. They are honest about product and service benefits and limitations, and they are honest in their business relationships. So, while there is no widely accepted screening procedure, oath or industry review procedure for most salespeople, they must ensure themselves, customer by customer, that they adhere to ethical standards. A salesperson who does not sell ethically will soon be without customers.

Set of Scientific Principles

Effective selling is based on the scientific principles of human behavior. These principles include economic exchange theory, the theories of motivation, the purchase decision process, behavioral style differences and communications research. These bodies of scientific research have resulted in principles of human behavior that help the salesperson work more collaboratively with customers and approach new accounts more effectively.

Body of Knowledge

There is a specific body of knowledge that successful agricultural salespeople possess. The process of selling is a part of this knowledge. Although many "hints" about effective selling can be passed along from professional to professional, the elements of an effective selling process can be refined and described so they can be learned by someone new to the profession. Process elements include territory planning, prioritizing accounts, planning sales calls, uncovering needs, formulating recommendations, and follow-up steps after a sale. Trade schools, colleges and universities have recognized the importance of communicating this knowledge about agricultural selling processes and have responded by creating an academic discipline of selling.

Effective salespeople also capture, maintain and update a considerable body of knowledge about their products and services, their marketplace, and their customers. These various types of knowledge complement the selling process itself, resulting in customer value. Research into better product and service solutions, new uses for current products and services, and improved access to all products and services is ongoing, not only at universities but also in the companies who live and die in the agricultural marketplace. Every day, salespeople add to their own knowledge as well as to the total body of knowledge concerning customer behavior and selling processes.

Systematic Procedures

Effective selling involves specific steps or procedures. Thorough research and analysis of customer needs leads the salesperson to choose solutions, approaches and activities that fit the customer and his or her business. Customer records and internal communications procedures must be maintained and regularly updated. A customer database may be used, or individual salespeople may keep their own records. These procedures are based in the body of knowledge about customer behavior, trends in customer needs and the marketplace, and available technology.

Common Language

There is a common language among salespeople. Anyone who has ever attended a sales conference can testify to the jargon that fills their sentences when they are talking shop. Many of the terms they use are the same across the industry – *close, objections, call opening,* or *prospect,* for example, are generally understood terms, although their exact definition may differ a little from company to company. Other terms may be unique to an industry or even to a specific company. For example, a complaint goes by a variety of names, including *product inquiry, non-performance problems, customer settlements and customer satisfaction issues.*

What Salespeople Do

Bill Walker has been marketing the farm's corn and soybeans since marrying into the Krakov Family Farm corporation twelve years ago. Playing the futures market has been a personal forte and Bill's expertise has really benefited the farm's bottom line. Since purchasing his latest Digital Data Superserver, the farm's corn and soybean trades have been smooth and accurate. Access to current grain and soybean market information has been better than expected. But this year, Bill feels out of his depth. The farm has planted some high oil corn. Yields look like they will be quite good – and Bill has heard that there might be a value-added market for this grain, since it adds energy to livestock rations. The problem? Bill is not sure where to market the crop. His traditional traders aren't set up for identity-preserved grain – and Bill doesn't want to let this special product go at #2 corn prices. "Better make a phone call," thought Bill. "Bet Dale Percey, who sold me on this high-oil corn, can suggest a grain marketer who understands its value."

In the above situation, wouldn't it be great for both Bill and Dale if Bill would say, "I have a problem. I think I'll call my professional problem-solver." In effect, that is what he did. When Bill bought the high-oil seed corn, he bought an added-value product. In order to capture the value of his purchase, the logical place to turn is his seed salesperson. And, if Dale wants to sell Bill this product again, he'll have an answer to his question or find an answer quickly.

Salespeople are Problem Solvers

Whether they are uncovering needs, presenting benefits of a solution, making a recommendation or following up with service, salespeople are solving problems. Their first responsibility is to determine needs and locate the products, services and information that help customers reach their business goals. They help people buy what they need – even if the need wasn't recognized by the customer before discussing the problem with the salesperson. All customers must buy some products and services to operate their businesses. The salesperson's ultimate goal is to help the customer make a good decision, thus creating satisfaction before, during and after the sale and opening the door to the next sale. Salespeople also use their problem-solving skills when they choose how to handle a particular customer, situation, meeting, competitor, etc.

Salespeople are Influencers

Throughout the sales process, salespeople act as catalysts – influencers of a decision. They influence buying decisions by providing the customer with alternatives and a body of technical and business knowledge that helps the customer fairly evaluate these alternatives. They apply their knowledge and persuasive powers to convince the customer that at least one of the solutions offered is viable – and profitable. While there are many sources for information on products, services, production practices and business practices, the salesperson has the wonderful opportunity to see all the different alternatives at work, through his or her daily contact with customers. Thus the salesperson is often one of the most trusted – and practical-thinking – influences on the decisions customers make.

Salespeople are Facilitators

Producers, retailers and distributors face a confusing array of choices. And, these choices change all the time, as new products and business systems enter the market each year. An effective salesperson makes it easier for the customer to make a sound decision, by helping the customer focus on their most important needs. This need may be hidden – even from the customer – under a web of misinformation, hearsay, lack of information or a hazy sense of dissatisfaction. It often requires a considerable number of skilled questions and careful listening, before a salesperson can uncover needs. As they talk and walk a customer through various priorities and various solutions, they hear the customer's needs and concerns. This information allows them to facilitate a sound and profitable buying decision for the customer.

Bob Woods
Penn Jersey Products, Inc.
Sales Supervisor
New Holland, Pennsylvania

Selling - especially at first—wasn't easy. There is still so much to learn. I guess that is what makes it such an interesting profession.

Selling is a lifestyle. I started my career teaching. I am still teaching. What better way to teach? Some people might just call them customers. But to me, these farmers I "work" for are the best. We have fantastic professional relationships. We help one another. I can hopefully make them more successful in their business through the product we get on their place. As long as the salesperson puts the customer's best interest first, they'll do well. It's a big, professional responsibility. It takes a big investment in time and energy and a true effort on the salesperson's part to really dig into what the customer is really about and what they really are asking for, but I think it's truly worth the long-lasting relationship you establish.

Responsibilities of Salespeople

For most of us, our first experience with responsibility probably came when we were about two or three years old. It was a simple task, assigned by Mom or Dad maybe something like "can you put your game away?" This simple responsibility had a purpose (although you may not have understood it at the time). The task itself had a beginning, a middle and an end, and when it was successfully completed, you were probably profusely praised. As you grew, the responsibilities assigned to you became increasingly complex, and the praise may have been increasingly random. By the time you took your first job, there were a variety of responsibilities you were expected to perform (and all too often these responsibilities are presented as "part of the job," rather than with their purpose attached.)

Sales responsibilities vary in different companies, but by and large many salespeople have similar responsibilities. Each of these responsibilities has a purpose. Each involves specific tasks - each with a beginning, middle and end - and many of these tasks must be completed on an ongoing basis. Why are there so many responsibilities for salespeople? As a professional salesperson, you are responsible for bringing products and services to the market, fitting them to customer needs, persuading customers that you bring good value for the price, and in the process building strong relationships. It's a complex job - perhaps one of the most complex jobs you could choose. While there are many factors you influence, in the end the customer has control of the decision. Understanding the many responsibilities of a salesperson helps you begin to organize your time and your activity to gain maximum positive influence and optimum sales success.

There are two types of responsibility: direct and indirect. Table 2.1 summarizes the responsibilities included in each category. Direct selling responsibilities are those that affect how you implement the sales process and work when you are face-to-face with a customer. Indirect responsibilities involve all of the responsibilities you must carry out to get yourself ready to sell, satisfy the customers you have sold, and to create a fertile climate for continued selling efforts.

Table 2.1
Direct and Indirect Selling Responsibilities

Direct Selling Responsibilities	Indirect Selling Responsibilities
1. Prospecting	1. Handling complaints
2. Pre-call planning	2. Maintaining customer relations
3. Building customer relationships	3. Market intelligence
4. Attracting customer attention and interest	4. Maintaining technical competency
5. Uncovering customer needs	5. Collecting accounts
6. Making sales presentations	6. Networking
7. Handling objections	7. Trade and public relations
8. Closing the sale	8. Office work
9. Servicing accounts	9. Managing information

Direct Selling Responsibilities

Direct selling is the first and foremost function of the salesperson. It is the set of activities most people associate with salespeople. Direct selling involves getting organized in your territory, finding new customers (called "prospects"), planning sales calls, building relationships with customers, uncovering their needs and attracting their interest in your solution, making a recommendation and presenting its features and benefits, handling any customer resistance, closing the sale, and following up after the sale with service. In "counter selling" (in a store) and in some telemarketing situations, these activities may all happen in a very shortened form all in one call. For most agricultural sales people, however, these activities happen over a period of several calls - often four to six and sometimes as many as twelve or even twenty. Some of these activities - such as uncovering needs - may happen in every single one of those twelve or twenty calls. They are that important to the salesperson's success in all the other activities.

Sometimes these direct selling activities happen in a formal, planned sequence over time. For example, a grain marketer may choose those customers with whom the company would like to work, work the "prospect" list until all have been contacted, uncover needs and opportunities to help them market their grain more profitably or more conveniently, present them with the advantages of working together, and follow up to make sure they understand their contracts, can fill them, and will contract again. On the other hand, a cattle breeder may work with a rancher for several years informally, meeting at trade shows[3] or auctions, sharing experiences and gradually learning about the rancher's breeding program and budget, before actually suggesting that they might work formally together through the purchase of breeding stock. In this latter case, the steps in the selling process may be so informal, so much a part of an existing relationship, and so drawn out that only another salesperson would recognize the skill with which they are being executed. Direct selling responsibilities are addressed in greater detail in Part Three of this book.

Indirect Selling Responsibilities

Indirect selling may be in the back seat of the sales vehicle, but it has the map to customer satisfaction and an ongoing business relationship. Indirect selling may also take more of the salesperson's time than direct selling, especially at certain times of the year. Indirect selling includes extended services performed for the customer, the company or the industry.

The customer may require more service at some times of year – such as when planting for a row crop farmer, when taking in large numbers of livestock in feeder operations, or when supporting planting or harvesting at the retail level. In addition, there are certain times of year when "touching base" with customers is very important – such as talking to a seed customer in late summer about his satisfaction with his hybrids and varieties and his cropping plans for next year.

The company may require that the salesperson "stay smart" on new technologies, and offer training through company sources or through public seminars. Even if the company does not require a certain number of hours of continuing education or a certain level of knowledge, successful salespeople spend several hours a week – the equivalent of 15-20 days a year – learning about "what's new" in their industry. Salespeople often also are asked to support market intelligence, sales forecasting and other activities based on customer needs and trends. Finally, many salespeople are involved in local, regional and national trade associations and philanthropic organizations. Let's look at each indirect selling responsibility in more detail here.

---

[3] For more about working at Farm/Trade Shows, see Appendix B.

Handling Complaints[4]

Complaints are a normal part of selling. When a customer has a problem with a product or service, he or she often wants to express dissatisfaction right back at the salesperson who sold the product or service. This is seldom the most popular or comfortable of a salesperson's responsibilities. However, complaints are really an opportunity in disguise. The way you handle the complaint can win you a customer for life - or cause a customer to begin looking for another supplier.

Most companies provide carefully-developed guidelines for handling complaints. The protocol to be followed is often different for each company, as is the degree of latitude the salesperson has to resolve the complaint without assistance from technical staff, sales management or marketing management. Resolving the complaint may involve several steps or repeated calls and/or visits with the customer. Experienced sales reps look at each complaint as a way to prove their worth as a trusted advisor. Even when they cannot (or are not permitted) to resolve the complaint immediately, they always respond to the customer's distress right away - usually within 24 hours.

Maintaining Customer Relationships

Salespeople are busy - so busy that it's easy to overlook or become insensitive to the feelings of established customers. When customers feel they are taken for granted, they become more vulnerable to your most aggressive competitors, who gladly give them the attention they deserve and are accustomed to receiving. Conscientious attention to the early warning signs of a deteriorating customer relationship can provide salespeople with the lead time needed to correct the problem. Such early warning signs include customers not returning calls, putting off appointments, dragging their heels on decisions, or even mentioning to you that they have been talking to your competitors. Professional agricultural salespeople recognize that every customer is unique - and that includes how much attention they want from you. If you suspect a problem with a customer, plan to spend some uninterrupted time together. Catch up on the customer's priorities and current issues. With a little effort, you can assure them that they are still very important to you.

Market Intelligence

Market intelligence refers to information about customer trends, competitor activities and programs, product performance (yours and others), markets, weather conditions and insect infestations - anything management needs to know about the market in order to make sound strategic decisions. Every good jockey in a horse race knows where the other horses are, as well as the condition of the

---

[4] For more about Handling Complaints, see Appendix C.

track. Sales is no different. You can't have the best competitive offer if you don't know the readiness of the market or the offers your competitors are bringing.

Market intelligence is often not a formally named responsibility in a salesperson's job description. Many agricultural companies have a Market Research Department or Market Analyst acting as their in-house "investigative reporter." Other companies identify research needs as part of the strategic planning process and contract for specific studies as needed. As a salesperson, you are your company's "front line" in the battle for the customer's business. For that reason alone, market intelligence is very important to your success. You should be have current knowledge of competitor actions, product performance, prices, incentives and discounts at all times. You should also keep a close watch on your top customers' moods, their general economic climate, commodity/livestock prices, business/credit conditions, and product use or inventory levels. Some companies require a short written report of such factors periodically.

Maintaining Technical Competency

Agriculture is a people business that rests on a highly technical foundation. Results – profits – are based on how technology is adopted, purchased, used, and evaluated. This holds true whether your customer raises corn, catfish, cattle or cucumbers, or is a retailer, distributor or manufacturer. New biological processes, engineered processes, inventions, chemistries, genes and breeding technologies have both environmental interactions and business applications. It is part of being "professional" to be up-to-date on current technology, particularly in your specific field. Whether you grow technical competence by choice or are required to increase your knowledge, your technical competence is both needed and noticed by your customers. Many companies provide training to help salespeople learn about their products and services, and some companies provide quite a broad base of technical training.

Increasingly, technical competence is measured and "verified" by some form of certification. This certification may require completion of a certain number of hours of continuing education, an examination, or both. For example, the Certified Crop Advisor (CCA) accreditation is now required of many sales representatives in the crop protection, seed and fertility industries. For many years, California has required an even more intensive education and certification process, the Pest Control Advisor certification, for anyone making crop protection recommendations. Registration as a Veterinary Technician can be attained by professionals selling pharmaceuticals and animal health products to veterinary clinics. These types of certification or accreditation by a professional organization add to the salesperson's credibility and reliability for the customer, and may add significantly to their ability to make sound recommendations as well.

Larry Barman
American Cyanamid
Marketing Specialist, IMI – Corn
Red Oak, Iowa

I am a regular computer user. It has saved me valuable time to do the administrative functions and to do the planning process and to keep current on technical information. Accessing newsletters and various other updates off the Internet, from universities and other sources is a key way for me to keep current. CCA certainly helps me keep current and knowledgeable on carrying that accreditation. The company also helps with their continuing education programs. I have a word of caution, however, as I have seen good salespeople who rely too much on the computer and sit at the computer and type up countless newsletters, brochures, mailings, etc., which in itself is good, but they lost contact with the customer. They became an office manager instead of getting back out into the field to generate business with the customer. You can overdo it.

Collections

The vast majority of customers pay their bills on time, but there are always those few who are unable or unwilling to do so.[5] Unfortunately, the sale is never complete until the money is collected. Many companies give salespeople the responsibility to identify "credit-worthy" accounts in the first place, and to complete the initial stages of the collection process. It is normal for salespeople to explain credit terms and policies, and to remind customers when accounts are overdue. Once a salesperson has to ask for payment of an overdue account, he or she will have a new appreciation for the need to extend credit prudently. With the size of many businesses in agriculture today, one large uncollected account can erase the profits of a salesperson's entire territory. The importance of this responsibility is obvious.

Networking

A professional agricultural salesperson is normally expected to maintain positive and productive contacts with county USDA personnel, university researchers, extension staff, and other opinion leaders in the area. For example, a seed salesperson may be expected to share experiences with other professionals (such as crop protection consultants) who have a major influence on the sales of seed products. The active utilization of viable, open lines of communication with other agricultural professionals and experts is called *networking*. Networking can provide a valuable pipeline for current information about pests, prices and

---

[5] For more about Collecting Accounts, see Appendix D.

products, as well as production trends, names of key producers, and other local influencers. These personal contacts can also help you influence some of your largest customers.

Educating Customers

As a problem solver and influencer, an important part of the salesperson's job is to educate customers. Needless to say, educating customers also puts your own expertise and your company's interest in new technologies in a very favorable light. Some salespeople have specific job goals to conduct a specified number of meetings, seminars, or field days. In other jobs, it's assumed that the salesperson will educate customers through daily sales and service contacts. Educating customers takes many forms. You might organize formal meetings, to which you invite all your customers and their top employees for a dinner and presentation on products and technologies available in the coming year. Or, you might organize a seminar on a first-come/first-serve basis to help customers and prospects understand the changes that will be required by new environmental regulations. And, of course, much of the most effective education takes place one-on-one, as you work with customers to solve their very specific needs and business issues.

Many customer education efforts are carefully planned in advance, and may be supported by slides, a videotape, or an outside expert. However, agricultural production is very vulnerable to problems that no one can predict - weather, diseases, and insects. For this reason, much education is done on an as-needed basis. The customer is most likely to listen when he or she has a problem that needs solving - right now. With experience, many sales reps find they are educating customers on the same topic many times and in many ways - from a banquet audience of one hundred people to a quick but intense conversation after church. Each educational effort is an opportunity to add value and create loyalty - and therefore each requires the appropriate use of communication and presentation skills.

Educating customers in such a wide variety of situations makes many demands on the salesperson's presentation skills. They must determine the audience - need to know, patience, need to interact, current level of knowledge and the appropriate depth of information. The most basic presentation skill is the ability to organize the information you deliver into a logical flow. Most salespeople also need to become comfortable with basic presentation tools, such as flip charts, electronic projection units, slide projectors, VCR hook-ups and overhead transparencies. In many situations, salespeople must also be able to create a personalized analysis, using detailed electronic spreadsheets and comparative data. A clear understanding of the customer's business needs _and_ education needs is critical.

Trade and Public Relations

To most people, the salesperson is the company. The salesperson may be the only contact the customer has with your company. Thus, salespeople must always maintain an image that is consistent with the desired image of their company. In fact, the way the salesperson conducts personal and business affairs casts a reflection on his or her honesty and integrity as a salesperson and on the company as well. This is an important issue for many customers, and one that is difficult to correct once the salesperson's reputation is in doubt. As one customer put it, "if you have to ask me how you can demonstrate integrity, you don't have enough of it." Salespeople must constantly keep the public nature of their profession in mind.

"Public relations" are specific activities, in addition to daily professional behavior, that a salesperson does to promote the business. These activities are usually done without expecting a sale as a direct result – at least in the short term. Typical public relations activities include involvement in community activities, participation in trade shows and exhibits,[6] field plots and farm/business trial programs, youth education programs, etc.

Office Work

Every salesperson's job contains some computer time, some paperwork, and some budgeting and administration duties. Many salespeople are asked to complete a weekly call report, summarizing their activities, sales calls, market conditions, order forms, and inventory reports. Sometimes salespeople are asked to complete surveys about their market, crop forecasts or competitive activities. Most salespeople prepare annual sales forecasts, and in some industries (such as seed), they may be asked to forecast product use two or three years in the future. Usually, there is a formal process for budget requests or exceptions to normal sales, and for credit and collection policies. At the very least, salespeople are required to file accurate expense statements and to keep meticulously organized records and receipts to support expense reimbursement. Salespeople may be required to file these expense reports on paper, electronically, or both ways.

Preparing for an important sales call also often requires some office work. There may be some in-depth research of products or services. If the company has a database or paper file of sales history, it should be consulted. Above all, many salespeople find that some "quiet time" to plan their next major calls is invaluable.

In addition to paperwork required by the company and planning time required for effective selling, there are a variety of communication modes to keep the

---

[6] For more information about Trade Shows, see Appendix B.

salesperson busy. It is critical to keep current on mail - both traditional letters and Email. Mail - the written word - is still the preferred choice for communicating policies, procedures, formal complaints and organizational changes. It goes without saying that customer correspondence should always be answered promptly and filed carefully.

The best salespeople also have an "in-box" on the desk which is regularly emptied and read - trade magazines, newsletters, company literature and other pertinent publications. Salespeople who travel frequently may have a "read file" where they keep such information, so they can quickly drop it in a briefcase as they run out the door. Reading a newspaper or two from different communities where you work also helps keep you current on local and regional issues, influential people and agricultural activities and forecasts. This "local flavor" provides you with lots of ideas when you are trying to begin a conversation with a brand new prospect, and shows all customers and prospects that you have an interest in their community and their local issues.

Managing Information

The quantity, quality and access to information have increased at an exponential rate in the last few years. In the future, more information will be available faster than in the past. Yet all this information can also create a certain level of "noise" in the customer's mind, making it difficult to sort out the most useful pieces of information and put them to work in the business. Many producers are now very adept at managing information about their own business, through computer-assisted record-keeping. Retail, distributor and manufacturer businesses usually manage business information quite well. As a sales professional, you need to get "plugged in" also.

As a bare minimum, you should be comfortable with several forms of information management. For example, you need to keep good sales records - but also use them to manage your territory. You need to be comfortable with the computer and with the Internet - but then know how to bookmark and locate key files or forecasts that you want to share with customers. You need to be comfortable with Email - but also have a system for filing information so that you aren't scanning a list of 600 saved messages to find the one you need.

The most efficient salespeople know much more than the minimum. They have learned to analyze financial information and translate product performance trials into electronic presentations, and to file these so they can quickly access them and present them or Email them to customers and influencers. They not only can write a good business letter – they know how to use merge functions in their database so that they can initiate and coordinate direct mail to targeted groups of customers.

Many salespeople also find "contact management" software helpful. There are many good contact management programs available. These allow the salesperson to manage daily contact, keep a record of important account information and retrieve it quickly and accurately, and set "calendar reminders" for follow-up activities. Other salespeople are amazingly effective with written, paper-based calendar systems to manage their contacts and make sure they meet their obligations. The system is less important than the result – managing information critical to your success, rather than being drowned in it.

How Salespeople Carry Out Responsibilities

The agricultural selling profession has a unique list of direct and indirect responsibilities. Each responsibility has a different priority, based on the type of selling you do and your company's organizational structure. *Whether* you carry out required activities determines whether you meet job responsibilities. *How* you carry out activities can mean the difference between mediocrity and superiority, between your success or failure as a salesperson.

One definition of the word "responsible" is to have the capacity for moral decision – to feel accountable. So far, we have identified numerous responsibilities that together make the agricultural salesperson's job a "profession." The degree to which you, as a salesperson, feel accountable for these responsibilities depends in part on your age, your experience, and the way you are managed. But regardless of age, experience and management, each of these responsibilities can be carried out well – or poorly. The quality of your performance, in each of these responsibilities, depends on the knowledge, skill and attitude you bring to the job.

Knowledge, Skill and Attitude

Each person is equipped with a set of "mental tools" in life. Some of us learn more easily than others. Some of us take a little knowledge and a lot of skills and are successful. Others have lots of knowledge but can't seem to apply it. Some salespeople would do anything to satisfy a customer – others could hardly be bothered. The knowledge, skill, and attitude you bring to the job of a salesperson interact to provide customers with results – and you with success.

Knowledge includes facts about your products and services, how these products and services perform in different situations, the "science" behind product performance and correct use, and typical customer needs. Knowledge also includes your understanding of customer business operations, the dynamics that affect their businesses, and your competitors' products, services and programs.

Skill describes how knowledge is used to help customers. A variety of skills is necessary for successful selling – not just "sales" skills. Effective salespeople have excellent problem-solving skills. They can dissect and analyze a situation and think logically about how to improve it. They have excellent communication skills – listening as well as talking. Many agricultural salespeople have some technical skills – whether it's teaching an application crew how to calibrate a new sprayer or helping a business set up a database. Skills get better with practice. Thus, the more a salesperson asks questions and listens, the better he or she becomes at asking good questions. Still, skill without knowledge can only go so far. Knowledge without skill is pretty useless. Knowledge and the skill to use it - that's a powerful combination.

Attitude describes the motivation to help customers – the desire to meet their needs. Attitude is what determines how often and with what intensity knowledge and skill are used. Two salespeople, with equal opportunities and an equal level of training and skill, may stand at the career starting line together. But by the end of the race, the one with a genuine desire to help and the persistence to persevere will win every time.

Professional Sales Competencies

A "competency" is an integrated description of knowledge, skill and attitude in the job environment. The competency gives us something *measurable* – how often calls are made, how much preparation, whether follow-up was done – to determine what customers want and what salespeople are currently providing. Competencies are not some strange idea dreamt up by a human resources specialist. They are very real-world descriptions of behavior – much as you might hear a customer describe salesperson activities. Let's look at an example.

> *Jaye is a new sales rep for an animal health company. He has a degree in Animal Science. One day he calls on a large hog operation and is told that they want to improve their NBA (number born alive per litter). Jaye knows that one of the products he represents can help keep sows healthy during gestation, so he shares the features of the product.*

> *A few days later, Nancy comes along – Jaye's competitor. Nancy also has a product in her portfolio that can improve NBA by improving sow health during*

gestation. However, Nancy <u>knows</u> more about practical treatment issues and the cost/benefit of treatment than Jaye does. She uses her knowledge and questioning <u>skill</u> to identify some other problems in the operation that could be contributing to lowered NBA. Nancy has the <u>attitude</u> that she is a consultant – not just a seller – and her attitude now is determination to get to bottom of the problem.

This customer will buy from Nancy, rather than Jaye – probably even if Nancy's product costs a little more. Why? With Jaye, the customer has a knowledgeable salesperson. With Nancy, the customer has an advocate who brings as much curiosity and caring to the problem as the customer himself. If we asked the customer to describe the difference between Jaye and Nancy, he could show us a continuum from "minimum skill" to "ideal skill" and then place Nancy and Jaye on the scale. For the example we just explored, the scale might look something like this (Figure 2.2):

Figure 2.2
Sample Competency "Scorecard"

Product Knowledge Competency

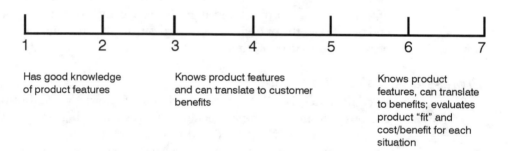

The competency that top customers expect is higher than it used to be. They expect more from their salespeople – and they can find salespeople who will deliver, although they may not live in the same community any more. If your organization has a list of salesperson competencies, study it. Evaluate yourself. Ask a few customers to talk through the "competencies" with you – or just to tell you in their own words what they expect, what you do well, and where they need more. You'll be amazed at how supportive they will be and how eager they are to help you grow. After all, no one knows better than a customer how valuable an excellent salesperson can be.

To Whom Do You Sell?

There are several different types of selling, depending on such factors as the industry, the company's structure, the brand and each individual's approach. One way to classify different types of selling is by the type of customer they serve, and the role of that customer in the distribution channel (Figure 2.3).

Figure 2.3
Distribution Channel

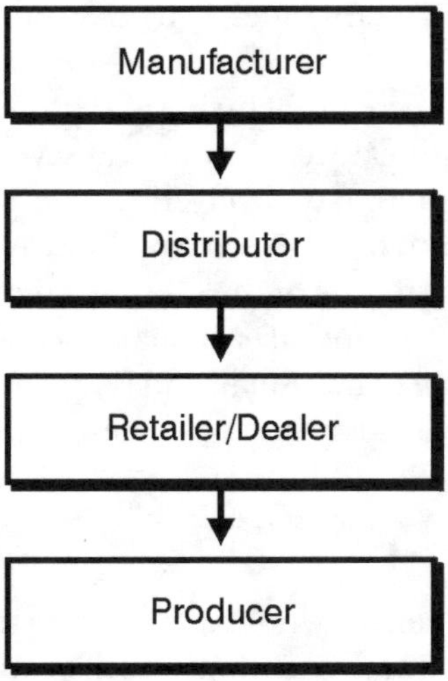

```
┌─────────────────────────────┐
│        Manufacturer         │
└─────────────────────────────┘
              │
              ▼
┌─────────────────────────────┐
│         Distributor         │
└─────────────────────────────┘
              │
              ▼
┌─────────────────────────────┐
│        Retailer/Dealer      │
└─────────────────────────────┘
              │
              ▼
┌─────────────────────────────┐
│          Producer           │
└─────────────────────────────┘
```

Each of these businesses is organized in a slightly different way. Each faces different challenges, has different types of relationships, and may have very different goals.

Manufacturing and Processing Companies

Manufacturing and processing firms typically take raw materials and manufactured inputs and convert them to products that are then sold at the wholesale, retail or farm level. Feed manufacturing firms, vitamin companies, crop protection companies and seed genetics companies are examples of firms that "manufacture" agricultural products. Depending on the manufacturer's distribution strategy, manufacturer sales reps may find themselves selling to distributors, retailers or directly to large farms. This has created a "blurring" of the identification of traditional distribution channel roles and responsibilities. As a manufacturer sales rep, be aware that the identification of your "customer" - distributor, retailer or farmer - is a strategic decision that your company will carefully review and discuss as part of their ongoing marketing strategy planning.

Manufacturing companies need salespeople with a sound technical understanding of their specific product line, as well as a knowledge of customer needs and customer business dynamics. Manufacturer sales reps typically are expected to have very good sales skills and good presentation skills, as well as a very persistent and competitive attitude. Distributors and local retailers often count on the manufacturer sales representative to train them on products, support their selling efforts, stand behind them when there is a complaint, and help them - but only as requested - to improve profitable business management practices. For example, some highly-trusted sales reps work with their customers on issues with high profit impact, such as inventory control, gross margin planning, advertising strategies, and occasionally even personnel issues.

Salespeople in some manufacturing and processing companies are responsible for a wide geographical area - as much as several states. They may travel by airplane to save time, but typically these salespeople spend a lot of time driving. Sales may be few and far between, but they can be very large when they occur. Because of the magnitude of the sale, the salesperson usually stays in regular contact with key personnel at each major account, using a combination of telephone calls, VoiceMail, Email and FAX. In many cases, these sales reps work out of their homes, and during peak seasons they may find themselves working very long hours.

Distributors/Wholesalers

Some salespeople sell for wholesalers and distributors. These businesses buy products from manufacturers and re-sell or "distribute" them to local retail businesses and large producer customers. The salesperson who sells for a distributor usually has a good knowledge of several manufacturers' product lines. They understand the retail environment and develop long-standing relationships with retail managers and others in their industry. Often, the distributor sales rep has the knowledge of the industry and the problem-solving skill to consult with retailers and help them grow their business. Some of these salespeople may travel in a larger geographical area. Regional contacts are made with relatively few customers, typically not farmers, where sales calls are fairly regular. Contacts are also made through trade shows and conventions, where the salesperson is expected to set up exhibits and "man" the booth during specified periods.

Salespeople who sell for distributors and wholesalers may work with buying agents or "brokers" who place orders for product. However, they also work with the retail level - not only to sell there, but also to understand the trends among producers and make sure they have the products and services needed by the market. They may help the retailer sponsor local public relations programs, co-promote specific products and services, train new salespeople in technical areas, and help troubleshoot product complaints. Some distributors also manufacture or "formulate" products that are no longer under patent protection.

Distributor salespeople may take orders themselves, but in many cases they "turn over" the order to a retailer or directly to a warehouse or manufacturing plant. In some cases, they never take an order personally. They also often work out of their own homes, and rarely travel for more than a night or two at a time.

Retailers

Some agricultural salespeople sell for retailers. Retailers sell directly to customers in a local community. Depending on the community, those customers could be farmers, ranchers, flower-growers, beekeepers or purebred cattle breeders – the only characteristic the retail customer has in common is that he or she is the *end-user* of the product.

Often, local retailers sell a variety of products, although they usually specialize in a specific area (such as crop, livestock, insurance, equipment, etc.) Retailers normally receive the products they sell from distributor warehouses or from brokers. For example, manufacturers develop a new crop protection product, and place it with distributors. The distributor sells the product to the retailer, who in turn sells it to the farmer. If the product is a "partner product" to a specific type of bio-engineered seed, the seed and crop protection product will be sold together as a "program approach."

In most cases, this traditional process is still in place. However, as mentioned earlier, some distributors will bypass their retailers to sell directly to large farms. Some manufacturers may try to bypass distributors and sell directly to dealers, or even to farmers. These "end runs" around the system happen because of pressure on profit margins at every channel level. The simplest way to increase profit margin – or so it seems at the time of the decision – is to eliminate one level in the channel and keep the margin they would have received, or use it to offer special incentives to customers.

Although people outside the industry often think of traditional inputs (fertilizer, chemicals, seed) when they think about retailers, there are a variety of individuals and organizations that service the end-user's needs. A partial list of these professionals includes loan officers, accounting services, insurance salespeople, grain buyers and marketers, farm building manufacturers, equipment manufacturers of every type, tradesmen of every type, petroleum salespeople and delivery people, computer services providers, remote communications providers, etc.

To many salespeople, selling to farmers seems like the ultimate in agricultural selling. This job has some distinct advantages, especially for people who want to live in a rural community and "put down roots" there. The close contact with farmers in a local service area provides a closeness to farming itself - one much appreciated by many salespeople who would like to farm but cannot, for whatever reason. Most salespeople at this level have a strong farm background. Whether or not the salesperson grew up on a farm, he or she must develop a sensitivity to current issues, current economics, and current opportunities for customers. A salesperson at this level listens and learns throughout a career, and develops lifelong relationships with customers. Local salespeople seldom spend many nights away from home - usually only for training, meetings and trade shows. However, they typically work very long hours during peak seasons.

Accounts with Multiple Decision Makers

Of course, within each of these businesses, there may be several people to whom you sell (Figure 2.4).

Figure 2.4
Individual "Buyers" Within Channel Levels

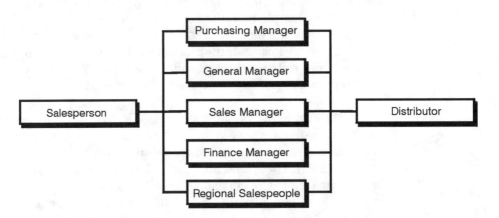

For example, within a distributor business a salesperson may work with product managers, sales managers, general managers, distribution/warehousing managers, financial managers and local or regional distributor salespeople. Each of these people are individuals, with a different set of personal and professional goals that must be recognized and met. As you can see - it gets complicated pretty quickly!

Summary

Agricultural selling is a profession. It has all the attributes of a profession – a code of ethics, a set of scientific principles, systematic procedures, a body of knowledge and a common language. Salespeople are problem solvers. They influence change and the adoption of technology and influence their customers to make sound business decisions.

The direct responsibility of salespeople is to sell products and services. This involves uncovering needs and opportunities with their customers, recommending products and services that will help the customer, and teaching the customer how to use those products and services for optimum effectiveness in their business. Salespeople also have many indirect responsibilities, including handling complaints, maintaining customer relationships, gathering market intelligence, maintaining their own technical competency, collecting, networking with other professionals, maintaining good public and trade relationships, and administration.

How salespeople carry out these responsibilities is extremely important. The best salespeople bring considerable knowledge, skill and a "can do" attitude to their work. Their customers recognize that these salespeople offer them more value and often are extremely loyal to them.

There are several different types of sales jobs, depending on the level of the industry in which a salesperson works. Selling for a manufacturer, a distributor/wholesaler, or a retailer puts the salesperson into contact with different types of businesses. Different types of knowledge are required to be successful in each level, but the skills of questioning, listening and solving problems for each individual and unique customer are important at every level of the industry.

Review Questions

1. The salesperson has a role in offering the customer a value bundle. Give an example of what a salesperson might do to offer that value bundle to the customer.

2. List and define the five building blocks of Professional Selling.

3. Appendix A further discusses the Agricultural Salesperson's Code of Ethics. Select one of the salesperson's responsibilities and explain why and how it is important in building a relationship with a customer in order to get the sale.

4. Choose an indirect responsibility of the salesperson and discuss how it contributes to the salesperson's overall professionalism.

5. What is a professional sales competency? Draw a competency scale of an indirect sales responsibility and evaluate yourself.

Chapter Three

Rewards of an Agricultural Selling Career

Learning Objectives:
Upon completion of this chapter, you should be able to:
1. accurately describe the demand for agricultural selling professionals;
2. recognize three different types of pay for agricultural sales professionals and be able to explain the differences between them;
3. identify six sales support functions and describe how they benefit the salesperson in the field.

Why Become a Salesperson?

The rewards of agricultural selling are as numerous and varied as the people, products and services of the agricultural industry. And, because of the changeable nature of agriculture, the many kinds of products and services, and

the many different types of salespeople, the job is one of the few that <u>never</u> has to be boring. Certain aspects of agricultural selling may be more valued by an individual during different portions of a lifetime or career. For instance, not working in an office may be more appealing to a salesperson during the early portion of a career. Long-term relationships with customers may be more valued during the middle or later portions of a career. The paycheck, although it may become fatter with experience, may be equally appreciated at any given moment of your career.

Salespeople are generally aware of and eager to receive the rewards of selling. Occasionally, a starry-eyed newcomer will eagerly anticipate the rewards without also considering the challenges of being an agricultural sales professional. In this chapter, we'll attempt to present both sides of the coin, with the understanding that we're likely to consider more pros than cons.

One thing about agricultural sales is absolutely clear – almost all successful salespeople love their job. They love the freedom, flexibility, and variety of the job. They love the feeling of helping their customers be successful. They love being technically competent and professional. And, they love getting paid well.

The Jobs Are Out There

Supply and demand is one of the primary economic principles upon which all of sales is based. Fortunately for agricultural sales professionals entering the job market, the law of supply and demand is strongly in their favor. In the U. S., the demand for college graduates in food and agricultural sciences is outstanding. For those graduates in Agricultural Sales, Marketing and Merchandising, demand far outstrips the anticipated supply.

During 1995-2000 in the United States, average annual employment opportunities for college graduates with expertise in the food and agricultural sciences should be 47,918. In contrast, some 45,675 graduates with expertise in agriculture, natural resources, and veterinary medicine are expected to be available to compete each year for these positions.

Projected average annual employment opportunities for college graduates in the food and agricultural sciences, for specific branches of the industry, are summarized in Table 3.1.

Table 3.1
Employment Opportunities for U.S. College Agricultural Graduates [7]

Type of Job	Number Available Annually
Agricultural Communication and Education Specialists	5,295
Agricultural Managers and Financial Specialists	5,613
Agricultural Production Specialists	3,873
Agricultural Sales Representatives, Marketing, Merchandising	14,353
Agricultural Scientists, Engineers, and Related Specialists	13,922
Agricultural Social Services Professionals	4,862

Figure 3.1 illustrates the additional jobs available for graduates of allied disciplines.

[7] Employment Opportunities for College Graduates in the Food and Agricultural Sciences, Agriculture, Natural Resources, Veterinary Medicine 1995-2000. Prepared and published by the School of Agriculture, Purdue University, West Lafayette, Indiana. Supported by Science and Education Resources Development, Cooperative State Research, Education, and Extension Service, U.S. Department of Agriculture, Washington, DC, and issued in furtherance of higher education in the food and agricultural sciences, the National Agricultural Research, Extension, and Teaching Policy Act of 1977, as amended.

Figure 3.1

Annual Available Graduates and Employment Opportunities

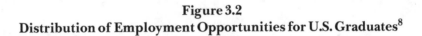

Figure 3.2 illustrates the distribution of jobs across the various disciplines. Note that, according to this report, 30% or almost one-third of the opportunities will be available in sales, marketing and merchandising.

Figure 3.2
Distribution of Employment Opportunities for U.S. Graduates[8]

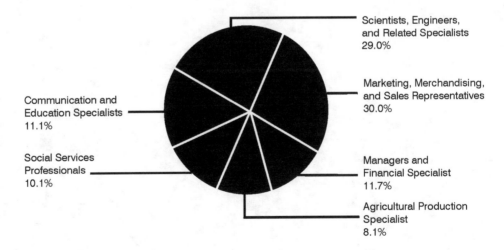

---

[8] ibid

It is encouraging to look at the opportunities available in agricultural selling jobs. Being one of the best salespeople possible will also help ensure a job is available for you, as your career develops and the industry further consolidates.

Snapshot of an "Average" Agricultural Salesperson

The salesperson's responsibilities, routines and remuneration will differ according to numerous factors. The area of the country plays a role, as do the product/service sold, the type and size of company worked for, etc. Even salespeople working for the same company, selling the same product, but working in different parts of the country may have a difficult time comparing customer needs and moods, or their roles and their competitors. In fact, compared side by side, the two may look like completely different jobs! This is natural, given the customer-focused, independent nature of agricultural selling.

While no two salespeople are exactly alike, researchers are able to provide statistically-accurate "snapshots" of a "typical" agricultural salesperson. One such study was conducted by Southern Illinois University economists Kim Harris and Anthony Sepich[9]. They conducted surveys of agricultural salespeople in the input/supply industry in 39 southern Illinois counties in November, 1997. They developed the following profile (Table 3.2).

---

[9] Harris, K. and Sepich, A.. Tomorrow's Super Salesperson: Man, Woman or Machine? Farm Chemicals Magazine .May 1998.

Table 3.2
Profile of Typical Agricultural Input Salesperson (Southern Illinois) 1997

Salesperson Characteristics	Job Characteristics
• 41 years old	• Has territory with 443,350 tillable acres (5.5 counties)
• 97% male - 3% female	• Works 55.1 hours per week
• Bachelor's Degree	• Sales of $3.35 million per year
• Farm Background	• Makes $43,310 salary + bonus
• Over 11 years selling for present employer	• Selling time is worth $3,998 per hour
• Sells chemicals and/or fertilizer and/or seed	

Of course, this is only a "snapshot" view of agricultural selling in one part of the country—a 39-county area in Illinois. However, it does provide some perspective.

According to Harris and Sepich, seven out of ten salespeople in the survey felt information technology made their jobs easier today than in the past. Eight out of ten salespeople believed information technology would make their jobs still easier in the future. Specific benefits cited by respondents included:

- saving time (65%);
- improving communications (63%); and
- increasing productivity (52%).

In addition, more than one-fourth of salespeople felt the adoption of information technology had increased their selling time.

Stacy Dunn
AgrEvo USA Company
Sales Representative
Indianapolis, Indiana

A lot of people who go into sales perceive their internship to be "what it is all about," but mine was totally different. When I completed my internship, I got the glory part of being a salesman. I saw what they got and what they did. It seemed very social and a lot of fun.

It is all those things, but there is a lot more office work than I thought there would be. There is a huge responsibility to discipline yourself not only in how you carry out the actual people contact and selling part of sales itself (what I consider the fun part), but to make yourself know, understand and do all the background work that goes into the sale – knowing the customers, the company, the company's goals, the products, who is a best prospect and why, what to do with dollar goals, money concerns, scheduling yourself, your meetings, your customers, etc. You have to be vigilant at keeping on yourself to keep all this stuff straight. It really makes a difference. No, selling is definitely not an 8-5 job!

I think the first couple years are the hardest. I believe you need that long to fully understand what you are doing and how to do it. I think if you don't have a sense of who you are, you may be in trouble. It gets lonely out there. There are not companions out there like in an office. You develop relationships with your customers, but you only see them for about a half hour and then you are on the road for an hour to your next customer. You don't always have people around you. You spend a lot of time alone. Not until you have those experiences under your belt do you fully start to reap the rewards of the selling business.

Rewards of Selling

Selling is the heartbeat of any business. Sales generate revenue for the company directly. Companies depend on salespeople for consistent effort. They entrust their future - their precious new products - to their care and cultivation. In some industries, the competition for high-performing salespeople is keen. Most professional salespeople can expect to take home a solid paycheck, especially when they are at their most productive levels.

Financial Rewards

Agricultural selling is generally a well-paid profession. Starting salaries in the field are particularly good when the beginning salesperson is a graduate of a university, college or technical agricultural program. Employers look for someone with an academic and work history that indicates such traits as leadership, ability to deal with people, and agricultural experience. When a firm is seeking to hire a more experienced salesperson, past performance is generally considered a reliable indicator of future performance and compensation. Table 3.3 summarizes starting salaries, as provided by the Bureau of Labor Statistics in 1996.

Table 3.3
Comparative Starting Salaries in Selling and Agriculture Related Jobs (1996)[10]

Industry	Starting Salary
Animal Science	$24,200
Plant Science	$22,500
Forestry	$20,950
Soil Conservation	$20,950
Biological/Life Science	$26,700
Farm Operator/Manager	$11,376
Agricultural Marketing	$25,400
Agricultural Advertising	$22,000
Agricultural Economics	$27,600
Agricultural Consumer Loan Officer	$27,200
Agricultural Residential Real Estate	$28,500
Agricultural Commercial Lender	$36,100
Average	$24,800

Types of Compensation

Incentive Compensation

Many companies offer some kind of direct financial incentive to salespeople. The type of incentive depends on the objective of the company and, to a certain degree, on what has been traditional within an industry. For example, a company that wants to increase sales volume might offer a straight commission on each sale. A company that wants to promote *profitable* sales (rather than volume of sales) might provide a commission on sales margin, or an end-of-the year bonus based on company profits over the last 12 months. Still other companies offer special incentives to encourage salespeople to call on certain targeted types of

---

[10] Bureau of Labor Statistics http://stats.bls.gov/

customers, or to sell a specific amount of a new product (accelerate its adoption). Finally, some companies offer a variety of bonuses and incentives, depending on their strategy and their financial situation.

Many salespeople find financial incentive programs appealing because they constitute a direct reward for successful efforts. However, sometimes such a program is difficult to administer fairly. For instance, a salesperson may assist dealers as they buy through a distributor. This is a common situation in agricultural chemical companies. The intermediary seller – in this case a distributor – makes it difficult to measure results from one salesperson's specific activities. In these cases, salespeople often work toward a team bonus, based on the collective results of their region or area.

Straight commission sales (no base salary) is not too common, and definitely not for the faint-hearted. It is more common for salespeople to earn a straight salary, with bonuses or raises given as a result of a supervisor's formal appraisal or evaluation. Salary plus commission is a combination of a lower base salary with the addition of a commission from products or services sold. Table 3.4 summarizes the different forms a salesperson's paycheck can take, and the degree of risk associated with each type of compensation.

Table 3.4
Types of Sales Compensation

Type of Salary	Explanation	Example	Risk
Straight Salary	Salesperson receivers guaranteed, predictable, annual salary usually paid by a bi-month paycheck	Jan makes $24,000 per year regardless of selling 1000 units or 10,000 units	Low
Salary Plus Commission	Salesperson receives a lower, set annual salary at the predictable bi-monthly or monthly interval and in addition, receives an agreed upon commission for what they sell	Jack sells tons of hog feed vita-mix for $240,000 in one year. Jack receives $16,000 base plus 5% commission - base plus $12,000 commission for a total of $28,000	Medium
Straight Commission	Salesperson receives a set percentage of the dollar value they generate through their selling efforts	Jon sells tons of hog feed vita-mix for $240,000 in one year. 15% commission means Jon's commission is $36,000	High

Many of the highest paid salespeople are on full commission. There is high risk associated with this compensation plan. The salesperson who sells nothing also makes nothing. The more is sold, the more is made. The employer has little risk because the salesperson gets paid based on only what is sold. Of course, if the salesperson is very good at selling, he/she stands to make a high income. It is not unusual for good commissioned salespeople to earn six digit incomes - and their employers pay quite willingly. On the other hand, a straight commission job is no place for an amateur or inexperienced salesperson.

Other Incentives

Some companies encourage, motivate, or reward salespeople with the possibility of earning trips, vacation packages, cars, or other bonuses. Usually, those rewarded with such lavish gifts are in the top sales bracket for the company. In almost every instance, the rewards are directly commensurate with sales performance—a fair distribution that many other professionals might well envy.

Occasionally, a salesperson might be offered an incentive in the form of a sales contest or special promotion. Holiday trips to exotic resorts for the salesperson and spouse, television sets, and sporting equipment are all common rewards for

winning contests. Perhaps even more important, for many salespeople, is the recognition that comes from the company and peers for outstanding performance. Competitiveness is a common trait of good salespeople. They love to win!

Sometimes rewards are offered by a manufacturer or supplier - not by the company itself. In order to motivate salespeople to higher levels of sales, a manufacturer or distributor may develop special programs. Most companies have formal policies that state whether or not it is appropriate to participate in such contests and/or to receive merchandise or incentives from someone other than the employer. These policies protect the reputation of the salesperson and the reputation of the company, by ensuring that products are sold to fit needs - not to win trips. If you are offered a special incentive or reward by a supplier, check with your manager first to determine whether or not you should accept it.

Non-Financial Rewards of Selling

Personal Rewards

In Chapter Two we established that salespeople are problem solvers, facilitators and influencers. The greatest reward, for many agricultural salespeople, is helping customers answer their production or business needs. They are energized and gratified when they can help a customer achieve success through their knowledge or problem-solving skills. This sense of personal satisfaction is the greatest single reward of selling, according to the most dedicated selling professionals. Immense satisfaction comes from meeting the challenges of making the sale. A satisfied new customer or a paycheck is not only viewed as meeting goals. It is tangible evidence that they have done a good job. They like the flexible schedule, independence to organize and run their daily routine to suit their individual style, and their self-image as manager of their own sales territory..

> **Martin Harry**
> **BASF Canada, Inc.**
> **Technical Sales Representative**
> **Ingersoll, Ontario, Canada**
>
> My favorite part of sales is making face to face sales calls. I love taking orders, completing the action, solving someone's problem, filling their needs. It gives me great satisfaction to be helping people, having a product they really want or need that fits their needs. Another big reward I get is when the dealer does something for you. In this business, they are my customers. I am always buying them lunch. Or, I am bringing stuff in. Sometimes they surprise me and buy my lunch or do something for me or when they ask me to help them set pricing. That's satisfying because then you know it is a true relationship.

Agricultural selling offers a degree of independence not matched in many fields. Managing your sales territory as if it were your own company is a great personal responsibility and provides a tremendous sense of accomplishment. If "variety is the spice of life," agricultural selling is the salsa of careers. In agricultural selling, no two days are alike.

There are two reasons for this variety and fast pace. First, selling means solving problems and creating opportunities – and no two customer businesses are alike. No two customers think in exactly the same way. You will always be challenged to come up with a fresh approach, to listen for an emerging need, and to fit new technologies into a unique set of existing systems. Second, agricultural selling is more challenging than some other selling careers, because so many factors are beyond the control of any one business. Commodity and livestock prices, weather patterns, crop conditions, world markets – all vary day to day, week to week, year to year. As your customers face each new challenge, it is your privilege to be the person helping them meet it successfully.

Agricultural salespeople work so closely with their customers that close personal friendships can develop over time. These are another reward of agricultural selling; such relationships can help salespeople build their own credibility. Everyone imagines, at the start of their career, that they will enjoy the respect of others as they develop skills, knowledge and solid customer relationships. Agricultural selling is one of the few careers where most of the factors that determine respect and relationships are <u>directly</u> under the control of the salesperson.

By their nature, salespeople also like meeting and dealing with a wide spectrum of people. Their interest in human behavior, science, technology, and innovation can be engaged every day of their careers. And many salespeople simply want the opportunity to work closely with agriculture and all the good things that implies.

Advancement

Traditionally, salespeople tended to view a sales job as the first step in a career path leading to more "important" jobs. This attitude is disappearing. It is no longer appropriate for many sales careers. More salespeople are realizing the intrinsic worth of a sales career. They don't want to trade a life of problem-solving, trouble-shooting, lifelong learning and community membership for a desk job in a big city. Many companies are responding to the challenge to keep good salespeople by building several levels of seniority into their field sales force structure. Today, there are increasing opportunities to earn an MBA in Agribusiness through weekend "executive programs" or internally, while continuing to work full time. Top salespeople are often asked to contribute their experience and their understanding of the market to strategic planning, new product launch planning, marketing program design and employee satisfaction advisory councils.

Senior salespeople are a critical asset for the company – and they are well-paid for the job they do. In fact, it is not uncommon that a promotion into a managerial position at company headquarters can mean a decrease in both the pay envelope and the general standard of living. A sales career can bring status and high financial rewards, while allowing the salesperson and his or her family to remain in the same area throughout a career. There are a <u>variety</u> of career paths open to successful agricultural salespeople, ranging from a financially rewarding career in field selling to upper management.

In their book, <u>Guerrilla Selling</u>[11], Jay Conrad Levinson, Bill Gallagher, Ph.D., and Orvel Ray Wilson point out:

> *Many salespeople earn more than doctors or lawyers, and the majority of Fortune 500 presidents started their careers in sales. It's the fast track to professional leadership, income, and prestige, because people who can generate business are the lifeblood of any organization.*

The aggressive, productive and effective salesperson can move on to more and more responsible sales-related positions, should they desire to do so. At first, this may simply mean an increase in sales territory, or responsibility for more crucial customers. But it may eventually include a move into sales management supervising salespeople. In the larger firms, advancement is usually well mapped out, with geographical relocation accompanying at least some of the steps. In local companies, by contrast, the chance of professional growth is less measurable. Here, it is tied to such things as increased respect (in the firm and in the community); broader market penetration; additional responsibilities within the company; and close, well-established relationships with customers.

It is also not uncommon for a successful professional selling experience to lead to opportunities in the broader field of general management or elsewhere in business. Because sales are the heart of the business, many firms put a premium on field selling experience. In fact, some agricultural firms (particularly marketing-oriented firms) require field selling experience for important management posts – with the exception of those highly technical fields like accounting or research. Therefore, field selling often is a good stepping stone into staff and line management, if that is the ultimate goal.

Ray McLaughlin
Blue SEAL Feeds
Dairy Product Manager
Dairy Manager at Bow, New Hampshire Facility
Londonderry, New Hampshire

I think selling is an excellent starting point to launch a lot of careers...but I think it doesn't have to just be a springboard to some other opportunity. Selling as a career, in my eyes, is a very exciting career in itself. I think agriculture is really exciting, even more so today than when I got into it. There are lots of rewards being out there on your own. You're on your own, you're answering to nobody, you're setting your own plan for the day. You are responsible. That's satisfying because then you know it is a true relationship.

---

[11] Levinson, J., Gallagher, B. and Wilson, O. Guerrilla Selling. Houghton Mifflin Company, New York, New York: 1992.

Challenges of the Selling Profession

Despite the glamour of setting one's own schedule, the lure of long-term satisfied customer relationships, and the enticement of the good monetary rewards, selling is still work. Agricultural salespeople must deal with the challenges of the job as well as its rewards. One of the most difficult challenges is the fear of rejection – of the customer saying *No!*

Rejection is a normal part of any sales job. Few people find it a pleasant experience. Everyone dreads hearing *No!.... Not now..... I'll think it over!..... I'm too busy!* You may invest a great deal of time, thought and sweat in trying to educate customers to a new idea or new product, and then see it rejected out of hand by six prospects in a row! Although there are many stories of famous people who failed many times before they succeeded, that doesn't help much when the door has just been closed in *your* face.

It helps to remember why you are selling: to solve problems. That means uncovering needs and new opportunities for customers. If they already understood what your product or service could do for them, they'd come to you. Change is not always comfortable for people. Their loyalty to current products and brands is a result, in part, of their loyalty to their current salespeople. Now – that's not a bad thing, is it? When customers reject your solution, figure out why (and no, it's not always the price). If you don't know why – ask them.

Then there are complaints. The only thing worse than having them is not having them, because the only way to completely avoid complaints is not to sell anything. But dealing with complaints is seldom pleasant. Handled properly, a salesperson may turn a complaint into a positive, but it often means dealing with a customer who is upset and disappointed. That can be difficult. It helps to remember that you can and should react to the customer's distress, even if you cannot resolve the complaint as he or she would like. Most customers hate complaints as much as salespeople. No one wants to have a failure, even if your company is willing to defray part of the cost.

The hours are often punishing in agricultural sales, especially in peak season. An agricultural salesperson covering a large sales territory may travel for weeks during peak season without spending many nights at home, or much time with friends or family on evenings and weekends. Travel combined with long hours can be very wearing. It helps to pace yourself – attend to personal business before peak seasons. If you have a family, talk to them about what is happening. Many children are delighted to learn more about what their dads and moms do, especially when their jobs involve helping people.

Stress can mount, especially during peak seasons. And, because every minute of the day doesn't have to be accounted for to someone, self-motivation becomes important. To keep going can be a very difficult proposition indeed when all is not going smoothly. Self discipline must be very high in these situations. Though salespeople generally work with many people, they are often geographically isolated from others in their own company, and even from those to whom they report. Consequently, if on the road for long stretches of time, many new salespeople begin to feel that they face the world alone. E-mail, phone, voice mail, and faxes help, but many salespeople miss the day-to-day camaraderie that is common in many other jobs.

Depending on the size of the company, salespeople may be required to move frequently. When you move to different areas, states, or territories, it requires a great deal of effort to reestablish personal and professional relationships. Many psychologists put "moving" on their top five list of most stressful activities humans can experience. This stress is compounded when there is a spouse who also has a professional career.

So, how "good" is a selling professional's job? It depends on each person's innate preferences as to activities, rewards and challenges. However, it is abundantly clear that the public's negative stereotype of "the salesperson" just doesn't fit in agricultural selling.

Sales Support Functions

Salespeople who approach their careers with an open mind and a learner's spirit seem to be supported by a cast of thousands. Company staff, university educators, extension employees, peers in non-competing businesses, hundreds of selling books and tapes, magazines – and even customers themselves are ready, willing and able to give them the help needed to close the sale and satisfy the customer. The most effective salespeople respect the professionalism and expertise of the different specialists who provide them with support. The number of company specialists supporting sales varies with the size of the company and the nature of its business. There may be one or two, or there may be several hundred. Whether you are working with people who support sales within your company, or with a wider network of support, there is always a need for a good two-way relationship. Ask – listen – learn. It works well with customers, and it is equally effective in getting support from peers, managers and company staff.

Supervisors

Supervisors are often the most accessible of all sales support personnel. They are also usually among the most helpful. Sales supervisors usually supervise a specific geography – a state, area or a region. Or, they may supervise a specific sales function, such as telemarketing. Supervisors carry such titles as "district manager" or "sales manager." They work closely with the salespeople in their area to ensure their success. Salespeople usually maintain fairly regular contact with their supervisors. Most talk to their manager at least once a week, and maybe every several days. For many salespeople, their manager is more than a boss. He/she is also a mentor, an advisor, a shoulder to cry on and a coach. Contact is often by phone, with less frequent face-to-face contact.

Often, the supervisor is the primary trainer for a new salesperson, explaining the duties and expectations of the job. The supervisor generally works closely with new people, especially in the very early months. This early training phase usually involves passing along specific procedures and product information, as well as a few days in the field introducing the new salesperson to regular customers and providing tips on selling methods and skills. Supervisors are ultimately accountable for success in their own geography, so they are almost always anxious to be as supportive and helpful to their salespeople as possible. The sales manager is the direct pipeline to company management, and so must be treated respectfully.

Training Programs

Chances are, in the first few months on the job, the company will make sure that new employees receive some form of training. It may be some type of orientation program - there are programs as short as an hour and as long as six months in different companies. Often new employees receive specific computer and task-based training, whether formal or informal. Formal training in selling skills is now typically offered by companies interested in maximizing the potential offered by the sales force.

Training doesn't stop when the employee learns the basics of the job. More and more, companies are also recognizing the value of regular, periodic training even for their more experienced sales staff as well. Some have professional company trainers or outside consultants to provide useful reviews of skills and techniques. Many companies offer - or even require - ongoing training in customer skills and technical knowledge. Other companies do not offer training "in-house," but allow employees to pursue skill improvement through supplier-paid training or local seminars and community college courses. Many companies have tuition reimbursement programs to encourage continued learning. Data from the U.S. Bureau of Labor Statistics shows that employees who work in establishments with 50 or more employees received an average of 44.5 hours of training in each six month period. Of that total, 70 percent of the training time was spent informally, and 30 percent was formal training[12].

---

[12] USBLS

Sometimes job training is accomplished through self-study materials that companies may pass along to new salespeople. These might include product information, general company orientation, fundamental selling tips, etc. At other times, the company may devote a few days or weeks at headquarters to such basics before sending new salespeople to the field. It is useful to remember, however, that nearly all companies expect on-the-job training to be the core of their training program.

Whenever customers have a special problem that is beyond the scope of a salesperson's expertise, the salesperson can count on technologists, specialists, scientists, etc. from the home or regional office to act as troubleshooters. Farm equipment companies, for example, might assign agricultural engineers to this task. The equivalent in an agricultural chemical company might be the entomologist or agronomist. Likewise, when a cattle feeder is grappling with problems of slow rate of gain, he can encourage the feed salesperson to bring along the nutritionist to help investigate the problem.

Advertising

Advertising adds credibility to the sales effort. Salespeople can use advertisements to arouse interest or "test the water" when talking about a new product's benefits. The salesperson's job is made easier when the customer's awareness of products and services has already been sparked by a company advertising and promotion campaign. In turn, the value of advertising, promotions and point of sales displays are all increased when they are supported by a face-to-face sales call. This is true in the case of both national and local advertising campaigns. In some agricultural industries, such as animal health, the advertising department may even personalize ad copy to fit individual dealers, and then run the copy in the dealer's local newspaper. In such cases, the parent company may split the cost of local advertising with the dealer. Whoever foots the bill, the ultimate winner is the salesperson.

Marketing

The marketing department often develops special incentives and programs that the salesperson can use to enhance the desirability of the product or service. Some companies develop elaborate programs, with special "thresholds" for ever-increasing discount, rebate or incentive levels. Others may have something simple, such as a travel incentive. When customers earn trips to exotic resorts from manufacturers, it is common for salespeople to accompany them. This can be an incentive for the salesperson as well as for the customer. It provides the opportunity for the salesperson to develop closer relationships with key customers.

Indirect support for the selling effort may come through efforts of the research and development team, who develop products and services for the salesperson to sell. The better job they do, the easier the job of the salesperson. For example, every salesperson likes to have a great new product to bring to customers. Let's assume the research department can develop a superior new variety of wheat. Product commercialization experts will work with agronomists and marketing experts to determine if the new variety has a profitable future. If they determine it does, the new product will be carefully shepherded and brought to market by a product manager. As a salesperson you may meet this product manager on a field visit, as he or she tries to learn more about selling challenges and competitive products. Eventually, when the product enters the commercial market, it may have a special sales incentive attached. Or, it may simply become the new "star" in the wheat portfolio. This whole process is guided, behind the scenes, by marketers and their research colleagues.

Credit

The credit department has the responsibility for helping grow "collectable" sales. Some salespeople make the mistake of viewing this department as more of an obstacle than a help. Yet, because the sale has not been completed until the money is in hand, the credit department often saves the salesperson from unnecessary headaches. One uncollectible bad debt can cancel out all the profit made from dozens, perhaps hundreds, of sales. Follow the credit department's credit approval guidelines carefully. The credit department can keep a salesperson out of trouble – and can serve as the "bad guy" when a customer must be denied credit.

Outside Agencies

Beyond the internal support services offered for salespeople, there are all sorts of outside sources that can be tapped by an alert and dedicated professional for information, problem-solving techniques, or other sales support. These sources include universities, the trade press, government agencies, the cooperative extension service and even dealers or customers themselves. Most salespeople in agriculture have used all these sources at one time or another in their career. Become familiar with them and learn how to get the most out of them.

Summary

Why do people decide to pursue a career in agricultural selling? The reasons are as different as the people who sell and the customers they serve. Many agricultural salespeople enjoy the high level of freedom to plan each day, strategize for each customer, and live "by their wits." Others like the systematic approach to information and accounts, and the fact that their relationships with customers can last for years. Still others choose sales jobs because the better they are, the more they can earn.

Regardless of the reasons for becoming a salesperson, it appears that the demand for qualified people will exceed the supply of agriculture and technical graduates for some time in the future. Many of the jobs to be filled are in the agricultural marketing and selling areas. This is particularly fortunate for job-seekers (and unfortunate for the industry), because technical change in all facets of production appears to be occurring at a faster rate than ever before. The industry needs well-educated, technically expert salespeople to help customers transition to new opportunities and new ways of doing business.

New salespeople are not the only ones valued by agricultural companies. While they need to constantly recruit, orient and train new salespeople, most companies depend on their experienced salespeople to consistently generate sales volume. These salespeople are especially valuable, because their long-term close relationships with customers allow them insight into changing moods, trends and issues in the marketplace.

Salespeople are generally well-compensated. This compensation may come as a base salary, a base salary plus commission, or a straight commission. In addition to salary (or commission), the salesperson may be eligible to participate in special promotions, contests, or bonus programs. Some companies have none of these special programs - others have many.

In addition to the financial rewards from selling, many salespeople find they are motivated by pride and sense of accomplishment in helping customers. Many also enjoy the lifestyle. They would prefer to stay a salesperson in the same geography, with a stable family location and community ties, rather than moving up the corporate ladder and moving out to a major city. In fact, there are so many satisfactions and such generally-competitive compensation for salespeople today that many no longer consider it a "stepping stone" to a management job. Although experience in field sales is still considered a very valuable background for management, career field salespeople may not always want to move.

The job of selling can be very challenging. Rejection, complaints, long hours, stress, and isolation from peers can all take their toll. Most successful salespeople develop a network of friends, experts and supporters to help them through the difficult times. While many of these supporters may be other company employees, some may be peers in the community, university experts, or even customers. Within the company, depending on its size, there may be many functions that support the sales effort. These include sales managers, trainers and training programs, marketing and product development, marketing communications and advertising, and credit services.

Review Questions

1. According to the report on Employment Opportunities for U.S. Graduates, what percentage of employment opportunities are available annually to those in sales, marketing and merchandising?

2. In Stacy Dunn's case study, she talks about the fact that there is a lot more to agri selling than meets the eye. Discuss some of the things she points out as challenging and explain how those challenges might affect a new salesperson.

3. Describe the differences between three types of incentive compensations.

4. There are three case studies in this chapter. Discuss the similarities and differences these professionals have regarding the rewards of agri selling.

5. List and define the six sales support functions.

Chapter Four

Why People Buy

Learning Objectives:

Upon completion of this chapter, you should be able to:

1. list two reasons people buy;
2. describe Maslow's theory on motivation and how it applies to agricultural selling;
3. identify the three buyer types and describe key characteristics of each type;
4. determine why selling to opinion leaders is important.

Why Do Customers Buy?

The Economic Exchange Model

The "economic exchange" model describes much of the selling and buying in the agricultural industry. When customers buy a product or service, they expect to give up something in return. In the U.S., they usually exchange money for products and services. In other parts of the world, they may exchange a portion of their harvested crop for product and service inputs. This basic exchange of goods, services, or currency is as old as civilization.

In the very beginning, when selling first began, the prehistoric cave-salesperson did not make a deal because he'd worked out a slick presentation. He had something – an extra club, an excess amount of antelope meat, a cave, a strange new thing called fire – that another caveman wanted. And the potential customer had something to exchange – something the first caveman wanted. Although the real trick in those days was to come to some mutually beneficial exchange agreement before the other person slugged you on the head and took your antelope meat, the basic element of a sale was there. Each person had something the other person needed. The person who was smart enough to initiate the exchange was the salesperson.

Buyers almost always behave rationally in this respect. They make a specific purchase decision because they believe they'll gain more than they expect to give up. What they gain may be measurable economic benefit, like a solution to a problem. In these situations, it's easy to see what the buyer gains. However, customers also buy because of their emotional and psychological needs. They may choose a product because it brings "peace of mind," or because it enhances their status.

Perceived "Need"

To sell effectively, a person must first understand <u>what</u> each customer wants and <u>why</u> they want it. People buy to solve problems or to satisfy needs. "Need" is, in one sense, an absolute concept. As a salesperson, you may correctly evaluate that a retailer "needs" to train employees, or "needs" to replace an old sprayer that has become undependable. Your evaluation is based on the facts. If you make a recommendation to the retailer based on those facts, you may or may not be successful. Why? Why can't the retailer see the need as clearly as you do? The incongruence between your evaluation of need and the retailer's evaluation of need has nothing to do with the facts. It comes, instead, from how those "facts" are interpreted.

We each see the world through a very unique and individual perceptual filter. A "clean" room means something different to a thirteen-year old than to an adult. A "good car" may mean something very different when you are in college than it does when you are twenty years into a well-paying career. Because of this perceptual filter, needs are actually *relative*, not absolute. One farmer "needs" a new combine with all the newest features. The next farmer may be perfectly happy to drive a combine for several years, until it becomes mechanically unreliable. This happens because these farmers experience their "needs" in different ways. As a salesperson, you want to meet the individual, unique needs of each customer. Doing so requires that you be able to recognize multiple types or levels of need – many of which may be different than those you personally perceive or those you believe the "facts" would dictate.

The Hierarchy of Human Needs

The pioneer in suggesting how individual perceptions of need could be organized and understood was Abraham Maslow. In his book, <u>Motivation and Personality</u>[13], Maslow suggested that human needs are arranged into a five-level hierarchy. The most critical needs, physiological survival needs, come first. Maslow proposed that, with rare exceptions, the needs at one level must be met before the next level of need was "engaged," or became a motivating force. If you

---

[13] Maslow, A.. Motivation and Personality. Harper and Row, New York, New York: 1954, 1970.

think about it, you can see this happening all around you. As a salesperson, you work hard to identify a need and offer a solution, only to hear the customer say, "I can't even <u>think</u> about that now...my first priority is to clear my operating loan or I won't even <u>be</u> here to talk to next year." The customer is operating at a different level of "need" than you imagined. And, unfortunately for salespeople, sometimes the motivating level of need can change fairly quickly.

Maslow named the five levels of need he identified and placed them in the following hierarchy (Figure 4.1).

Figure 4.1
Maslow's Hierarchy of Human Needs

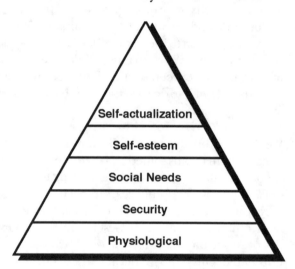

Physiological Needs

The most basic need is to survive, and thus the most fundamental level of needs are physiological, or driven by the needs of the body — air, water, food, shelter, warmth, sleep and sexual fulfillment. Unless these needs have been met, a person will not be motivated to fulfill needs on the next levels. For example, when smoke begins to fill a room and with it the sounds of choking and calls of "fire," a person's highest priority and need is to get out of there quickly. The need to escape danger is more powerful than concern about finances, reputation, or dignity.

Another example is the issue of worker safety. Agricultural production in highly industrialized countries is often more concerned about worker safety issues than in developing countries. A country that is struggling to produce enough food for its inhabitants (and has little money to buy food on the international market) may exercise many instances of "unsafe" practices – according to an industrialized nation's standards. However, when a country or person is struggling to survive, safety becomes a "nice to have." Enough food remains a "must have" – the primary motivating need.

Security Needs

Once a person is not immediately threatened, he/she begins to think about safety and security in the future. While many North American and European farmers don't normally worry about meeting survival needs, they may worry about security. For example, in times when the agricultural economy is poor, farmers buy very conservatively. They are acutely aware of how their decisions in one year affect their ability to keep their farm and stay profitable 2-3 years down the road. Farmers may buy only the equipment they absolutely must have, and may buy used equipment rather than new. They may buy generic (unbranded) weed control products, even though they are older technology, because they work fairly well and cost much less. They may save seed for wheat or soybeans, to keep their costs down, even though they "know" that this seed may not produce as well if used year after year. Salespeople selling to farmers concerned with survival or security needs must recognize that these customers are less interested in the "latest, best" product and more interested in a product they can depend on at a low price.

Social Needs

Once survival and security needs have been met, people start dealing with more complex social needs. They want to be accepted by other people. They find enjoyment in belonging to a group. Families, social cliques, clubs and agricultural organizations help fill these needs. Peer acceptance can be a very strong motivator for some people. They are motivated to "keep up with the neighbors" or at least choose a course of action that is accepted by their friends. If selling in a rural community, the salesperson must recognize and meet these needs.

Social needs can make the salesperson's job easier – or harder. For example, let's say a salesperson is selling a new transgenic seed product with excellent insect resistance. Let's assume a few leading farmers use the product and like it. A few leading input retailers talk about it with customers. The salesperson may find he/she is selling insect-resistant seed to farmers who have had economic damage from insects as well as to farmers who feel these products are "the thing to do." Their need for this specific product trait is minimal – they buy simply because everybody is doing it.

On the other hand, in communities where social needs are very strong, the seller must also recognize and accept his/her role in becoming part of the customer community. Selling in a rural community often means participation in and support of the community and the local customer groups. For example, the salesperson had better be at the County Fair 4-H auction, and some farmers will watch to make sure their salesperson bids on the champion – even if it's not their daughter's or grandson's project. The money is less the issue here. Rather, this event is a chance to demonstrate support of the local agricultural community. Some farmers watch to see who understands this.

Self-esteem Needs

Self-esteem needs are even more complicated. These involve the desire for respect by others and a need to feel important. Once a farmer feels reasonably accepted by peers, he/she may be motivated to do something to be noticed by others in their group or to enhance status. Being elected to a leadership position, being recognized as a top farmer, or driving a new combine can all help fill this need. A dealer may buy new variable rate technology equipment not because it is *a profitable* decision, but because it fits the image of the dealership as forward-thinking and professional.

When selling to self-esteem needs, the salesperson is helping a customer excel. A cash grain farmer may want the highest yields in the county, or absolutely "clean" (weed-free) fields. Cotton farmers still like to have the first bale in their area, as well as to produce fiber that grades high. A fruit or vegetable farmer may want his produce to grade at top quality levels. A livestock or poultry producer may want top rates of gain, or lowest rates of disease, or fewest days to market. These farmers are motivated not only by the economic rewards, but also by the respect their results bring from other farmers and from their suppliers. Some salespeople find these customers challenging, but other salespeople find them the most enjoyable. When a customer asks you whether his or her product, equipment, facility or staff is the "best you've ever seen," you may well be dealing with someone who has strong self-esteem needs. In such a situation, you also need to "be the best around" or bring someone with you who is. Recognized superiority in technical knowledge and skill may become important to meeting this customer's needs.

Self-actualization Needs

"Self-actualization" needs are the most complex of all. These involve the need for a sense of self-worth or personal accomplishment. Self-actualization comes about not because others note a person's accomplishments, but from the good feeling a person gets inside about himself or herself from doing something he or she believes is important. A Peace Corps Volunteer, a school board president, and a person who contributes to local charities are fulfilling their needs for self-actualization. They provide a service not for prestige, but because they feel it is an important and worthwhile contribution.

The Hierarchy of Needs and the Salesperson

How does the Maslow hierarchy of needs apply to the salesperson? Among the salesperson's peers and friends in agriculture and business, most people will probably have their basic needs for physical survival already met. While making ends meet is a challenge for much of the working population at some point or another, people generally have enough food on the table or know how to get some. Most salespeople spend most of their effort selling to people who are acting on their needs for social acceptance and self-esteem. This can be an important factor in how the salesperson tailors the sales presentation or approaches a prospect. Let's look at some examples.

Kevin was an experienced salesperson, representing a line of livestock buildings and feed storage facilities. Over the years, he had worked with a variety of customers, and it never ceased to amaze him how two people could look at the same set of facts and draw two totally different conclusions. Why, just last week, he had made calls on two large hog operations not ten miles apart.

At the first, his customer Tim met him at the office, which was neat as a pin. Kevin noticed a new plaque on the wall, thanking Tim for several years of service in the state Pork Producers Association, and Kevin congratulated him on it. They continued a conversation they had begun a few weeks before, planning for replacement of a sow barn. This was part of Tim's eventual transition to a multiple-site facility, to reduce disease and improve baby pig production. Turns out, Tim had talked with one of the best ag engineers in the state, who agreed that their plans were sound. Kevin collected the final details he needed to make a bid, and reminded Tim that he was making a good decision. "I know," Tim replied, "This place will be a real showplace when we're through."

The second farm looked totally different. Entering the office (which looked like it had been furnished from army surplus), Kevin passed a pile of dead baby pigs out front. This customer, Wally Jameson, had battled high death rates in the nursery for years. And for years, Kevin had preached the message of multiple sites to control disease and improve productivity. Yet, as Wally walked in, Kevin could see that today wouldn't be any different than any other. Wally was exhausted. His son had taken off in a huff because Wally'd yelled at him; his hired man had hurt himself a month ago; and the hog market was falling. Wally just couldn't seem to get a solid foundation under his operation – he was always just about three months away from not being able to make it. Kevin mentioned his "message" on *multiple site production, but Wally just rolled his eyes. Wally asked Kevin to give him a "lowest possible" bid on replacing a sow barn – right next to the one he had. As Wally put it, "I'm just not interested in some new approach – not until I have the business under control will I even <u>think</u> about spending money on an idea." As Kevin left, he assured Wally that the building he proposed would do the best job for the least money, to which Wally replied, "Yeah...well I sure hope so...otherwise we may not even be here in a year."*

In these situations, Kevin is selling the same product to two farmers with the same *technical* problem - baby pig health - but with two very different buying motivations. He can sell successfully to both, but only by recognizing and accepting the needs they feel.

Jack hung up the phone with a surprised look on his face. In the five years he'd been working around Pauckacett as a crop consultant, he'd never expected to get a call from old Harry Sangstrom, manager of one of the best independent local input dealerships. Turns out, Harry is close to retirement. He feels he's seen too many young farmers in his area go broke because they didn't know the difference between a new idea and a good idea. Before he quits the business completely, he wants to do something about it. What's more, he wants Jack's help.

Harry asked Jack to consider working with him to create a "model farm" - one with a diversity of the fruit, berry, hay and row crops common in the area. They could use his old place as a location – Harry had always dabbled around in farming and still ran the family's small orchard. Harry made it clear that he was hiring Jack to <u>teach</u> other farmers - not just consult with Harry. Harry would take care of recruiting the farmers he had selected for this opportunity. If any of them decided to hire Jack on their own, that was fine. Harry's only request was that Jack spend a little extra time with him and the young farmers he'd selected, walking through the orchard and the fields, and explaining the reasoning behind every recommendation.

The more he thought about it, the more excited Jack got. Most of his customers were concerned first, last and always about Jack's ability to improve their bottom line. A few were interested in working with him because "having a consultant" made them feel important. But Harry - well, he just seemed to want to give something back, to find a way to thank the community for their support and also ensure that there would always be room for younger farmers to succeed. Jack had to admire that.

In this situation - which is admittedly more rare - the salesperson has recognized a customer's need for self-actualization. This is the need to make a contribution to farming and to the community as a "capstone" to a successful career. To meet this need, Jack must adjust the way he positions his services (more education, less profit) and the way he delivers his services. Jack has a wonderful opportunity here. He will be a part of a very special community effort. He will work alongside one of the most respected professionals in the area, and he will have a chance to build relationships with some of the best young farmers in the county. To capture this opportunity, he needs to remember at all times <u>why</u> Harry wants to buy his services – his primary motivation.

Customers Buy Based on Wants

We have talked about needs. But let's not forget another important factor – *wants*. Lets begin this section by asking the following questions:

If you want something, do you need it?
If you need something, do you want it?

Customers often equate needs with wants and vice versa. They almost always *want* a product they think they need, but also believe they *need* many products they in fact only *want.* The argument about the difference between wants and needs is purely academic. In either case, the "getting-more-than-you-give" rationale still applies. The sale will occur only when the fulfillment of needs – or wants – will provide the customer with more than the cost of buying the product.

Who decides when the benefits are higher than the cost? In our society, it is the customer who chooses. Of course, there are some areas where laws and government regulations limit consumer choices, but the decision by and large is left to the customer. Only he/she knows his/her needs and desires intimately enough to make a buying decision. As long as the salesperson is ethical and honest in what is said about the product, the burden of making a correct buying decision rests squarely on the customer's shoulders.

While a good part of the buying decision in agribusiness is increasingly based on facts and rational thinking, humans are not completely clear-thinking, logical creatures. Emotions do play a part – a big part in some cases. In surveys of salespeople from coast-to-coast, selling all types of products, they report as much as 90 percent of the buying decision is based on emotional rather than logical reasoning (which is an extension of research indicating that people hear and see what they want to see and hear)[14] These results may sound a bit extreme, since farmers today are indeed relying more and more on sound business judgments when they make purchases. Certainly the impact of emotion and feelings varies between customers. But the salesperson cannot ignore the emotional aspects of the buying decision.

---

[14] William W. Consumer Behavior. John Wiley and Sons, New York, New York: 1986.

Consulting psychologist Gail Eldrige,[15] notes: "All behavior is caused – goal directed – and a salesperson is in some way satisfying some need at some level...man only acts when moved through fear, hope, love or greed. Human beings are basically emoting creatures. Emotions arouse, sustain and direct behavior."

Eldrige helps us understand that, no matter what superficial needs or desires are expressed, beneath them lie powerful emotions. When a farmer trades combines, it is true that a new one is needed to harvest the crop. But behind that primary "need," there may be some important emotions. Perhaps the farmer fears break-downs on the old machine and the inability to complete harvest before bad weather. Perhaps the prestige of having a new model is a factor. Or, new safety features may make him/her feel better about family helping with harvest. The salesperson who can find the underlying drive or need, has gone a long way toward making the sale.

When customers decide what and where to buy, they don't think consciously about their level of need (survival, social, self-esteem, etc.). They usually don't analyze their emotions (fear, greed, or hope). Most customers believe they are making the best possible *business* decision. What complicates matters is that this "business" decision is made through their very unique perspective on what "best" means, what a "business" should do, and what results they anticipate as a consequence of their decision. For example, assume a retailer buys a new piece of variable rate equipment. The underlying need is a desire to "be one of the best in the state" – a self-esteem need. Does he need the equipment to cover more acres? Maybe not. Does he need to replace older equipment? It could probably last a few more years. But the self-esteem need is so tied up with who the retailer is, and what kind of business he runs, that it becomes a motivating want. He wants the equipment and, if he can afford it, he'll buy it.

What results does this retailer expect from the new equipment? He expects to get the business of the best, most forward-thinking farmers in his area. He expects to be a supplier of choice, because he so obviously is the most technically advanced and most professional. He *anticipates* a higher level of respect and success with this purchase. Will he actually receive what he expects? He may. If this retailer is truly one of the first, and if he can use this equipment to meet the needs of top farmers in his area, he may receive the results he expected. His *actual* results – the degree of satisfaction – will be colored by how he uses the equipment in his selling efforts, as well as by how strongly he believes he is now "special." It's complicated, isn't it?

---

[15] Eldrige, G. Industrial Psychologist. Blueprint for Professional Selling seminar. San Antonio, Texas: 1972.

- Product needs are recognized by customers within the larger context of their life needs – survival, security, social acceptance, self-esteem and self-actualization.
- Even within these levels of needs, customers are still very influenced by their emotions. Their need level and their emotions can cause them to want products they don't technically "need." The salesperson must remember that the responsibility for the buying decision is the customer's, once all information has been given.
- Customers anticipate positive results when they buy something. Whether *actual* results match *expected* results depends on more than product performance. It also depends on whether the set of needs that drove their decision is met.

Bill Brockett
Virginia Beef Corporation
Owner and President
Haymarket, Virginia

Always try to give the customer what he wants. I guess that's number one for anybody in selling. Without a customer, you don't have a sale. Everybody has to remember that.

I try to preach that to the National Cattlemen's Beef Association right now. Some producers in the cattle business keep forgetting they are producing a product for a customer. They have to have a customer to sell their beef to. Beef sales have gone down dramatically over the past twenty years. The amount of beef an individual consumes has declined. Some of these producers have their own ideas of what they want to produce, but they keep forgetting they have to produce what the *customer* wants...not what *they* want to produce. It's a really tough one. Whatever the customer wants, if it is within reason, you've got to meet it. Plain and simple. If you don't meet the customer's needs and wants, somebody else will. I think that's the long and the short of it on any sales thing. If a customer wants a product, if you don't have it, somebody else will have it or will make it.

The thing you gotta do is be flexible. You've got to be willing to listen to what he's saying. Sometimes the impossible becomes possible when you have to do it. Communication is essential for determining that customer's needs each and every time.

How Customers Evaluate Their Options

It seems clear that customers buy for a variety of reasons, and that sometimes these reasons can be very complex. Most salespeople are not psychologists. They have neither the time nor the training to analyze the underlying need structure

and ego motivation of each customer. Nor, many people believe, is that their right or their responsibility. However, salespeople <u>do</u> need to understand how customers evaluate their products. It helps the salesperson to recognize patterns of needs and expectations among customers, so that he or she can develop strategies to address those needs and expectations.

Sometimes needs might be quite straightforward — better control of pests, or better resistance to variable weather, or for improved productivity. Sometimes needs are more complex. Clearly, the quality of the solution depends on the quality of products, services and recommendation. Even more importantly, a quality solution depends on the salesperson's ability to uncover the real issues and concerns of the customer and then to develop and recommend a solution that will work on *that* farm, in *that* greenhouse, in *that* retail business, or for *that* distributor.

The best salespeople are able to look at a sales situation from the buyer's perspective. How do customers define quality in the sales relationship?[16]

> *I want my supplier to keep me advised as to what I need to know. I want them to help me be a better business professional on my place. I read and have good input, but I like to have the salesperson knowledgeable about what their products and services do for me toward a better bottom line. For instance, we spent two hours the other day discussing the new rules on a product that has to be kept 60-65 feet away from everything. I like them to go over my operation with me, finding the areas that we need to be careful with. That's what they need to do...keep us informed about the rules, keep us legal. I think they need to keep us up on the latest innovations, whether it is equipment, or fertilizer, or types of insecticides, or new herbicides. They're the ones that are supposed to learn all this new stuff. Then they educate us.*

> *Make sure you offer service...I think service is the most important part of it. And I think, to me, keeping it light is as important as anything. I realize that wouldn't necessarily be true for everybody. I like them to come out and feel like they want to*

---

[16] Taken from market research completed by Synergy, a Division of Agri Business Group, Indianapolis, Indiana.

help me in my business – I think that is the main thing. You have to have that feeling there and not all salespeople do.

If they can offer me a complete package at a low price, with good service, I am happy.

These customers are typical of many from all over the country. Each customer is different. What works with one, doesn't work with the next one. Yet, there are some overriding truths about human nature that can help you understand the customer. Once you understand why customers buy and how they evaluate their options, you can better answer their particular wants and needs. It is up to the seller to determine how to address customer's unique needs. Market research can identify differences among customers – from the emerging young producer or the super farmer – but when it comes right down to it, the salesperson has to meet needs one customer at a time. This is why the salesperson is so important.

Earl Bell
ELANCO Animal Health, Eli Lilly & Company
Sales Representative
Rocky Mount, North Carolina

Customers have to know why you are there, but at the same time, you have to use an artful technique of not coming across with so much pressure that they get defensive. They have to know that you bring solutions to their business and you are not just going to come in and pound them on product and price. Your job is to help them understand how your product can help them be more successful.

Calling on different segments within a company (big customer) can be confusing as to the task that must be accomplished. A purchasing agent needs to get the best possible price because that is the way he will be measured within his job. The veterinarian's need is to use a product to help his animals, to prevent or treat disease. A nutritionist is going to be focused more on the product's effect on improving feed efficiency. You really have to be able to sort out the needs of each individual to the point that you get your sale. You are trying to sell all those different components. A lot of people get very frustrated trying to sell large accounts because of all those different components.

A supplier company has to have a good understanding of their products and how they will be utilized in the market so that they can effectively price the product. When the situation is handled properly the supplier will profit and their customers will have additional profits because they strategically utilized the product.

Suppliers need to have a coordinated management team from the top down to salespeople who can clearly understand the implications of developing the right products for the markets they serve. A supplier's long term success depends on clear open lines of communication and commitment within their company that allows everyone to focus on fulfilling the needs of their customers. When this process happens, you see companies that are successful.

The Three Types of Buyers

There are excellent theoretical model describing need. But what does the salesperson do with these models in the real world? Whether selling to distributors, retailers, or farmers; and whether selling seed, feed, chemical, pharmaceuticals or livestock products, the salesperson works with several types of buyers.

Since 1988, market research conducted by Agri Business Group, Inc. (Synergy Division)[17] has completed a wide variety of buyer type studies in fertilizer, agricultural chemicals, feed, animal health and seed, both in the U.S. and internationally. The results of this research were, of course, somewhat different depending on the type of product, the production dynamics (livestock vs. crop), and the geography. However, three distinct buyer types could be identified (Figure 4.2).

Figure 4.2
Buyer Types

Relationship   *Economic*   *Business*

As we will learn in subsequent chapters, effectively understanding and classifying buyer styles allows a salesperson to better identify which prospects are the most likely customers, and, ultimately, successfully gain that person's business. Once the customer is buying your product or service, having a knowledge of their buyer type can allow you to service their needs and wants effectively, and keep them as a happy customer.

The salesperson must realize that each of the three buying motivations - relationship, economic and business is represented within each individual customer. It is through determining the customer's <u>predominant</u> motivation that you can better understand how that customer will likely evaluate your products, services, programs and prices and buy from you. Salespeople interviewed by Agri Business Group, Inc. agree that the buyer type is sometimes almost more important than the program itself. The salesperson must be able to bring the program or solution "to life" for each customer in his/her operation. If the salesperson cannot do that, selling will be a real uphill battle.

---

[17] Agri Business Group, Synergy Division. Customer Segmentation Method.

For instance, some customers may like their salesperson to organize on-farm trials, or to take them to see a company or university research facility and talk to the experts. Others trust the salesperson to provide the expertise, and would rather do things to build their relationship, like a hunting trip or a fishing trip or just having lunch together every once in a while. A third type of buyer wants the best deal.

When you learn what makes the customer tick as a person, you can build the kind of total relationship, or total partnership, between the customer and your business that makes you both feel comfortable. The customer whose salesperson brings them the things they want, who trusts their salesperson, and whose salesperson's selling style "suits" their personal style is usually very loyal. Interestingly enough, these buyer types are usually not correlated to size of operation. Relationship farmers may be large or small. All economic buyers are not large farmers. The following paragraphs briefly profile each of these buyer types.

The Relationship Buyer

The classic Relationship Buyer is one to whom the relationship with the salesperson is critical. As an example, a Relationship Buyer may have been involved with a local farm supply organization for years, and purchases inputs only from that business. The Relationship Buyer expects the salesperson to be a trusted confidant, a friendly, dependable "buddy" who looks out for his/her best interest. Relationship Buyers look for regular contact with the salesperson, whom they trust and accept. Both formal and informal contact is appreciated.

Relationship buyers are predominantly concerned with or influenced by human characteristics such as:
- trust;
- personality;
- common style;
- attitude.

Let's look at an example.

> Nicholas appreciates "one of the boys" down at the co-op stopping by to let him know he saw his kids' soccer game over the weekend. The salesperson continues, "And by the way, Nicholas, there's a new herbicide that may be coming in sometime soon. I think you might be interested in it. I will bring by the background information to you, if you want, sometime.

Relationship Buyers trust information sources they know – friends, neighbors, etc. For instance, Nicholas may talk about the new herbicide with a couple of neighbors and then trust that his salesperson is giving him a good, fair recommendation. He may not even compare price, if he trusts the salesperson. Relationship Buyers like and often want full service, because they like to feel well cared-for.

Key Relationship Buyer characteristics include:

- like regular contact;
- want to spend time chatting;
- trust information sources they know;
- like informal and formal contact;
- accept rep, trust rep;
- may not compare price if trusts;
- like full-service packages.

The Economic Buyer

This customer is tuned into product and/or service cost. They typically have little or no time for flashy, lengthy displays or discussion. They do carefully look at the product or service they purchase. The Economic Buyer is quick to react, competitive and often wants the cheapest possible price for the product they have selected. They are not particularly interested in service, and would rather rely on their own information sources. The Economic Buyer is very pragmatic and self-reliant.

The Economic Buyer tends to focus on specific attributes of a product or service such as:
- price;
- convenience;
- product characteristics;
- availability;
- time saving.

The Economic Buyer often quickly bases his/her buying decision on "factual" product attributes without spending time and/or effort on deep analysis. Sometimes, salespeople avoid the Economic Buyer because they sense that this person is less influenced by their expertise, or less easily persuaded by their selling skill. However, if a salesperson can quickly and effectively show increased results or reduced expenses through a product or service and can offer a very fair price or a performance guarantee, he or she may be able to sell this type of buyer. Again, let's look at an example.

Jim does not attend chemical company field days because he sees them as plain and simple opportunities for the companies to sell product. He doesn't trust that information. Rather, he relies on his own resources for information. Jim wants the try a product before he has to pay for it. Then when he does pay, Jim wants the best price around for that product. It makes Jim feel really good to get a good price on a product or service he determines is satisfactory for his operation.

Key Economic Buyer characteristics include:

- always consider cost in a decision;
- like to compare price;
- react quickly;
- not interested in service;
- competitive;
- rely on own information sources;
- pragmatic;
- self-reliant.

The Business Buyer

The Business Buyer usually looks beyond cost or elements of the relationship alone. In a way, the Business Buyer synthesizes the dominant motivations of economics and relationship. The Business Buyer looks at what an "investment" in a product or service will produce. Business Buyers value good human relationships. However, they are also attuned to the economics of this business transaction. This customer runs a business – and thinks of business first and foremost and throughout all dealings. The Business Buyer is very bottom-line and results-oriented. Let's look at an example.

When offered 25 bags of seed corn free if he bought 100, and those at less than the price of his current brand, Mark refused based on what that seed might yield. The seed dealer couldn't believe his ears. "Wait a minute," he said, "you're refusing free seed?" Mark's reply? "That "free seed" could be the most expensive seed I ever planted, if it doesn't yield."

A Business Buyer is often interested in facts and research. Trying a new technique or product is intriguing, if the customer is convinced through third-party trials, objective research by various institutions, trade press and trusted experts. The Business Buyer is usually very organized with details and information, and may be very brief and to the point. This buyer demands appointments, likes expertise, and considers the total value package you offer. If a supplier or salesperson is not meeting their needs, Business Buyers will switch to one who better serves their business. As mentioned earlier, however, the Business Buyer still values good human relationships. In the absence of a relationship, economic attributes of the product or service may weigh more heavily. It is clearly in the interest of a salesperson to get to know this buyer's business operations, goals, challenges and record-keeping systems, so that a relationship can be built on delivering profitable results.

Key characteristics of a Business Buyer include:

- bottom-line results (not what it costs, but what it produces);
- brief, to the point;
- facts and research;
- appointments;
- organization;
- expertise;
- comparison shopping;
- considers value "package."

Debbie Stiles
BASF Canada, Inc.
Senior Marketing Associate, Soybean Products
Guelph, Ontario, Canada

You have to adjust your style by customer to make it work. What I find is that the bottom line makes more difference to some than others. Sometimes, it becomes important to modify what your emphasis is in relating to that person. If you are with a bottom line person, the bottom line will be your emphasis. Some may be more concerned with added value and still others are primarily interested in service....You can spend a whole lot of time beating your head on the wall if you are talking about what doesn't matter.

Summary

The reasons why customers buy are as varied as customers themselves. The Maslow Hierarchy of Needs suggests that human needs have five levels and that each level of need must be fulfilled before a person can recognize needs at the next level. The levels of need are physiological, safety/security, social, self-esteem, and self-actualization. Salespeople need more than technical knowledge to recognize a "need" for a product or service. They must understand (and accept) the basic level of needs that underlies specific product or service decisions, so that they can help customers make a good choice.

"Needs" and "wants" sometimes get confused, even in the mind of the customer. They almost always want a product they think they need. But sometimes they think they "need" products that they only want. When this happens, they are operating at a level of emotional or psychological need that overrides technical factors or sometimes even economic factors. While this can be a difficult situation for a salesperson, it helps to remember that the customer deserves your honest and best recommendation – the final decision is always theirs alone.

With so many things to consider, salespeople could spend all their time analyzing customers instead of helping them solve problems. Fortunately, research has identified three types of buyers and has described the purchase evaluation characteristics common to each. Relationship Buyers like regular formal and informal contact with the salesperson, want a long-term relationship, and accept recommendations and information provided by people they trust. Economic Buyers are more skeptical of salespeople; they are pragmatic, rely on their own judgment and experience, and often prefer to react quickly or "based on facts." Business Buyers are also factually oriented, but they use facts to plan for profit (rather than reducing cost). They are bottom-line oriented, to the point, have high expectations of their salespeople, and need to respect the knowledge and skills of their most important suppliers.

Review Questions

1. Customers buy based on two primary reasons. What are they? Explain how and why they contribute to customer buying behavior.

2. Explain Maslow's hierarchy of human needs and how it affects buyer behavior.

3. As a salesperson selling a single product to two different customers, it is your job to determine the customer's needs. Discuss how selling to a customer whose needs are security-based may differ from selling to one whose needs are self-actualization-based.

4. Distinguish the primary behavior differences between an economic buyer and a business buyer.

5. Salespeople sell. They are not psychologists. Why do salespeople need to understand how customers evaluate their products?

Chapter Five

How People Buy

Learning Objectives:

Upon completion of this chapter, you should be able to:

1. recognize that buying involves a five step decision procedure;
2. discuss need recognition, information search, examination of alternatives and decision, and post purchase evaluation;
3. define "buyers remorse";
4. describe the Farmers Buying Decision Model;
5. explain how technology is adopted within the farm community;
6. explain the three types of buying classes: new task buying, modified re-buy and straight re-buy;
7. define "opinion leaders" and give an example of their influence;
8. list the five steps in Rogers' adoption process model;
9. describe the adoption of innovation curve;
10. determine why selling to opinion leaders is important.

How Do People Buy?

Chapter Four examined the nature of people's wants and needs – the *why* part of buying. Now, to further understand agri selling, the salesperson must understand *how* the agribusiness customer buys. First, the salesperson must understand that no purchase is ever made unless some sort of problem or need is perceived. If a person does not believe he/she is sick, it's unlikely that person will be in the market for medicine. But suppose that a new vitamin supplement is discovered that can remarkably increase one's stamina and greatly reduce the frequency of colds. If someone is to sell this new vitamin, they will first have to make the customer aware of its existence and then convince that customer that it can, in fact, increase stamina and reduce colds. That is, the customer first must become aware of the product and be convinced of his/her need for it.

Gloria was a salesperson with a mission. Her company had just introduced a new product against several tough fungal diseases, and she couldn't wait to introduce it to her top greenhouse managers. But, before she could sell it, she knew she had to identify the diseases prevalent in her area against which the compound was active, assess their probability of occurrence, and evaluate their consequence to flower growers – both the aesthetic and the economic loss from lower quality flowers. She knew she had to do this "homework" before she could present the product as a solution and possibly make the sale. That is, she had to convince the flower producers of the size of the problem and that her solution would make them appreciably better off. Unless her customers perceive the problem – and its economic impact – they will not likely be interested in a solution.

Gloria understands the salesperson's job very well. Many times, the customer is not aware of a problem or need, or doesn't believe there is a cost-effective solution available. It is up to the salesperson to show the customer the problem or the additional potential that is possible and then present a solution. In order to make the sale, her ultimate goal, Gloria has to "walk" her customers through a logical decision-making process – the buying process.

The Buying Process

Before any selling or purchasing is done, there is a logical thought process that every customer completes. In some cases, such as impulse decisions, these steps may occur very rapidly. In other cases, as in changing management practices or suppliers, these steps may take months or years. In every case, it's the seller's job to help the buyer through each step as ethically as possible. Figure 5.1 summarizes the steps of the buying decision process.

Figure 5.1:
The Buying Decision Process

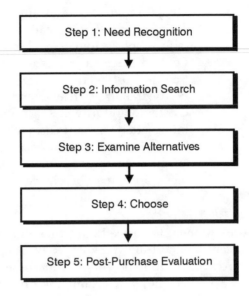

Step 1: Need Recognition

Step 2: Information Search

Step 3: Examine Alternatives

Step 4: Choose

Step 5: Post-Purchase Evaluation

Step 1: Need Recognition

No purchase ever takes place until or unless a problem or need is recognized. The customer must become *aware* that a change might bring improvement. The problem or need can be real *or* imagined. When customers feel a need strongly enough, they will aggressively search for a solution. But often, customers are not aware they have a need until it is pointed out to them. How can that happen? They may not know there is a better way that can make them more money, increase their satisfaction, or decrease their risk. Therefore, the salesperson plays an important part in helping customers recognize the need to change. This may involve changing brands, changing suppliers, changing business practices, or adopting new technology. The salesperson is a very effective agent of change – but only when he or she makes sure the customer recognizes a need to change first.

Step 2: Information Search

Once a need is felt, customers look for information about their problem and about alternative solutions. That search may be extensive for large, infrequent purchases like buildings or equipment; for customers who are cautious or highly analytical; or when money is tight. The information search may be minimal for small, frequent purchases like cleansers, iron supplements, etc.; for customers who are impulsive buyers; or, when there is a high level of trust with a supplier.

Managers and employees of agribusinesses use a variety of information sources. Some of the most commonly-used sources are listed below.

- Media – radio, TV, satellite information delivery services and print are very important in creating an image, especially for new products, or for whole technologies.
- Public contacts – agencies and university publications are significant for some customers.
- Personal contacts – friends and neighbors have a high level of credibility and are widely accepted; they are a key source of information for many customers.
- Professional contacts – service reps, consultants and veterinarians are an important source of specialized information, especially with the increasing impact of science and technology on production.

Step 3: Examine Alternatives

Once customers feel a need and are comfortable with their understanding of the problem or opportunity, they are ready to analyze alternatives. Here, customers compare and contrast how one product or service might fulfill a specific need or solve a problem they have. Examination of alternatives might be the point when the customer makes a checklist of each product's advantages and disadvantages. They compare this product against that one, trying to determine which one does the job or accomplishes their objective most satisfactorily. Their analysis may be deliberate and lengthy, using projected profits vs costs. Or their analysis may be instantaneous, relying on experience, "gut feeling," or a salesperson's recommendation. Analysis is likely to be more thorough when:

- the customer has a larger business;
- the customer is more progressive – interested in innovation;
- the purchase involves considerable risk;
- the customer is financially conservative or risk-averse.

Step 4: Choose

In step four, the choice is made. Engel, Blackwell and Miniard define step four as that in which "the customer acquires the perfect alternative or an acceptable alternative if necessary."[18] When the customer arrives at a solution, he/she makes a choice to select one product and reject others.

Many customers are not knowledgeable about all of their choices, or experienced in their use. The salesperson can offer valuable assistance. In fact, the salesperson is often critical to a good decision. Salespeople can clarify information, correct

---

[18] Engel J., Blackwell, R., Miniard, P. Consumer Behavior (6th Edition). Dryden Press, Chicago, Illinois: 1990; p. 27.

misconceptions and explain the benefits to be gained. Therefore, the salesperson plays an important part in helping customers examine alternatives and decide on an appropriate course of action.

Step 5: Post Purchase Evaluation

Once the purchase is made, there is a strong and logical tendency to justify the decision. The customer is looking for information that reinforces their decision, and for early "clues" about results that can provide information for future purchases. Research into *dissonance*[19] shows that if a person makes a commitment to change, they do <u>not</u> want to know that their commitment was not worthwhile. In fact, they will ignore information that might indicate they made a bad decision, or rationalize it away if it cannot be ignored. The need to feel that a good decision was made is so great, that the person will go to great lengths to not accept any contrary information. In agri selling, understanding dissonance may help explain why some people go to such great lengths to protect the decisions they've made to date.

A customer's decision process can just as logically lead to a rejection decision as to adoption.[20] For example, Rogers points out that it is possible to reject an innovation - a new idea — at each stage in the purchase decision process. At the knowledge stage, rejection may come from simply forgetting about the innovation after initial awareness. Rejection can occur even after a prior decision to adopt or, in this case, purchase. People "change their minds" about a purchase in part by the motivation of dissonance, or an uncomfortable "gut" feeling the person hopes to decrease or eliminate.

When a customer has "second thoughts" after buying, the feeling they have is called "post purchase dissonance" or "buyer's remorse." The customer wonders if he/she did the right thing - if it was a smart buy. He/she needs to rationalize the decision. He/she will need reinforcement from you, the salesperson, and may also seek reinforcement from friends or neighbors whose opinion is trusted. In their sixth edition of Consumer Behavior,[21] Engel, Blackwell, and Miniard point out that buyer regret or remorse is a common initial outcome under various circumstances. However, dissatisfaction problems resulting from "buyer's remorse" usually can be corrected by a follow-up call or visit by the salesperson. Since many agricultural products and services are on-going repetitive purchases, a positive post-purchase evaluation is especially important for the next sale.

---

[19] Holschuh, M.K. Working Class Participation in Adult Education. 1985; pp. 69-70.

[20] Rogers, E. Diffusion of Innovations. The Free Press, New York, New York: 1983; pp. 184-185.

[21] Engel, J., Blackwell R., and Miniard, P. Dissertation: Indiana University Bloomington: 1990; p. 544.

Same Process, Different Buyers – Information Search

The buying decision process is a problem-solving procedure. Most customers ask the following questions, consciously or subconsciously:

1. Do I have a problem or opportunity?
2. What is the problem? Is it worth fixing?
3. What is causing the problem?
4. What are the possible solutions to the problem? How should I evaluate them?
5. What is the one best possible solution?

While most customers think through a problem or opportunity using a similar process, the *speed* of the process, the *depth and quality* of the analysis and the *type* of information that is most powerful may differ sharply from customer to customer. The buyer types introduced in Chapter Four provide one way to illustrate some of the differences. Let's focus on the "information search" step, Step 2, of the Buying Decision Process.

- A Relationship Buyer may base the information search on word of mouth from several friends, peers or neighbors. The customer's deliberation may be short when there is a high level of trust in the supplier or salesperson. When trust is high, the customer says, "Why waste time looking around. I know my salesperson will treat me right."

- An Economic Buyer will conduct an extended search only if the stakes are very high or the competition for his business is very strong. In general, he or she will search for a cost-effective solution, and then conduct a second "search" for a deal or program that stretches the business's dollar as far as it will go.

- A Business Buyer may make an extensive information search. This buyer may want to take the time to look at every possible solution and how it impacts the bottom line now and in the long run. This is especially true before making large, infrequent purchases such as buildings or major pieces of agricultural machinery, or before making major changes in production or business systems.

Same Process, Different Buyers — How Customers Weigh Alternatives

As customers gather information (Step 2), they begin to weigh the alternatives (Step 3). What are they looking for? They don't consider every possible solution, product and supplier. Instead, they use a "scorecard" that has worked for them in the past. Their attitudes, characteristics and information - obtained, perhaps, from a magazine, trade show, organization or neighbor - determine what is on the "scorecard" and how heavily each factor weighs.

Contrary to what advertising would have us believe, most customers don't look only at products and their attributes. Most begin with the attributes of the salesperson - is the person who brought the need to their attention trustworthy, knowledgeable and credible? If not, the need may still be valid, but the solution may require finding a more credible and knowledgeable salesperson.

They then consider the business with whom they will be working. This consideration often has two levels. The first is the business selling the product, and the second is the manufacturer - the brand of the product. Most business customers understand that successful product use and repurchase depends on product performance <u>and</u> on the kind of service received.

The third influencing factor is product performance, though the salesperson still has a strong impact. In fact, the farmer is so dependent on the salesperson that if the farmer finds the product unsatisfactory, he/she may question the choice of sales personnel as much as the product. This points up the importance of following ethical selling practices and not trying to "put one over" on the customer or "sell them a bill of goods." Someone may be fooled once, and maybe even twice, but the dishonest agribusiness salesperson will not likely see that same customer a third time.

The most important of these influencing factors, especially in the purchase of a specific product such as an herbicide or seed, is the salesperson. The farmer tends to choose a person to deal with first and choice of product or brand follows. Research conducted by Dr. Michael A. Humphreys and Dr. Michael R. Williams[22] of Illinois State University showed that buyer/seller interaction (interpersonal process attributes) is as critical to achieving true "customer focus" as any benefits received from the product (product performance attributes). Their research underscores the significant role played by the salesperson in optimizing customer value and satisfaction.

Inside the Customer's Mind – Pre-purchase Attitudes

Ultimately, in most all agri selling, the customer is the end-user. Even the chemical representative selling to a local co-op must understand the processes by which the *farmer* makes purchase decisions. The retailer you sell to must re-sell your company's image, brand and products based on their understanding of end-user attitudes and their end-users' "scorecards." This scorecard is based on the

---

[22] Humphreys, M. and Williams, M. Journal of Personal Selling & Sales Management (Vol. XVI, Number 3, Summer 1996); pp. 47-57.

cultural, economic, social, legal, environmental and technical background of the end-user.

Figure 5.2
End-User Scorecard

- Confidence in the salesperson
- Desire to buy products that are complementary or go together
- Desire for a nearby supplier
- Concern about safety hazards and dangerous chemical misuse
- Need for technical knowledge
- Desire for services
- Desire to be well-regarded by friends and neighbors
- Degree of habit
- Need for respect or recognition
- Degree of aversion to risk

Inside the Customer's Mind – Salesperson Attributes

With these concerns in mind, customers set out to find a good salesperson, retailer, or wholesaler, often before deciding which is the best product or brand. Some things the customer looks for in a "good" salesperson include these characteristics:

- reputation for credibility;
- accurate and dependable information;
- good management at the sales location;
- salesperson support of product;
- prompt, satisfactory handling of complaints;
- complementary or backup services;
- convenient location;
- good personal relationships with customers;
- understanding of farmers' problems;
- a broad product line;
- neat and attractive site;
- reasonable credit policies;
- fair pricing.

Inside the Salesperson's Mind – Brand/Business Attributes

Once the customer is satisfied that he or she has an expert "ally" to help navigate the confusing array of product and service choices, information about manufacturers (and local dealerships) and brand image begin to influence the decision:

- recognized name with a good reputation;
- company support of product;

- product quality;
- readily available supplies;
- credible company representatives;
- factual product information;
- access to representatives for problem solving;
- good appearance and attitude of sales representatives.

Finally, the customer considers the attributes of a specific product, program or service – he or she evaluates the *solution* offered by the salesperson. Factors that customers consider might include:

- good quality;
- dependability;
- good performance;
- safety;
- product/service availability;
- price.

Understanding Customer Loyalty

Loyalty is something that every salesperson and every company wants. When customers are loyal, they are willing to accept minor concerns and temporary problems because they believe in the salesperson and the company. They have faith that a solution will be found. Many customers are as loyal or more loyal to a salesperson with whom they have worked for many years, as they are to a company or brand. Over time, the customer may come to depend heavily on information supplied by the salesperson and will often rely on salesperson recommendations. Where does loyalty come from?

First, all customers like to do business with people upon whom they can depend and whom they trust. The closeness of the relationship appears to be the most important element of salesperson loyalty. Relationship buyers and some business buyers like to do business with their "friends." As described in the list of salesperson attributes above, the salesperson "friend" will be reliable, can be trusted, and will often be able to provide services and offer credit. In addition, most customers are aware that technology is changing rapidly – almost faster than they can keep up with. Reliable access to topnotch information encourages a customer to stick with certain select salespeople.

Second, loyalty comes from the ability of a trusted salesperson to help a producer or retailer avoid penalties, costs or hazards. Agricultural customers have an intensifying awareness of the potential environmental impact of powerful fertilizers, herbicides and pesticides, and genetically altered and engineered products. With the attendant increasing regulation, more and more producers and retailers want to ensure proper handling of all products. They expect their salesperson to advise them correctly and specifically on amounts to be used, as well as on handling and storage precautions and dangers. Similarly, for livestock operations, the correct disposal of waste is a growing issue. Customers may expect their salespeople to be able to provide expert support to help them handle this challenge.

In all, the buying decision is a process that is unique to the individual and the sale. Successful sellers first understand customer needs, then recognize the process through which the customer goes to arrive at a decision to buy. Individual people go through the process of a buying decision at different speeds and use different types of information.

One of the most important areas of customer behavior for an agricultural seller to understand is how new technology is accepted. As technology continues to enter agriculture at an increasingly swift pace, the acceptance and integration of new technologies in production and in agribusinesses will be critical to the health of the industry. A great deal of research has been done to describe the general attitudes toward new products and new technologies that determine when - or if - a customer will adopt a new idea.

Adoption of Technology

Adoption refers to the process by which new technologies or ideas are embraced, accepted and implemented by the customer. Understanding how farmers and retailers consider and adopt new ideas can be very important to the selling process. Successful salespeople are sufficiently aware of the customer's needs and wants to gauge how easily the customer will adopt a new idea or technology.

George Beal, Everett Rogers and Joe Bohlen[23] of Iowa State University studied how farmers react to new ideas. A set of adoption theories resulted. This theory proposes that, with some degree of consistency, the *same* small group of risk-takers tend to try a new idea first. A large "first wave" tries the ideas that survive the experiments of the risk-takers.

[23] Beal, G.M., Rogers, E.M., and Bohlen, J.M., Validity of the Concept of Stages in the Adoption Process. Rural Sociology, Volume 22(2), (1957); pp. 166-168,

This second group often refines the use of the product, and learns how to make money with it. They are followed by the majority, and finally by those few very conservative customers who are the last to try anything. Let's imagine how this would work if you - a salesperson - were the customer.

Just sit back for a moment and think about how quickly salespeople might shell out hundreds or even thousands of dollars on a newly introduced "salesputer," a computer developed especially for salespeople, that might help dramatically in a selling job. The salesputer incorporates the fastest computations of sales schedules, databases of customer information, voice-mail, e-mail, Internet and Intranet technologies, and more, all coordinated and organized with your selling job in mind. Most salespeople would probably rather wait and see whether the idea catches on or whether fellow salespeople had purchased such a product and were happy with it. Still, there would be a few brave souls who decide that buying a salesputer would be a good idea.

In his book, <u>Diffusion of Innovations</u>,[24] Everett Rogers placed farmers into five groups: innovators, early adopters, early majority, late majority and laggards. He also theorized that these five groups were distributed in a "normal" curve, with each group representing one standard deviation from the mean (except laggards, who take up two standard deviations).

Table 5.1
Innovation Adoption Groups

Innovators	2.5%
Early Adopters	13.5%
Early Majority	34.0%
Late Majority	34.0%
Laggards	16.0%

Innovators

Innovators are defined as the first 2.5% of farmers anxious to try an untried brand or idea. Innovators are risk-takers - willing, even anxious, to try out new and sometimes risky ideas. They see themselves as keeping in touch with new ideas, and are well-read. They frequently read research bulletins, are well-educated, have a scientific approach to problem solving, and have an ability to deal with abstract ideas. Often enough, they hold leadership positions in regional, state and national farm organizations rather than in more local groups.

---

[24] Rogers, Everett M. : 1983, pp. 172-173.

While innovators sometimes enjoy a high social status and are highly visible, they are often viewed skeptically by the folks around home and may not have a great deal of local influence. Innovators travel a great deal and are well networked with other innovators. They are venturesome risk takers who test out new ideas, knowing that some or many will fail.

Early Adopters

Early adopters are defined as the next 13.5% of all farmers willing to try a new idea or technology. This group, while not the very first to embrace a new product or idea, is surely in the "first wave" of adopters. In fact, they often refer to themselves as "one of the first." They are alert to the possibilities in new ideas being tried by the innovators. They tend to have a higher success rate at adopting "good" new ideas because they learn from the success and failures of the innovators. Like the innovators, early adopters are well-educated and keep up-to-date by attending Agricultural Extension and company meetings, subscribing to trade publications and reading Agricultural Extension and other research bulletins. Early adopters' farms are slightly smaller, less specialized and may be slightly less efficient than those of the innovators. But their peers see them as "good farmers," and they enjoy high social status. They are involved in many community organizations - often in leadership positions.

Early adopters are well-respected in their community. They often are aware of that fact. As a result, they may not broadcast to everyone that they're trying out the new idea. They may maintain a low profile - at least until they're sure an idea will work. Nevertheless, they are watched closely by other, less bold farmers. They are proud to have influence in the community, viewing it as a responsibility. Because early adopters are well regarded, they are good target customers. Consider the possibilities of selling to the "leader" who has a large influence on other farmers.

Tom Giese
Cenex/Land O'Lakes
Livestock Production Specialist
Canby, Minnesota

It is really important to take a look at the people, the kind of customers you are working with. You've got to go to the innovators first. No doubt about it. You get them talking about it and they'll help sell it for you. You get the big players to the meeting and give them a voice and make sure it's open so everybody else that will be following can hear. And you make sure everything is what you're doing, you can't hide anything because you are going to get caught. You've got to throw everything on the table that you're doing and why and then prepare to get shot down if it isn't right.

But, that's where the learning comes in. If you go to the innovators, the early adopters, you go to all those people and you can sell it to them, your job is done. It really is. Then it is just a matter of following up. Because they are going to go to the coffee shop and they are going to go to their town council meetings and they are going to go to township meetings and the school board. Those guys, they are involved in all that. You and/or your product...it's going to be discussed.

Early Majority

Early majority farmers are the next 34% of the farmer population willing to try a new idea or technology. These socially-oriented people, with many contacts in the community, watch for a successful pattern in the innovator's and early adopter's acceptance of a new product or program. When there is enough evidence for them, they jump aboard the ship too. When they switch to a new method, product or service, they may feel they are making a deliberate decision to break with tradition. Members of the early majority also rely on neighbors and friends for information and, of course, read trade publications. Their education is slightly above average, and their farms are slightly larger than average.

Late Majority

Group number four, the late majority, is defined as the next 34% to adopt the product or service. As can be seen from their position, they have a wait-and-see attitude. They are often skeptical about new ideas. They also tend to be less progressive farmers, less well-educated, and less well-read. They have smaller farms, rely more on friends and neighbors for information, and travel outside the community less frequently than more progressive farmers.

Laggards

Laggards are the last 16 percent of farmers to adopt a new idea. These are the least progressive farmers, averse to taking risks, less educated, and afraid of debt. Their feet are firmly planted – maybe cemented – in tradition. They may wait to adopt a product or service only if it becomes necessary for survival or when the product is so widely used that they have to switch over. Laggards are not heavily involved in community groups – and almost never in a leadership capacity. They are less well-read than almost everyone else, depending mostly on friends and neighbors and on the broadcast media for information. Figure 5.3 summarizes the adoption diffusion curve.

Figure 5.3
Adoption Diffusion Curve[25]

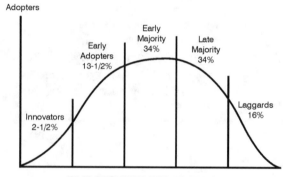

TIME REQUIRED FOR ADOPTION

Over the years, as technology has become an increasing powerful determinant of success, and as current technical information has become more pervasive and routine, it is believed that the time axis of the equation is shrinking. Managers of today's agribusinesses are more aware of the technology surrounding their industry, and thus may adopt it at a quicker rate than 10, 20, 30, or 40 years ago. Everett Rogers' innovation-decision process suggests that an individual passes from first knowledge of an innovation, to forming an attitude toward it, to a decision to adopt or reject it, to implementation of the new idea, and to confirmation of the decision. The innovation-decision period is the length of time required for an individual or organization to pass through the innovation-decision process. The length of time it takes to adopt a new idea or technology does vary from innovation to innovation. For instance, according to data

---

[25] Rogers, Everett, Diffusion of Innovations. The Free Press. New York, New York: 1995, p. 262.

generated in 1942 by Neal C. Gross,[26] there was a nine year average period for the adoption of hybrid corn in Iowa. The average time period for adoption of 2, 4-D weed spray in Iowa was 2.1 years in 1960 (Beal and Rogers, 1960)[27]. Beal's and Rogers' work reminds us that innovations with certain characteristics are generally adopted more quickly. For example, Rogers[28] points out, "innovations which are relatively simple in nature, divisible for trial, and compatible with previous experience usually have a shorter innovation-decision period."

In addition, Beal and Rogers show there are also important individual differences in length of the innovation-decision time period based on adopter category (innovator, early majority, etc.). The first individuals to adopt a new idea (the innovators) do not do so only because they become aware of the innovation somewhat sooner than their peers, but also because they require less time to decide to adopt a new idea or technology.

The Power of Opinion Leaders

An *opinion leader* is a customer (or potential customer) who is respected by his or her peers for business success. Other potential customers watch the opinion leader, and often try to emulate his or her decisions. Recognizing opinion leaders is not terribly difficult, especially if you take a close look at the description of the early adopters and identify them in your sales territory. Opinion leaders can be found on the boards of directors of cooperatives, school boards and churches, and attend a wide variety of public meetings. Or, if you are in a new territory, you need only ask people who the "best farmers" or "best managers" or "best businesses" in the community are. Most of the fingers will point to early adopters. Other good sources of information for identifying opinion leaders are County Extension personnel, Farm Services Agency personnel, farm credit managers, bankers and non-competing peers who supply some of the same customers as you.

It may be easy to find opinion leaders, but it may not be so easy to sell to them. They are high-profile people – that's likely why they were made known to the salesperson in the first place. There are quite a few salespeople calling on these people. Because they are approached by so many people, opinion leaders are often wary of strangers. They may feel a responsibility to their community as leaders, and also do not want to ruin their reputation with too many foolish choices. Opinion leaders may not easily be swayed.

---

[26] Gross, N.C. The Diffusion of a Culture Trait in Two Iowa Townships,. M.S. Thesis, Ames, Iowa State College; 1942, p. 57.
[27] Beal, G.M., Rogers, E.M. The Adoption of Two Farm Practices in a Central Iowa Community. Ames, Iowa Agricultural and Home Economics Experiment Station, Special Report 26; 1960, pp. 4,6,8,10,19.
[28] Rogers, E.M. : 1995, pp 199-203.

However, opinion leaders are usually curious about better ways to do things and sometimes seek out the information on their own. They are willing to examine ideas and listen to a salesperson who knows what she/he is talking about. In most cases, they won't waste their time with an unprepared salesperson. Some salespeople have found that a good approach to opinion leaders is to establish an advisory group or "council." Most opinion leaders, as early adopters, enjoy getting together with others of their kind to trade ideas, and everybody comes out a winner.

It is a good idea for the salesperson to develop strong relationships with opinion leaders for a number of reasons. First, they often can bring you a sizable amount of business themselves. Second, the opinion leader may prove helpful as a source of extremely well-respected testimonials. A third reason to pay special attention to opinion leaders is their potential for <u>negative</u> influence. If they are not well-serviced, the positive community-wide recommendations you hoped for can become a powerful negative force that warns other community members away.

Because opinion leaders seem to revel in adopting good new ideas and products, it is not always necessary to offer special rewards or deals to get them to use and recommend the product. It is sufficient to offer the opinion leader what they want: a good new idea. Always be careful to respect their intelligence, their management skill, and their influence. To act arrogant or to focus only on price and deals might cause them to feel manipulated, which could result in a negative, often vocal reaction.

Decision-Making Process in Larger Businesses

Understanding an individual customer, as evaluated thus far, takes on a broad matrix of considerations: knowledge and classification of the individual, their preferences, style, operation, etc. Still, many agricultural salespeople today find that they are dealing with an even more complex buyer – an account that contains multiple decision-makers, with sometimes differing personal needs and professional priorities. Selling to a large industrial account or large integrated operation may offer the salesperson a veritable index of individuals to whom he or she must sell. It's no longer enough to know one contact person within the organization.

Many large farm operations have individuals responsible for distinct input decisions: crops, livestock, machinery, etc. Others may be in charge of recordkeeping, marketing, etc. and/or other combinations of arrangements. The motives of each of these decision-makers must be understod to best allow the salesperson to effectively communicate the sales presentation to them. Large businesses – from a $60 million local retailer or co-op to the much larger regional distributor that supplies it – routinely involve several people in major purchase decisions. Often, there are decentralized offices, compounding the logistics of calling on all decision-makers. There may be multiple addresses/phone numbers involved in the same account. The bottom line is that, as the salesperson for this customer, you can't do enough homework.

A word of caution: customers in large or multi-part farm organizations or business may fool even a savvy salesperson as to just who makes what decisions. Even though a title may imply that an individual would likely be the key person responsible for the buying decision at hand, clarification of individual customer roles/responsibilities through tactful questioning is often beneficial to the salesperson.

- Pedro may make buying decisions or partipate in decisions regarding taxes, marketing, accounting or GPS.
- Kelly may be the chemical expert and agronomic decision maker in the business.
- Tyson may know what animals are ready for breeding stock sale.
- Nicholas may know which animal was vaccinated for what on which day and balance treatment withdrawal periods vs marketing needs.

Bob Woods
Penn Jersey Products, Inc.
Sales Supervisor
New Holland, Pennsylvania

In many selling situations on the farm, you usually have 2 buyers, the husband and wife. If she is involved in decision making, get her involved from the very beginning. Sometimes it is an ego thing. Give them time to make decisions and tell them you'll be around. When a spouse is a partner in the business it could be suicide to neglect them in the purchase decision. In some cases, I've even had the spouse be the one who wanted the product and actually helped me sell the other spouse. Be straightforward. Don't be fake. They're in business. They'll work it out. They sometimes sell themselves.

New Buy, Modified Rebuy, Straight Rebuy

Another way to look at the purchase decision is to consider your degree of familiarity - as a salesperson and as a company - through past business with an account. Three classes of buying processes are identified in *Marketing*, by William

F. Schoell and Joseph P. Guiltinan[29]. Each "class" represents a different level of familiarity and history surrounding the current buying situation. A newer situation involves more problem solving, whereas a familiar buying situation may only involve a routine response. A *new task* (little or no prior history) requires an extensive problem-solving process. A *modified rebuy* (some history) still requires some problem-solving, but it is usually more limited. A *straight rebuy* may require only a routine response. Let's look at each type of decision in more detail.

New Task Buying

A new task situation is one in which the customer has little experience or knowledge of the product or service. Because it is a brand new solution, it requires that the customer exert a great deal of thought, calculation and speculation as to how the product/service or new idea fits into the operation. New task buying situations often spur the customer, hungry for advice, to seek out the salesperson.

Modified Rebuy

The buyer making a modified rebuy is one who considers making changes in an existing product order or service, price or supplier. The customer has some experience with the solution, but has become dissatisfied – and is now looking for something new or different. A modified rebuy may bring less consternation for the buyer than a new task buy, but still involves considerable thought and may involve multiple buying influences.[30] A person making a modified rebuy may find alternative suppliers who better fit his or her needs. In essence, the customer is "shopping" for opportunities to take business away from the present vendor.

Straight Rebuy

A straight rebuy is the purchase of a standard item from the same vendor on a regular basis. Two common straight rebuy purchase agreements are the annual purchase agreement and the blanket purchase order. A blanket purchase order is commonly used with low cost items. Buyers contract with suppliers to accept delivery of an agreed-upon quantity of an agreed-upon quality of product at agreed-upon intervals. A purchase order is signed upon contract agreement, and delivery is made on the set schedule. Annual purchase agreements usually require the supplier to agree to provide a specific quantity of products or services over the contract period.[31] There is often a discount attached. If more products or services are used, the customer may qualify for more discounts. There may be a formal contract (such as "preferred provider" or "preferred customer" agreement), or there may simply be a verbal agreement with a salesperson or manager.

[29] Schoell, W.F. and Guiltinan, J.P. Marketing. Allyn and Bacon, Needham Heights, Mass.: 1992.
[30] Marx, R. Personal Selling: An Interactive Approach. Allyn and Bacon, Needham Heights, Mass.:1994.
[31] ibid.

These straight rebuy situations can be very advantageous for the salesperson-that is, if *you* are the salesperson of choice. The straight rebuy can be a difficult situation for a salesperson who is *not* that salesperson of choice. To get a chance at this customer, a salesperson may have to thoroughly, carefully and strategically plan - examining the prospect's operation and the advantages he/she and his/her product or service can offer that customer.

Buying Classes in Action – A Case Study

Read the following case study carefully. Consider Wilhelm Van Eyck's thought process. Determine where the types of buying classes apply. What kind of purchase choices did Wilhelm Van Eyck have? When could he have made a decision in each of the buying classes? What, ultimately, did he decide?

A Case Study: Wilhelm Van Eyck[32]

Wilhelm Van Eyck turned his pick-up into the lane of Eyckline farms. He surveyed the orderly spread of Eyckline Farms and admired the new chicken house built this year. "Yes sir, if you make a dollar, you sometimes do well to put it back into the business," he said to himself. Wilhelm stopped at the mailbox. Pulling out the day's mail, he found, among the usual collection of items, an advertisement from his feed supplier, Master Feed. "I wonder what they want. I just saw old Jim yesterday and he didn't seem to have anything to say - seemed in a hurry as usual." Master Feed had been his broiler feed supplier for two years, despite two price increases. The last price increase annoyed him because it seemed to cover additional services he didn't use. Still, results had been reasonably good. He did, however, wish his salesman, Jim Sellars, would have stopped by to check his results.

Wilhelm gave no more thought to the letter from Master Feed until after dinner that night when he and his son, Harold, looked over the accounts. He noticed again the relatively poor returns from the last crop of chicks and the latest price increase of Master Feed. Harold suggested they might do better with something less expensive. Then, Wilhelm opened the letter from Master Feed, discovering a form letter for contract growers. Wilhelm had never contracted and it annoyed him that he should have received that letter. Jim Sellars should have taken the time to make sure his non-contract customers didn't receive the letter. The next morning, Van Eyck was on his way to the barn when his neighbor, Fritz Lonsdorf, stopped by. Lonsdorf was one of the larger broiler producers in the area and Wilhelm enjoyed comparing notes with him. Wilhelm mentioned the new Master Feed policy and their carelessness in sending him the form letter. They had discussed the price increase earlier and Wilhelm's disappointing crop.

---

[32] Condensed from Funk, J.G. and Thomas, F. Wilhelm Van Eyck Case Study, University of Guelph, Guelph, Ontario, Canada, 1981.

Case Study, continued

Fritz suggested trying his Domar brand. "My birds weighed over 4 lb. at 7 weeks on the last crop." (That was a darn sight higher than Wilhelm's last average, even with that expensive feed.) Wilhelm and Fritz continued discussing the latest research in the Poultry Review and university information and made plans to attend the London Poultry Show later in the month.

That afternoon, Wilhelm reevaluated his account books, calculating the cost of the poor results on the last crop - not bad, but certainly not something he wanted to continue, especially given Master's price increase. Fritz's results kept running through his mind...Master's quality, price and disappointing performance; his new, state-of-the-art poultry barns and equipment; his son's excellent management; and the good quality chicks. That left feed. The latest price increase would cause a significant decrease in return per bird.

Wilhelm evaluated other suppliers he had used in the past as well as other types of feed. As he was lost in thought, a car drove in the lane. It was Dave Crawford, the salesman for Martin Feeds in Elmira, walking toward the house. Crawford was a young salesman, about Harold's age. He'd been with Martin Feeds for about a year and had been trying to get Wilhelm to consider their Domar brand feeds. Crawford was a nice fellow; it would be pleasant to pass some time with him.

"Hello Wilhelm, I was in the neighborhood and thought I'd stop by to give you this article on the new feeding system. I saw it in a trade magazine and thought you would enjoy reading it." "Thanks, Dave, that's thoughtful."

They chatted a while about local events, marketing news, and disease conditions of some flocks in the next county. Then Dave said, "Wilhelm, the mill is taking a group of growers to the London Poultry Show and I thought you might be able to join us." Wilhelm replied that that was nice, but he already had plans to attend with Fritz. Dave then casually remarked, "I hear Master upped their prices again."

Wilhelm acknowledged this was so, and Dave went on, "They've got good feed, no doubt about it. Are you still pleased with the results?" Wilhelm admitted his last crop was disappointing.

"I can understand your feelings, Wilhelm. I really believe Domar can give you equal or better results. You know our quality and feed conversion ratios are competitive and our price is a good $5 a ton lower. Someone as experienced as you knows we have to offer a quality product to stay in business. Why not let me drop by a ton on Tuesday and you can give us a try?"

Case Study, continued

"Dave, I'm not ready just yet to make a change, but I sure will give your offer some thought," Wilhelm answered, "I'll let you know in a couple of days." "Sure, Wilhelm," Dave replied. "I appreciate you considering us. I'll talk to you in a couple of days."

During the next couple of days, Wilhelm met one feed salesman who questioned his choice of ventilation systems in his new chicken house, suggested he try a new hatchery and was pushing his product on Wilhelm besides. Wilhelm continued thinking abut his feed situation but made no move to change suppliers as he had some Master Feed left. He did know he'd have to decide soon. Crawford stopped by several times, as did the pushy salesman. Wilhelm knew there were other feed suppliers in the area and he was not opposed to traveling a few miles further, although he knew local feed was fresher. Prices were all pretty competitive. "Maybe it isn't worth it to change," he thought. Just then Jim Sellars passed him on the road and waved. Wilhelm thought he might be coming for a change, but Jim drove on. With that, Wilhelm made his decision. He would place the call after supper.

Summary

Chapter Five examines the nature of how people buy. Every salesperson must realize that no purchase is ever made unless some sort of problem or need is perceived. But before a decision is made, there is a logical thought process that every customer must complete. This "buying decision process" involves need recognition, information search, examination of alternatives and decision, and post purchase evaluation. A salesperson who understands these steps may better understand what the customer is experiencing, and thus be better able to respond to the information needs customers are experiencing at each phase.

The speed with which people make a purchase decision and the depth of their analysis can be quite different. Depending on the type of buyer, the analysis of information may be very detailed, or almost cursory. Similarly, when evaluating alternatives, customers consider a variety of factors. These include their expectations (formed by their past experiences), the type of salesperson they want to work with, the type of business they want to work with, and finally the product or service itself.

Because the adoption of new technologies is so critical to the success of the agricultural industry, the rate at which customers adopt new ideas is worth special consideration. Their adoption of new ideas and new technologies can be "mapped" according to five categories of customer. The most likely to adopt a new technology is the innovator, followed by early adopters, early majority, late majority and laggards. Each category of customer tends to approach new ideas in fairly consistent ways – either consistently excited and curious about them, or consistently skeptical, etc. Opinion leaders, who have considerable influence over others in their circle, are often early adopters. They deserve special attention from a salesperson; their knowledge and their influence power can both be quite helpful.

The purchase decision process includes the period immediately post-purchase. Buyers remorse (post-purchase dissonance) is a common outcome under several circumstances. The salesperson has an opportunity and responsibility to support the customer through their decision to purchase and the post purchase period, to sustain their business for future sales.

Each individual goes through the purchase decision process in a unique way. However, large accounts may contain multiple decision-makers. In this situation, it's not enough to know one contact person within the organization. The motives of each decision-maker must be understood to best allow the salesperson to effectively communicate solutions.

Finally, the purchase decision process will be strongly affected by the level of history and experience between buyer and seller. Three classes of the buying process have been identified: new buy, modified re-buy and straight re-buy. A newer situation requires more intense problem solving, whereas a familiar buying situation may only involve a routine response. In all situations, consistent contact and attention to future needs increases your chances for success.

Review Questions

1. What are the steps in the buying process?

2. Explain dissonance and how it factors into post-purchase evaluation.

3. List and describe the five groups of adopters. Why are these groups important to the agri salesperson?

4. Describe a situation in which an interaction with an opinion leader would be an advantage to an agri salesperson.

5. Wilhelm Van Eyck had to consider making a new buy, a modified rebuy or a straight rebuy. Which did he select? Why? Why should the salesperson be aware of the decision-making processes customers go through?

Part Two:

Customer Value and Your Role

Part Two is about recognizing and understanding customer value *and* recognizing and understanding *your* role in developing those critical components of the selling process.

Knowing and understanding what a product or service is worth to someone else makes communicating with them much easier. What do they value? Why is it important to them? By getting to know and understand your customer's past experience, goals, etc., you learn what they value and why. You learn to communicate how your products and services can effectively fulfill their individual values and needs. Ultimately, this translates to more successful selling.

It is a key role of the salesperson to learn how to best determine what the customer needs and wants. Delivering value to the *right* potential customer and in the *best* possible manner is a function of the salesperson's strategy. A strategy is the salesperson's plan to assemble his/her resources and decide how to use them. It is a further analysis of one's territory, local market, and individual customers. By developing those analyses, the salesperson is better prepared to successfully plan and effectively reach the customers of choice.

In the chapters that follow, value, marketing and strategy are discussed at length. The case study that follows illustrates how value, marketing and strategy are linked as key elements of agri selling and valuable tools to the agri salesperson.

Martin Harry
BASF Canada Inc.
Technical Sales Representative
Ingersoll, Ontario, Canada

Value, Marketing, Strategy

My company is important but sometimes you have to fine-tune what comes out of the office. They have to know what the customer values, needs and wants. Then, marketing programs have to be translated into what works. Sales is that final link.

For instance, some things that come out of the office may not be for every customer...as is, anyway. It is the salesperson's job to adapt and customize the philosophies and goals of marketing to fit the sales I offer my dealers. As the salesperson, I am the translator who delivers what the dealer values, what the company wants and needs to accomplish their marketing strategies and what I want to accomplish by answering that individual's specific situation and needs. There is a lot of responsibility involved – especially for a new salesperson in interpreting the company philosophy and goals. But, you really treat people how you would like to be treated.

I want to fully understand the programs that come out of the home office. If there is a need to change a program that comes out, get it changed. Explain why. I am always curious and probing to find out why we do this <u>this</u> way, why we do this <u>that</u> way so we can do it <u>better</u> for the customer. I like to get people in the company, peers and management, marketing too, to think about what will be the best fit to get the most impact. I really like to remind them that it is critical to not lose focus and forget about the customer. It has to fit together.

In the field, I am the ears and eyes of the company. Yes, I am the company to those I sell to. But that makes my input valuable to the company as well. I am the entity which translates and determines what the customer values, what their wants and needs are. Sure, that's important to the customer for their individual purchase. It is also just as critical to the company to know and understand that clearly so they can best develop the plans and strategies that relate back to that same customer.

So, personally, I work to make sure the company understands how to best take care of my number one-and that's my customer's needs.

Chapter Six:

Customers Buy Value

Learning Objectives:

Upon completion of this chapter, you should be able to:

1. understand that value is a relative, not absolute, concept;
2. define *tangible* vs *intangible* value and give some examples of each;
3. describe how value may be seen differently by relationship, economic and business buyers;
4. recall four different levels of value that contribute to a strong customer relationship.

What is "Value"?

Value is a term used so often, it's to the point of being over-used. For many people, it has lost a lot of its original meaning – not because it isn't critically important, but because there is often so little substance behind the claim to value. For example, what does it mean when you hear that a product or service is:

- "more value for the money?"
- "a good value?"
- "the best value on the market?"

Value is a term that means different things to different people. It's not a term people consciously think about often. But every day people <u>act</u> based upon what they value.

What did you value the last time you rented a hotel room? Was it conveniently located on the sales route? Was it reasonably priced? Was it clean? Did it provide soap and shampoo? Was it noisy, or smelly? Were the hotel employees friendly, efficient, helpful?

In some cases, an individual's choice may be influenced by circumstances or by someone else. But in all cases, once something has been purchased, people are able to recognize whether the purchase was a "good value" or not.

For both salespeople and customers, _how_ an individual defines value determines _what_ the individual values.

> For someone who hates to stand in line and likes convenience, paying $.50 to $1.00 more for milk or butter at a "quick-stop" is not a problem.

In sales, the challenge is to find out exactly how the customer defines value. To do this, it is necessary to understand their past experiences, their current situation and their expectations. Only then can their expectations be met – and value delivered. That process takes time and perseverance.

Value And Worth

Selling is defined as solving people's problems and addressing needs. Customers buy based on their wants and needs. Value is a relative concept for each customer, a measure of how important something is to them. Some salespeople find it helpful to think about "value" as actually containing two related concepts – value and worth.

Value is an interactive experience.

    a) It is comparative in that it depends on a rating or ranking of one object against another.
    b) It is personal in that it differs among individuals.
    c) It is situational in that it hinges on the context within which an evaluative judgment occurs.

Ultimately, it is perceived value (worth to the customer) that attracts a customer or lures a customer away from a competitor. Value can be encounter-specific or a more enduring, overall perception. Value may be thought of as arising from both quality and price or from what one gets and what one gives.[33] Generally, perceived value increases as quality increases and as price decreases. Yet exactly how quality and price combine to form value is not well understood.

Value is personal preference and therefore assumed to be essentially subjective. However, the perception of value is susceptible to being altered by objective changes. Let's look at an example.

---

[33] Zeithaml, V.A. Consumer perceptions of price, quality and value: A means-end model and synthesis of evidence. Journal of Marketing, Volume 52: 1988, p. 2-22.

Ron Jakes had been growing corn for almost twenty years now, making all the decisions since taking over from his Dad. In those twenty years, he's only seen about three bad infestations of European corn borer. So when the seed companies came out with some new transgenic hybrid with corn borer resistance, Ron wasn't too excited. Sure, he saw the value in the resistance – for someone who had real problems with corn borer. But it just wasn't worth it to him to spend an additional $10 per unit or more to get protection for a problem he only had every seven years or so.

Ron's opinion changed pretty rapidly when severe corn borer infestations began happening every two or three years. Maybe it was all the no-till – he didn't really know for sure – but there just seemed to be a reservoir of the insects that were able to overwinter now. There was always a low level of them present – and his seed dealer showed him some data that convinced him he was losing 10-15 bushels an acre to that low infestation. When weather conditions were right, though, there were severe infestations now – more often than before, with higher yield losses. Ron began to re-consider his decision about ECB corn...maybe insect resistance was worth something to him after all.

This example illustrates how value is an interactive concept. Value, for each customer, depends on:

- the characteristics of the product or service;
- the situation of the customer;
- the awareness of the customer that product or service characteristics.

The critical role of the salesperson is to help the customer understand the current situation: how product and service characteristics can "go to work" for them - to make them aware of the value of a product or service <u>for them</u>.

Clues to Value

In agricultural selling, perceived value is all that counts. You might say that value is *always* in the eye of the customer. The salesperson must be able to understand the clues to value that customers give them: what people want, why they buy, and in what they believe. So often, salespeople discount or rationalize what they hear. In the example above, a salesperson might have classified Ron as a laggard - someone who isn't too interested in innovative products. That might not be true at all - it's just that the innovation of ECB resistance wasn't worth anything to Ron until he recognized the cost of his problems with corn borer. When a salesperson makes a customer aware of a need, he or she is preparing the customer to understand and perceive the value of a product/service solution.

Aaron McWhorter
Sports Turf Co., Inc., & North Georgia Turf, Inc.
Owner and President
Whitesburg, Georgia

I define value as exceeding expectations...anybody's expectations...customers, public, mine. Customers can't tell if they're buying value unless the salesperson does his/her job. Customers can't tell if they are buying value unless you can eventually prove to them that your product offers them something unique that satisfies their needs or expectations. It is the salesperson who makes that connection for most customers – who explains or communicates what value their product is to the customer.

Types of Value

Value is not only dollars and cents, although "economics" is certainly important. Value can also mean a preferred way of doing business. It can be associated with the positive or negative feelings or outcomes that result from the selling relationship. Morris B. Holbrook, in *Service Quality*,[34] suggests that products contribute to customer value insofar as they provide services that create *desired consumption experiences*. For example, that expensive 4-wheel drive sport utility vehicle allows the driver to have the "desired consumption experience" of off-road, wilderness travel and adventure, with all the comforts of an automatic transmission.

Visionary Selling, by Barbara Geraghty,[35] discusses the role of value as an *insightful idea* offered by the salesperson. She points out that, too often, the customer's idea of a business solution and the salesperson's idea of a business solution are two different ideas. Geraghty explores how the salesperson can creatively answer the customer's needs by insightfully delivering value in the form of a good idea or solution.

In her book, Geraghty shares a comment offered by Bob Peebler, CEO of Landmark Graphics. His comment is in response to how salespeople aligned with his company's vision of how it could offer value through an idea.

> *I have not yet had one salesperson approach me with a "higher level" idea. They always come with features/functions or just a "canned" solution that is looking for*

---

[34] Holbrook, M.B. The nature of customer value. Graduate School of Business, Columbia University, 1994. From Rust, R.T., Oliver, R.L. Service quality: new directions in theory and practice. Sage Publications, Inc., Thousand Oaks, California: 1994.

[35] Geraghty, B. Visionary selling. Simon and Schuster, New York, New York: 1988.

a home. I would enjoy just once having a salesperson start the discussion with a better understanding of what we are trying to accomplish and probe me for a deeper understanding of our challenges. We have plenty of them, but I sometimes feel as if I am in a desert where original ideas are water. I am still waiting for the innovative visionary sales approach versus a mirage called a solution that is designed to benefit the selling company versus mine. I suspect most CEO's are just as thirsty. Can you imagine having a lemonade stand in the desert?

Value, in this illustration, is a fresh idea offered by a salesperson – one that is based on an understanding of needs and that benefits or is worth something to the *customer* company and not just the *seller* company. This customer expects the salesperson to bring that value – to interact with the customer's situation and concerns <u>before</u> trying to present the "value" of a solution. While most of agricultural selling is not done at the CEO level, this exact same situation happens every day. The "fresh ideas" you bring as a salesperson are worth as much or more to your customers as the specifics of your product, described in some brochure.

The perceived value of a product or service, as mentioned earlier, is increased by *quality*. In many industries (including agriculture), there are some national brands, as well as some local retail businesses, that "set a standard" for quality.

Why does a Mercedes cost more than a fully-loaded Cadillac? How have our perceptions of "value" been influenced by products like:

- Sony TV's and stereo components?
- Toyota cars and trucks?
- Chanel No. 5 Perfume?

These products are considered leaders in the public eye, yet everyone doesn't drive a Toyota wearing Chanel No. 5 perfume, while listening to a Sony stereo! Quality is an important component of value, but it only becomes "worth something" to a customer who appreciates that quality, "needs" or wants it, and can afford it.

Intangible and Tangible Value

There are many ways to define, measure and enhance value, but for the sake of discussion, let's focus on two types of value: tangible and intangible.

Intangible Value

Intangible value is hard to measure objectively. It may involve emotions or feelings such as pride in ownership, prestige or status associated with a particular product. Several of the types of value described above are examples of *intangible* value. The "feeling" or consumption experience described by Holbrook is certainly a personal, objective experience that is hard to quantify. The "fresh idea" described by Geraghty has an intangible value, although when translated into concrete action steps it may take on tangible value. Certainly "quality" has an aspect of personal judgment that makes it somewhat intangible.

A Mercedes may not last longer than a Cadillac, but some people pay more for it anyway. Why? Because the Mercedes image creates a perception of value in the buyer's mind that is strong enough to command several thousand dollars more in price. Its image as a "high-value" automobile is carefully supported by advertising that promotes the consumption experience (status and comfort), the "fresh ideas" of safety features and engineering, and the "quality" of its construction. These intangibles, taken together, drive the perception of greater value. The salesperson delivers intangible value by understanding the customer as a person - their experience, their hopes, their dreams, and their definition of quality.

Tangible Value

Tangible value is concrete, real and easily measured. Product safety or availability are examples of tangible value. The ability of a specific feature to "go to work" and create added profits or reduced cost for the customer is tangible value. For example, a product with a good repair history, lower fuel consumption, control of a specific problem, or demonstrably higher yields delivers tangible value. The salesperson delivers tangible value by understanding the business situation of the customer - whether that business is a farm, ranch, greenhouse, accounting service or livestock operation.

David Suttle
WorldCom Advanced Networks
Director, Network Channel Sales
Hilliard, Ohio

Value...I think that is the toughest thing to teach or explain when we teach our salespeople. Value is sometimes very tangible and sometimes, it becomes difficult to impossible to explain or display intangible value. In that case, your product is viewed as close to a commodity or as similar to any other product out there. And for you not to be compared dollar for dollar, you have to establish either what makes your corporation different, your individual sales effort different, or your follow-up and support of the customer different. All of those add to the perceived value of the product.

...continued

> You can look at your own internal corporation and your product to try to find value points that are "differentiators," but to really get a sale, you have to be able to really translate your specific value points into the bottom line contribution or value for the customer.
>
> Here's an example. We provide services to a lot of the transportation industry, airlines, cargo, that type of thing. Most of these companies have some type of data network themselves. But where they trust us to run the network for them is typically whenever it has something to do with their customers...because what they've found is that we can do it more cost-effectively but also more reliably.
>
> Until you can determine what is value to the customer, you don't necessarily have anything to sell.

The Economics of Value

The discussion of value would not be complete without considering the "economics" of value. How does a customer weigh product features, services, price, and anticipated results? How can a salesperson influence the customer to "see" that his or her solution offers more "value" than those of competitors?

The Value Equation

We have identified that value has an individually determined worth. Fundamental economic exchange theory tells us that people expect an equal or better exchange: what they get must be worth as much as (or hopefully more than) what they give. As a salesperson, you know that your product or service can deliver value in many ways to your customers. Your job is to make sure that it delivers more of what *they* value than the competition. Then, they are often willing to do business - for a fair price. This dynamic can be expressed as a simple value equation:

Perceived Product Performance +/- Additional Services - Price = Value

Perceived Product/Service Performance

A favorable (or even neutral) perception of product and service is "baseline" or table stakes. It is the minimum required for a customer to even consider doing business with a company or individual. Remember - it is not the *absolute* or "brochure" value of your products and services that counts here. It is the *perceived* value, depending on how well you have uncovered needs and matched needs to the tangible and intangible ways your product has value for this customer.

Additional Services

These are services that go beyond basic expectations. They can "add value" to the total solution you offer. For example, many manufacturers may offer a similar weed control product, but only *you* are willing to train retail staff on how to use this product in conservation tillage situations to improve farmer yield and reduce farmer costs. Many animal health suppliers may offer feed-grade antibiotics, but only your company also offers a feed assay service to make sure they are mixed appropriately and the resulting feed satisfies FDA guidelines. Many grain marketers may be willing to take grain, but only your company has a program to help farmers select and grow special high-value output trait crops, and then collect, store and market those crops for a premium. Through additional services, the company or sales representative has the opportunity deliver more value than the product or service alone could generate.

Price

The price of a product is generally regarded as a "negative." However, any negative feelings about price can be "neutralized" if the customer perceives the value received to be equal to or more than the price paid. Value and price are *always* intertwined. While some customers want the "lowest price," most want a "fair price." A "fair price" is a price that fulfills the customer's expectation of a fair economic exchange – the products/services return more to the business than they cost.

Value

In "Managing Customer Value,"[36] Bradley Gale calls customer value "the most important concept and the most important target in business management." This is particularly true in agriculture, because salespeople must approach the same customers year after year. Making sure that the customer perceived "value" from your solution in your key to future business.

Even within an economic model of value, it's important to remember that perceived value has several sources:

- economic benefits;
- functional benefits;
- psychological (dynamic) benefits.

Economic benefits of value include prices, discounts, or programs. This is the area most people typically think of first when considering "value" issues. While it is certainly important in some cases, economic value usually is NOT the only type of value to emphasize as an overall sales strategy. Selling on price leaves the salesperson's business vulnerable to every competitor in every sales situation.

Functional benefits come from other basic features (besides price). Availability, reliability, control, ease of use, and safety are all examples of this type of value.

---

[36] Gale, B.T. Managing customer value. The Free Press, New York, New York: 1994.

Functional benefits offer many opportunities to differentiate from competitors and give people rational reasons to pay more for one product or service than a similar item. Psychological (dynamic) benefits are probably the most difficult to predict and understand. However, they are often the benefits that the buyer cares most about, and thus they offer the best opportunity to sell the right products at the right price. Examples include peace of mind, security, status, perceived risk, relationship with the seller, and the like. It is much more difficult for a competitor to duplicate the psychological benefits of your particular solution - and the relationship with you.

Value As Business Results

"The way to win the value revolution is to exceed your customers' expectations at the particular level you position yourself." So says author Robert Tucker in his book, "Win The Value Revolution."[37] In order to exceed expectations, you have to understand them. Agricultural selling is a curious hybrid of industrial (business-to-business) selling and consumer selling. When you sell to an agricultural business, you are selling business results - but expected and desired results are heavily colored by the person making the purchase, and what is important to them.

Your customer may want reduced costs, more technical knowledge, greater access, or less "hassle" from your products and services. These "value factors" all mean something different to each customer...and are held in different priorities. While generalizing about value may not be prudent, it is very productive to tone selling points to the business results that determine the "perceived value" for each customer or prospect.

Increased Revenues

 Increased revenues affect the customer's "top line." Increased revenues may come from higher yields, better prices for what is produced, or higher sales. In any event, the customer's revenue is growing and with it, assuming additional revenues are higher than additional costs, the bottom line also grows.

Decreased Costs

Many customers are looking for reduced costs of operation as a way to greater profits. This may come from lower purchase prices or, more often, from the

---

[37] Tucker, R.B. Win the Value Revolution. Career Press, New Jersey : 1995.

impact of the salesperson's products or services on the customer's operating efficiency. By using a certain product, the customer may be able to replace and reduce current costs. Decreased costs can come through your expertise and advice or through tangible product benefits.

Enhanced Relationship

Customers often switch products or suppliers because of dissatisfaction with the interpersonal or business relationship with the current supplier. These relationship deficiencies are likely caused by something other than poor product performance or economic results. Perhaps customer service or response time is poor, attention is lacking, or communication difficulties abound. In any event, the customer is vulnerable to making a change.

Reduced Complexity

With the increasing technical and environmental demands on agriculturists and those who serve agriculture, simplifying the lives of many of our customers can lead to increased satisfaction and/or more sales. Reducing customer complexity may mean more accurate invoices, simpler user instructions, keeping customer records on supplier database systems, having that information accessible to the customer via computer, or providing products or services which are a better fit for the customer's expertise level. Reducing complexity is growing in importance for many customers. Often, greater access to technical information specific to the product offers customers an invaluable source of reduced complexity. Less hassle in product use, care, handling, and maintenance are also of strategic importance to simplifying the busy life of an agricultural customer. Time is money to the customer, just as it is for the salesperson.

It is critical to understand which one or combination of these results is most important to customers, particularly since many benefits can lead to more than one result. For example, a customer who values "more, better information" could be seeking any of the four results. Moreover, the result being sought will change from sale to sale, year to year as circumstances change. So, salespeople must assemble a "value package" to meet customer defined results.

Levels of Value

Perceived value is a function of customer expectations. These expectations are specific to the customer, dynamic (they change from situation to situation and year to year), and determined by the customer's experiences, hopes, awareness of need, and business demands.

It may be helpful to think of perceived value as having several different levels. As a customer determines what a product or service is worth, he/she considers both types of value (psychological, functional, economic) and the level of value ("how much") you can deliver. Each customer has a slightly different pattern of thought, because each starts from a different point in terms of their past experiences and their understanding of what is available. Four levels of value can be identified.[38]

Figure 6.1
Levels of Value

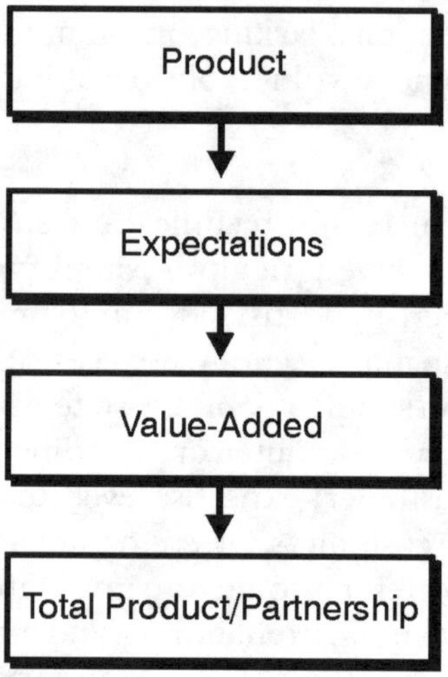

```
┌─────────────────────────────────┐
│            Product              │
└─────────────────────────────────┘
                │
                ▼
┌─────────────────────────────────┐
│          Expectations           │
└─────────────────────────────────┘
                │
                ▼
┌─────────────────────────────────┐
│          Value-Added            │
└─────────────────────────────────┘
                │
                ▼
┌─────────────────────────────────┐
│    Total Product/Partnership    │
└─────────────────────────────────┘
```

The Product – Level One

The product itself is represented by the bottom level. A quality product is the foundation of customer value. Quality may be defined differently by different types of buyers, but usually product quality adheres to fairly universal definitions for a specific product category.

Within each industry, there are specific attributes for baseline product quality. Over time, these basic expectations tend to increase. If, twenty years ago, "quality hybrid seed corn" could be depended on to yield 120 bushels per acre under favorable growing conditions, today "quality seed corn" may be expected to generate 150, 160 or more bushels per acre. Fifteen years ago, basic manufacturers of animal health products could arguably claim that their products had a higher

---

[38] Based on information compiled from Levitt, T. The Marketing Imagination. New, Expanded Edition. The Free Press, A Division of Macmillan, Inc., New York, New York: 1983.

quality than generic products. Today, with improved quality of manufacturing across the industry, both branded and generic products offer "good" quality.

Every customer has a set of "quality criteria" they use to judge products available to them. If a product doesn't meet the baseline quality level they have established for their business, it won't even be considered. The message to salespeople is clear: before you can sell a product or service, you must make sure that it has the level of quality that meets customer minimum standards. That not only requires you to know the quality of your product, but also to be able to compare it to the quality of other products on the market and to uncover the standards of each customer. If your product is not even in the "consideration set" of the customer because of quality issues, your customer may not care to hear about your low price, your expertise or even your value-added services.

Expectations – Level Two

Baseline quality is often not enough, particularly when the salesperson's products are higher in price than competitive products. To be judged favorably in a competitive environment, products and services must not only perform as claimed, but must also meet the expectations of the customer. These expectations are often greater than quality or performance minimums, especially for those large and profitable accounts that every salesperson wants.

For example, having "average" yield, particularly if competitors have influenced the market with "record yield" claims, may not be enough. Having "good control of broadleaf weeds" may not be enough if competitors have developed a product that performs better in some way. Offering genetics for pigs that gain quickly may not be enough if most genetics companies can promise pigs that put on lean gain and are thus more marketable. Expectations also change with time, for both product and service components of your "value bundle." Many components that, at one time, added value are now simply expected. For example, at one time a good retailer financing program could add significant value to a distributor/retailer relationship. Now, it is expected. At one time, special input traits such as herbicide tolerance or insect resistance added value to a seed brand; now, having transgenic products is expected for most major brands. Again, the salesperson must know his or her marketplace. Positioning a product feature or a service as "something special" when everyone else is already offering it makes the salesperson look naive or even manipulative.

Value-Add – Level Three

The third level in the "total product" concerns activities and services the individual salesperson brings to "add value" to the product. Many selling and marketing activities are designed to create competitive value at this level.

Examples would be sponsoring customer outings such as fishing trips; retailer seminars such as Certified Crop Advisor training; significantly higher customer rebates or volume incentives; or yield guarantees from a crop consultant.

As indicated, the level of services that "add value" is always rising. Services that were used to add value a few years ago have become expected now. One of the most exciting areas for salesperson creativity is to develop new services, expertise and cross-industry relationships that can "add value" in unique, hard-to-imitate ways. Let's look at an example.

> *A few years ago, Larry was ready to tear his hair out. He had been asked to focus his efforts on larger farmers in his area, and they had become really difficult to deal with. In one area of the county after another, large farmers had formed buying groups. With their combined purchasing power, they were able to get the lowest prices from any retailer they approached. Product quality was much the same everywhere – and they, of course, still expected all the services they had been used to as individual customers. It seemed like a no-win situation. Then, about eighteen months ago, Larry had a brainstorm. Instead of fighting these farmers, why not join them? With the agreement of his manager, he began to take an active – almost aggressive – role in organizing top groups of farmers himself. When a group with enough buying power came together, Larry met with them and determined which services they needed. He offered to keep their crop records for them, bring in manufacturer reps to share the latest ideas with them, brokered the services of a local crop consultant at a reduced rate – really tried to develop a "value bundle" that would help them get where they wanted to go. In return, they agreed to do all their business with Larry, as long as his prices were competitive. As a result, Larry is now the highest-volume salesperson in the company. True, the margin on each sale is a little less. But he has "locked in" enough business at a high enough margin to contribute to his company's profits. And, instead of spending his time trying to sell these top farmers, he can spend his time looking for low-cost ways to improve service to them.*

Total Product/Partnership – Level Four

This fourth level of value is the most difficult to attain. Yet it can be done, and it is worth the effort. Larry, in our example above, is well on his way. At this level of value, you and your business have become mental "partners" with your customer's business. The partnership is not formal, and does not involve the sharing of profits or costs (although it could eventually evolve to that). However, you allow the way you work - products, services, expertise - to be influenced by the customer's needs. They, in turn, allow their business to be influenced by you. This "partnership" can happen in one product area or several, and can be more or less formal. For example, a retailer could approach his top vegetable growers and offer to invest in a new piece of spray equipment, saving them the cost of each buying one, in return for an agreement to buy product and spraying services. Or, a distributor customer could agree to invest additional time and resources in training salespeople to introduce a new animal health product in return for a limited distribution agreement.

At the retail level, these "partnerships" evolve naturally over time for the most successful businesses. The retail business exists in its current form - products, services, people - to meet the needs of its major customers. They, in turn, feel that their needs have a significant impact on the retailer's business decisions. Together they stand profitably - divided, they might both be less successful.

The salesperson is *always* critical to the development of a "partnership" with the customer and a "total product" that meets the customer's needs and expectations. In an era when many retailer businesses are absorbed or bought by larger regional cooperatives and distributors, local businesses may find that the salesperson is their *primary* tool to creating these powerful partnerships with top accounts.

Delivering value at all four levels is necessary to create loyalty in today's market - and it can be quite a challenge. Like a retail buyer, a customer may be attracted by certain advertising campaigns, low prices, or product features. While their business sense tells them they'd be better off with a supplier who understands their business and wants to be a true "partner," their consumer mentality can make free goods and wearables hard to refuse. Increasingly, however, the customer needs and expects performance from the products, services and the business relationship with a salesperson and the company he/she represents.

Donald Upton
United Cooperative Farmers, Inc.
General Manager
Fitchburg, Massachusetts

We bring value to the customer. I think we've been doing this for many, many years. The interesting part is how the definition of what is "value" to the customer has changed over time and how as a company and as salespeople, we just get better at it and more technically oriented in response to what customers value.

Something our customers value most is a high tech approach to livestock, dairy and poultry nutrition. All our salespeople have laptops. Almost on an annual basis we upgrade the software so that they can do programs for the farmers on

...continued

their farms at a faster rate then they've done in the past. Then the customers can adjust their feeding program either financially, depending on the commodity markets, or on nutrient value, depending on what their nutrients are in their home-grown forages and so forth.

Our technical value-adds of getting them price adjustments on the farm and locking them in from there make the timely visits another added value. That's a tremendous value because the dairy man can say each morning that he knows what his feed will be, and if he feels it is good then he can order it. Or, he can further negotiate and change the price and maybe either increase the value or decrease the value through the programming from there on the site. But, it's pretty rapid service and I think that's what our customers consider one of the real value-addeds that we bring to them. And because of that, we're unique in the Northeast.

We do a number of innovative things over all, that each contribute to a great value that we can bring the company better, more efficiently and more effectively than competitors. Also, the value we are offering the customer is of specific value <u>to them</u>, because of these things: knowing how to and conducting accurate analysis; time spent with sales representatives; and accuracy. These are all special values to the customer; we can deliver special value to them on their terms. Knowing what they value and delivering it to them, in turn, makes the salesperson more successful – the company as a whole more successful.

Customer Value Patterns

In Chapter 4, the three buying styles of Business Buyer, Relationship Buyer and Economic Buyer were introduced. These buying styles are ways of grouping customers with somewhat similar values. It is important to recognize that in each situation, customers must perceive that *they* got the *best value bundle*...and that they did, based on *their* value system. Let's look at an example.

A husband and wife were talking about getting a new Ford Explorer. They were busy and each decided to do their homework on their own. Both wanted a new Explorer.

Karen went auto shopping on the Internet. She found all the information she needed in a matter of hours. She joined a chat room of new vehicle owners, discussing models and options. Her detailed print-out included product information, price comparisons, financing and delivery options. All that was left in her shopping effort was the credit card number and the vehicle would be delivered to the door.

Alan, on the other hand, went to see Steven at the dealership. He and Steven spent 3-4 hours talking, drinking coffee, taking test drives, kicking tires, etc. He also ended up with enough product information and price comparisons to make a decision. They arrived at the same solution: the same make, model, same price, same color vehicle. Same deal.

This couple valued different means of vehicle shopping. Karen didn't need to go to the dealership. She valued the ease of never leaving her desk, and also determining what best suited their needs, wants and budget in what she considered an "objective" way - without interference from a salesperson. Alan valued the physical and personal interaction with the car and the salesperson. He needed to talk and interact with someone about needs, wants and budget to arrive at the vehicle that satisfied their needs.

Let's briefly review the buyer types introduced earlier.

Table 6.1
Buyer Types

Business Buyer	Economic Buyer	Relationship Buyer
• bottom-line results • facts and research • organization • brief, to the point • likes expertise • compares price/value package • wants full service to meet needs	• very discriminating • efficiency oriented • very price conscious • "knows" what he needs • demands tailored programs • shops around • exacting details	• likes regular contact • trusts info source he knows • accepts rep, trusts • wants to spend time chatting • likes informal and formal contact • may not compare price if trusts • likes full service

A Relationship Buyer may place a great value on the insights and ideas offered by their salesperson or others - about farming, a product or service, even raising kids! That relationship with their salesperson may be part of the overall value of their association with one another. It's an important connection the Relationship Buyer has with the world outside the business. Their salesperson is a valued partner in their life. Because of the strength and relative value of that relationship with <u>you</u>, the Relationship Buyer buys <u>your</u> company's product.

An Economic Buyer may determine that a discounted price or "free" product is an important part of a purchase they make. The big seed company representative may say they can't offer free seed. But Pat, down the road, who sells for a home state seed company, can bonus him one bag seed for every five he buys. Because of that, and because of the lower price per bag in the first place, the Economic Buyer will trust their own practical, gut instinct and buy Pat's lower-priced seed.

The Business Buyer wants both a solid relationship with someone he/she can trust and a product or service that will improve profits. He or she is always concerned about a "fair price." But a "fair price" for the Business Buyer is the one that results in profits that outweigh costs - even if it is not the cheapest product or the lowest-priced service. In fact, the Business Buyer may often be somewhat suspicious of the "lowest-priced" product or service.

These different types of buyers have different "patterns" of value perception. For example, a close and warm relationship with the salesperson is worth a lot to a Relationship Buyer. It may be worth very little to an Economic Buyer. A Business Buyer may place little to no value on the "partner points" they can receive for a purchase and redeem for merchandise through a catalog. What is more important to a Business Buyer is the increased profit resulting from having used the best product for the job.

In each case, value is determined by the buyer, based on their personal wants, needs and personalities. Again, in each situation, customers perceive they got the best value bundle based on their own value system. Friendliness, price, and profit are important to every individual buyer. However, one of those factors may be *more* important.

Summary

Value is a tough concept to describe, because it means something different to everyone. When a salesperson learns about the products and services he or she will represent, many aspects of value seem clear. These may be intangible - such as innovation, brand quality, or the feelings or status that having the product confers. Or, these value aspects may be quite tangible, such as specific features, demonstrated results, or the product's ability to reduce customer costs. Yet, in a one-on-one selling situation, the salesperson must not only understand these aspects of value; he or she must determine what each is "worth" to the customer and sell accordingly.

Selling in agriculture means selling to businesses and business needs, as well as to the people who manage those businesses and to their personal needs. Business needs differ from customer to customer, but many "business benefits" fall into the categories of increased volume or yield, reduced costs, enhanced relationships, and reduced complexity.

Customers expect that a product or service will return as much or more value to them as the cost of the product. That value might come through the product itself, or it might come through value-added services and the relationship with the seller. In order to create customer loyalty, it is critical to offer products and services that meet customers' basic criteria for quality, meet their expectations for "normal" service, add value in ways that are meaningful, and eventually to create such a strong relationship between the salesperson or company and the customer that a feeling of partnership exists.

The way customers define value is related to their general approach to the buying decision. Some customers are motivated primarily by the relationship they have with the salesperson and his or her organization. Others are motivated by economic considerations, and like to find the best "deals" from among those products that meet their other criteria. A third type of customer approaches the decision more analytically, and judges "value" based on the results a product or service can generate for the business.

Review Questions

1. Value is a relative concept for each customer. Describe the critical role of the salesperson in helping the customer understand the value a certain product or service has for them.

2. Define tangible and intangible value. Give examples of both.

3. Discuss the four value factors listed as business results. How do each of these impact the potential sale?

4. In this chapter, four value levels are defined. Explain how the fourth level (a total product/partnership) is developed and what the salesperson can do to enhance this level.

5. Choose either a car sale or a seed sale scenario. Explain what a relationship buyer might "value" in purchasing that product from a salesperson.

The Market System

Learning Objectives:

Upon completion of this chapter, you should be able to:

1. compare and contrast differences between selling and marketing;
2. define marketing as a set of functions organized in a systematic way to satisfy customers;
3. explain value bundles and their role in marketing;
4. distinguish between product, customer and sales' driven marketing;
5. recall the major outputs from a marketing system (e.g., product strategies, pricing, etc.);
6. name the five components of the marketing mix.

Marketing Defined

The new salesperson may have a question about why marketing is even included as a chapter in a book on agricultural *selling*. It is because sales and marketing are so closely related. Marketing develops the goals, strategy, and tools necessary to satisfy customer needs (profitably). Sales is the field-level implementation of those strategies. The company marketing mission, vision, strategy, and plan often identify the market within which the salesperson will work and drive the programs which guide sales.

The marketing plan and strategy are important because they give the salesperson direction, information, tools, programs, processes and other resources to satisfy customer needs. The salesperson then becomes the critical, intimate connection with the customer. Using marketing programs and strategies, salespeople can best "close the loop" by connecting with the customer, satisfying their needs and wants and, ultimately, closing the sale.

What is *marketing*? Why do organizations have marketing departments, marketing managers and market plans? Marketing is the system a company uses for identifying and satisfying customer needs and wants profitably. Marketing is, therefore, at the very heart of your business, because it defines:

- who customers are;
- what they need;
- what they want;
- how your products can meet those needs and wants;
- how services satisfy customers;
- how to make a profit (and stay in business) doing this.

Agribusinesses are not only in business to make a profit selling their current products. They are also in business to help customers accomplish <u>their</u> own goals through the use of those products and services. In fact, putting the customer's needs first is the best way to plan for long-term selling success. If the customer's needs are not being met, it is pretty difficult for the agribusiness to be successful for long. Most highly successful agribusinesses know that putting the customer first is the best route to generating profitable sales, because this sincere interest in the customer creates trust and credibility. Agribusinesses that are primarily focused on "selling stuff" to customers in order to make a lot of money often don't do very well in the long run.

Larry Barman
American Cyanamid
Marketing Specialist, IMI-Corn
Red Oak, Iowa

Marketing and selling, I think, go hand in hand. In many ways, talking about marketing and selling, it's hard to tell where one ends and the other begins. I think as a sales rep, in a way, you do both.

Selling, I guess, I would define as describing the features and benefits of a particular product or program. Marketing is the other part of incentives and programs that further benefit the grower. Marketing takes into account a bigger company scheme – but needs sales to click. Still, they do go hand in hand.

In a specific conversation, I think a key role of the salesperson is to identify what a customer is looking for in a product. You have to be adept at determining whether it is the product that's selling or if you are selling on the relationship. Still the salesperson has to do that with the overall marketing picture in mind.

...continued

> I think, anymore, a lot of selling is done as consultative-type selling, where the salesperson helps the customer identify their problem and, through two-way communication, come to a solution. This kind of sales seems to plug in more of the marketing ideas/concepts better. As a result, it helps address a bigger picture of concerns and solutions for the customer while at the same time advancing the company's marketing ideas/concepts better.

Why Understand Marketing?

Marketing is all about understanding customer needs. When we understand the needs and values of the customer, we are better able to develop product/service "bundles" that meet those needs. We can price them competitively and for a fair profit. We can sell a broad range of products more efficiently. When our customers can buy value "bundles" that meet their needs and match their values, they benefit. So do we.

Let's look at an example of how this works.

> *Brian and Regina have been married for seven years and have two small children, Dane and Bridget. Brian recently took a new job and they decided to move and buy or rent a new place. Brian's primary need was safe and dependable housing at a fair price. Regina felt they needed a house with plenty of space for growing kids. Since Brian travels in his job, she wanted a house near neighbors, good schools, and her sister. She wanted most services available locally, at stores that made her feel comfortable, even if she didn't know many local people.*

> *In addition to their needs, Brian and Regina agreed that they wanted a place that was bigger than their current apartment. However, they didn't want to look all over town for the best deal, and they didn't want to hassle with a builder over price, options, timelines, etc.*

What do you think Brian and Regina chose? They chose a large, sunny condominium in a new building across from a school and a park. Why? While many houses probably offered the space they wanted, the condominium offered the space along with a living experience and image that matched their values and their priorities.

How did Brian and Regina find this condominium, from among the many houses and apartments available? They saw an advertisement:

Sunshine and Laughter
Large, open condominium in a new, modern building. Walk to park, schools, church, shopping. 24-hour security protects your family. Day care available.

They contracted an agent, saw the condominium, and fell in love with it.

The agency representing the building didn't attract Brian and Regina by accident. They had carefully developed a product, a package, a pricing strategy and a promotional strategy that, as a value "bundle," was targeted to appeal to customers like Brian and Regina. The result? Brian and Regina are satisfied customers.

Remember the definition of marketing: *a system for identifying and satisfying customer needs and wants...profitably.* While there are many different models or systems for thinking through a company marketing plan, most companies use a system that involves these basic steps (Figure 7.1).

Figure 7.1
The Marketing Process

Mission/Vision

A company's marketing plan begins with the mission/vision. Usually, this marketing mission or vision is drawn directly from the company's overall corporate mission. The mission statement is a broad-based statement indicating the general parameters within which the company wants to operate.

A mission or vision statement often defines the kinds of problems for which the company wants to find solutions and for whom. For example, an agronomic supply company may have a mission statement that reads something like this:

> *The mission of our company shall be to successfully find profitable solutions for farmers' agronomic seed and production needs.*

A microbial feed supplement company may have a more technically-based mission/vision statement.

> *Our company mission is to continually research and develop the latest technologies that lead to improvements in microbial feed supplements for customer's livestock feed needs and to provide those to our customers in a cost effective and timely way.*

Simply put, the broad-based mission or vision statement clearly states kinds of problems for which the company wants to provide solutions and for whom they would like to develop these products and services.

Earl Bell
ELANCO Animal Health, Eli Lilly & Company
Sales Representative
Rocky Mount, North Carolina

As a new salesperson it is important to understand the company you work for as well as know your product or your customer. Ask the questions of the company early on. What do you expect me to do? It's so key. I think the most critical thing for new salespeople coming on is who are they going to work for? Who would be their manager? I feel like salespeople are pretty well set for the rest of their life probably two years into their work. They are so easy to influence at that time. They are looking at their boss as the successful person in that company. You just hope that boss has a good set of skills and values.

...continued

I've seen people's whole careers change because they had maybe a bad manager and he didn't teach them and protect them, he was looking out for himself rather than a company. When you're talking to young/new salespeople, everybody in that company has a responsibility to see that they are trained properly, that they have the right image of what the company ought to be and it is so important those first two years.

Situation Analysis – Evaluating Strengths and Weaknesses

A thorough *situation analysis* is the first step to developing a customer-centered market plan. Analyzing the situation usually involves looking at two types of factors: external or "marketplace" factors, and internal or "company" factors.

External or Market Analysis

Marketing is a long look – a three to five year plan or more. Marketing is also discovering and exploiting opportunities. The "long look" or extended time period covered by the marketing plan defines the selection of the *external* or "marketplace" factors to consider. These are factors that affect everyone in the marketplace. Depending on the type of solution (seed, agricultural chemicals, dealer service, etc.) a company has to offer, the market environment may affect some companies more than others. In general, though, the external analysis looks at the current economic environment, political situation, cropping or livestock numbers, the regulatory environment, technology, etc., in which your company works. It also looks at trends in each of these areas, and may include a detailed analysis of customers and their needs. Thus, the external or marketplace analysis usually includes five components:

1. the political/economic situation;
2. customer demographics, psychographics and trends;
3. regulatory changes and trends;
4. impact of technology;
5. competitor activity/strategy.

Discovering and exploiting opportunities is the essence of marketing. It is critical to anticipate customer needs so that your company can prepare for the moment when the customer is ready to buy. Fortunes are made in a free enterprise system by companies that correctly anticipate customer needs. Many companies invest millions in research and development activities, using the latest technology to find solutions to problems their customers already have or may have in the future. If you were only concerned with selling what you have today, you would only need to look at today's environment.

It is *critical* to be able to see where today's trends will lead you. No one can predict the future absolutely. But the most effective marketers know how to read today's trends and estimate the products, services and competitive environment of tomorrow.

1. Political/Economic Situation

The general political and economic situation <u>always</u> has an impact on your market, because your end-users own and/or operate businesses that must survive economically. Political and economic factors are increasingly intertwined, especially as we move to a more global marketplace through trade agreements such as NAFTA[39] and WTO.[40] Economic and political factors that will have tremendous effects on crop protection markets in the next few years include the following:

- changes in farm policy, farm bills, and impact of the phase' out of subsidies;
- the strength of the local currency (for example, a high-valued U.S. dollar means importing U.S. grain and meat is more expensive; a "low" dollar means that U.S. commodities are cheaper to other countries and are easier for them to buy);
- for non-agricultural markets, strong and consistent performance in the stock market increases discretionary income people spend on golf, resorts or even their own back yard; and
- legislation to protect family farms or to encourage conservation of marshlands or erodible land takes acres out of production.

The general health of the economy also plays an important role. In the 1980's, many North American farms went out of business because they could not meet the high interest rates on funds borrowed for operating expenses and/or for land. The bottom dropped out of the land market, and with it the value of their collateral, forcing many farms into bankruptcy.

The result of a serious economic downturn in the farm market is not only fewer farmers. It can also lead to a political backlash. For example, in the USA in the 1980's it led to state laws designed to protect the family farm. Some of these laws unfortunately prohibited or delayed new products. An example is bovine somatotropin (BST), a product injected into dairy cattle to increase milk production. The introduction of BST was delayed partly because of the fear that it would put additional economic pressure on smaller family farms at a time when small farms were already under great economic stress.

---

[39] North American Free Trade Agreement
[40] World Trade Organization http://www.wto.org

Analysis of political and economic factors should include such considerations as the world economic situation, including need for feed, fiber, grain, livestock, dairy, poultry, aquaculture, fruits and vegetables and specialty crops; world trade laws, agreements and their impact; the U.S. political environment, including tax laws; and the U.S. economy's strength, inflation, etc. All of this must be factored into the estimated demand for the products and services you sell.

2. Customer Demographics and Trends

Customer demographics refers to the type of information about customers you might find in a census: the number of customers, their ages, the size of the farm, the proportion of acres planted to one crop vs. another, the type and amount of equipment they may own, etc. This information is crucial to companies because it tells them the potential need for their products.

Often, this section of the market analysis also includes information about the number of acres planted to a specific crop nationally and regionally, as well as trends in cropping. For example, some analysts believe that the release of many acres from government conservation programs (i.e., idle acres) will have a significant impact on the market. Other analysts believe that, since many of these acres are less productive land, the impact on production output will not be major, although the increase in acres treated with crop protection may be high. There is often conflicting information and viewpoints that make these predictions quite complex. Cropping practices should also be considered. For example, different products are used when crops are grown using minimum tillage vs. conventional tillage. Thus the type of cropping practices used, such as the trend toward minimum tillage, can have a significant impact on the number of acres where a given company's products or services would be appropriate.

Psychographics are a different way to describe customers' needs and trends in those needs. Psychographics describe how customers buy. For example, it is important to know how customers evaluate new technology, how quickly they will adopt it, how they weigh service vs. price, how they process information about products, and how they evaluate whether they got "fair value" for the price they paid.

Many companies are now doing extensive research on psychographics, benchmarking current findings and watching carefully how buying habits and values are changing over time. They believe such information will be invaluable in designing marketing programs that are in sync with changing customer needs.

For example, in the U.S. agricultural marketplace, many studies have seen a trend toward more of a business orientation among large farmers, as opposed to farming "as a way of life." This is an important trend, because it affects how products are developed and introduced, how your company trains its re-sellers in local markets to position products, and the degree to which everyone at the company needs to understand farm economics.

3. Regulatory Changes and Trends

The regulatory environment has affected everyone in the business of agriculture, whether they sell products that involve sunflowers, soybeans, pigs or poultry. In plant protection, for instance, new products developed for food crops must undergo rigorous testing to make sure they will be safe when used according to label directions. The Environmental Protection Agency (EPA) evaluates the test results on every new crop protection product, and can also require that old products be re-registered or re-tested using today's analytical procedures. The regulatory process can take many years and cost many millions of dollars – $70 million or more just to get a single new crop protection product approved for use by farmers. The situation is not much different for animal health products, which are regulated by the Food and Drug Administration (FDA).

Products that are currently registered are not exempt from regulation. The EPA collaborates with companies to develop a product *label* that clearly spells out when the product should be used, in what quantity, with what equipment, under which weather conditions, and what to do in case of a spill or injury. Over the last 20 years, EPA regulations have become more and more stringent, in an effort to protect drinking water supplies, surface water quality (lakes and streams), the worker, and the consumer filling his grocery cart.

In addition to national regulations, many states also have put still more strict regulation in place. Some states (such as California) may even require that product recommendations be made only by a person with post-graduate education in pest control and certification. One response to increasing regulation has been a national industry effort to improve and standardize the expertise level of people who recommend and/or sell plant protection products. This certification is called the Certified Crop Advisor (CCA) and includes a certification test (national and state) as well as documented continuing education.

Increasing regulation means that some old products will be discontinued, because of the expense of re-registration. In other cases, companies have had to develop special carrier or application systems to meet the EPA's demands for safe product use. It also means that there is an opportunity for companies to add value by helping re-sellers achieve CCA certification, and/or become more expert in product use and safety.

4. Impact of Technology

People outside agriculture often believe the industry consists of many "Ma and Pa" type farmers and a few large factory farms. Nothing could be further from the truth. North American farmers, or farmers in most developed countries for that matter, are among the most technology-hungry businesspeople anywhere in the world. Technologies such as hybrid seed technology, mechanization, chemical fertilizers and crop protection have made North America highly productive and are feeding new mouths in every developing country as well.

Today, analysts are keeping their eyes on two trends that have the potential to change the industry. The winning agri salesperson must include both of these trends in any analysis of market opportunity:

1. biotechnology and the development of crop protection solutions through genetic research (such as insect-resistant plants, herbicide-tolerant plants, etc.);

2. information technology, including:
    -   precision farming (on-farm decision-making support through computer-assisted targeting of inputs and evaluation of outputs);
    -   electronic information sourcing, from Internet chat rooms to Email with university experts;
    -   electronic commerce, or ordering and paying for products by computer, with or without the support of local dealers.

5. Competitive Activities and Strategies

In the market situation analysis, competitor strategies and activities are evaluated also. Later, when looking at strengths and weaknesses, specific comparisons of competitor products and programs can be made. The market analysis is more concerned with where competitors want to be in a few years, and what evidence we see of that today.

For example, the merger of Sandoz and Ciba into Novartis created the largest agricultural chemical company in the world, something other companies must take into account in planning their strategies. By the same token, the purchase of Sandoz corn products by BASF expanded its product line and made competitors sit up and take notice. The purchase of some of Pioneer Hi-Bred by DuPont told the industry that DuPont had decided to be a player for the next 10-20 years, and that they would be involved in biotechnical product development.

Internal Analysis

The *external analysis* portion of a situation analysis deals with the marketplace. The *internal analysis* portion deals with your company specifically. There are two major components: strengths and weaknesses. Strengths and weaknesses cover any item or factor that can influence your success in working with customers. Examples include product performance, warranties or guarantees, services, competency of service staff, effectiveness of salespeople, company image and reputation, information systems, distribution and delivery, facilities systems, financial strength, and technical credit policy. The list can go on and on.

Strengths and weakness are always considered relatively – that is, your strengths compared to those of your primary competitors. Even though your company may be doing a good job in some areas, if it does not measure up to what the competition is offering, you are not as strong in the customer's eyes. Some weaknesses can be corrected as soon as they are recognized. Some strengths can easily be enhanced. Others may require years or a significant shift in corporate strategy. In any case, if a strength or weakness will affect the performance of a company in the marketplace, it should be noted and dealt with in the company's strategy.

SWOT Analysis

How does a marketer know whether market segment(s) can be served profitably or that a differential advantage can be found or developed? Many companies complete a formal analysis called a SWOT Analysis:

- **S**trength
- **W**eakness
- **O**pportunity
- **T**hreat

Strengths and Weaknesses

A strength is something a company is good at doing or a characteristic the company has that gives it an important capability. In other words, a strength can be a skill, a competence, a resource or something the company has done which puts it in a position of market advantage (e.g., stronger name recognition). A weakness is something a company lacks or does poorly (in comparison to others) or a condition that puts it at a disadvantage.

Once a company's internal strengths and weaknesses have been identified, the two lists have to be carefully evaluated. Some strengths are more important than others, because they count for more in determining performance, in forming a strategy, and in competing successfully. Likewise, some weaknesses can prove fatal, while others might not matter much or can be easily fixed.

Opportunities and Threats

Market opportunity is certain to be a factor in shaping a company's strategy. Unless a company is well-positioned to pursue a given opportunity, and unless

the opportunity is interesting enough to pursue, it usually makes more sense to choose some other strategic course. The prevailing and emerging industry opportunities that are likely to be most relevant to a particular company are those in which the company in question can capture a competitive advantage.

Very often, certain factors in a company's external environment or internal resourcing pose threats to its well-being. These threats may stem from the emergence of cheaper technologies, adverse economic trends, restrictive government action, changing customer values, organizational upheaval and the like. Identifying threats is important, not only because they affect the attractiveness of a company's situation, but also because they drive the forming of a business-level strategy.

Putting It Together

SWOT analysis is much more than making four lists. Here are some of the key questions to consider, once the SWOT listings have been compiled.

- Does the company have any internal strengths around which an attractive strategy can be built? Specifically, do you have a distinct competence that can produce a competitive advantage?
- Do the company's weaknesses make it competitively vulnerable and do they disqualify you from pursuing certain opportunities? Which of your weaknesses does your strategy need to correct?
- Which opportunities does the company have sufficient skills and resources to pursue, with a real chance of success?
- What threats should the company be worried about most, and what should be your key defensive strategies?

The purpose of the SWOT analysis is to identify profitable opportunities that fit your company's resources and long-term strategy.

Marketing Objectives

Upon successfully identifying the strengths and weakness of your company relative to other companies and the total marketplace, and evaluating your opportunities and threats, marketing objectives can be developed. Marketing objectives take into account the findings of the SWOT and apply them within the window of the company mission or vision. Marketing objectives more specifically address what the company wants to accomplish.

In *Marketing Management*[41], Philip Kotler points out that two types of objectives are made at this point. The first are the *financial objectives.* A company's management wants each business unit to deliver good, sound, financial performance. Often higher-level management in a company sets financial objectives for strategic business units, or different areas of the company that become targets for those units. For instance:

- earn an annual rate of return on investment of XX% over the next five years after taxes;
- produce net profits of $XXXXXX in this fiscal year;
- produce cash flow of $XXXXXX in this fiscal year.

The financial objectives are then converted into marketing objectives. The marketing manager takes financial objectives and determines a sales volume goal, a gross margin goal, and an expense level goal that will be sufficient to generate target profit levels. For example, if the company expects the Northwest sales region to generate $100,000 profits for the year, the Northwest sales or marketing manager may determine that the division will need to meet a sales goal of $1,000,000 while maintaining a 25% gross margin and keeping expenses to 15% on each dollar of sales during the year.

Of course, the Northwest Division manager does not make these important decisions without a great deal of analysis and planning, using all sorts of accounting data, trend information, and projections. It is very common for field salespeople to be asked to do analysis and projections for their local areas to help in this process. After all, who knows the local situation better than the salesperson who works a territory?

The marketing objectives often include more than just financial goals and some sales and gross margin objectives. Many companies also track market share, i.e., the percentage of the total market sales for a product that their sales represent. They may set customer turnover goals (lost customers compared to new customers). They may establish market concentration ratios (the percentage of each customer's total business). They may set market penetration goals (the percentage of all customers with whom the company does business). There are many other possible marketing objectives that may be established. All of these, of course, are designed to help lead the company toward meeting their financial objectives.

---

[41] Kotler, P. Marketing Management: analysis, planning, implementation, and control, 9th edition Prentice-Hall Inc., New Jersey: 1997, p. 99.

When these objectives are set, there is usually a lot of discussion about the best pricing strategy, and what kinds of marketing support must be developed, at the company, regional, and local levels, to accomplish objectives. Of course, the field salesperson will be directly impacted by all discussions. When the company has firmly established the marketing objectives for each business unit or region, these objectives are then reinterpreted in terms of sales goals for each salesperson. It becomes the salesperson's responsibility to help the company accomplish marketing objectives by meeting sales goals in the territory. In some companies, these goals actually become "quotas." Sales managers work with each salesperson throughout the year to insure that each person is on track in meeting their quotas or goals.

Segment, Target and Focus

Once there is a clear understanding of the situation and objectives, the company will "target" or identify those customers with whom it wants to do business. Sometimes companies identify important segments very early in the marketing strategy planning process and then establish marketing objectives for each segment. If customer groups or *segments* were not identified before, they are now.

Segmentation

Let's review the concept of segmentation. Segmentation means organizing all potential customers into groups of customers according to how they make the buying decision. That is, a market segment is a group of customers that will respond similarly to a given offer, because they have common needs or values. For example, customers who buy most of their clothes at a discount store like Wal-Mart are different in some ways from customers who buy most of their clothes at an exclusive fashion store like Nordstrom's or Eddie Bauer. But how are they different? If you were a marketer at Wal-Mart or at Eddie Bauer, that would be a burning question. Figure out who buys where and why, and you would know how to advertise, what products to stock, and even how to organize your store. It is no accident that these two examples, the discount store and the high-end fashion store, are different in so many ways. Location, store design, product quality and style, service, and pricing are all the result of much research into the value structure and needs of the customers each has targeted. The trick is to identify groups of customers with common needs or values and then build a "value bundle" that matches those needs. If you can do this cost-effectively, you have the ingredients for success.

Some companies decide to target multiple segments and develop very different approaches for each segment. For example, in the USA, Holiday Inn provides three very different styles of overnight lodging accommodations.

The Holiday Inn Crown Plazas and Holiday Inn Selects are high-end luxury accommodations designed for the upscale business traveler and for conventions. The traditional Holiday Inns are more modest and appeal to the overnight business guest and vacationing families. The Holiday Inn Express appeals to the budget-conscious. Each of these businesses can be highly successful if they are operated efficiently and are perceived as a "good value" to the segment of the market for which they were designed. There are three common methods for segmenting customers:

- demographics (size, age, income level, education, etc.);
- product usage (crops grown, pest problems, livestock raised, equipment used, etc.);
- psychographics (buying behavior and value structure – business buyer vs. relationship buyer, for example).

To be useful, a segment or customer group must meet three standards. It must be measurable (how many people, animals, acres there are in the segment). It must be accessible (can we find and reach those in the segment). And it must be profitable (a sufficient volume of business in the segments to warrant treating the segment in unique ways). The purpose of segmenting markets, of course, is so that special approaches and programs can be designed to meet the needs of each segment. If you can't identify which customers are in the segment or sell to them profitably, it is not worth pursuing.

If a segment does not meet these three tests, it will likely not be a good decision to develop a special or unique program designed for that segment. It often takes a great deal of effort and resources to design special marketing programs for a segment. But even if an agribusiness chooses not to design special programs, it is very convenient and useful for agricultural salespeople to think of their customer base in terms of segments. Often a salesperson will organize their own activities differently for different segments. For example, you might want to make a special effort to invite the more progressive, high-tech farmers to a producer meeting designed to demonstrate a new technology. Or you might decide to send a letter describing a new volume discount program only to large customers in your market.

Targeting

The point of segmentation, as all marketing, is to identify and act on opportunities. Once segments are identified and described, the company can choose which segments it wants to target as "high opportunity." "Targeting" allows a company to channel its resources (time, energy, programs, etc.) into areas that are believed to be most profitable over the long pull and get the most "bang for the buck." Targeting or prioritizing some segments does not mean that the general market is not important. Indeed, the general market is important and will continue to generate important sales. But focusing some extra attention on some market segments provides opportunities for making a bigger impact where it is most important.

In today's competitive markets, many companies can't afford to target just one or two groups of customers. They need to do business with many or most customer groups in order to meet their profit goals. However, this situation makes segmentation, targeting and focusing even _more_ important, not less. Let's look at an example from retail marketing.

> *Let's again take a consumer market example that everyone knows – McDonald's. Why do you go there? If you watched all the McDonald's commercials during an entire day, you would see that McDonalds is the restaurant for kids. It is also the restaurant for grandparents. It is the restaurant for teenagers, for working parents, for Dads who are away all week, etc., etc. McDonald's has identified multiple segments that it can serve and that are profitable. Depending on the market, it has adjusted the products it sells, the "look" of the facility, and even the prices.*

Understanding your company's target market segments is very important. Your company is probably spending a lot of time and resources developing products, incentive programs, support materials, distribution systems, and pricing schemes that are designed to appeal especially to targeted segments. To be most effective, these programs and products must be taken directly to those for whom they were targeted. If you ignore these strategies and simply call on prospects randomly or do not apply the programs and products appropriately, you lose a lot of your potential effectiveness. And the company is much less likely to meet its marketing objectives.

Of course, you will also take a more general approach with customers who are not in the high priority or targeted segments. You must do a good job with them also. But customers in segments that have been targeted by the company marketing strategy should receive special attention.

Focus: Determining Differential Advantage

When marketers identify a segment, target it, learn all they can about it and begin to strategize to get that business, they are searching for a differential advantage. A *differential advantage* is something that makes your product/service value "bundle" better than the competition's – enough better that customers will buy from you.

Marketing Mix

When managers think about marketing strategy, they often think about five key components of the *marketing mix* (sometimes referred to as the "five P's" of marketing). These are the variables that the marketing manager controls to accomplish the marketing objectives. Each of these areas represent major decisions that the marketing strategy addresses and that directly impact the salesperson's job:

- **P**roduct;
- **P**rice;
- **P**romotion;
- **P**lace (distribution);
- **P**eople.

Product Strategies

Product strategies govern and guide *everything* a company sells. This includes tangible products and services as well as the intangibles: the people, reputation, tradition and history associated with the product or service. Product strategies also determine the breadth and depth of a company's product lines and services: how many product lines; how many products within a line; and in what sizes, packages, etc. Product strategies can also include plans for introduction of new products. They should also include tactics to *cross-sell* products: to encourage sales of a second product when a first is bought. For example, a tactic might be "buy four jugs, get half off on surfactant" or selling a "total weed control program" by cross-selling select products across the product portfolio.

In practice, there are often two levels of product strategies. The first level is the corporate strategic decision on product research priorities, product development priorities, commercialization, forecasted manufacture, and profitability goals. This decision involves corporate planners, company leadership, research and development and the group responsible for regulatory approval and commercialization of products. Once this decision is made, there may be many field strategies or tactical plans for product marketing. This second level of strategy is usually under the guidance of the product manager or higher level company executives and has the support and involvement of sales management.

Pricing Strategies

Price is the only element of the marketing mix that brings money into the company. Everything else in the marketing strategy costs money. Price is a very critical and important issue that gets lots of management's attention. If price is too low, the product may sell more easily, but there may not be enough money left over after expenses are covered to make any profit. In fact, if price is too low, the more you sell, the more you may lose! On the other hand, a company can't just arbitrarily set a price "high so it can make a profit," because the competition may quickly attract a lot of business away from you. Pricing is a very sensitive issue that can generate much emotion in the marketplace very quickly.

In the early part of your selling career, you may not be involved in pricing products. In some situations, you may be allowed or required to creatively address pricing issues. Meantime, as part of the company's marketing mix, the headquarters office is making the pricing decisions, usually by one of several means of "pricing" products. The pricing strategy must be in line with your company's core strategy; the values of your target segment(s); competitors' prices; and demand for your product. Prices must be in line with the customer's perception of the value they will receive from your product, your services, and doing business with you. And pricing must be sufficient to cover the cost of producing and distributing the product and related services. These are complex and dynamic issues. The following pricing techniques are commonly used:

- *mark-up pricing* adds a set amount or percentage to the cost of the product;
- *going-rate pricing* follows the competition;
- *profit margin pricing* prices for a given % profit on the sale of each item; and
- *ROI or gross margin target pricing* sets price so that [targeted price] x [targeted volume] will achieve company profitability goals.

Pricing strategy must be based on the concept of <u>value</u>. The cost of manufacturing and distributing a product is only the *floor* for price. Its value is the *ceiling* because customers will never pay more than they perceive the product is worth to them.

For some products, there may be a huge difference between cost of manufacturing and price. The profit from these products goes to research, to strengthening products and services, and to shareholders. A good example is the animal health industry, where the actual cost of production and distribution may be small, but millions of dollars may be required to do research and development and meet regulatory requirements before the product gets to market.

In other cases, there may be barely enough difference between cost of manufacture/distribution and customer price to justify the product. In this case, overpricing the product could create a negative image. Yet pulling the product from the market could also create a negative image. The answer to this dilemma lies in the core strategy of the company. Is it their core strategy to provide low-cost products that meet needs? Then keep the product and find the profit somewhere else. Or is it their strategy to bring only the highest quality products and services to market? Then pull the product and divert resources to a new product or service.

Pricing decisions are commonly made by product managers with the collaboration of market research (to understand competitive "value") and sales management. Budget and finance staff may support major pricing decisions to make sure that selling targeted volumes at the targeted price will achieve the target ROI for the year.

Promotion Strategies

Promotion describes all the things a company does to communicate its value to the customer. Promotion activities are numerous and varied, but again, all return to the who's, what's, where's and how's of the customer base. A great deal of time, effort and research may go into any one of these ongoing promotional background or foreground efforts. It is important for the salesperson to realize that these efforts are under way at any given time throughout the year.

While many of the promotional programs are designed and managed by company level marketing managers, there is one extremely important aspect of promotional strategy: the field salesperson. In fact, most people believe that the field selling effort is far and away the most effective method of communicating the company's value to the customer. Certainly, the field salesperson is the most expensive promotional strategy for most agribusinesses. (Thankfully, most companies believe that good value is received for the money spent on field sales efforts.) But it is important for you to understand where you as a salesperson fit into the total company marketing strategy.

There is another important way that promotional strategy impacts the field salesperson. Many or most of the promotional tools developed as part of the promotional strategy are valuable tools you can use in your selling activities. They can make you far more effective if you use them the correct way with the customers they are designed for. So it is very important to understand the promotional strategies and plans of your company. Some of the more common tools you will have include:

• database marketing; • tracking of customer purchases; • identify customer demographics • segment-specific direct mailing; • response tracking and follow-up: • fact-to-face communications.	• personal sales calls; • meetings; • seminars; • advertising; • radio: • trade press.	• WEB-pages • Internet promotions; • samples; • gifts; • purchase incentives; • community activities.

In order to put together a promotion strategy, the marketer has to understand how customers in target segment(s) want to communicate. For many manufacturers, promotion may be complicated by the fact that they are dealing with a two-tiered customer base. It includes re-sellers and end-users.

In this situation, promotion often has a two-pronged strategy. One strategy is to "push" the product through re-sellers to end-user customers by making re-sale of the product attractive (incentives, marketing programs, discounts, etc.). The other is to encourage the end-user customer to "pull" the product through the re-seller by creating demand in the marketplace.

For example, every Spring across the Midwest you will see TV advertisements for crop protection chemicals. All Winter, farmers receive mailboxes full of promotional gifts, from videotapes to popcorn. These promotional tactics are meant to create awareness of a product and demand or "pull" for it. At the same time, manufacturer reps are calling on re-seller dealers in the farmer's county, training them on product benefits and use, encouraging them to stock product, and offering incentives for aggressive selling and servicing of the product ("push" tactics).

Promotion decisions usually involve multiple functions in the business. Decisions might include communications (database, media and public relations activities); sales (personal selling), product development and commercialization (technical support of new product introductions); or outside agencies and training companies to help implement promotion plans.

Distribution Strategies

Distribution refers to how products are shipped, stored, and delivered to re-sellers and end-user customers. The *distribution channel* describes the path that products take from manufacturer to grower. Every channel level that touches a product by warehousing it, or billing for it, or selling it wants a small percent of the product's *margin* (the difference between manufacturer cost and customer price). The basic theory behind distribution is that each channel level (manufacturer, distributor, local dealer) will add more value to the product/service package than they cost in margin.

Distribution strategies have changed as the market has consolidated. Today's market is dominated by large regional cooperative distributors and large "linked" distributor/retail organizations. Some of these organizations sell only to re-sellers. Others will sell to large farmers directly. Many distributors and re-sellers are fighting for a hold on their customer base, fearing that basic manufacturers might bypass them altogether and sell directly to the farmer. That will probably not happen soon, however, since many large farmers report that they still want and need local product service and support.

Product distribution can be a very complicated undertaking. In most companies, there are several functions involved with product distribution. Their job functions and daily work must be closely coordinated, so that the response to the customer is uniformly high quality, regardless of which person or office they call upon. Distribution may involve:

- manufacturing or formulating (to provide product in the right sizes and containers);
- shipping (including international shipping lines for product ingredients manufactured outside the U.S.);
- warehousing and re-shipping to regional distributors;
- tracking/billing for product shipped;
- customer service/telemarketing (take and ship orders);
- coordination of product sales records with promotion/communications staff who administer purchase incentives.

People Strategies

When product marketing was king, *people strategies* were often not even a topic of discussion. As more and more products flood a market with fewer and fewer customers, the power of individual marketers and sellers has become clear. In the end, every strategy is only as good as the people responsible for implementing it.

What do customers expect? Customers expect:

- understanding of their need and wants;
- understanding of the role products and services can play in their business;
- expertise about the product – how it works, when and how to use it for maximum effectiveness;
- expertise in forecasting, distribution and logistics so that products are available when needed at a fair price.

Every function in the business should have a people development strategy. This strategy begins at the very top of the business, as corporate leadership sets the direction for the business. It trickles down through the management structure, with each supervisor responsible for setting performance goals, monitoring performance, coaching, and performance review.

Here again, the salesperson plays a critical role. This is because of the value that the salesperson personally can generate for the customer. Many companies today believe that the primary differentiation or advantage their company may have over competition is directly related to the technical expertise, service, and customer relationships of the salesperson. While the demands on the salesperson are often intense, they are very important to the success of the company.

Rob Vincent
American Cyanamid
Sales Representative
Iowa City, Iowa

When you are out there selling, you *are* the company's eyes and ears about the customer. You are the customer's eyes and ears about the company and its products. You are the conduit. That makes you valuable to both the customer and the company. It's a big responsibility. It's a good one.

Bottom line, you have to know the company market strategy, and how you fit into the company market strategy. Nobody may tell you that when you start working for a company, but it is up to you to find it out to effectively represent that company, that market strategy.

Action Plans

Action plans are more specific marketing activities that are developed at this stage in the marketing strategy. Action plans help the company and management determine, for instance, what they want to tell the public, what media they want, when they want messages released, how they will reach the ultimate customer and hopefully, positively influence their buying decisions and attitudes about the company and/or its product/service.

Salespeople may be involved in several or many of the action steps. You may be asked to organize educational meetings, make specific sales calls on targeted customers, collect information, trouble-shoot product complaints, make suggestions on pricing, and a wide array of other activities that need to be localized to your territory.

Measure Results

The final piece of the marketing process is to measure and monitor results. The company's goals provide a benchmark against which sales performance and market penetration can be measured. Image research and customer satisfaction tell us whether the core strategy was appropriate and whether it was fully understood and communicated.

Companies need a way to measure results more often than once a year. After all, if results aren't monitored until the year is over, managers and marketers can't use their experience to change tactics and potentially improve results. It would be a little like a sports team that didn't know if it had won the championship until the last game was over. Interim performance is monitored by companies as reviews of monthly or quarterly performance vs. budget; product performance complaints; distributor and key customer satisfaction research; and by tracking key account performance.

Monitoring involves many functions in the business. Billing departments, customer service, and shipping can help determine how much product has been delivered to re-sellers. Communications/database departments may be able to track sales to individual customers. Sales representatives and their managers have a good sense of progress for their specific geography. Product managers track sales, satisfaction and distribution of specific product lines.

As a field salesperson, you may also be asked to become directly involved in measuring the results of various marketing strategies. You may be asked to do surveys for the company, collect information from your customers, or to complete a variety of other activities designed to provide necessary information to company marketing management.

needs,
This is all part of your role as a salesperson. Marketing today means developing a system of information flow and planning throughout the business: customer product research, analysis of competitive opportunity, and the delivery of win-win solutions to customers.

The Role of Selling in Marketing

Marketing is a long-term process dealing with customers as segments or groups of customers. Sales, on the other hand, is a short-term <u>and</u> long-term practice for dealing with customers on an individual basis. However, it is imperative for the salesperson to realize the interconnectedness of these two functions.

In John Crosby's book <u>Managing the Big Sale</u>,[42] he points out that, "Marketing involves a long planning horizon and, broadly speaking, is primarily responsible for such functions as: the definition of technologies, identification of products and services, delineation of served markets, product positioning, product pricing and the definition and achievement of specific revenue and profit goals." Crosby concludes that sales and marketing are clearly two different functions, yet they are interdependent.

Figure 7.2
Interdependence of Sales and Marketing

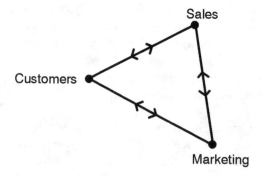

---

[42] Crosby, J.V. Managing the Big Sale. NTC Publishing Group. Chicago, Illinois: 1996, p. 5.

- Sales success is dependent on marketing strategies and customer needs.
- Marketing success is dependent on sales efforts and customers needs.
- Satisfaction of customer needs is dependent on sales efforts and marketing strategies.

Figure 7.2 illustrates how sales and marketing are interdependent. The synergy necessary for customer satisfaction comes from each function acting with the other. Successful interdependence continues in "recursive patterns of interaction,"[43] with sales helping marketing understand customer needs, and marketing helping sales to deliver better solutions.

Summary

The focus today is on <u>customer needs</u>, rather than the company or the product, for marketers and salespeople alike. Professional salespeople recognize that fulfilling customer needs is their primary objective. Today, marketers recognize the customer not as something to be used, or an object to sell to, but as their very reason for being. They recognize that meeting customer needs is their only way to operate profitably, or even survive.

Although sales is only one part of the total marketing process in most companies, it is the focal point around which the total marketing program is built. The last three feet are the most critical in the marketing process. That is the three feet between the salesperson and the customer. Bridging <u>this</u> distance is the critical link to making marketing and sales programs successful. The professional salesperson learns how to capitalize on the total marketing program, and uses it to bridge the final three feet to the customer.

Review Questions

1. Define marketing. How is marketing different than selling?

2. The case study with Larry Barmann in this chapter discusses similarities and differences in marketing and selling. How does Barmann describe why and how these contrasts are important to the agri salesperson?

3. List the steps of the marketing process. Briefly describe them.

---

[43]ibid.

4. Explain a SWOT analysis. What types of questions might the company consider in this type analysis?

5. What are the five "P's" of the marketing mix?

Chapter Eight

Selling With a Strategy

Learning Objectives:

Upon completion of this chapter, you should be able to:

1. understand how to construct a territory strategy that complements and implements your company's marketing strategy;
2. understand the role of different types or *segments* of customers in your market according to what they most value;
3. evaluate the value of your products and services through the customer's eyes;
4. evaluate your competitive strengths and weaknesses.

Strategy Defined

A *strategy* is simply a plan to assemble your resources – skills, knowledge, energy, time, people – and decide how to use them to accomplish your objectives. In selling, an effective strategy requires you to understand your customer and your market, assemble the product benefits and services that meet customer needs better then anyone else, decide how to use your support team, evaluate the competition, and <u>then</u> call on accounts.

A strategy can be very simple or it can be very complex. It may be something you do without much input from others, or you may develop your strategy with others on your "selling team." No matter how complex or how simple your sales strategy is, it is always done with thought.

It is intentional and should contain the following elements:
- a clear link to your company's marketing efforts;
- an analysis of your local market;
- an understanding of what customers value and/or need;
- identification of key customer segments or groups;
- specific sales goals, if possible for each group of customers;
- an analysis of your competitive strengths (and weaknesses) with each group of customers;
- a written plan describing how you will achieve your objectives.

Sales strategies begin with a very broad, long-term plan called a territory strategy and then become more refined or "drilled down" to specific key account., strategies, and eventually to a call strategy for a specific call on a specific customer. Sales strategies may include "action plans" describing how you will organize your sales effort - whom you will call on, for example. We'll introduce a process to help you prioritize your accounts in the next chapter. Sales strategies may also include specific account plans. These more detailed plans contain profiles of key accounts and your own personal selling "calendar" for getting and keeping their business. Key account plans are described in more detail in Chapter 10.

Territory Strategy

Your "territory" is the geographical area or group of customers from which you are expected to generate sales. A territory strategy is based on your personal analysis of all customers' needs, your local market dynamics, and your competitive situation - your opportunities and your barriers. It includes a statement of your goals, the identification of top customer groups or "segments" with whom you must be successful to meet your goals, and what portion of your goals you think you can achieve through each customer group (or segment). In some companies, a territory strategy is written by individual salespeople, with little input from managers or others. In others, there may be a formal plan format for the territory strategy. A few companies even provide territory-specific market information on potential customer names and specific information about them, such as size, location, type of business, past purchase history, etc. This information, combined with an understanding of market trends, helps you develop your plan.

How Do You "Fit" Into Corporate Strategy?

Each salesperson's territory strategy is part of the company's larger strategy for their market. This larger strategy outlines the company's goals and sets broad guidelines for how they will be achieved. It may identify key segments or groups of customers with whom the company wants to increase sales or strengthen relationships. These broad strategies are executed through the company's "marketing mix."

As identified in Chapter Seven, the "marketing mix" is the combination of specific strategies, tactics and actions that each company plans to help them achieve their sales goals. To review, the marketing mix includes five distinct areas:

1. product strategies;
2. place or distribution strategies;
3. price strategies;
4. promotion strategies;
5. people strategies.

Many of the major decisions in each of these areas are made above the territory level – maybe at the regional level, but most often at the company level. Thus, there is usually a basic set of company marketing strategies in place that serve as a foundation for regional and local territory selling strategy.

In theory, the sales function is part of "promotion" strategies, because it primarily involves communicating benefits of the company and its products to customers. This is a critical marketing job that is assigned to salespeople. No one else has the function of face-to-face discussion with customers about their needs and product solutions. However, salespeople often like to be involved in other elements of the marketing mix, when possible. Why? First, they often learn information from customers that could help "fine-tune" pricing, distribution, product or promotion strategies. Second, their own success locally may be affected by decisions on price, distribution, etc., that are made at a regional or company level.

The degree to which salespeople are involved in marketing mix decisions varies widely from company to company, and even from year to year within the same company. Whether the salesperson is involved in *making* decisions or not, it is critical to understand these decisions and support them. Consistent implementation of marketing strategies by salespeople helps the company spend its marketing dollars more efficiently, ensures that customers are treated fairly and equitably, and reinforces a consistent benefits message to the market.

As a salesperson, you will be expected to know the basic strategies in your company. Companies expect the cooperation and even the enthusiasm of their salespeople in implementing corporate strategies, because the more consistent strategies are, as seen by customers, the greater their impact.

For example, a company may want to communicate the message that they – as a company – are *different* from other companies. The product itself is only a part of what they promote. They must promote a buying "experience" that is highly personalized, on the one hand, and very low-pressure, on the other hand. Their pricing, distribution, product and promotion strategies are all targeted toward a certain type of buyer – one who values his/her own ability to make a decision and then, having made a decision, wants full service and friendly support.

Salespeople are on the "front line" with customers every day. If the salesperson can't communicate this approach to each customer – including pricing guidelines and service offers – face-to-face, the strategy can't succeed. Does this mean that the salespeople are all robots, stamped out with the same backgrounds, sales "pitch" and benefits statements? No. On the contrary, the salesperson is expected to interact with each buyer in a highly individualized, customer-focused way. Once the sale is made, customer support and service staff are expected to continue meeting the needs of each customer in unique ways.

What Do You Need to Know?

New salespeople naturally have many questions about the marketing mix. The answers to these questions allow the territory plan to be *aligned with* company strategies. When territory strategies and company strategies are aligned, the salesperson can take advantage of momentum created by others' efforts in the marketplace, rather than trying to "swim upstream." The following questions will review the marketing mix and help a new salesperson get started.

Products	Which products or services should be emphasized?
Services	Which products or services will we be phasing out? Which products or services are most profitable?
Place (distribution)	Who is my primary customer or segment? Do I also pursue customers above or below my target level? To what extent do I sell direct vs. help reseller efforts?

Pricing

Are prices set, or can I negotiate?
If I negotiate, what are my guidelines?
In what situations should I adjust price?
What are the gross margin objectives?
How do we get paid for services?

Promotion

What is the theme of our marketing program?
What promotion program will we offer?
How can I use our promotion programs with customers?
What advertisements will run locally?
How should I follow up on them?
Is there any customer database information I can use?
Who can I call on for help in selling?

People

What competencies should I have? What do customers expect?
What are my priorities?
What training or development is available?

New salespeople also need to make sure they understand what customer groups or segments the company has selected as their highest priority. These "target" segments or groups should get more time, more attention, and more creativity from everyone involved in marketing and selling. As a result, success with high-priority customer groups or segments is often more visible.

New salespeople can ask the following questions to learn more about the company's highest-priority customers or segments.

- Which types of customers do we most want?
- How do I identify these customers?
- What are their needs?
- What special advantages do we offer these customers?

Where to Get Information

The best source of information on these questions is your direct supervisor. Experienced salespeople on your regional, district or dealership team can also help you, if your company is large. Major changes in strategy are often communicated at national, regional or dealership sales meetings. If you don't understand your company's strategies, you must ask. These strategies are your company's "map" from where they are today to where they want to be tomorrow. The roadside is littered with salespeople who didn't bother to find out about strategies or who didn't think they mattered. As a salesperson, you can be much more effective if you understand your company's overall marketing strategy as it applies to your area – and can build on it. Ignoring this strategy or going your own direction makes you much less effective or, worse, can cause you to fail.

Unfortunately, not all companies have well-developed company-level strategies. Or, the strategy may not be well-communicated to the field. Where that is the case, answers may not be clear even when the salesperson asks for clarification, and it may be necessary to make some decisions independently. Clearly, the salesperson must have a sense of direction on these important issues in order to develop a solid selling strategy. One approach is for the salesperson to develop a *territory strategy* and then present ideas and plans to a manager for discussion and approval. This process works – it generates increased selling success and is well worth the effort. The following steps describe the process.

Territory Strategy

Analyze Your Local Market

Your territory strategy begins with an analysis of the factors at work in your local market. Some large companies spend millions of dollars each year to find out about market trends, customer needs and competitive strategies. Yet no one can do a more accurate analysis of your local market than you. Market analysis should look at your situation this year, but should include a understanding of what will likely happen two years in the future. A basic local market analysis includes at least three elements:
- local market dynamics;
- customer needs;
- competitor activities and trends.

Local Market Dynamics

In this section of your analysis, you want to identify all the factors that could affect your local customer's business, as well as your own.

Market trends	What is the economic outlook for your customers?
	Will exports rise or fall?
	Is the demand for certain types of products growing faster than for others?
	Is production capacity increasing or falling?
Farm production trends	What is being produced?
	How much is being produced?
	What is "standard" productivity?" "Excellent" productivity?

	How are customers achieving it now?
	Which customers are growing and which are scaling back?
Technology	What new technologies will enter the market?
	How will new technologies impact your customers' business?
	How will new technologies impact your business?
	How rapidly will new technology be adopted?
Information	What are the most trusted customer sources for information?
	What new sources of information are becoming accepted?
	How fast are customers adopting new information sources?
	What type of records are kept on productivity?
	What type of records are kept on profitability?
Regulatory trends	What new regulations will affect your customer?
	What new regulations could affect your business?
	What regulations are being enforced more stringently?
	How will these regulations affect producers?
	Do producers understand how to comply?

Understanding the dynamics of the local market provides the salesperson with important clues to identifying marketing and sales opportunities.

Customer Needs

The market analysis first helps the salesperson see the dynamics of the total market and its effect on customers. The next step is to identify specific needs of customers, as they work to reach their individual production and profit goals.

In the past, when salespeople could simply sell a product that was unique or was superior in some important way, products were easier to sell. They just needed to find people who needed or valued the unique characteristics of their product. Selling the uniqueness of a superior product is still a good strategy if the product is clearly superior. However, the market today is filled with good quality products,

We have reached the point as an industry where product *parity* (similar performance) has become common. Therefore, it is a better strategy to build your advantage on your ability to understand customer needs and to tailor your approach and services to meet those needs.

An understanding of customer needs offers you an opportunity to expand your product or service offering, adding value to your current products and creating a *differential advantage* for you in your local market. A differential advantage is simply a set of products or services you offer which sets you "head and shoulders" above your competition - a difference that customers recognize and for which they'll pay. Let's look at two examples.

> *Kerry has been selling agricultural chemicals for the last three years. When he prepared his territory plan this year, he realized that new state environmental regulations would require his farm customers to pass a new certification test before handling certain restricted use products. He knew that several dealer organizations were preparing their applicators to pass the exam, but he also knew that many of the largest farmers in his area preferred to apply their own products. Kerry took this need forward to his sales manager. With his manager's support, Kerry developed a "farmer certification" training program through local dealerships. Dealers like the fact that large farmers get the service through them – meeting Kerry's goal to strengthen partnerships with his dealers. Large farmers like the idea that Kerry's company is helping them manage their business the way they want to, by applying their own pesticides, and by doing so safely and in compliance with the law.*

> *Samantha has been a sales rep for a feed company for about 5 years. She has had increasing difficulty selling complete feeds to large swine producers, because they have the facilities to grind and mix feed on-farm. However, these same large producers are increasingly limited in their profits because they can't get the same results with baby pigs using their own feeds as they could with manufactured feed. Samantha was able to meet the needs of her largest producers and also meet her sales goals by working with producers, local animal nutritionists, and feed company nutritionists to develop starter and nursery feeds that could be produced more economically at the local feed plant than on-farm, with higher quality and resulting better weight gain and survival rates for weaned pigs.*

Today's market is very fluid. Almost every company is looking for new ways to differentiate itself with top customers. Many companies are searching for alliances with local experts and even with former competitors in order to meet top customer needs. Every customer need is an important need for that customer - and a salesperson should keep track of every need, whether it can be met with today's products and services or not.

How do you identify customer needs? First, make sure you have a general understanding of both the production dynamics and the business goals of customers. Second, talk with customers about their needs – not just about your products. Keep track of what they say, and use every opportunity offered to you to share this information with company managers and planners. If you have an idea for how to meet a need, share it also with peers and your boss. Keep in mind that many of the most important needs are for value-added services that come directly from the salesperson.

Competitor Trends

No salesperson sells in a vacuum. Everyone has competition. In crowded markets with mature products, there may be many companies offering similar solutions to common customer needs. In new markets, your toughest competition may be the *status quo* – farmers' inability to see the need to do things differently. In both cases, you need to track trends in your competitors.

In a later section of this chapter, we'll deal in more depth with how to evaluate your competitor's specific strengths and weaknesses compared to your own, in the customer's eyes. In this section, let's look at a more general analysis of competitor trends. Here, you are looking for competitive information that tells you the strategies and tactics your competitor is planning to use in your market. This analysis should include product line, distribution, promotion, pricing and segmentation.

Product line	Was the competitor's performance generally strong or weak last year? If they are expanding, what product lines will they add? Is the competitor merging or acquiring another business?
Distribution	How are products distributed to customers? Is their distribution dependable? What is the image of this business as a professional supplier? If wholesaling product, how strong are dealer/distributor relationships? Is any change expected?
Promotion	How aggressively will they market and sell their products? Are they co-marketing products with anyone? How will their sales efforts support their strategy? How good are their salespeople?

Pricing	How does their pricing vs. value compare to our own? Will it be tougher (or easier) to compete against their prices?
Segmentation	Which customers have they targeted for their best efforts? What are they offering these customers? Where are their strongest relationships in the market? Where are their weakest relationships in the market?

The analysis of competitor trends provides you with the information needed to do an accurate evaluation of your strengths and weaknesses for the coming year vs. each competitor. It also provides you with some insight into their future strategy, so that you can prepare now for next year's selling battles.

Donna Berry Hines
Pfizer Animal Health
Swine Industry Representative
Quincy, Michigan

Knowing your competition's products is really important. You have to know your competition. Part of it is being out in the field and seeing what has and hasn't worked for customers. Part of it comes from being able to ask my technical service vet questions, and part of it is asking other people – colleagues, professional contacts, customers – these questions and respecting their opinions, particularly if they are a key influencer of my customer.

Knowing and understanding the competition helps you best place your products and services in front of the customer. Where a product may be neck-and-neck in competition in a customer's mind, by knowing the competing product and the salespeople and company of that competing product, you may be able to achieve the sale through better positioning your service and other things you bring to the customer that enhance their business.

Understanding the competition *has* to be part of your selling strategy. To be successful selling, you've got to know your customer's business. Everything out there on the market is part of a consideration he/she must make in running their business. Make it your business to best place your product in front of that customer.

Confirm Sales Goals

Once you have completed your local market analysis, you are ready to set or confirm your sales goals. In some companies, salespeople have a lot of influence over their goals. In other companies, goals may be set for you by a sales manager or the owner of your business. Even if goals are set for you, your analysis of the local market will prove useful. Your analysis may uncover an opportunity you hadn't seen before, allowing you to meet or exceed goals. Or, you may find you need to ask for additional support from marketing programs, company promotions, internal experts, etc. in order to sell competitively and achieve your original goals. Achieving sales goals can make the difference between staying employed and looking for work elsewhere. And, in some companies, exceeding sales goals may make you eligible for extra, incentive compensation.

There are many types of sales goals beyond dollar or unit sales. Since your goals help you prioritize how you spend your time, sales goals should directly reflect the strategies of your company. They often include:

- sales volume goals;
- profit goals;
- product goals;
- penetration goals;
- concentration goals.

Sales Volume Goals

Sales volume goals are by far the most common and most trackable of all sales goals. They are useful because they are so easily measured and relate to the core of the sales function. Sales volume goals set a performance target measured in dollars or units. For example:

- *sell $1,000,000 in agricultural inputs;*
- *sell 500 units of seed corn.*

Profit Goals

Profit goals are more sophisticated sales goals. In profit goals, the salesperson is asked to reach a target level of profit dollars or *gross margin dollars*. The gross margin is calculated by subtracting the cost of the product from the price of the product. For example, a product that is sold for $100.00 and costs $70.00 to manufacture has a gross margin of $30.00. Gross margins for all products sold are added together and should equal or exceed the gross margin goal. This calculation may be made at the level of a territory, a region, or for the company as a whole. For example:

- *achieve $300,000 in gross margin dollars.*

Companies who set profit goals use several different strategies to encourage salespeople to reach these goals, depending on the company and the industry. For example, in equipment sales, the value of the trade-in may be deducted, as well as the cost of the equipment to the dealer, to get the gross margin figure for each sale. By subtracting the value of the trade before calculating profit, the dealership encourages salespeople to make a fair trade but not to give more than necessary for trade-in equipment. In businesses that sell many products, such as fertilizer/chemical dealerships, a gross margin goal encourages salespeople to sell more of high gross margin products, such as seed, rather than lower-profit or "commodity" products.

Product Goals

Product goals are set to encourage the salesperson to sell more of a specific product or product line. Product goals often emphasize high-margin items, and thus they resemble profit goals except that the salesperson does not need to know the profitability of each individual product. Product goals are also used to emphasize specific products in accordance with the company's product strategy. For example, if your company is introducing a new product, it will encourage quick adoption of the product, before competitors imitate it. You may have a specific sales goal set for this new product. Or, your company may have too much of a product, through a forecasting error or a production overrun. In this case, you might also have a product sales goal, to encourage salespeople to "move" the product. Product goals do not mean that you should sell products customers don't need or don't want. While that might get you short-term results, it is not good for the customer and certainly is not good for long-term success. Goals do encourage you to spend time selling products which will help your company accomplish its strategies.

Examples of product goals include:
- *to sell 100 units of the new XYZ rootworm-resistant hybrid;*
- *to sell 4 new 9000-Series 4-wheel drive tractors;*
- *to sell $300,000 of your company's new nematicide.*

Penetration Goals

Market penetration describes the proportion of customers you are selling to within a given market area. High penetration means that you are selling something to almost everyone. Low penetration means you are selling to relatively few potential customers. Penetration goals encourage the salesperson to talk to *all* potential customers, not just to those with whom he or she is most comfortable. Penetration goals may be for a market in general; they may be by segment (customer group); or they may be for a specific product. For example:

- *(general) to do business with 75% of all potential accounts;*
- *(segment-specific) to sell to 50% of dairy herds with 20,000 lbs+ rolling herd average production;*
- *(product-specific) to sell some high oil hybrid seed corn to 25% of the county's hog producers.*

Concentration Goals

Market concentration refers to the amount of business you are doing with each customer. For example, if your business has been selling a product to dealers for many years, you probably will continue selling that product for some time. However, you may find that competitors are "eating away" at your share of the business from each customer. Your concentration is falling or, said another way, your market share of each customer's business is dropping. A subset of concentration goals are *retention* goals. Retention goals describe how many customers you completely lose (they go to 0% concentration) each year. Some customer turnover is normal. However, as the number of large commercial farms shrinks, companies are increasingly concerned that they not lose any customers they currently serve.

Salespeople can sell more either by selling to new customers (increase penetration) or by selling more to current customers (increased concentration) or both. The best choice depends on your products, your customers, your competition, and the direction you are given by your manager. Sample concentration goals might include:

- *to increase our percent of each customer's breeding business by 10% on average;*
- *to increase the % greenhouses planted to our hybrids among current customers by 15%;*
- *to increase the % total inputs purchased from our distribution organization by current customers from 55% to 57.5%.*

> **Dan Puck**
> **Dow AgroSciences**
> **Sales Representative**
> **Madison, Wisconsin**
>
> When I get my goals, I go back to a customer and basically propose to them where I think our opportunities are, and where I think our best areas to grow together are. Then, I ask them what they feel they could accomplish and try to get their feedback/input. Then, sometimes, they come back to you with a stronger figure even than you had planned. And it's a stronger number and you just run with it.
>
> A lot of times, however, they'll come back with a number that's a little more modest than you had in mind. And then, in that case, what we try to do is propose to them whether the number I had in mind is realistic and if not, why not, and explore that area more. What other products/packets were they thinking of, etc.? Then re-sell what you think your advantages are.

Key Customer Segments

A *segment* is a group of customers who are similar in the way they make decisions, the needs they express, and the types of products they buy. Segmentation is based on the concept that, while every customer is unique, there are certain recognizable patterns of behavior that help us group or "classify" customers. Many experienced salespeople have been selling "by segment" for many years, even though they may not have a formal market research study to back up their informal insights.

When Jim started selling seed for GreenGro, he was determined to succeed and felt he needed little direction. He began calling on every farmer in his territory, but most told him they already had a local seed dealer – neighbor or friend – and that they didn't need Jim's high prices. After 3 months of little or no success, Jim talked it over with his manager, Frank Thomas. Frank explained that, even though GreenGro seed would work well for any farmer, not just any farmer was a good candidate for GreenGro seed. He explained that, in his 10 years experience, farmers who understood GreenGro's benefits were top producers, kept good records, liked GreenGro's information services, wanted top yield, and understood the value of a top product. In fact, you could almost identify them by the top equipment they drove, the neat, professional appearance of their farm, whether they marketed their grain themselves, and whether they had a computer they used in the farm business. As Frank explained it, there was a "type" of customer who understood value – and appreciated GreenGro products and their value.

In this example, Frank is describing the "segment" or group of customers that are the best candidates for GreenGro seed and the salesperson's time. Some companies identify key customer groups or segments by talking with their salespeople. Other companies prefer to complete formal market research studies, called *segmentation research*. They use the results of this research to fine-tune the marketing mix, and may also share "segment descriptions" with salespeople.

Segments are very useful to salespeople. Few salespeople have time to call on everyone in the territory. If you can identify or target the most profitable, accessible segment of customers, you can spend your time where you are likely to get the highest return. Of course, understanding segments in your market <u>doesn't</u> mean you stop treating each customer as a unique and important individual. Nor does it mean you don't sell outside the targeted segment. It simply means you give more energy and resources to those in the targeted segment. Each customer wants and deserves to be treated according to their needs. Segmentation studies can't predict exactly what each customer will do at each moment. However, they help you predict general needs and trends — much like the game films your favorite team watches during the week between competitions. They predict the general strategies and decision-making patterns that will be used.

Tom Giese
Cenex/Land O' Lakes
Livestock Production Specialist
Canby, Minnesota

You've got to target...early, often, well. You've got to target farms, and what I've tried to do is target the farms you want to be doing business with or target the people you want to be doing business with. Whether it is with someone who is on the dairy council or local dairy board or somebody that is very active in the pork producers council or Pork Producer's Association or whatever business you're targeting. Find the people that are going to help you sell. Find the people that are going to really promote you and what you do. Because, again, everybody's got a product. As competitive as it's gotten, unless you really come out with something new and innovative, there really isn't a lot in the ag industry. Whether it be machinery, feed ingredients, it doesn't really make any difference, it's gotten so uniform. It's the people that sell the product, people that place product, position products with the right people.

Segments in Your Territory-Review

Demographic segments describe farmers according to the type of information that the Census Bureau might collect – age, education, size of farm, labor, etc. Again, these segments have limited usefulness because such factors as age or education may not have a significant effect on how the buying decision is made, at least for commercial farmers.

Product Usage segments group customers according to the products they use – corn farmers vs. bean farmers, for instance, or hog farmers vs. cow/calf farmers. This is useful in determining what level of sales you can expect from each type of farmer, but doesn't tell you how to sell each farmer if he or she can choose from multiple products and companies that meet product usage needs, as is the case today.

Psychographic segments describe what the customer values and how they make decisions. Psychographic segmentation commonly looks at other factors that we believe affect the buying decision, such as attitude toward farming (is it a business or a lifestyle); how information is recorded, used and stored; who influences the farmer; and whether the farmer is growth-oriented or not. Psychographic segments are very useful to salespeople, because they group customers according to how they buy.

Let's review psychographic segments once more. Over the last 10 years, segmentation studies in many branches of the industry have been completed by the Synergy Division of Agri Business Group[44], a company that specializes in agricultural research and strategy. As introduced in Chapter Four, Synergy research has identified three psychographic segments that seem to underlie many of the product or company-specific segments.

- Relationship buyers – buy from people they know and trust; value the seller/buyer relationship sometimes more than price; value high service;
- Economic buyers – buy based primarily on price or "the deal;" profit-oriented but measure profit based on input cost rather than output value;
- Business buyers – buy based less on cost and more on the productivity of the input; bottom-line oriented; require trust and a sound buyer-seller relationship, but the decision is made based on overall profitability.

---

[44] Agri Business Group, Synergy Division, Indianapolis, Indiana.

Whether your company provides you with a method for segmenting customers or not, you need to develop an understanding of the different types or groups of customers in your territory. This helps you determine where your efforts will pay off, who is likely to appreciate your products and services, and what "value bundle" you need to create to get their business.

If your company has provided you with a method for segmenting customers, by all means use it! Begin by assigning customers, by name, that match the characteristics of each buyer group or segment. This helps you "see" the segments in your own market, and adjust your approach to be more effective. If you want to try segmenting customers on your own, the following thinking process will help get you started (adapted from Cooper and Inoue, 1996).[45]

Customer Segmentation Process

1. Determine how customers currently evaluate competitive brands or competitive suppliers in your market. What *attributes* (characteristics) do they use? Make a list of these product/service attributes.

2. Determine how different types of customers weigh the *relative* importance of each attribute when evaluating a company. Use the three buyer types or segments described here (relationship, economic and business buyers), and make a list of what they value most. For example, price may be very important to economic types of buyers. Price is also important to relationship buyers, but personal service may be the most important for them.

3. Develop an *ideal profile* of products, services or the company, according to preferences of each type of buyer.

4. Determine which *ideal profile* you can deliver most profitably – which segment you want to do most of your business with.

Often, an analysis of segments tells a company as much about itself as about customers. For example, if your company is a low-cost, low-service supplier, you will probably most easily attract the economic buyer. However, that may not be the segment with whom you could achieve the highest sustainable profit. Yet, if you want to work more with

---

[45]Cooper, L. and Inoue, A.. Building Market Structures from Consumer Preferences. Journal of Marketing Research, (Vol XXXIII); August 1996, pp. 293-306.

business buyers, you may need to find a way to increase your service level, supply dependability, expertise, and other attributes these customers value.

Prioritizing Segments

Once you have determined what customer groups or segments exist in your market – and which customers belong to which segment – you're ready to prioritize segments. Your goal is to select or "target" the most productive segment(s) and focus your efforts on getting their business. Keep in mind that the reason for segmenting your market is so that you can concentrate your selling efforts in a more precise manner utilizing resources more effectively and getting better results.

If you have identified segments or customer groups in your market, you know which types of customers have the most need for your products and services. You know which types of customers have a similar price and service or "value" philosophy similar to yours. These are the customers with whom you have the greatest chance of success. These are the customers who should provide most of your business. And these are the customers with whom it is worthwhile to build a long-term partnership, by developing products and services that continue to meet their needs.

When you evaluate your customer segments, you should target one or two as "top" segments – worth more of your attention and time than other segments. This does not mean that you will ignore customers who don't fit into one of your top segments. However, it *does* mean that you will spend significant time and effort with your top segment, because you believe they will provide the bulk of your current business and the future growth of your business.

At this point in your plan, you need to do a "reality check." Can you meet the needs of your top segment(s)? Are they accessible to you – close enough to you, willing to talk to you, etc.? If you got their business, could you sell to them profitably?

Top or target customer segment(s) should:
- be able to provide significant progress toward your sales goals;
- be profitable to sell to;
- have needs that match your products and services;
- be measurable – you could identify farmers in this segment.

Many experienced salespeople speak of an "80-20" rule: you get 80% toward your sales goal with 20% of your customers. Your top segment(s) must include the 20% of your customers that will help you reach your goals.

Identify Value for Key Segments

Once you have identified your top segment(s), you should focus on their current needs, understanding their business, helping them recognize future needs, and helping them achieve their business goals. Your job is to find out <u>in detail</u> what they value and then find a way to deliver more of it than any competitor. Recall the "Value Equation" from Chapter Six? It can be described with this simple formula:

> Product benefits
> + Service benefits
> + Added value
> - <u>Price of your product or service</u>
> = Value to the Customer

While we often find it difficult to put actual numbers on all these elements in the equation, the concept helps us appreciate how customers see the value. Let's look at an example:

> *(Sales rep) Dr. Johnson, I stopped by the clinic to tell you about a new feed antibiotic we have developed. It does a better job against E. coli scours in the nursery and ileitis in older pigs than anything you've seen so far* (product benefit). *And we have also developed a new sensitivity disc, so that you can easily determine whether the offending "bug" will respond to this new product* (product benefit). *I would be happy to teach your lab worker how to use them properly* (service benefit). *As an introductory offer, we could provide some of these sensitivity testing kits to you, so that you could introduce the product to your customers with full confidence and also be the person they look to for more advanced diagnostic services* (value-add). *We think you'll find the price is very fair, considering the results you'll see* (value).

Unfortunately, some customers (particularly economic buyers) may be thinking this formula through in precisely the reverse order:

> *(Dr. Johnson) New antibiotic, huh...wonder if it really is all that good a deal* (value). *Maybe they could give me a special introductory price* (price). *Would they really spend time with my lab? And would the diagnostics make much difference to my farmers* (service benefits)? *I'd like to see proof of performance before I buy* (product benefit).

Remember: in order to sell the value of products and services, you have to understand what customers in your top segment(s) value, and then make it your business to deliver that value. Value can be broken into two general categories: tangible value and intangible value.

Tangible Value

Tangible value is value the customer can measure. Many product benefits and some service benefits fall into this category: product performance, competitive quality, service quality, output quality and quantity, billing accuracy, financing and price. In the example above, tangible value would include:

- absolute product performance (effective against *E. coli* and ileitis in pigs); can be backed up by scientific data including laboratory trials and field trials;
- relative or competitive performance (better than other available products); can be supported by field trials and testimonials from other customers;
- service quality (effectiveness of the diagnostic/sensitivity test);
- output quantity (less disease means more pigs survive for this veterinarian's customers); can be documented through field trials;
- output quality (less disease and better gain rates for operations using the product); documented through field trials;
- price ("fair"); needs to be presented as a cost/benefit to the user.

Intangible Value

Intangible value is not as measurable as tangible value, but it is no less important to the customer. Intangible value includes such factors as reduced time or hassle, ease-of-doing-business, increased flexibility, problem-solving expertise, and dependability (freedom from worry). In the above example, intangible value could include:

- reduced time or hassle (feed antibiotics are easier to administer);
- ease of doing business *(I'll be happy to work out a testing protocol with you if you like, and monitor the effectiveness of the product for you);*
- increased flexibility *(with less danger of E. coli and ileitis, your customers may be able to improve their throughput and overall productivity, mostly through your help – that's good for business);*
- problem-solving expertise *(according to our vet advisory board, this should really help producers; the sensitivity test was developed with some new technology that makes it easier to use, too. As always, Dr. Phillips at our regional office will be available for any questions);*

- dependability *(as you know, we won't introduce a product until we're convinced it will work for you...you can count on this product going through the same rigorous testing you've come to expect from us).*

As in this example, most sales reps do a much better job of explaining <u>tangible</u> product performance and service benefits than the <u>intangible</u> benefits. Yet the intangible benefits may be what make or break the sale – add enough value to justify the price.

Relative Value

Of course, "value" doesn't exist only for <u>your</u> products and services. Every competitor is trying to bring value to the customer, although their methods may be quite different from yours. To understand how the value of your product/service offer "stacks up" against the competition, you must return once more to understanding what the customer values. Competitive value is not decided in some abstract way – it is decided by real customers who decide to buy one product rather than another. This decision always makes sense to the customer – he or she will always choose what they believe to be the best alternative available at that moment, given his or her specific needs and values.

How Do You Stack Up? Measuring Relative Value

When a customer is looking for a new supplier or considering a new product, they evaluate each option against a "mental list" of the tangible and intangible benefits they need. Some of the tangible benefits may be quite specific, such as *kills lambsquarter* or *protects against intestinal parasites.* Intangible benefits are often much less specific, such as *easy to work with* or *reasonably responsive when I have a question.*

To evaluate how you "stack up" to the competition consider the following:

1. Talk to your top customers and to people you'd like to have as customers about their needs for products and services (tangible benefits).
2. Ask them how important some of the "intangible" benefits are to them.
3. Ask them who their "best" supplier is – in any branch of the industry.
4. Ask them who their "worst" supplier is – in any branch of the industry.

When you have talked to a number of customers (10-20), you are ready to build your own competitive scorecard. Do you have to compare your company to <u>every</u> possible competitor? No – your customers don't. They use their needs and values, in the order of their importance to them, to develop a "short list" or *consideration set* of suppliers or companies that could potentially meet their needs.

Which competitors make it onto the "short list" for your highest-priority segment? If you know what these customers value, you will be able to choose easily. For example, if you are selling inputs for a local dealer in a fruit and vegetable area, location may be an important factor, because proximity to the farm is important for chemical or fertilizer application services, soil sampling and scouting. If you are wholesaling fertilizer or feed microingredients, the location of your business may not be important to customers at all.

On the following pages are sample "competitive scorecards."

Construct Your Competitive Scorecard

- Put all the value factors in the left-hand column.
- Weight each factor 1-5, depending on how much it impacts purchase behavior for your target segment.
- Put the names of up to 3 competitors across the top in the first three columns.
- Put your company's name in the last column.
- Give your competitors and yourself a score from (-5) to (+5) on each factor.
  - A score of (+5) means the company is performing as well as the most demanding customer could wish.
  - A score of (-5) means the company is performing so poorly it could lose business on this factor alone.
- Multiply scores x weight to get an impact rating.
- Add impact ratings to determine the strongest competitor.
- Look at ratings to see where your selling challenges (and opportunities) are.

Table 8.1
Construct Your Competitive Scorecard

Value Factor	Weight	Competitor		Competitor		Competitor		Your	
		Score	Impact	Score	Impact	Score	Impact	Score	Impact
Product performance									
Competitive product quality									
Service quality									
Improves out put quantity									
Improves output quality									
Easy to do business with									
Quality of expertise from salesperson									
Saves time or hassle									
Financing									
Dependability									
Level of contact from salesperson									
Complaint resolution									
Other									
Other									
Other									
TOTAL SCORES									

Let's look at examples from two industries.

Table 8.2
Feed Manufacturer/Distributor Scorecard (Sells to Dealers)

Adds Value	Weight	Competitor		Competitor		Competitor		Your	
		Score	Impact	Score	Impact	Score	Impact	Score	Impact
Product portfolio (# of products)	4	+3	+12	+2	+8	+3	+12	+3	+12
Competitive product quality	3	+4	+12	+4	+12	+3	+12	+4	+12
Service quality	5	+2	+10	+4	+20	+2	+10	+3	+15
Improves # of dealer sales	5	-1	-5	+2	+10	+2	+10	+4	+20
Improves profitability of dealer sales	5	-2	-10	-1	-5	+1	+5	+1	+5
Accurate billing	3	-2	-6	+1	+3	+1	+3	+2	+6
Easy to do business with	4	-2	-8	+2	+8	+1	+4	+3	+12
Improves dealer flexibility to work w/new customers	3	+2	+6	+1	+3	+1	+3	+1	+3+-
Quality of expertise from salesperson	3	+3	+9	+4	+12	+2	+6	+3	+9
Saves dealer time or hassle	5	-1	-5	+2	+10	-1	-5	-1	-5
Financing	2	+4	+8	-1	-2	-1	-2	+2	+4
Product delivery	3	+2	+6	-1	-2	-2	-6	+2	+6
Level of sales support from salesperson	4	+2	+8	+3	+12	+2	+8	-3	-12
Support of complaint resolution	4	-1	-4	+2	+8	-1	-4	+2	+8
Other									
Other									
Other									
TOTAL SCORES		13	33	24	96	13	56	26	95

In this situation, you can see how your competition stacks up very clearly. You have several areas of strength (service quality, improving the number of dealer sales, improving the profitability of dealer sales) that are very important to dealers. However, you need to find a way to contact these top accounts more often. Let's look at one more example.

Table 8.3
Combine Sales Scorecard

Value Factor	Weight	Competitor Score	Competitor Impact	Competitor Score	Competitor Impact	Competitor Score	Competitor Impact	Your Score	Your Impact
Product performance	5	+1	+5	+3	+15	+5	+25	+5	+25
Competitive product quality	4	+1	+4	+2	+8	+5	+20	+5	+20
Service quality	5	+3	+15	+2	+10	+2	+10	+3	+15
Improves output quantity	3	+1	+3	+1	+3	+3	+9	+3	+9
Improves output quality	2	-1	-2	+1	+2	+2	+4	+2	+4
Easy to do business with	2	-1	-2	-1	-2	-2	-4	+2	+4
Quality of expertise from salesperson	3	-2	-6	+2	+6	-2	-6	+1	+3
Saves dealer time or hassle	3	-2	-6	-1	-3	-1	-3	+1	+3
Financing	4	+3	+12	+4	+16	+4	+16	+4	+16
Dependability	5	+1	+5	-1	-5	+5	+25	+5	+25
Level of sales support from salesperson	1	-2	-2	+2	+2	-3	-3	+1	+1
Complaint resolution	3	-2	-6	+2	+6	-2	-6	-3	-9
Other									
Other									
Other									
TOTAL SCORES		0	20	16	58	16	87	29	116

In this situation, we see that product performance and other product features play a great role in the customer's decision. However, the ability of the dealership and the salesperson to follow-up, to meet service needs, and to ensure dependability are also very important to farmers in this segment. These factors are under the control of the salesperson.

Building Competitive Selling Strategies

Once you know your competitive strengths and weaknesses, you can "fine-tune" your selling strategies to sell more competitively. Experienced salespeople find that three strategies work well:

- lead with your strength;
- set the quality standard;
- if you can't fix it, feature it.

Lead With Your Strength

If you find, after your competitive analysis, that you are strong on a factor that customers value, make sure customers know about it! Talk about your strengths when you call on customers. Feature your strengths in company newsletters. Place an article in the local paper, showcasing your strength and the value it has for customers. Gather testimonials from customers to share, showing new prospects how that strength can go to work for them. Organize a customer meeting, and make sure your strength comes through clearly.

For example, let's assume that your customers value expertise. You know that your nutritionist is one of the best people in the country in beef nutrition and feedlot operation. You could offer a seminar on feeding programs for incoming cattle. You could offer ration balancing services to farmer-feeders in your area. You could place an article, authored by your expert, on the economics of feeding a particular commodity that is cheap this year, in your company newsletter or a local trade journal. You could arrange for this expert to speak at trade shows and local seminars, or ask them to moderate a panel of experts for large feedlot operators. The possibilities are endless. The key is to capitalize on the strengths you have.

Set the Quality Standard

You may find one or more value factors where no company in your area is meeting top customers' expectations. This situation provides you with the opportunity to set the quality standard for this service or value factor in your area. For example, perhaps no one is following up with customers as often as they would like. You could develop a plan to follow-up on every sale, regularly measure customer satisfaction, and contact current customers on an ongoing basis.

Setting the quality standard for a value factor does not guarantee you a competitive advantage forever. Competitors will eventually notice what you are doing and will imitate it. However, if you choose to set the quality standard in an area you can perform more effectively or more efficiently than your competition, you may be able to maintain a competitive advantage for much longer.

If You Can't Fix It – Feature It

If you are weaker than your competitors on a value factor and you can't "fix" your performance, find a way to turn the situation to your advantage. For example, your price may be higher than your competitor. You may not be able to change the price of your products or services — but you can show customers how your company uses research and development to improve the quality and performance of products, and how you can support customers through educational seminars. Perhaps you are not as close as another dealer and the customer fears working with you would be inconvenient. A selling strategy should include featuring your radio-equipped delivery truck and your toll-free 24-hour service.

Above all, if you have a weakness on a factor important to customers, don't simply ignore it. They won't. If you can fix it, do so. If you can "re-arrange" your business around it, do that and then sell the value of a "new" way to serve customers.

Summary

A strategy is a plan to assemble your resources and decide how to use them. Your territory strategy is linked to your company's direction and also to the needs and values of local customers. Thus, you need to know your company's strategies in key areas such as which products to emphasize, pricing guidelines, preferred distributors and promotion support. Talking to your manager is a good place to start.

Next, you need to analyze your local market. What are key trends? Is your sector of the industry strong right now, or depressed? How is technology accepted? What information sources are most powerful? Your analysis should result in a clear understanding of your customers' business and production environment, and their needs. Once you understand those needs, you can begin to develop a "differential advantage" (something that sets you and your company apart in a crowded, competitive field).

The strength of your differential advantage, along with company goals, will lead you to realistic, achievable territory goals. These goals should include territory development, not just sales for the coming year.

As you learn more about key accounts in your territory, you'll notice certain patterns of decision-making. Certain types or segments of farmers seem to buy for similar reasons. Sometimes, these similarities relate to a shared business practice - for example, conservation tillage farmers share many needs. Sometimes, the similarities relate to buying motive - relationship, economic or business motives.

When you have identified your most important segment of accounts, you should analyze what they value and your competitive strength for that segment. Weaknesses can often be remedied (and strengths better communicated) once you know what they are.

Review Questions

1. What do sales strategies help salespeople accomplish? How?

2. Define a territory strategy and describe how it fits into the company's marketing mix.

3. Give three examples of questions a new salesperson can ask to learn about the company's highest-priority segments.

4. In the past, products were sold based on <u>finding</u> people who needed that specific product. Discuss why it is a better strategy to sell products based on the salesperson's ability to understand customer needs and to tailor his/her approach and services to meet those needs.

5. List and define the five types of sales goals discussed in this chapter.

6. Give an example of how a new salesperson can measure relative value.

Effective Selling Skills

Part Three explores basic selling skills. Consistent and well-considered use of these skills can help a salesperson transform selling from a random happenstance to a planned, organized process that builds customer trust and sales success. The selling process includes a series of steps. Although, for the sake of the logic, these steps are presented in the following chapters in a sequence, in the real world, salespeople find they may occur in almost any order. In fact, some steps (such as probing for needs) may occur several times.

For many salespeople, the first step is to determine whom to contact, through prospecting for new accounts. Top salespeople then prioritize their prospects, so they spend time where they will be most successful. Top accounts usually require some planning – a sales *strategy* – to ensure that a relationship with them begins well and continues to be consistently above their expectations. Each sales call within this strategy should have a concrete objective and a mini-plan, whether it is a formal visit or "just bumping into" the account at a community event. This planning allows best use of salesperson *and* customer time.

Planning is critical to success, but face-to-face selling skills are extremely important, too. In order to build a strong relationship with a new account, you must consistently behave in ways that make the *customer* most comfortable – whether it's how fast you talk, the way you ask questions, or even the clothes you wear. The cornerstone skill is the ability to ask good questions – and really listen to the answers. What you learn about customer needs and values can then be reflected back to the customer in the solution or "value bundle" of products and services you present for their consideration. Even with the best possible solution, a few objections are inevitable. These objections are also invaluable in moving you toward a sale, when you understand why they occur and how to use them to delve deeper into needs and build trust. As you prepare to "close" the sale – and *you* will usually need to initiate the close – you can gauge the customer's readiness to buy using a variety of verbal and non-verbal cues. Your final step should always be to set expectations for product or service performance, and then to follow-up after the sale to make sure expectations have been met or exceeded.

Together, these planning and face-to-face selling steps ensure that your customers get the products and services they need, that fit their values, and that

Bill Stuever
Consolidated Nutrition, LLC
Regional Director of Operations
Springfield, Missouri

A Point on a Continuum - Know Where You Are

Being a good salesperson is all about understanding exactly where you are at any given point in time in the sales presentation and being able to react or respond in a conversational manner that leads the call to your desired results.

For example, if you are an experienced running back, and you run up to the line of scrimmage and you see a linebacker waiting to tackle you, and it's just you and him...you may have already made a bad decision. You forgot to look at his hips or knees to determine which way he was leaning so you could go the opposite direction and pick up a half a step. Great running backs do that. Even the experienced ones look at game films over and over and over again with their coach saying, "Did you see the mistake you made? You forgot to look down at his feet or waist to determine which way he was leaning. If you had given him a head fake one way and gone the other, he had no chance to tackle you."

A running back has only a split second to make that decision and he has to learn how to anticipate the opposition to be a great ball carrier. New salespeople can learn skills that help them reach their goals as well.

My comparison from carrying a football to making a sales call is this. Once you learn how to analyze all parts of a sales call, you'll be able to determine whether the customer is skeptical, indifferent or just has an objection. Or, it may be that he's ready to buy. Unless you practice sales calls and learn to observe different personality traits, and have good coaching, you'll never be able to make reaction decisions on the spot and make them correctly. That's the art of selling. That's the experience sales training and coaching can give you...to be able to recognize exactly what's going on at any one point in the sales call. You have to get to the level of knowledge that if you could freeze frame any moment of a call and if your coach would ask you, "OK, what's going on with the prospect right now?" Or, "What's the prospect really telling you?" If you can answer these questions, and know exactly where you are at any given moment, then you are on the way to success.

perform as expected. Over time and with consistent use of these skills, you may well find that your relationship with key accounts has undergone a transformation. They *want* to see you. They *anticipate good ideas* from you and high performance from your product. They may even begin calling *you* when they need something. And you will be on the way to a successful selling career, because you have helped customers achieve their goals.

The following case study sums up the perspective of one of our panelists on effective selling skills.

Prospecting

Learning Objectives:

Upon completion of this chapter, you should be able to:

1. explain the role of prospecting in a successful sales effort;
2. explain how to use prospecting to grow market penetration or market concentration;
3. develop a system to prioritize prospects within a market or segment into A, B and C-level action priorities;
4. describe three methods of prospecting;
5. use a Prospect Priority Index to identify immediate action accounts;
6. describe the type of account information or "profile" that can support prospecting or result from it.

The Role of Prospecting in Strategic Selling

"Prospecting" is the term used to describe activities the salesperson undertakes to identify potential new accounts. A "prospect" or "prospective account" is an account with whom you are not doing any business yet, or with whom you are doing business only occasionally. A good way to think of "prospects" is from the customer's perspective: if you asked all the people who could potentially buy your products and services if they were your "customers," who would say they are

not? Even if a farmer or dealer has bought from you at one time in the past, if they do not "feel" any loyalty as your customer, you can count them as a "prospect."

Identifying prospects and converting them to customers is one of your most important tasks as a salesperson. In all markets, there is a certain amount of customer turnover - customers who leave the business entirely or take a portion of their business to a new supplier each year. In agricultural markets, the loss of business from normal customer turnover may be compounded by the existence of fewer customers overall in the total market, because the number of farms and dealers that support them is still falling. Even if your business were able to keep all of today's customers, at their current level of business, prospects would still be critical, because they represent the potential growth of your business.

Prospecting is therefore a valuable skill. It helps you identify new customers who can replace those who leave, and who can be added to those who remain to grow the business. A systematic and planned prospecting process also helps you, as a salesperson, to make the most efficient use of your time. The fact is, all prospects are not equal! Some may take years to cultivate into productive accounts. Others may immediately see the benefit of working with you, or of regularly giving you a much higher proportion of their business.

Five Rules for Successful Prospecting

Successful prospecting is not a one-time activity. It is a process that is integral to your short-term and long-term success. You will begin prospecting your first day on the job, and should still be prospecting when you retire. Salespeople with a record of year-in, year-out success organize their prospecting effort around these five guidelines.

1. Make sure your prospecting plan will help you achieve your sales goals – not only sales volume, but the type of customer you want, the proportion of business you want from them, and the degree to which you will have to work to re-sell them each year.
2. Use a prospecting process that enhances your knowledge of your market and how it is changing, helping you refine your list of "top account" criteria or characteristics.
3. Use a variety of prospecting methods.
4. Prioritize your prospects so you know where to spend your time.
5. Develop a system for profiling prospects – the specific information about their business you need to organize your effort and to prepare for your first call.

Prospect to Achieve Sales Goals

Sales goals can be stated in a variety of ways, depending on the type of business, the product(s) you are selling and the conditions of the local market. Some salespeople have highly defined goals. Other salespeople may simply have a list of 200 names handed to them with instructions from their manager to "sell as many as you can."

Your prospecting effort will be much more effective if you have clearly defined sales goals. Even if these are not provided by your manager, you should have developed them from your territory strategy. If you don't know which type of customer you want, how your products and services might "fit" their needs, or who your competitors are, your prospecting effort can't be focused enough to do you much good. Wanting to sell something to everyone may mean you don't spend enough time with anyone to really cultivate loyal, profitable business relationships.

1. Do you want to increase your market *penetration*? If so, you need to identify and cultivate new customers for your products and services.
2. Do you want to increase market *concentration*? If so, you need to identify customers who are doing much lower levels of business with you than they could be, or who are buying from only one part of your business.
3. Do you want to combine increased penetration and increased concentration for maximum growth? If so, you need a system to organize all potential customers, including those who are doing some business with you, and begin calling on those who offer the greatest sales growth.

Jim Jackson
Land O'Lakes, Inc.
Swine Program Manager
Indianapolis, Indiana

Talking prospecting, it is important to take a step back and really understand the producer segments and target the right accounts. Understanding segmentation and knowing the targets help us determine who, where and how to prospect.

In our business, the most rapidly growing segment is made up of those producers who want to align with companies like ours, who want us to share risks with them and through this are willing to share in the business's profits and losses. We have targeted this segment as key to growing our business and because of this we have developed our programs and products and trained our salespeople around their needs.

In segmenting and targeting, like many companies, we develop market data and know the basic details of the prospects and their businesses. The second step is to identify producers interested in sharing risks (financial or production) with companies such as ours. We further look at the producer's business goals, their

continued...

ability to grow business, their financial resources, etc. and out of this processl, we create our targeted prospect list.

This is a change in how we have done business because we can now partner with these operations rather than operating in a typical customer supplier relationship. Focusing on this segment has caused our sales force to think differently about how they target and prospect, but those who have accepted this change have been successful.

Let's look at an example of how prospecting can support each type of market growth goal.

Prospecting to Increase Penetration

Maxine thought back to a year ago – some days she had felt like the luckiest person in the world, and other days she hadn't known where to begin. About two years ago, Maxine was hired by a regional feed company and given the "opportunity of a lifetime": to grow feed sales by developing a farm-based integrated swine production network. Maxine's company was ready to offer young, aggressive producers an outstanding line of complete nursery feeds and supplements for on-farm feed manufacturing for growing and finishing pigs. Maxine had a joint venture agreement with one of the top swine genetics companies to provide high-lean breeding stock. She was authorized to help secure financing for multiple-site farrowing and finishing operations, and to support the development of a local multiplier operation.

Maxine started the job excited and full of energy, but after six months of knocking on doors, she wasn't sure she could make it work. She had worked through a list of producers who currently used complete feed, but there weren't enough of them interested in expansion to build a network. A few young producers had come to her and expressed interest, but she usually found they were more interested in her facilities financing program than in forming a network.

Maxine decided she had to find a way to work smarter – not harder. She gave herself four weeks to learn all she could about successful networks like the one she wanted to build. She talked with animal science professors, some leading swine consulting veterinarians, and producers in a swine production cooperative in the next state. She found that the type of people who could make a swine production network successful had very similar characteristics, no matter which part of the country they lived in. They were well educated, strong and profitable managers, interested in farming for profit, looking for ways to integrate into the food system, and willing to adapt to new production practices. Many of them were also experimenting with other new technologies, such as early weaning, contracting identity-preserved specialty feed grains, or computerized tracking of feed intake and gain. When Maxine returned to prospecting, she focused her efforts on the producers who fit these criteria, rather than the ones her company had sold before. And three weeks ago, she hosted a kick-off dinner for producers in her first swine production network.

Prospecting to Increase Concentration

Kevin was hired by a San Joaquin Valley cooperative agronomy department with one clear goal: grow the business. The cooperative was doing well now, but they wanted to expand into the next county and Kevin had been given the job of adding business from that geography, which would be serviced by a small office the cooperative had bought and converted to a depot. Kevin had a demonstrated success record from his former job selling on-farm computing systems, and he approached his new job with the same process that had worked for him in the past. He identified some of the top farmers in the area, and began setting appointments and calling on them.

Within the first year, Kevin had been able to attract a few of the prospects he'd targeted to the co-op, but his success was less than his boss had hoped. He was having trouble convincing the large citrus producers he'd targeted that his co-op could provide the level of service they wanted, since it was headquartered in the next county.

Kevin's wake-up call came one day when he was manning the counter at the main store. He began talking with a customer who had stopped by to see if he could get some insecticide and have it applied in the next day or two. As they talked about how the product needed to be applied, Kevin realized that this producer was located in the heart of his new territory. Yet Kevin hadn't met him yet, let alone called on him. Kevin asked how the farmer happened to stop by their store, and learned that he had been buying petroleum for some time from the co-op – in fact, he'd stopped by today primarily to pick up fuel filters and oil. While this farmer wasn't as large as the ones Kevin had been targeting, he quickly realized that a bunch of medium-sized citrus  *farmers like this could bring the cooperative a sizable amount of business, and help him establish a base from which the business in the new county could grow.*

Kevin started revising his prospecting plan immediately. He talked with the other PCAs, the petroleum route drivers, and the co-op's bookkeeper. He developed a list of medium-sized farmers who were doing some business with the co-op, but very little business (usually just emergency orders) with the agronomy department. He used others' knowledge of these farmers and their buying habits to plan his first calls. Now, one year later, he has a broader base of customers in his new county, and a list of testimonials he can use with his largest prospects to back up his claims for quality service.

Prospecting to Increase Penetration and Concentration

Gerry is a salesman for a national distributor of animal health products. His goals are to increase sales volume by increasing the proportion of products customers purchase from his company (concentration) and also by adding new accounts (penetration). Gerry spent the first few weeks in his new job learning about the market – talking to his peers, visiting major customers and non-customers, and looking at livestock production trends in his new territory.

Gerry found that his company had a good reputation with the clinics they served, although veterinarians looked to them primarily as a "warehouse" from which they could draw what they needed... they rarely saw the distributor as a viable source of advice on one brand over another. He found that several co-ops and feed stores they were supplying were satisfied with the service they received, but that they basically didn't "sell" animal health products, preferring to wait for walk-in traffic to ask for products and move inventory. As a result, they had many problems with aging inventory and felt the product line wasn't very profitable – more of a nuisance. Gerry found that larger swine production units – and there were several big 600-1000 sow operations in the territory – were not being called on at all.

After meeting with his manager, Gerry put together the following prospecting strategy to meet his business growth goals. First, he talked with major clinics to make sure they understood the full product and service offering of his company, and showed them how centralizing their purchases could save them money. Second, he developed a prioritized list of feed stores and co-ops, so that he could call first on those businesses with a desire to grow animal health sales. Finally, he developed a short list of producers who were large enough to be worth his sales time, and began calling on them. Two years later, Gerry had increased the share of animal health products sold through his company in his territory by 15%.

The Prospecting Process

As you can see from the above examples, there are many ways to approach prospecting, depending on the sales goals to be achieved. However, all of these approaches have a similar process at their foundation.

1. Confirm territory strategy goals – penetration, concentration or both.
2. Analyze the current market and develop a list of characteristics of the type of customer who can help you achieve your sales goals.
3. Plan your prospecting time – many salespeople find it helpful to look at A, B, C-priority accounts.
4. Use a variety of prospecting methods – leads, cold calls and segment-specific prospecting.
5. Develop a system for prioritizing action accounts – which "A" account you will call on <u>today</u>.
6. Develop a set of information you can maintain on prospects and enrich as you begin working with customers – a "profile" that helps you stay current with customer needs and decision makers.
7. These steps in the process can be summarized as a system flow (Figure 9.1).

Figure 9.1
The Prospecting Process

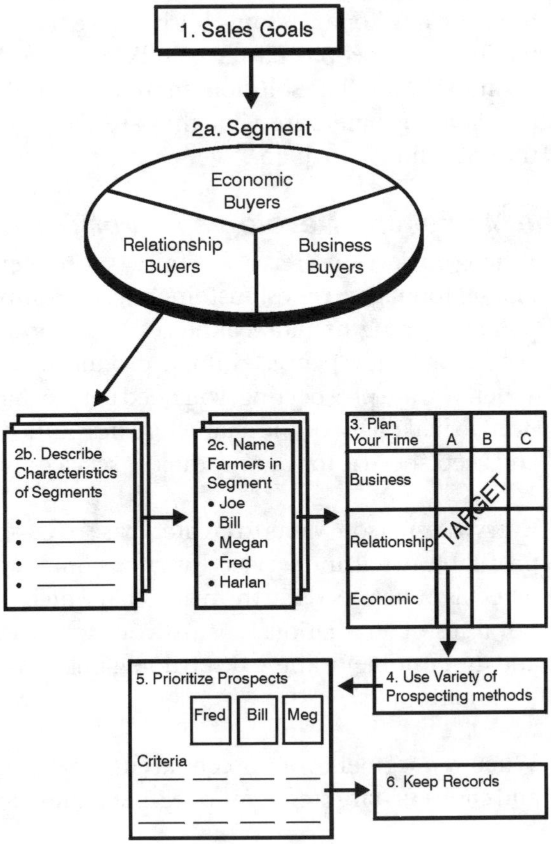

1. Confirm Sales Goals

In the first section of this chapter we described how critical it is that your prospecting strategy be aligned with the rest of your territory strategy. But for many salespeople, there may not be a business strategy in place that defines penetration and concentration goals. Or, such a strategy may be in place at the company level, but it doesn't "filter down" to all salespeople. For example, consider Phil's situation…

> *Phil was hired as a new sales rep for a major equipment manufacturer's local dealership. The dealership was large and influential, covering a 3-county area with agricultural, industrial and lawn and garden sales, as well as an active service department and a large after-market parts business. Phil was hired to grow the agricultural equipment business, with emphasis on whole-goods sales of a new product that had just been introduced. He had a list of farmers that his sales manager had compiled, and was told to "sell as many of them as you can."*

Phil's situation isn't unusual. In the past, many agricultural businesses sold to the same customers year after year, often selling much the same products in much the same way. Today, as some businesses exit and others expand their sales territory, salespeople may face Phil's task – developing a new market with little or no information. The solution: analyze the local market to determine where potential customers are, what they are likely to buy, and how likely you are to be the one selling it to them.

2. Analyze the Market and Develop a List of Top Customer Characteristics

When you develop a territory strategy (Chapter 8), you begin to analyze your market for major trends, customer needs, competitor activities, and your potential strengths and weaknesses. You choose one or more target segments, according to how people evaluate products and supplies the buying motives. When you are prospecting, you need to take that analysis one step further. You need to make a <u>list</u> of the characteristics of the type of customer you want to get and keep, specific to your product or service and your competitive environment.

Every salesperson wants to create a base of customers who are loyal and profitable to sell and service. Every customer wants to buy from a business that meet his or her needs, in the priority in which the customer sees those needs. Loyal customer relationships are a two-way street – you want to keep the customer and the customer wants to keep doing business with you. How do you identify these customers?

When you segment your potential customer base into different types of customers and choose a "targeted" or top segment, the characteristics of customers in the top segment make a good place to start. For example, if you have chosen "business buyers" as your target segment, you will probably be looking for customers who:

- are average to larger than average in account potential;
- keep good records;
- understand where their profits come from and want to increase them;
- are concerned about price but more concerned about profit;
- want and expect you to get to know their business;
- are financially sound.

Aaron McWhorter
Sports Turf Company, Inc. and North Georgia Turf, Inc.
Owner and President
Whitesburg, Georgia

Like anyone in sales, good prospecting is and always has been important to us. When we started the Sports Turf business, we started some doing some calling on some people we knew in the industry. Those calls/contacts worked into renovations, renovations worked into construction.

We prospect like most people in the building industry prospect. We use the Dodge report, CMD, all the typical building construction reports on a daily basis. We go through them, call and then make initial calls.

The part of prospecting we do a little differently than many salespeople or companies may do is this: while we are prospecting, we are also developing that prospect as a potential customer. We don't just call on the owner or company who may be footing the bill for developing a new sports field, we spend a lot of time with architects who design and write specifications for facilities so they can write and design a facility that's probably above the expected norm. We've found the higher quality the facility, the better off we are. For example, if the architects put requirements in there that your average landscaper or grading contractor can't perform, that leaves us a place to get in and do the work.

We have been doing analyzing of clients or prospects over the years...we were doing 1-2-3- thousand dollar renovation projects and now we don't think we have time for that anymore. Now most of what we do is $100,000 or more. By paying close attention and developing those prospects into good customers, the business has grown as a result.

You may need to "customize" this list for your local market. Then list customers who ought to fit into each segment. You'll notice that there may be some customers in this segment with whom you are currently doing business and others with whom you do no business today. Some may have a good opinion of your company, others may have had a bad experience in the past and a third group may not know you at all. Some may require technical support and service from you, while others may have their own consultants or advisors. Some may be open to changing suppliers – switching to you – while others may be very loyal to their current suppliers.

Plan Your Time

For most salespeople, the target segment often still represents too many customers to call on all with the same high level of resources and energy. Let's look at two extremes you might find within your top segment – "customers for life" and "single-purchase customers."

"Customers for Life"

In the long term, you want to develop a list of customers who are yours for life, assuming you continue to meet their needs. These customers will always consider you as their "first option" when buying the products and services you sell. Such a customer might look like this:

- value philosophy similar to ours;
- does business with us now;
- needs products and services we offer;
- pays on time;
- easy to service;
- loyal;
- has influence with other potential buyers.

If most of your business came from customers like this, your life would be a lot easier, wouldn't it? You wouldn't have to spend so much time developing new business each year and you could focus on servicing customer needs. You would have the time you need to really get to know their business. They would appreciate and value your products and services and would tell others about you. And, over time, they would contribute many thousands of dollars in profit to your business. In short, they would be worth the effort to get them and keep them.

"Single-Purchase Customers"

These customers buy from you only when they really need something you have. They would be just as willing – in some cases more willing – to buy from someone else if they could. They see no difference between your business and most of your competitors. If you want their business again, you have to sell them all over again, or wait for them to come to you again. These customers may not care if you understand their business or what is <u>really</u> important to them. They simply expect you to have the products or services they want at a fair price and with a minimum level of service.

If most of your business came from these customers, would that be bad? Not necessarily – it depends on the business. WalMart, after-market parts stores in the equipment industry, providers of commodity feed ingredients, and many propane companies all have a healthy business working primarily with this type of customer. And almost every salesperson counts on some sales from customers like this each year to meet annual sales goals. Sometimes, these customers are essentially "single-use" customers with everything they buy. In fact, you could think of them as a specific segment of buyer – one who looks at price and convenience and values little else. However, *some* of these customers may actually be your "ideal" customers in disguise. Your own behavior as a consumer will illustrate this "hidden ideal customer" phenomenon very well.

> *You normally buy what prescriptions you need from a drugstore near your home. You are satisfied with their service and your doctor has their number on file as the place to call in new prescriptions. You are a "customer for life" – a loyal customer unless something happens. Now assume you get sick on a weekend. You need to have a prescription filled, but your drugstore isn't open. You find one a few miles farther away. Your intention is only to buy that one prescription and then return to your normal drugstore. You don't expect much from them except a competent pharmacist and a reasonable price. You intend to be a single-purchase customer in this situation, although you clearly prefer a more stable customer/seller relationship.*

In this situation, you are a "hidden" ideal customer. How can the drugstore uncover you? They might ask you a few questions to determine what you value. For example, the pharmacist could ask what information you would like about the drug you are buying, or whether you would like them to check for any interactions with other medications you are taking. He/she might offer to keep your insurance on file. The pharmacist might recommend some symptomatic medication – aspirin or cough syrup – to make you feel better, and might point out brands that are especially cost-effective. He/she might even ask if you'd like a call later, in case you experience any side effects.

Your list of top prospect characteristics should describe your "ideal" customer, but it should also allow for customers who are not ideal and yet could help you meet your sales goals.

Table 9.1
Top Prospect Characteristics –An Example

Account Potential	How much potential business could this account give me?
Need Your Products	Do my products match this account's needs?
Need Your services	Do our services meet this account's needs?
Can be serviced efficiently	Do we have time and equipment to service this account well?
Influential with others	How well is this account recognized as an opinion leader in the market?
Current customers	How much of this account's business an I getting today?
Open to change if not current customers	How vulnerable/dissatisfied is this account with its current supplier?
Similar value philosophy	How closely does the price/value philosophy of this account match our own?
Not frequent switchers	How loyal will this account likely be?
Can sell profitably	Can we sell and service this account at a profit?
Good credit risk	How likely is this account to pay?
Business stable/growing	Will this account be at least current size and strength in 5 years?

The list of characteristics of top accounts contains a combination of "ideal" customer characteristics (such as similar value philosophy and large size) and highly practical characteristics (can we sell them profitably, will they pay).

The list of key account characteristics as a refinement of your "segment strategy" should reflect the current business, your product, your market, and your sales goals. This list of characteristics can be used in at least three ways:

- to prioritize your prospects into A, B, and C accounts;
- to decide which account(s) are your highest action priority today;
- to help you profile each account to help you get and keep their business.

3. A, B, C Priorities

The next step is to put your potential accounts into a rough priority, based on your understanding of their characteristics and your goals. Many salespeople use a simple system of "A," "B," and "C" categories of accounts. Depending on your business, its strategies, and your specific goals, you select some of the most powerful characteristics from the list you developed and use these to organize your customer list within each segment. To review, segments describe how customers buy. A, B, and C accounts describe the <u>impact</u> of each customer on your business: the ease with which each customer can be sold and the potential size of their business.

- "A" accounts are the highest priority - they offer the most potential and deserve the most time.
- "B" accounts offer good potential, but they are usually smaller, harder to sell or harder to service profitably.
- "C" accounts are those you are least likely to sell without significant effort, or accounts that are so small they cannot be sold at high profit.

Some companies prefer to use segment (customer type) descriptions instead of A-B-C priorities - for example, a luxury car company may segment according to whether luxury or dependability or status is most valued. Although they advertise to segments, local dealers may not classify and actively call on prospects.

Other companies include their understanding of segments in the way they choose A, B, and C accounts. For example, high quality/high price manufacturers may identify their highest potential segment of customers as those who value the quality and business performance they offer. Most of their "A" accounts may be in this value segment, but there may be others who buy every few years because of resale value.

Finally, some companies use A, B, and C priorities <u>within</u> their target segment, for maximum targeting efficiency. For example, a crop protection company may identify dealers with loyal no-till corn and bean customers as their top segment, and then prioritize within that segment according to the dealer's ability to explain and sell conservation tillage and the value they place on their relationship with the manufacturer. Table 9.21 illustrates how a company could organize its A, B and C account priorities.

Table 9.2
"A," "B," and "C" Account Priorities

Account Priority	New Accounts		Existing Accounts	
	Size/Revenue Potential	Probability of Getting Business	Size/Revenue Potential	% of Current Business
A	Large Medium/Large	Medium/High High	Large Medium	50-100% 100%
B	Large Medium/Large Small	Low Medium/High Very High	Large Medium Small	<50% >50% 100%
C	Large Medium/Large Small	Very Low Low Medium		

4. Use a variety of prospecting methods

Once you have categorized accounts by buying motive and prioritized them by potential, you should begin prospecting. A variety of methods is most effective. There are three basic methods of prospecting, and each has some specific advantages. The three methods are:

- cold calls;
- leads;
- segment-specific prospecting.

Cold Calls

"Cold" calls are calls you make on customers you don't know or haven't worked with before. In rapidly-growing markets – like long-distance services – cold calls are the preferred method of prospecting. In these markets, the product is usually one that almost everyone could use, and therefore the best way to sell is to contact as many customers as possible.

Agriculture is not a rapidly growing market. In fact, the number of commercial farms is shrinking, and the number of dealers and elevators serving those farms is shrinking also. However, cold calling still plays an important role in your prospecting effort. When you cold call, you have an opportunity to learn a lot about perceptions of your products and your company, as well as learning about a potential customer. You may know that a certain customer is currently happy with a competitive supplier, but *never assume that this customer wouldn't be better off with you.* Your competitor's customers should always be prospects – just as your customers are their prospects.

No matter how sophisticated a customer database is, there will still be some accounts in your area that no one in your company knows enough about. Calling on these accounts as part of your prospecting effort helps you "fill the gaps" in your targeted prospecting effort. It allows you to learn about management changes, mergers and joint ventures that may turn an average account into a high-potential account. Finally, cold calling keeps you "sharp" - ready and able to ask questions and learn something new to add to your territory strategy:

- the potential of accounts currently served by a competitor;
- why accounts prefer your competitor;
- how/if you could serve them better than your competitor;
- strengths or services of your business that haven't been widely-enough communicated.

Trade shows[46] represent a special type of cold call. When a salesperson works a trade show, the objective is to attract potential accounts and to enhance the image of the company as a whole. The relative importance of these two objectives depends on the company, the type of person attending the trade show, and the degree to which the company wants to sell directly or generate "pull-through" demand for its products. Let's look at two very different examples.

Peter was assigned to work the trade show booth for his company at the World Dairy Expo. Peter's company makes computerized feeding systems. They had a demonstration set up, and encouraged people to stop by and learn more about the system by playing a "quiz bowl" game on one of the computers out in front of the booth. Their objective was to increase awareness of their new product among dairy professionals, and to create some demand or at least some questions that top dairymen could ask their equipment supplier. Peter had a great time - enjoyed helping people play the game, did several demonstrations, and talked to a lot of people. When they tracked the number of "hits" on their game after the trade show, they had interacted with 200+ people. Fifty of these were farmers who wanted more information. The show was a success - as effective as several days or weeks of cold calling.

Suzanne was assigned to work the trade show booth at a regional Farm Show. Suzanne's company develops and sells farm structures such as pole barns and grain bins. She had a display behind her, showing pictures of the buildings, and a table with free literature in front of her. She also had little plastic key chains, in the shape of three different types of buildings, to give out to passersby. The objective of Suzanne's company was to attract producers to their new grain storage products, because the increased interest in identity-preserved grain could

---

[46]For more information on the trade shows, see Appendix B.

mean a need for more separate storage facilities. Suzanne talked to lots of people and gave away lots of key chains, but she felt that the trade show had not been a success for her company. Many of the people she talked to were not farmers – they were just out for an afternoon. Those that were farmers didn't seem interested in hearing a sales pitch about the buildings, and it was impossible for Suzanne to talk to anyone long enough to know if they were a good prospect or not. When the show ended, she had only 5-6 people who wanted a personal call – not much for 3 days on her feet!

Trade shows <u>can not</u> take the place of all cold calling. There's nothing quite as exciting as sitting down with a total stranger at his/her place of business and learning all you can about their needs and their priorities. But trade shows <u>can</u> be a part of your cold calling effort, provided you have these factors in mind:

- you have realistic expectations about the type of person attending the show;
- you create a way for customers to interact with your exhibit;
- you create a way to track who was there and what interested them;
- your booth - from demonstrations to giveaways - reflects the image you want to present to commercial customers.

Leads

"Leads" are references or prospecting "clues" that help you identify accounts that might fit your "A" prospect category. Leads are often offered spontaneously to the salesperson as a gesture of support from current customers. If they like working with you, they will recommend you to their peers and tell you where you might have the most success. Salespeople with the most prospecting success are systematic and persistent in collecting leads. In fact, in some industries (such as insurance), asking for a "lead" before leaving a current account is standard practice: *John, who else might you know who would be interested in this type of crop insurance?*

Other professionals in your business are an excellent source of leads. If you sell to producers, talk to others who work with them. Don't neglect to talk regularly with delivery personnel, route drivers and applicators. They see the customer often and - because they are <u>not</u> selling - they often hear a lot about customer neighbors' needs. If you are selling in a wholesale business, make sure you talk with anyone else who has contact with the account, including customer service and finance. You may discover a question or a need you could fill, and be able to convert a low-priority account to a major account.

Professionals in related, non-competing businesses are also good sources for leads. For example, in a local community there can be a regular exchange of "leads" among:

- input dealers;
- ag lenders;
- consultants/veterinarians;
- equipment dealers;
- seed reps/DSMs.

Of course, in exchanging leads, salespeople must respect the confidentiality of the customer at all times.

5. Prioritize Action Accounts

Once you have agreed on the characteristics of high-potential accounts, it's time to name names and make plans. Your next step is to select specific accounts for immediate action. Use your list of key account characteristics to develop a *Prospect Priority Index (PPI)*. The PPI allows you to list the characteristics you believe are most important in selecting accounts, and then rate each potential "A" account to determine your highest potential prospect. You can use the PPI as a filter to determine which accounts to call on today, this week, or – if you have dozens of accounts to call on – to plan your prospecting for a month or a year.

Prospect Priority Index Instructions

1. Enter the names of specific "A" accounts – select those you intuitively believe are important.

2. Review the characteristics in your PPI. Add any that are new to your market; delete any that no longer apply.

3. (Optional) Assign a weight to each characteristic if you believe some characteristics should carry more weight than others. (For example, "willing to pay" may be more critical in a poor economy).

4. Rate all prospects on the first characteristic. Use a 1-10 scale. "10" is the most favorable rating and "1" is the least favorable rating. Consider the variation between prospects as you go, to make sure true differences emerge.

5. Continue rating prospects on the second characteristic, third characteristic, etc. until you have rated them on all characteristics.

Rate each prospect on a characteristic before moving onto the next characteristic.

6. (Optional) If you have weighted the characteristics, multiply each rating X each characteristic's weight for a weighted rating.

7. Total the scores for each prospect.

8. Identify your "action" prospects by their high PPI scores.

Prospect Names

Rate each Prosepect,
0 - 10 on each of
these factors
(0 is least favorable,
10 is most favorable)

FACTOR

1. Potential account size
2. Credit evaluation
3. Current business
4. Product match
5. Service match
6. Time availability
7. Distribution/Delivery
8. Opinion leader
9. Open to change
10. Loyalty
11. Price/value philosophy
12. Potential profit
13. _____
14. _____

Prospect Priority Index

(Total Score)

Explanation

1. How much potential business could this prospect give me?
2. How likely is this prospect to pay?
3. How much of this prospect's business am I getting now?
4. Do my products match this prospect's needs?
5. Do my services match this prospect's needs?
6. Do I have the time to serve this prospect well?
7. How conveniently is this prospect located?
8. How well is this prospect recognized as an opinion leader in the market?
9. How vulnerable is this prospect in his relationship with his current supplier?
10. How loyal will this prospect likely be?
11. How closely does the price/value philosophy of this prospect match my own?
12. What is the potential profitability of this account?

6. Develop Information on Top Prospects

You have now identified top prospects you should call on as part of your strategic selling effort and a subset of prospects you will call on first. One more step is needed before you make that first appointment: gathering all available information about that account, its history with your business (if any) and its potential needs. This information may be sketchy now, but as you build a relationship with the account you will be able to add to it until you have a *profile* of each key account. <u>The profile is the basis for your preparation for each call</u>. It is invaluable if you must at some point pass the account on to another salesperson.

A good account profile should contain as much pertinent information as possible. You won't know all this information by your first call, but eventually you should know it. Use this list as a basis for you first few "backgrounding" calls with a prospect and to qualify the account. "Qualifying" means making sure your prospect has the <u>authority</u> and <u>resources</u> to work with you.

- decision maker(s)
  - ➤ name(s)
  - ➤ addresses
  - ➤ telephone numbers (include the mobile phone)
  - ➤ FAX numbers
  - ➤ Email address
  - ➤ personal information

- information about the business situation
  - ➤ type of business
  - ➤ size (acres for farms, dollars sales for dealer businesses)
  - ➤ business goals, if known
  - ➤ names of key employees

- information about potential needs
  - ➤ profit goals
  - ➤ current suppliers
  - ➤ satisfaction with current suppliers
  - ➤ factors this account may use to evaluate suppliers

- past history with this account
  - ➤ purchase history and trends
  - ➤ any historical problems or barriers

- current challenges in selling this account

Debra Warman
American Cyanamid
Master Sales Representative
Minnesota Lake, Minnesota

For customer profiles, I try to make notes and a lot of times if it is a customer that I haven't spent a lot of time with in the past, I'll just come right out and ask if it is all right for me to write a few things down so that I can remember these things better. No one has ever said "no" and some guys feel that I am concerned enough about this to write some things down.

After the call or that evening, I try to sit down and go over my notes and organize my thoughts. Then, I put it in a file. Right now I just have a paper trail. I should do it electronically, but I haven't yet. There's a real science to carefully picking out the information that is important to profiling that customer. It is critical to carefully log the information that is going to serve you well in serving the customer. Personally, I feel like I do a better job with people that I haven't worked with a lot. When you get to know some customers well, sometimes you get a little lazy or over confident and may start to make some assumptions about what is important to them, based on last year.

People change and their needs change over time. Last year farming may have been all that was important to a particular customer and maybe this year s/he has a new baby in the family and wants to stay home more. Likewise, some customers may have an operation which has made a shift to more of a hands-on type program due to a different family corporation structure, landlords, or absentees, etc. You really need to keep up on those shifts.

Keeping tuned in and maintaining a current profile, however you do it, is a really good point for new salespeople to pay attention to-even people that have been out there a long time. Sometimes you get in a rut and need to find a way out. You have to constantly explore new avenues. Everyone changes over time and recognizing that is very important.

A Word About Multi-level Accounts

Many salespeople today find that a substantial portion of their business comes from "multi-level" accounts. These accounts may have several decision makers at the same level and location. For example, if you are selling vitamins or anticoccidials to an integrated poultry operation, you may find you need to sell the value of your products and your company to a purchasing manager, the nutritionist, the veterinarian, and potentially the manager of grower units. The salesperson may face a hierarchy of decision makers, some of whom work several states away. If you are selling crop chemicals though a large distributor with linked retail, you may find you must sell to local dealers, area managers, regional managers and potentially company product line managers. When working with multi-level accounts, keep the following tips in mind.

- Identify decision makers as soon as possible – all of them.
- Ask about (and keep a record of) how decision-maker success is measured internally, by the company or business – you must meet each person's needs as well as product needs.
- Ask about the decision process.
- Begin thinking about others on your sales team who could help you create or strengthen decision-maker relationships.

Sample Prospect Profile – Single Decision Maker

The following prospect profile is an example of how you can arrange profile information on one sheet. Your company may provide you with much more detailed records of past purchases or even a pricing and service history. Or, you may need to assemble the customer history yourself, from invoice files and discussions with other sales reps or your manager.

Figure 9.2
Sample Prospect Profile

Date _____

1. Key Decision-Maker _____ Age (approx.) _____

2. Address _____
   _____ Phone _____

3. Family Situation _____

4. Other Decision-Makers (Mgr., Owner) _____

5. Address _____
   Phone: _____ Fax: _____
   Mobile: _____ E-mail: _____
   Family Situation _____

KEY DECISION-MAKER PROFILE:

6. Personality Description _____

7. Interest, Hobbies, etc. _____

8. Off-Farm Income _____

9. Educational Background _____

10. Business Situation:
    • Acres Owned, By Crop _____
    • Acres Rented, By Crop _____
    • Program _____
    • Labor Situation-Employees _____
    • Major Equipment Line _____
    • Tillage Practices _____
    • Current Supplier(s) _____
    • Years With Current Supplier(s) _____
    • Current Program By Supply Area _____
    _____
    _____
    • Problems With Current Suppliers _____
    • Background With Us _____
    • Non-Business Contacts _____

11. Factors Likely To Be Important To This Prospect In Purchasing _____
    _____

12. Past Experiences With Prospect _____

13. Anticipated Problems In Selling And Servicing This Prospect _____
    _____
    _____

Summary

Strategic prospecting is a critical skill for successful salespeople. Prospecting involves analyzing the market, determining the characteristics of your highest potential accounts, organizing accounts into high, medium and low-priority call groups, identifying the best accounts to start calling on, and developing a system of customer profiling.

The best prospecting systems are built on a strong foundation from the territory strategy. They allow the salesperson to organize efforts so that prospecting time is invested in those accounts that will help meet sales goals.

Prospecting never stops. Even the most experienced salespeople still make cold calls, because talking with the accounts you <u>don't</u> yet serve is the best way to find out how you could improve your sales effort.

Review Questions

1. Explain how prospecting is used to grow market penetration. How does that differ from using prospecting to increase market concentration?

2. What are three methods of prospecting discussed in this chapter? Describe them.

3. Categorizing accounts into A, B, C accounts can help the salesperson adequately prioritize the segments they need to fulfill sales goals. What are two ways companies use A, B, C accounts to prioritize accounts?

4. Explain the Prospect Priority Index and how it helps refine prospecting efforts.

5. List and describe ten factors you consider relevant and important to include on a prospect profile. Why do you consider these relevant?

Chapter Ten:

Planning and Organizing for Success

Learning Objectives:
Upon completion of this chapter, you should be able to:
1. understand the role of key accounts in your sales success;
2. describe the steps in developing a key account strategy;
3. set objectives for each call in the sales strategy;
4. develop a projected flow or plan for each key call in the sales strategy;
5. make optimum use of selling aids such as people, product performance data, programs and sales literature.

The Role of Key Account Strategy in Your Selling Success

A successful selling career is built on successful, mutually beneficial sales relationships with individual accounts over a period of years. Each of these accounts has slightly different needs. Each expects and deserves to be treated as an individual. Ideally, the salesperson wants to be successful with every account that could benefit from his/her company's products and services.

A *key account* is "a customer deemed to be of strategic importance" to your company.[47] Strategic importance depends on your expected level of concentration with an account. Or, as one chief executive put it, "To lose customer x, permanently or temporarily, would be unthinkable. We become hysterical if our share of their purchases falls below 40%.[48]

---

[47] Millman, T. And Wilson, K. Developing key account management competencies. Journal of Marketing Practice: Applied Marketing Science, Vol 2 No. 2, 1996, p. 8.
[48] ibid, p. 10.

At some point, every salesperson must face this tough truth: all accounts are not of equal importance. Some offer significantly more potential than others. This is especially true in agriculture, where the economics of the industry are consolidating the management of more and more land and livestock into fewer and fewer hands. Your job as a salesperson is *not* to approach all accounts as if they offered your company equal potential, but rather to determine which accounts you must gain and keep in order to maintain and grow your market share. These are your *key* accounts, so called because their business is key to your success today and key to growing your business in the future.

If the salesperson or the company has developed a segmentation plan, a subset of potential customers whose needs and values fit your products and services has already been identified. Most key accounts will probably come from this segment or group of customers. In addition, consider potentially high-volume customers where you offer a differential advantage – a strength in products or services that puts you head and shoulders above the competition.

How many "key accounts" are enough? Many experienced salespeople report that they do as much as 80% of their business with as few as 20% of their accounts. Meeting the needs of these accounts is clearly critical to their success.

In addition to the sheer size of the account, there are other facts to consider such as:

- accounts with high influence in your marketplace;
- how much time you have to sell;
- where you can invest that time for maximum results;
- how much support you have from your selling team (managers, nutritionists, veterinarians, agronomists, etc.);
- how you can make the best use of the support you have.

What is a Key Account Strategy?

A key account strategy is a plan for capturing and retaining all or a part of the purchases from that account. It contains the salesperson's sales goals, the account's key business goals, major activities to be undertaken to build those sales, the personal relationship between the salesperson and the account, and the salesperson's plan for using any expert resources or programs your company makes available to support the sales effort. This key account strategy works like a "game plan" – it doesn't detail every interaction with the account, but it does guide the salesperson's week-to-week or month-to-month activities with the account over a two to three-year period.

Many salespeople base key account strategy on information they can collect on the account before their first sales call – sales history with the company, conversations with other non-competing suppliers and current customers, what you can observe by driving by or by looking at plat maps (maps showing the ownership of land in each county, available at the county courthouse). Then they adjust the strategy as they learn more about the account over time – or as the account changes. For that reason, the key account strategy should never be seen just as a document. It is a *working* plan. Expect to change it and refine it many times. In fact, if adjustments are not made to the key account plan as you learn more about an account, you probably aren't finding out enough about them to do the best possible job for them.

Basic Steps in a Key Account Strategy

1. Set account goals.

2. Collect information/history about the account.

3. Learn the account's business needs and goals through a questioning process.

4. Develop and present products and services that meet account goals.

5. Decide how to use your support resources.

6. Measure satisfaction and revise account goals.

The key account process will be repeated many times over the course of the salesperson's relationship with the account. Even if you are successful far beyond original projections in your first year or season with the account, the process of understanding needs and goals, evaluating current performance, and revising your approach and your goals should be reviewed and revised in each sales cycle.

The Selling Strategy and Selling Cycles

Jill was hired last year by a basic chemical manufacturer to work with smaller distributors and retailers. She was excited about the opportunities and the chance to get back in the country, after several years working as a manager of communications in the home office. Jill started the job in September, and set about getting to know her

key distributors and as many of her retailers as possible. While she had been told there was a customer database, she didn't spend a lot of time looking at customer records. She felt like that was the past, and it was up to her to build a future. By Christmas, Jill had seen almost everyone. She had even gone out with some of her retailers to visit their top farmers. She had sent everyone the marketing program for the coming season, and had encouraged everyone to call her with questions.

With the new year, Jill was ready to get out there and close some sales. To her absolute surprise, and growing disappointment, she found that several large customers had already made commitments to other companies. Their bulk tanks were full of someone else's product, and some of the same top farmers she had met had already signed a purchase agreement for competitive product. Jill was not only disappointed – she felt almost cheated. She had definitely had the impression, when she met these guys, that they were going to give her a chance. She decided to call her manager and let him know the bad news before he read it on a sales report. He wasn't happy – but to Jill's surprise, he took some of the blame himself. "I'm really sorry, Jill," he said, "I just thought since you had been with the company several years you understood that most of the decisions are made before the new year, any more. You just weren't out there selling at the right time."

Every product and service has a distinct selling cycle. If you sell with the cycle, your chances of success are increased. If you sell against the cycle, you'll be disappointed at every turn.

It's helpful to think of the selling cycle from the customer's perspective. First, the customer becomes aware of the need for a product or service - aware that there might be a better way of doing things. Then, there is a period when the customer is evaluating alternative products, services and suppliers. There is a period when the customer needs to make a decision on what to buy. The next period is the choice and use of the product or service. Finally, the customer will evaluate whether the choice of product or service was a good one, or whether they need to look around for a new alternative.

Each of these steps or periods in the customer's decision making process should have a corresponding step or process in your selling cycle (Figure 10.1).

Figure 10.1
Basic Selling Cycle

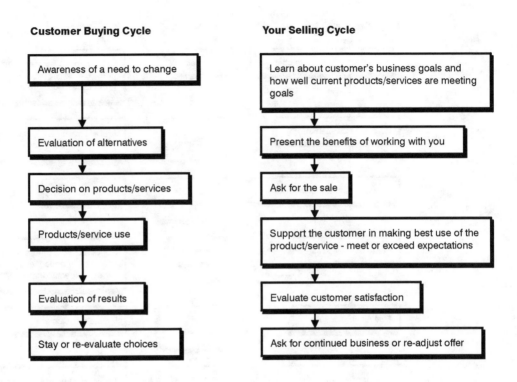

A specific selling cycle depends on what is being sold. With a salesperson selling a seasonal product to farmers, such as seed, fertilizer or chemicals, the selling cycle will mirror the production seasons of planning, purchasing, planting, growing and harvest (Figure 10.2).

Figure 10.2
Agronomic/Seasonal Selling Cycle to Farmers

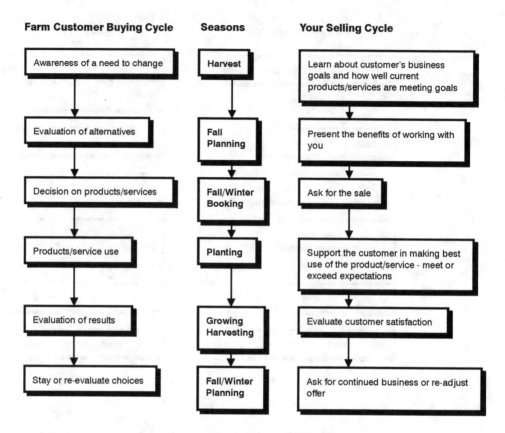

Salespeople selling for a manufacturer or distributor of agronomic products must support the dealer/retailer selling cycle. Thus the salesperson will sell to retailer customers a few months *ahead* of the farmer selling cycle (Figure 10.3).

Figure 10.3
Agronomic/Seasonal Selling Cycle to Retailers

Retailer Customer Buying Cycle	Seasons	Your Selling Cycle
Awareness of a need to change	Growing Season/Harvest	Learn about customer's business goals and how well current products/services are meeting goals
Evaluation of alternatives	Early Fall Planning	Present the benefits of working with you
Decision on products/services	Fall Ordering	Ask for the sale
Products/Service/Sales to Farmers	Winter/Early Spring Sales to Farmers	Support the customer in making best use of the product/service - meet or exceed expectations
Evaluation of results	Growing Season/Harvest	Evaluate post-sale satisfaction of dealer and user satisfaction for farmers
Stay or re-evaluate choices	Early Fall Planning	Ask for continued business or re-adjust offer

Different products may have totally different cycles. For example, the sales of equipment is related to the seasonal cycle - a farmer may want to buy a new combine before harvest. But a salesperson won't sell a new combine to most customers every year. Their need to consider a new combine is the result of how many hours of use they have put on the equipment, whether it was bought new or used, what current repair costs are, and whether the current financing program allows them to buy this year. The most careful planners may decide on a new combine right after harvest!

In every case, if you are selling to the farmer, you must organize your selling cycle around his or her business needs. Similarly, if you are selling to the retailer - a feed dealer or agronomy department of a local input business - the selling cycle must be adjusted so customers are fully aware of the benefits of the products and services offered *before* they start selling to farmers.

Larry Barmann
American Cyanamid
Marketing Specialist, IMI - Corn
Red Oak, Iowa

One doesn't always come in to the selling cycle at that opportune time (for instance when you start working for a company). If one starts selling in the middle of the growing season, one certainly does have somewhat of a disadvantage. You almost feel like you are never catching up with anything. I guess words of encouragement are: hang in there until that cycle reaches around full circle again and things will certainly be more manageable. I guess if you could think of things in that circle instead of the straight-line continuum, it will help you in planning and organizing and thinking of the big picture plan.

The selling cycle is very dynamic. In the past, many farmers bought what they needed just a few days or weeks before they needed it. Today, large row crop farmers often make their purchase decision months before they will use the product. They may decide as soon as they harvest and can measure the results of last year's decision. They may try to make a final decision before December 31, so that the cost of the next year's inputs can be subtracted from this year's profits before paying taxes. The introduction of transgenic seed products that contain herbicide tolerance or insect resistance has pushed the chemical crop protection decision to early fall. If a farmer has ordered herbicide-tolerant soybeans in September, he or she will buy the herbicide they were developed to complement – it's just a question of where to get it. It's critical to understand *when* your customers and prospects make their decision, and to adjust your selling cycle accordingly.

A key account selling strategy may include several selling cycles (for feed or agronomic products) or it may include only one selling cycle (for single major equipment purchases). In fact, *when* to talk about *what* is one of the key decisions the salesperson will make in planning a strategy. But before going any further, it's imperative to plan the selling strategy with the end in mind – the account goals.

Basic Steps in Key Account Strategy

1. Key Account Goals

The salesperson should have a specific set of goals for each key account, based on realistic assessment of that account's needs and potential and your company's assessment of market potential. <u>These goals should come directly from your territory goals.</u> In this way, each goal achieved with a key account puts the salesperson one step closer to achieving overall territory goals. For example, if you have a dollar sales volume goal, the dollar sales you plan to achieve with each key account should contribute significantly to your overall sales volume goal. If one of your sales goals is to increase market penetration (doing business with new customers), then several of your key accounts should be net new customers. If one of your territory goals is to increase the proportion of each customer's business, then the goals for each key account who is a current customer should indicate the level of business with you to be achieved.

Table 10.1 is an example of how a salesperson could "distribute" or break out their territory goals into key account goals. In this example, the salesperson has divided key accounts into current customers and new customers (those not currently doing business with the company). The territory sales volume goal is broken out into goals for each key account. This salesperson also has goals to increase concentration and penetration. Therefore, the sales goal with each current customer represents an *increased* share of this customer's total business. For new customers, the salesperson has estimated what percent or *proportion* of their total business he or she wants to achieve – increased penetration.

Table 10.1
From Territory Goals to Key Account Goals

Territory Goals	Goal: Current Customers		Goal: Non-Customers	
	BJ Farms	Lundgren	Bjorklund	Thomas
Increase concentration	goal = 10% increase	goal = 10% increase	--------	--------
Increase penetration	--------	--------	10% of farm purchases	15% of farm purchases
$1,000,000 sales	$125,000	$80,000	$25,000	$18,000

To summarize, goals should be set for each key account. You base the account goal on a realistic analysis of needs and potential. These goals help focus the sales strategy and help measure effectiveness with the account. Upon learning more about your key accounts, you may uncover more needs than you expected, and you can revise your goal upward. Or, you may uncover more resistance than you expected, and you must revise your goal downward. If you keep your goals for key accounts current at all times, you will find it easier to know where to spend your time, and you will have a clear sense at all times of your progress toward territory goals.

Some salespeople resist setting key account goals, especially for new accounts, until they have had a chance to talk several times with the account and learn about the account's needs. That is not only acceptable - it is to be recommended when the account is very large or very new, or when you have little background information. However, whether key account goals are set during your planning process or only after you have begun implementing the first few calls in your strategy, they should be set and then regularly reviewed. And remember - together, your key accounts should provide the bulk of your sales in your overall sales goal.

2. Key Account History/Information

Whether or not you have personally worked with an account in the past, it's a good idea to assemble as much information as possible about the account before planning your strategy. You need to learn all you can is so that you can make the best use of your time and the customer's time in each sales call. For example, if the account has been recommended to you by another supplier, someone in your business, or a current customer, ask some basic questions.

- What is important to this account?
- Why do you think they might fit well with our business (products or services)?
- What can you tell me about how this business makes decisions?
- Are there any topics or areas I should stay away from?
- What kinds of products or services might be a good "fit" for this business?

One of the most critical pieces of account information is that of sales history. If this is an unfamiliar account, try to find someone in your business who has knowledge of the account's purchase history. Often, in local retail businesses, the most wasted resource is a fellow employee who has worked with the customer in the past, or the bookkeeper who could share purchase history with you.

Sometimes, reviewing account histories or customer records can be a challenge, even if the customer has bought from you in the past. Increasingly, companies are filing detailed customer purchase histories in an electronic database. If you cannot access this directly, find someone who can help you get the information you need.

In many organizations, important key account information is filed "between the ears" of the last person who worked with the account. It is worth your time to talk to that person, even if he or she has since left the business (assuming he or she didn't go to your competitor). The more information you have about each key account, the better job you will be able to do for them.

It is useful to have the following detailed information on key accounts:

- purchase history by product;
- average price paid vs. list price (discount history);
- timing of purchases (remember, purchase decisions happen earlier each year);
- quantities purchased;
- services used;
- payment record;
- complaint history.

3. Learn Key Account Business Goals and Needs

The salesperson has goals that guide how time and resources are spent. Your larger accounts have business goals also. In today's market, many large farm accounts may produce grain, fiber, specialty crops, milk or livestock worth $500,000 or more each year. They have budgets and cash flow statements, just like any other business their size. They have close relationships with their banker and their accountant, and most of them have a firm idea of what they want to achieve in their business. If you are selling to distributors or retailers, or buying grain contracts, you are working with businesspeople who may manage millions of dollars each year. These accounts know how they will measure their success or failure: growth, profitability, market leadership, or safeguarding their assets.

In order to be successful with these key accounts year after year, the salesperson needs to find out what the key account wants to achieve in their business. Only then is the salesperson in a position to help the customer meet business goals – not just sell them products or services. Unless you understand the business goals of your customer, you will simply be pushing your products – and your goals – on the customer. As a result, you will find yourself re-selling them each year instead of being able to use last year's success as a building block to your future together. What are some typical business goals for larger accounts?

Farmers/ranchers
        Increase yield (bushels, animals finished, pounds milk)
        Expand the operation
        Improve financial position (reduce leverage)
        Reduce labor/equipment expenses
        Improve profits
        Maintain the operation for the next generation

Dealers/Retailers
>
> Increase sales
> Increase business with top farmers
> Sell more of the most profitable products
> Improve expertise
> Reduce expenses
> Upgrade equipment/rolling stock
> Improve financial results

Distributors
>
> Increase sales
> Strengthen dealer relationships
> Grow manager skills to strengthen the business
> Improve inventory control
> Purchase more efficiently
> Improve return on investment

The motivation and needs that underlie the goals of each key account will be specific to that account. They may be very different from other key accounts in your territory. These goals greatly affect their purchase decisions – what they buy, when they buy it, how they pay for it, and what services they want. Each set of key account goals requires a different selling approach. For example, a farmer who is interested in maintaining the operation for a son or daughter has very different goals than an aggressive young farmer who is rapidly expanding. Your selling strategy must reflect those goals.

Debbie Stiles
BASF Canada
Senior Marketing Associate, Soybean Products
Guelph, Ontario, Canada

Sit down with account first...go in with no predetermined notions about the account...find out everything you could want or need to know about their business...dollar volume, etc. You have the option as a new person to ask a lot of questions that someone more experienced to that area might not be allowed or reasonably be able to ask. Once you've found out, look at the sales figures, the history of that dealer in their business. Find out from others about that customer...then create your own customer profile. Who are key contacts, sales figures, history, competitive advantages, strengths and weaknesses of each dealer.

I have a database in my computer for each of my dealers. I organize my year from four pages: overall sales rating of dealers, dealer profile, dealer history and the rebates back to them.

The first one, the overall sales rating of all the dealers, shows whom I need to spend my time with. It helps break out who are movers and shakers and who needs to be pushed a little. Then, for each key dealer who collectively moves 80 percent of my business, I create a profile of the dealer that states who are key contacts, what are the different contracts or programs they are working with us on...and a quick summary of their sales dollar volume and the rebates that we may or may not give back to the dealer. I usually compare current year to previous year. And that gives me a starting point there.

On the next sheet, I have sales history in a table and in a graph which shows me where their trends have been going for the last 4-5 years. It is also a good tool to show them to get their feedback and input on where they think they are going.

The last sheet on that dealer is broken down by program: the number of dollars per unit and the number of units that are involved with that program and the total dollars...Then I can show the dealer the rebate margins. I keep a hard copy so I can write notes and then I can get current information from dealers. I update those databases three times a year. It's probably not enough, but it's what works now. That's what I build my whole year on. It is a system.

I like to, no, really <u>need</u> to approach this business as a business and keeping good records and keeping organized data on accounts is the best way I've found to do

continued...

that. If I am organized and understand where I am with whom, I am better prepared to approach my customers in a business-like manner. They are in business to make money. I respect that. Organization helps me plan and develop effective strategies to conduct business with these customers.

4. Develop a Product and Service Bundle That Supports Key Account Goals

Once a goal for a key account has been set, and you have learned as much as you can about the account's history, goals and needs, you can begin developing a "bundle" of products and services that meet identified needs better than anyone else.

In some situations, you may have worked with a key account before, and may have a good idea of their needs. You'll want to confirm them and update your knowledge, rather than assuming you already know what's important. In other situations, you may not know the account well, and you must devote several sales calls to learning about needs, priorities and values. (See Chapter 11 for more detailed information about asking questions and uncovering needs.) Let's look at an example.

> *Elaine worked in an area with 15-18 very large dairies (500-2000 cows). She had called on each of them several times in the first few months in her territory. They slowly started warming up to her and began sharing some of their business goals and production challenges. As Elaine began to work with the first two or three dairies, she found that she was creating a few "special programs" to meet their needs. She also found herself calling her manager more than once, asking to make a few exceptions in other areas such as the limit on financing, or product delivery policy. As she added accounts from his "top 20" list, she soon found that she was negotiating much the same type of product and service package with all these large accounts. One day it hit her: these dairymen were really as much alike in their business needs as if they all belonged to the same club, or had learned dairy farming from the same source, even though they were 20 unique personalities. She decided to develop a "21st Century Dairy" program that was especially appealing to this group of dairies. The program created a package or "bundle" of products, services, educational events and discounts designed to fit these farmers' needs. While anyone was eligible for the 21st Century Dairy program, essentially only the larger, more progressive dairies purchased the volume necessary to be included. Elaine got approval for the program from her manager and looked forward to her best year ever.*

Whether a value bundle is created for one key account or a group of key accounts, it should:

- meet the business needs of the customer (or needs of customers in the segment for which it was designed);
- differentiate you from the competition;
- be profitable for you to offer;
- help you achieve your territory goals and your company's strategies.

5. Make the Best Use of Resources

When planning a strategy for key accounts, you may find that you don't personally have all the resources you need to meet their needs. Perhaps you need technical expertise from a veterinarian, a nutritionist, an agronomist, or an engineer to help in developing a facility. Perhaps you need business expertise from a specialist in commodity marketing, grain purchasing, farm inheritance planning or farm corporations. Perhaps you need other marketing resources, such as purchase incentive programs, cooperative advertising support, newsletters, brochures, or caps and jackets.

In almost all larger companies, one can find someone who has the expertise or the resources needed to answer a question or solve a problem. Even in smaller companies and dealerships, there are often technical support services offered by basic suppliers, and sometimes you can form alliances with other companies who specialize in complementary products/services that help you get the job done. In most cases, even though your company's experts and marketing managers have many duties already, they enjoy spending time talking to customers about your products or helping you think through a creative approach.

To find these resources, start by asking your manager. If he or she does not know whom to call, ask the Marketing Department at your company's regional or home office. Be ready to explain your opportunity and to ask specific questions about resources. Or ask the manufacturing sales rep who calls in your dealership for help in locating specialists or product literature.

You can also search the Internet for articles that will help your customer or interest him/her. At your local land grant university you will find many experts. Some of these specialists are specifically employed by your tax dollars to provide their expertise to farmers and other agricultural businesses. To locate someone near you, call the university switchboard and ask for the Cooperative Extension Service.

Whether you are using company personnel, manufacturer support, university professors or extension agents, you need to allow time to assemble your resources. Your needs will have to be fit into their already busy schedules. In general, you should allow:

- 2-6 weeks to schedule a conference with a company expert;
- 3-4 weeks to schedule a university person;
- 1-2 weeks to schedule an extension agent.

6. Measure Satisfaction and Revise Account Goals

When putting together a key account strategy, the salesperson needs to plan ways to measure the account's satisfaction. In spite of what many salespeople believe, customers don't always change suppliers because they find a similar product for less money from a competitor. More often, they leave a company because their expectations haven't been met, however unrealistic these expectations may have been. They may feel they didn't get the service they expected, or simply that you take them for granted. (We'll explore these issues more fully in Chapter 16.)

Satisfied customers are those whose expectations have been met or exceeded. It follows, then, that you must set specific expectations, together with your key account, so that you know the standard against which your company's performance will be judged. This also provides the opportunity to "manage expectations." If your customers' expectations are unrealistic, you can bring them back down. It is infinitely better to *slightly exceed* expectations than to *slightly miss* them.

Once you know the customer's expectations, satisfaction can be measured in several ways. Regular contacts with the customer - even if you have nothing to "sell" that day - are one of the best ways to monitor the account's satisfaction and to identify areas of misunderstanding or irritation while they are still minor. Specific follow-up calls after a sale help ensure that the account knows how to use your products and services, and allow you to reinforce the expectations you set when the product or service was sold. With the permission of the decision maker, you can also talk with farm or ranch employees about their experiences with your products and services. Finally, many of the best salespeople complete a formal "satisfaction audit" every year, to reinforce the benefits of doing business with your company and to uncover any dissatisfaction.

It is amazing what you can learn from a customer just by asking them! Finding out that a key account is dissatisfied isn't always pleasant, but telling you about their problems is a whole lot better than if they tell their neighbors...or worse, simply go to your competitor without giving you a second chance. And, just taking the time and having the courage to ask communicates a powerful message to your account - that you really care.

Making It Happen – From Account Strategy to Call Planning

Your key account strategy is your plan for building a relationship, selling, servicing and growing a key account. Within this overall "game plan," you will have many contacts with your key account. Some may be formal sales calls. Others may be "accidental" or informal contacts, such as bidding on your key account's 4-H steer at the county fair, or arranging to be at a seminar he or she will be attending. Formal sales calls and informal influence and relationship-building activities must flow together seamlessly – that's the whole point of having a key account strategy. Each activity with a key account should build your understanding of their needs and their trust in your professionalism. Each activity or sales call should also have a plan. This plan doesn't need to be elaborate, and often may not even be written down. Yet the *thinking process* of planning each contact or call is critical.

Again, each individual call, like bricks in a foundation, builds on the call before and anticipates the next call. The results of a series of well-planned calls include a thorough understanding of customer needs, the development of "value bundles" that meet those needs, and customer satisfaction. The blueprint that ties all these calls together into a sound structure is your key account strategy. And, much like an agricultural engineer who designs and then supervises the building of a conservation structure (pond) or a new farrowing barn, you must be alert to how the knowledge you gain, as you build this relationship, should alter and strengthen the design of the strategy.

Figure 10.4 on the following page illustrates how each individual call and its call objectives integrate into the key account strategy. This example describes a manufacturer sales rep selling crop protection products to a retailer.

Figure 10.4
Planning Call Objectives Within a Key Account Strategy

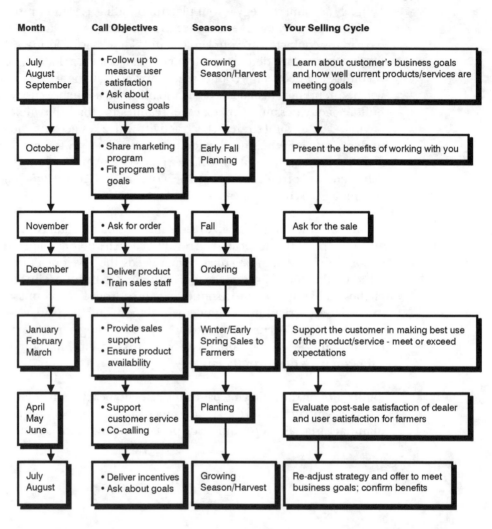

Month	Call Objectives	Seasons	Your Selling Cycle
July August September	• Follow up to measure user satisfaction • Ask about business goals	Growing Season/Harvest	Learn about customer's business goals and how well current products/services are meeting goals
October	• Share marketing program • Fit program to goals	Early Fall Planning	Present the benefits of working with you
November	• Ask for order	Fall	Ask for the sale
December	• Deliver product • Train sales staff	Ordering	
January February March	• Provide sales support • Ensure product availability	Winter/Early Spring Sales to Farmers	Support the customer in making best use of the product/service - meet or exceed expectations
April May June	• Support customer service • Co-calling	Planting	Evaluate post-sale satisfaction of dealer and user satisfaction for farmers
July August	• Deliver incentives • Ask about goals	Growing Season/Harvest	Re-adjust strategy and offer to meet business goals; confirm benefits

Planning Each Sales Call

Each sales call should involve a *thinking process.* There are five steps involved in that thinking process: the objective of the call; your plan for the call – how it will flow; the results you anticipate from the call; the evaluation of whether you achieved anticipated results; the adjustment of your call strategy and follow-up activities.

Figure 10.5
Call Planning Elements

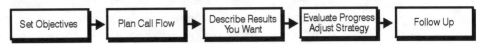

Clearly, different types of sales activities will have different objectives, plans, anticipated results, and follow-up steps. A call on a new customer will flow differently than a call on an old friend. A call to handle a product complaint certainly feels very different than a call to deliver a rebate check or a voucher for product the customer has earned through your marketing program. Regardless of the type of activity or call, however, there should be an objective, flow plan, anticipated results, measurement and follow-up activity in place before you call. Actually, most people are quite good at this sort of planning in those areas of their life that are <u>really</u> important to them. Let's look at two examples.

> *David first met Stephanie when they were assigned to the same case study team in college. From that first meeting, she knocked his socks off, and he was determined to get to know her better. Maybe there really was such a thing as love at first sight, after all. He decided that, at the very worst, they could become good friends, and began to think about how he could begin building this friendship (overall strategy). He started by asking her out for coffee after a study group. His goal was just to learn a little more about her, outside the classroom (objective). He was pretty nervous, and he thought they might start by talking about their interests outside of school (flow plan). He hoped that, after this non-date, she might be willing to see him again on a "real" date (anticipated results). To his surprise, they both loved canoeing, and they agreed to get together with a few friends the next weekend and spend the day on the river. True, it wasn't really a "date," but David felt pretty happy about it anyway (measure). He called her in mid-week to tell her when and where the group would be leaving (follow-up), and they had another good talk. Somehow, talking to Stephanie seemed like the most natural thing in the world, and David thought they might become friends sooner than he had thought (strategy adjustment).*

> *Peter's "dream career" was to work with one of the large feed companies, helping forward-thinking swine producers build their businesses through new genetic, feed and facilities technology. His overall game plan (strategy) was to get hired by one of the top companies as a sales or marketing rep, and then build his business base through top-of-the-line products and services. Eventually, he wanted to be located near the town where he grew up, but he was content to live somewhere else for 5-10 years first. The first step in the strategy was to decide which company he wanted to work for (objective). His plan was to meet with on-campus recruiters and also to talk with the local reps of each company in his home area (flow plan).*

He anticipated that, at the end of this research, he would be able to make a good choice (anticipated results). He decided he would judge a "good choice" by whether he got hired and then was able to work with customers in the way he liked (measure). When Peter received an offer from one of his top choices, he called the field rep he knew from home and asked a few more detailed questions before making a final decision (follow-up). Peter accepted the job, and began planning the next step in his overall strategy – building a local base of loyal, forward-thinking customers.

Let's look at some examples of how call objectives and call plans might vary for different types of sales activities (Table 10.2).

Table 10.2
Sample Call Plans

Plan Element	New Customer	Re-selling	Service Call	Complaint Handling	Customer Satisfaction
Objective	• Get acquainted • Learn about needs	• Confirm last year's purchase • Sell same or more	• Add value to product by providing planter calibration	• Investigate complaint • Resolve if possible	• Assess customer satisfaction with weed control
Plan	• Visit farm • Discuss needs and goals • Leave literature on new product	• Arrange time to meet w/all decision makers • Evaluate last year's performance • Get order	• Make appointment • calibrate planter for our product • Test calibration for accuracy • Discuss benefits	• Meet in the affected field • View damage • Assess loss • Determine cause • Discuss resolution	• Scout field in June and again in August • Report results to farmer • Discuss any issues
Anticipated Results	• Customer agrees to 2nd call	• Order	• Customer understands how to calibrate • Customer tells neighbors of value-add	• Customer knows we will help	• Customer appreciate our commitment
Measure	• Set appointment for 2nd call	• Size of order	• Customer re-purchase • Customer neighbors purchase	• Customer agrees to plan to handle the issue	• No unexpected problems • Easier sale next year
Follow-up	• Send any requested information	• Send note to thank customer	• Call during planting to answer any questions	• Contact manager • Call customer with resolution	• Submit scouting report

Now, let's look at each element of the sales call plan in more detail.

Call Objectives

Every call should have a specific objective. The objective states what you want to accomplish with the call. The objective should be stated so that it can be clearly understood and measured.

- Be clear and concrete - can you determine if you achieved it? Could you state it to your customer as the reason for calling?
- Be realistic - sales success with large commercial accounts is a process that can take months or even years; know what you want to achieve in this call as you build toward a key account relationship.
- Keep it simple - wanting to achieve everything in one call may mean you don't achieve anything very well.
- Be action oriented - does something specific happen as a result of the call? What will you or the customer do - what action will result?

Calling on a key account without an objective firmly in mind is the mark of an amateur - someone who hasn't yet understood that a key account's time is his or her most precious commodity. Salespeople sometimes resist this notion, because they like to "stop by" and visit with key accounts, often without having something specific to sell and sometimes without an appointment. However, if you ask these salespeople *why* they stop by so frequently, they might respond with something like this:

- *This customer just likes to see me when I'm in the area.*
- *It's important to keep the relationship strong.*
- *I can learn a lot from this guy about what's new in the area.*

In fact, some of these salespeople <u>do</u> have objectives for their call firmly in mind! However, they are not "selling" objectives as much as "learning" or "relationship-building" objectives. These objectives are important, too, especially with key accounts for whom a strong personal relationship is a prerequisite for a loyal professional relationship.

Traditionally, sales objectives were written from your point of view as the salesperson - what <u>you</u> wanted to achieve with the call. That is still valid, because it helps you see how each call builds toward achievement of your key account strategy. However, it is also critical to think about the objective for each call from the <u>customer's</u> perspective. We've all heard this old expression: "You can lead a horse to water, but you can't make him drink." You can have the objective of presenting benefits of your products and services, but if the customer doesn't see how these fit his or her business, you won't achieve much!

Stating your objectives from the customer's perspective is a good "reality check." Are you offering something of value - information, services, an analysis - in every call? You should be. Let's look at some examples of how you can "check" your objective by re-stating it from the customer's perspective.

Table 10.3
Objectives: Your Perspective, Customer's Perspective

Your objective is...	The customer will...
...to introduce yourself and your organization	...see me as a supplier worthy of his or her consideration
...to communicate to the customer how our products and services can benefit his or her business	...see that we offer solutions to his needs and more value than other choices
...to give the customer a competitive bid for his or her business	...see that we offer the best bundle of products, services and prices
...to demonstrate our knowledge of production dynamics	...accept that our expertise would be useful in solving production issues of problems

Notice that some discussion - asking questions, listening to the answers, and building a solution together - is necessary to achieve your sales objective from the customer's perspective. Your call plan spells out how that will happen - how you will guide the call so that it is more than a presentation. It helps you learn more about your customer each time you work with him or her.

The Call Plan

A call objective helps the salesperson focus on why he/she is calling and what he/she wants to achieve. A call plan helps the seller think through the actions to take, the questions to ask, and the sales aids to use to reach the objective.

One word of caution - if you are new to selling, you may assume that a good call objective and a detailed call plan will work like a road map - follow the plan and you'll be successful. Real sales calls are lively and dynamic. One can never predict which issue is at the top of the customer's priorities at the precise time of the sales call. You can't control whether a competitor called the day before, or a tank broke, or they just lost an employee. However, a call plan helps the salesperson assemble what is known about the account and then think through the logical next step for the relationship or the sale to follow. You may change it the moment you walk through the door, but without it you will likely fumble, or forget to ask a key question, and waste both your time and your customer's time.

Earl Bell
ELANCO Animal Health, Eli Lilly & Company
Sales Representative
Rocky Mount, North Carolina

Customers basically have to know why you are there, but at the same time, you have to use an artful way of not coming across where they get defensive. They gotta know that you bring more to the party and you are not just going to come in and pound them on product and price, information, etc. You are going to really try to help them be more successful, when you are calling on these different segments within a company (big customer). A purchasing agent, his need is to get the best price. A veterinarian, his need is to use a product to help his animals be less sick. A nutritionist is going to be looking at it from the standpoint of, is my feed efficiency going to be any better because nutrition is my side. You really have to be able to sort those out. That's three different groups and you have other people with different needs within a big company you call on. You are trying to sell all those different components. A lot of people get very frustrated trying to sell large accounts because of all those different components.

It can be done and done well. A company has to have a really good understanding— are they a price company? Are they a high price company that has to sell value, image, all these things that they do as problem solvers? You have to have that from the top down or else, you can go out here as a salesman and be doing the right thing and if your company doesn't understand it from the top down, you may be out here spinning your wheels.

A call plan can be very simple. The key element is to plan how this call will help each decision maker see that a partnership with you can help them meet their business goals. In order to put a good plan together, you'll want to consider the account's probable needs; personal characteristics; and how you compare to the competition. The best call plans consider:

- probable needs of this account at this point in their relationship with you
  - ➤ expertise
  - ➤ product solutions
  - ➤ service
  - ➤ relationship support

- important personal characteristics:
  - ➤ where they are in their unique decision process
  - ➤ how quickly they make a decision – impulse vs. analysis
  - ➤ how they source information
  - ➤ your personal value to them as a professional salesperson

- how you stack up to the competition
  - ➤ other businesses they use
  - ➤ other businesses that are actively selling to them
  - ➤ your differential advantage
  - ➤ relationship support

The call plan describes what you will do or bring to the account during the call that will result in value for the account. For more complex calls, such as those on multi-level accounts or integrated businesses, your call plan may need to be more complex. This is particularly true when you are calling with someone else (such as an agronomist, engineer or your manager), or when you are calling on several decision makers at the same time. Figure 10.6 shows an example of a more complex call plan.

Figure 10.6
Oak Hill Farms Call Plan

Account Name: Oak Hill Farms **Key Contact:** John James, Purchasing Mgr.
Business Goals: Production and processing of high-quality pork for hotel and restaurant market.
Calling on: John James, Manager; Ben Archer, Nutritionist; Gil Williams, Nursery Manager.

Probable needs of this account at this point in their relationship with you:
Identified need to improve nursery productivity and reduce mortality:
- expertise to achieve better weights for pigs entering grower phase;
- product solutions that return more value than they cost;
- service to support implementation of any new feeding regimen.

How they buy: Considering change in feed program; need to see data before deciding; purchasing manager most interested in cost; nutritionist and nursery manager most interested in solving nursery mortality and increasing throughput.

Objective: To gain agreement that our medicated nursery feeds can improve weight gain for young pigs and reduce nursery mortality in similar situations, and to demonstrate how these results could thus improve nursery productivity and allow faster throughput for Oak Hill.

Sales Team: Self, our nutritionist (specialty in nursery feeds), our veterinarian

Other Sales Aids: Data from similar operations on productivity gains using our medicated early weaning program

Plan:
- Ask for meeting of our experts and theirs to discuss ways nursery productivity could be improved (re-state objective to customer)
- Coordinate date for meeting with our team and theirs; get 2 hours blocked

Call:
- Introduce everyone
- Ask Oak Hill Farms team to confirm some of the challenges they have shared with me, so our experts can make sure they understand the issues from their experts
- Discuss some potential strategies for improving nursery productivity and where we might be able to help
- Share data we will bring, as it fits the discussion and supports our suggestions
- Ask permission to put proposal together, outlining the solutions discussed and their cost

Anticipated Results: Permission to put together a bid for their nursery feed business

Measure: Set date for receiving bid from us and date to review it with them

Follow-up: Send any additional information requested during the meeting. Send proposal as scheduled and set date to review with the purchasing manager or designee.

Anticipated Results

When you plan for a call, stating the results you want from the call makes it easier to measure your progress. Anticipated results are not always exactly the same as your call objective, but they should always be related to your call objective. Let's look at some examples (Table 10.4):

Table 10.4
Call Objectives and Corresponding Anticipated Results

Call objectives	Anticipated Results
...to learn about this customer's business - size, number of employees, decision-making process, goals if possible	...to be able to have enough information to plan a "fit" for our products and services in this business
...to discuss how our products and services could increase rolling herd average	...to be able to put together a formal sales proposal for the business
...to show the dealer how our marketing program could maximize profits	...to improve efforts to sell and service our products with local farmers
...to teach dealer feed reps the features and benefits of our new medicated calf starter	...to increase higher sales of calf starter and increase penetration of local market
...to provide value-added service to our corn rootworm insecticide by calibrating farmers' planters	...to see better "pull-through" of our corn rootworm insecticide at the dealer level

Measures

The measures included in the call plan are always closely linked to the results anticipated. For example, if the result you anticipate is "better pull-through of corn rootworm insecticides at the dealer level," how will you measure that? You could use a variety of indicators:

- records of dealership sales of your product;
- records of walk-in or telephone requests for information (you may have to provide a small incentive to collect these);
- discussions with farmers who have bought the product – where they heard about the calibration program, what value they think it has, whether they found it added enough value to give your product an advantage;
- discussions with dealer sales reps.

Measures are often very simple – if you wanted to get enough information to write a proposal, did you get it? Either you can write the proposal or you can't. If you wanted to sell a certain amount of product, did you sell it? Either you did or you didn't. Why go to the trouble of setting specific measures as you plan each call? Most agricultural salespeople work with customers day in and day out with little contact or coaching from their manager or more experienced peers. It is simply the nature of the industry – relatively few people trying to meet the needs of customer through products and services over a broad geography.

In addition, when you call on farmers, you are calling on lots of independent business people who are not nicely clustered in a shopping mall or downtown, but who may live 100 miles or more apart. Although dealers are consolidating, that doesn't mean they are any closer together. All agricultural salespeople find they spend a lot of time in the car. In essence they are alone except for the radio and maybe a car phone. As a result, they learn to become their own coaches and teachers, with the help of their customers.

The best salespeople analyze every call, trying to figure out what they could have done differently or better. If you have set specific measures for your call's "success," this analysis is much more focused. And, you will find you often have the opportunity to pat yourself on the back for bringing your key account relationship one step closer to a true partnership.

Follow-up

The salesperson's key account strategy is designed to build strong and loyal customer relationships. Each call, each promise, each expectation met or un-met works like a "moment of truth." If the salesperson delivers on the promise, he/she builds trust. If he/she doesn't deliver, trust will develop more slowly – if at all. It often seems unfair, especially to new salespeople, that they can do everything "right" in the first five calls in their strategy and then lose the sale this year because they forgot to call the customer back and answer a question. Yet it happens.

The follow-up portion of your plan is usually quite simple – to get back to the account with any information requested:

- Anticipated result: Customer understands how our product could improve yield.
- Measure: Customer asks for information or analysis of how profit would improve.
- Follow-up: Send requested information.

Occasionally, if your objective was to create another opportunity for contact or for selling, your follow-up will be to execute this opportunity.

- Anticipated result: Customer will see the value of allowing us to bid on the design of his new multiple-site production facility.

- Measure: We are asked to submit a bid.
- Follow-up: Deliver the bid within 2 weeks and schedule a time to discuss it.

Specific follow-up strategies are discussed in more detail in Chapter 16.

Summary

Your key account strategy is your "game plan" for getting and keeping the business of a key account. It includes the sales calls and sales activities you make when first establishing a relationship with the account, when making your first sales, and when servicing those sales. It usually spans a period of several years, and so it eventually also includes your strategies for managing the satisfaction of your key account.

The key account strategy is as good as the quality of information used to build it. Therefore, you must uncover all possible relevant information before putting a key account strategy together, and you must constantly adjust and re-adjust your strategy as you learn more about the account's needs and decision making processes.

Within the key account strategy, individual sales calls and activities are planned. These calls may be of many different types, depending on your relationship with the account, the time of year or where they are in their buying cycle, how they make decisions, and whether you have one buyer or many decision makers in the account.

Each activity or sales call should have an objective – a statement of what you want to achieve with this call, and why it will be worth the customer's time to talk with you. The objective is not always to "sell" – it may be to share expertise or build the relationship. Again, the objective should be appropriate for the selling/buying cycle, the customer's decision making process, and your overall strategy.

Many experienced salespeople find that, while a call objective is both necessary and helpful, it is not enough. They prefer to spend a little time thinking through how the call will flow, so that they can be as prepared as possible. Planning the call flow is particularly advisable if you are calling on an account with more than one decision maker or if you are calling with others from your company.

Along with the call plan and call objective, many salespeople state the results they anticipate from the call, and how they will measure these results. This gives them a sense of progress toward their ultimate goal of getting the key account's business, and also helps them uncover ways to improve.

Finally, every call or contact should have some follow-up. It might be as simple as a thank-you note or sending an article you saw on the Internet. It might be as complex as a business proposal. The key to follow-up – as with all key account strategy elements – is to send your key account a consistent and unmistakable message that you are the best possible solution to his or her business needs.

Review Questions

1. Describe a key account strategy. List the steps that outline a key account strategy.

2. What is a selling cycle and why is it important to the agri salesperson? How does a key account selling strategy relate with a selling cycle?

3. What vital piece of information does the salesperson need to learn from a key account? Why is it critical information?

4. Define sales call objectives. Why is it important to have sales call objectives for each call?

5. How do you develop a sales call plan? What are some key elements to include in your plan and why?

Chapter Eleven

Opening the Call to Build a Customer Relationship

Learning Objectives:

Upon completion of this chapter, you will be able to:

1. understand that a sound personal relationship is at the heart of every sound business relationship;
2. understand the power of first impressions in setting the tone for a productive business relationship;
3. be able to create a positive first impression;
4. recognize that customers have unique and different behavioral styles that affect how they evaluate salespeople, products and services;
5. use your knowledge of customer styles to more easily build rapport with a new account;
6. transition from building rapport to opening a sales call.

The Power of Personal Relationships

The foundation for every successful sale is the relationship with the customer. A good business relationship begins with and is built on a sound human relationship.

When you meet a prospective customer for the first time, everything you do and say will have an impact on your relationship - your appearance, your body language, what you say and the way you say it - everything. Even when you already know the customer, all of these things are important. Each time you make contact with the customer you have the opportunity to maintain and grow the relationship.

People seldom buy from people they don't like – unless they have no alternative. Relationships can deteriorate unless some effort is made to maintain them. Many a good customer has been lost because the salesperson has taken the customer for granted. It is clearly in the salesperson's best interest not to let this happen, but rather to start each relationship off with a positive first impression and then to continue to build on that positive impression in each succeeding call. A good relationship often generates a great deal of loyalty. Very often, customers have more loyalty to the person they buy from than they have to the brand or company. In fact, it is common for customers to evaluate a product more favorably because of their positive feelings for the salesperson. So there are many good reasons to focus on getting off on the right foot – and cultivating a strong relationship with customers.

Martin Harry
BASF Canada, Inc.
Technical Sales Representative
Ingersoll, Ontario, Canada

I really strive to be a partner of the customers I serve. That's a nice way to look toward a goal of being a partner with the dealer. I may pick up something of interest that may help them. And they may share something with me, like the dealer yesterday showing me his new plans, new philosophy, new direction for the business. That's not something they need to share with me, but it's a partnership sharing.

I was in a place two weeks ago where they just got a new DTN and they weren't happy with it sitting back there for the employees and nobody was using it. He said to me, "I don't see the advantage of this thing. You've seen a lot, what do you think?" I told him, "What you want to do is get it up here on the counter for the customers to use." Yesterday I went in and he said, "Hey, thanks for your input on this...it's working out really well."

That kind of relationship doesn't happen overnight. You have to build that partnership – the kind of partnership or relationship that helps you pick up on their cues. There's a rapport, a trust, a connection that makes them feel they can offer a cue to me and I will know them and their business well enough to pick up on it.

Building customer relationships happens throughout each sales call, but it is most critical at the beginning of a call and especially in the first call. Therefore, we'll deal with building relationships and opening the call in the same chapter.

To open a call successfully, you must do five things:

- create a positive impression;
- get the prospect's attention;
- arouse their interest in your product or service;
- build rapport;
- bridge to a discussion of needs.

These objectives are listed in logical sequence - but in the real world of selling they may not occur in precisely this order. They may overlap, or a particular technique may help you achieve two or more of these objectives at once. However, all of these are clearly important to developing a solid relationship with each account, and in building on that relationship to provide business solutions.

There is no one type of call opening that works "best" across all branches of agribusiness and with current customers as well as prospective customers. For example, a small farmer whom you've known for years may want to visit with you for awhile before getting down to business. A veterinarian in a large, busy clinic wants to know - right away - if you have information she can use. A vegetable/truck market customer may want to talk about yield goals and disease problems right away. An information service customer may already have decided what he wants when he enters your dealership and wants to talk "Internet" almost before you've said hello.

Opening a call successfully is not only different in different branches of an industry; it is different for different types of businesses (farmer, dealer, distributor). There are also critical differences between customers within each industry. These differences depend on the basic behavioral and communication style of each customer.

The biggest single factor that determines the nature of how each call is opened is the previous relationship with the customer or prospect. Your opening with a long-time customer will, of course, be very different than with a new account you have never met before. But personality (yours and theirs), the situation, the time of day - and a host of other factors - will impact your sales call opening. Common sense must prevail; no one knows your customers as well as you do.

There are, however, some keys to developing strong customer relationships, as experienced salespeople have learned. New salespeople often are intimidated by the huge task of building relationships with a large group of potential customers, especially if they represent large commercial operations, often with more technical knowledge and management "savvy" than the salesperson. Is there any hope for a new salesperson? Are the only successful salespeople the ones who come to the job with excellent communication skills, excellent product knowledge and excellent knowledge of the local market? No. While communication skills, product knowledge and market knowledge are all very important, anyone can learn to build solid customer relationships.

The key to a sound customer relationship and a successful sales effort is to adjust your communication to the customer. This is wise at every point in the call, but especially when you open the call. Salesperson performance depends, in large part, "upon their unique interactions with each buyer" rather than any tendency on their part to perform consistently well or poorly.[49]

Creating a Positive First Impression

The impression the salesperson creates in the first few minutes of the call is crucial. Creating a favorable impression will not necessarily make the sale. However, allowing a negative impression to form in the prospect's mind may be enough to block the sale. Fortunately, everyone has a comprehensive set of experiences *as a buyer* that helps them recognize some obvious pitfalls – such as being too pushy, or assuming too much too soon.

Begin with the golden rule – but with a twist: most customers want you to treat them the way they would like others to treat them. That means you need to understand how they normally act, and then adjust your self-presentation to make them as comfortable with you as possible.

In agricultural selling, there are three levels of "adjustment" the salesperson will need to make in order to create a positive impression and begin building a relationship:

- meet the basic expectation of any consumer relationship;
- meet the "cultural norms" of the business or person to whom you are selling;
- meet the customer's personal behavioral "norms."

[49] Cronin, J.J. Analysis of the Buyer-Seller Dyad: The Social Relations Model. Journal of Personal Selling and Sales Management, Volume XIV, Number 3 – Summer 1994), pp 69-77.

Meet Basic Consumer Expectations

As a consumer, you may have experienced more than one situation when a salesperson treated you poorly. They may not have listened to you. They may have seemed distracted. They may even have seemed disinterested. The result was a poor first impression – and often, although you never complained to their manager, you tried to find the item you needed somewhere else the next time.

We all have certain basic expectations when we are the customer. As the retail market has become more competitive, many businesses have responded by improving the customer relations skills of their employees – and our expectations have increased. Even a large discount chain like WalMart now has a "greeter" at the door. The local supermarket may have someone to carry out customer groceries. Many department store clerks will call you by name when they hand your charge card back.

The salesperson must meet or exceed the basic expectations of the customer for salesperson performance. To put it another way, if you are selling a $150,000 piece of equipment, you should be able to behave at least as well as the best clerk in your local drugstore or the telemarketer who answers the phone at your favorite catalog. What are the basic expectations for personal selling?

How You Look

Comedian Billy Crystal had an act portraying a character who repeatedly stated: "It's not how you feel, it's how you look – and you look marvelous...." Creating a positive impression begins with good hygiene. You should be neatly dressed, in appropriate clothing (more about this later). Evaluate yourself carefully, and if you have a question, choose the more conservative alternative. Your vehicle and your briefcase or sales notebook are a part of how you look. Both should be clean, free of clutter, and in good repair.

How You Arrive

Above all, be on time. Distributors and dealers have many responsibilities, and often spend half their time or more out of the office. Farmers also have many good choices for where they could be, other than spending time with you. This is as true for cash grain farmers in the Midwest as for corporate farmers in the Imperial Valley. If you have made an appointment (highly recommended), they will notice whether you are on time. You want your customer to trust you with the future of their business – so make sure you keep the first promise you make. If your customer happens to be one of the many who are sticklers for promptness, you can absolutely ruin your chances if you show up late, even if you have a good excuse. "Not fair," you say. But the customer sets the rules and deals out the consequences.

Many salespeople consider the start of the sales call to be when they pull their vehicle into the parking area. Don't announce your arrival with a screech of brakes and a cloud of dust. Apply common-sense courtesy. In a business, don't take a parking place away from customers, or park where your vehicle will block access to a drive or garage. On a farm, don't park where trucks need to move in and out. If you're not sure where to park – ask. The act of asking – especially if it is a prospect you don't know well – helps create an impression of sensitivity.

How You Greet the Customer

Your greeting should be more than a mumbled "Hello, how are you" that neither of you takes seriously. Try to greet your customer or prospect with friendly confidence. In order to do this, you have to develop the "right" frame of mind before ever making contact. Regardless of how your day has gone, your customer will evaluate this call beginning with your greeting. Be positive.

State your name slowly and clearly. Many people find it difficult to remember a name the first time they hear it. Make it easy for them. You can help them by speaking in a strong voice and counting "1, 2, 3" quickly to yourself between your first and last name. This may seem corny at first, but you will be surprised how natural it sounds in practice. For example: " Hi...I'm Kelly (1, 2, 3) Spencer, with FastGro Feeds. I have a two o'clock appointment with Jack Hays." Introduce yourself to the first employee you meet – you need to know them, too, and they can direct you to your prospect. Some salespeople even choose to wear a professional-looking name tag to make it easy for the customer.

What do you do if this is a second call? You still don't know the prospect well and they will likely have trouble recalling who you are or your name. Don't assume that just because you have an appointment they will know who you are. He or she has had many other things to accomplish that day and probably hasn't been sitting there just waiting for you to stop by. Introduce yourself again – just as slowly and clearly as you did the first time. That means stating your name, the company you are with, and the time of your appointment. You may want to hand them your business card when introducing yourself, unless you are quite certain they know you well. Even when they act like they know you, they may be rapidly searching their brain to figure out exactly who you are. Remember the cardinal rule – make it easy and comfortable for them.

It is a very good idea to learn how to pronounce the prospect's name correctly. You can check with other salespeople in your company, others who know the prospect, or ask the prospect directly. If your prospect gives you a nickname, make a note of it and use it, whether it's "Sam" for Samantha or "Moose" for that lumberjack sitting across the desk. However, experienced salespeople know it's wise not to get too familiar too fast. If you have never met Mrs. Horner and you hear her subordinates call her Mrs. Horner, then you should call her Mrs. Horner as well. If you choose to use the last name of your customer and she is female, you'll have to choose Mrs., Ms., or Miss. If you're not sure - ask. You can't build a relationship with someone you consistently call by the wrong name. Besides, it's embarrassing.

Should the salesperson shake the customer's hand? In most cases, yes. Your customer may read a lot into that first handshake - make sure it is firm. If you have small hands, aim your handshake at the "web" between your customer's thumb and first finger - that avoids the pain of a too-firm handshake or from a ring on your customer's hands. If you are female, be aware that some male customers will give you "half" a handshake - clasping your fingers briefly and then letting go. Recognize that this is their attempt to be polite and make sure they don't hurt you by shaking hands too firmly. It may also signal, for male prospects, that they are uncomfortable and not quite sure how to deal with a female sales rep. A firm handshake initiated by a female is an excellent way to signal your professionalism and self-confidence. Occasionally, you'll meet someone who doesn't seem to want to shake hands. Don't force them to.

How You Converse

Getting a conversation started is one of the most difficult parts of opening a sales call with a new customer. You convey a weak impression if you awkwardly fumble around for the right words or seem to lack purpose. On the other hand, an overly aggressive start could cause your prospect to put you in the stereotyped "pushy salesperson" category, which they probably consider about as attractive as pond scum. Experienced salespeople usually have a clear idea of how they will open the conversation before they ever pull in the drive or walk in the store. Usually, they accomplish two things in the first minute or two. They break the ice (weather, humor, and news of work) and they state the objective of their call. This sets a professional but friendly tone for the meeting.

How You Act

Maintain good eye contact from the beginning to the end of the call. But "good eye contact" doesn't mean an unmoving stare. Show your interest and openness. Focus your full attention on the prospect. Consider what non-verbal messages you are sending as well. Your posture should be open, attentive, and neither too familiar nor too distant.

Your customer may offer you coffee or a snack. Accept if you like, but make sure you put cups and plates where you won't knock them over or leave rings on a beautiful natural wood finish. And, at the end of the sales call, make sure you remove any trash yourself. Leave your tobacco and/or gum in your car - you shouldn't chew or smoke in your customer's home or place of business, at least in the early stages of your relationship. And you should never indulge unless you are absolutely certain it is quite acceptable.

If you wish to take notes, it's a good idea to ask your prospect's permission ("I'd like to write some of this down, if it's OK"). Make sure you have your own paper and pen, and don't move anything on your prospect's desk to make room for your notepad, unless they invite you to. Taking notes is not a bad idea. Some salespeople new to the profession seem to think it makes them look unprofessional or it is impolite to take notes during a sales call. Not so. Taking notes lets the prospect know you are taking them seriously and makes them more secure that you won't forget some of the things that are important to them.

Meet the Cultural "Norms" of the Industry Branch

If you follow all the guidelines listed for meeting basic consumer expectations, you will be able to create a neutral impression - about as good as a well-trained salesperson in any retail store. You, however, are not working in any retail store. You are working in agriculture - an industry where farmers, as independent business people, and retail managers routinely purchase $100,000's of inputs each year. To build a relationship with your customers, you need to dress, act and converse in a way that shows your respect for they way they live, work and do business in their part of the country and their branch of the industry.

Clothing/Attire Selection

Think of your clothing as a kind of "uniform" you wear to work every day. Depending on where you are and what you are doing, you want to wear clothing that identifies you as "one of the group" but that looks professional and is also appropriate for the job at hand. Experienced sales reps often develop at least two and often three very distinct wardrobes over time.

- They have one set of clothes they wear to the company office - usually sport coats and slacks, or suits/dresses, or nice business casual clothing for companies that have adopted this policy.
- They have a second set of clothes they wear on customer calls - usually business casual for dealers and farmers, and sometimes suits/ties or suits/pantsuits to call on purchasing agents and veterinarians.

- They may have a third set of clothes they wear when working with the customer on-farm or in the dealership. For example, they will have disposable coveralls and boots if they work in confinement hog operations. They will have warm coveralls and boots if they spend much time helping "heat-check" dairy cows in Northern Minnesota. They will have a set of personal protective gear in the truck if they plan to help calibrate a sprayer.

The type of clothing you wear should make sense for the work you plan to do <u>and</u> should match or very slightly exceed the clothing worn by the person you call on. Wearing a dark, navy suit to call on a dealer is not just unnecessary – it can actually communicate the message that you don't know how people in that business dress and that you arrogantly assume it doesn't matter.

How You Arrive

If you are calling on a farm, drive in and park where you will be out of the way. Unless you see your prospect right away or she has given you a specific place to meet, go to the office, if you can see it. If you see no office, go to the house. Most large farmers carry 2-way radios and/or cellular phones, and your prospect may well be in the field or hog barn, waiting for someone at the house or office to call him when you arrive.

Never go in a barn or livestock facility unless you are invited. Most large hog confinement facilities have some type of bio-security – security against accidental contamination with biological organisms such as bacteria. Your shoes, innocent though they make look to you, could introduce micro-organisms into a hog barn that could cause disease and even death among your customer's pigs. The farmer may require you to "suit up" in gear he/she provides, or even to "shower-in" and to "shower-out" again when you leave the facility. At a minimum, you should have clean paper boots in your car, and always ask about bio-security measures <u>before</u> asking to see the facility.

For dairy farmers, the situation is slightly different. The dairy farmer is still concerned about protecting the health of the herd. However, dairy farmers have learned through experience that tranquil, "mellow" cows give more milk; when cows are upset, they give less milk. In a dairy barn, you rarely hear shouting, and animals are moved fairly gently from their stalls to the milking parlor and back. Your job, should you be invited into a dairy barn, is to stay out of their way (they're actually very polite animals), and let them go about their business.

What if you are calling on a farmer who has no livestock, but is simply out in the barn fixing something? You may even hear the roar of a truck motor or see the arc of a welding torch. Before you walk in and stretch your hand out, remember that farming is one of the most dangerous occupations. Countless fingers have been lost because someone looked up from their work before turning off the power tools or equipment they were using. If you must interrupt a farmer at work, try to call out or knock loudly and step clearly into view. Wait patiently until they can safely stop their work and talk with you.

If you are calling on a dealer, distributor, or purchasing agent, you will probably meet with them in an office. You may speak to a receptionist first. You should be as polite to this person as to the customer – they may have more influence than you expect. (They are often called "gatekeepers" for a good reason.) If you have time to talk with them, you can often learn quite a bit of useful information, from the correct pronunciation of your customer's name to the history of the company.

Calling on veterinarians presents special challenges. People often say "Time is money," but this is truly the case for a veterinarian. The time spent with you is time that cannot be billed to a customer. As a result, many veterinarians, especially in large clinics, have delegated most sale contacts to a veterinary technician, who manages the purchases for the clinic. This technician is extremely knowledgeable about the clinic and its normal usage of current products, but he or she may not have the authority (or the scientific training) to recognize the benefits of a new product and trial its use. Although this technician is not your ultimate customer, you must treat him or her with the same respect you would treat the veterinarian. Be on time, ask if you have parked in an appropriate place, etc.

How You Greet the Customer

If you are calling on-farm, greet and introduce yourself to everyone you meet. You may meet the spouse of the farmer, a brother-in-law, a Mom or a hired man. In every case, you are dealing with someone who may not be able to make the decision to buy from you, but who absolutely can block the decision to buy from you if they feel you are rude.

Shaking hands is still a traditional way to greet people – and not just the first time you meet them – even if it is not your customer. However, there are two exceptions to this traditional greeting. First, in some parts of the country, some women may not be accustomed to shaking hands. Second, there are an alarming number of farmers who have sustained some injury to their hands or arms that makes it difficult for them to shake hands. A farmer with this type of injury has faced this situation many times before, and they may either take a half step back (no shake) or shake hands with their left hand (be alert for the switch). If someone seems uncomfortable shaking hands, don't force it but _do_ acknowledge the introduction in another way. You could touch the brim of your hat (real or imagined), or restate the name ("Mrs. Johnson") and nod. In many parts of the country, in rural areas, a simple "Ma'am" or "Sir" and a smile still go a long way.

If you are calling on a distributor, dealer, clinic or purchasing agent, similar rules apply. Again, you must acknowledge anyone to whom you are introduced – whether they are a receptionist, a computer programmer or the CEO. Remember as many names as you can, but be sure to make a note of the receptionist's name, the customer's secretary's name, and/or the veterinary technician's name. This is a person you'll speak to quite often. One additional note: always address a veterinarian by their proper title – "Dr." – unless they tell you otherwise.

How You Converse

The basic rules still apply – break the ice and state your call objective. However, it's a good idea to also confirm the amount of time the customer has for your call. Agricultural customers – whether farmers, ranchers, dealers, distributors or veterinarians, always seem to be "fighting fires." Your customer may not have as much time as originally planned. Find out before you start.

Most agricultural customers like to "talk shop" for a few moments. Some like to visit for considerably longer than that. In most cases, veterinarians are an exception to this rule. They usually prefer to get down to business and learn about your products or offers quickly, so they can get back to their paying customers.

There are two important rules to follow when you open a conversation with a prospect or customer. First, keep your comments positive. If it has been a bad year – from weather or from the commodity exchange – your customer probably knows it. Don't be the bearer of bad news. Second, never gossip. Building rapport with one customer by sharing information about another is a cheap trick – and can quickly ruin your reputation as a professional. Sometimes, general information that seems quite innocent to you might cause the customer to wonder what kinds of things you might tell others about them.

Meet the Customer's Personal Behavioral "Norms"

Chris had called on four customers in one day, and though she'd tried the same basic opening with each of them, it hadn't always worked equally well. She was more confused than ever. The first customer had been abrupt, kept cutting her off, and wanted to get down to business right away. The second just seemed to want to talk – she hardly had time to talk about business at all before she had to leave for her next appointment. The third was a really nice guy, and listened carefully, but kept talking about where he did business now. At the last farm she called on, she'd talked to a nutritionist who had given her the "third-degree" – she'd have to study up before calling on her again.

Each person approaches the seller-buyer relationship in a highly unique way. Some customers like to talk – they'll answer any question you ask and then some. Others are more reserved, and the more questions you ask the more reserved – or even irritable – they become. Some people like to develop long-term loyal relationships, while others like to shop around every year. Some make decisions only after they have digested mounds of data, while others seem impulsive — almost charter members of the "ready-fire-aim" school of decision making.

These variations in behavior are all normal. As a salesperson, you might wish that your reserved customers would talk more or that your analytical customers could make decisions faster. But for each of these people, the way they react to you, the way they make decisions and the way they communicate is "right" – as natural as breathing. Your job as a salesperson is not to change them. Your job is to accept and understand them as they are, and develop a way of working together that is comfortable and productive. Your job is to adopt a style with a particular customer that is most conducive to developing a good relationship.

Social psychologists have studied these different ways of looking at the world and behaving. By asking many thousands of people to describe themselves and how they make decisions, they have developed systems that describe patterns of behavior. Several such systems exist, but most look at behavior along four different scales:
  * how quickly and firmly the person makes decisions;
  * how easily the person shares information about the business, their needs or their values;
  * how the person reacts to change – in circumstances, products, or the community;
  * how firmly the person believes in "rules" – whether they be rules of behavior, rules of evidence, or a "proper" decision-making process.

One of the most useful systems for classifying and understanding patterns of customer behavior is the DISC, developed by Dr. Russ Watson of Target Consultants, Inc. of Oswego, Ill. The DISC system looks at behavior from four perspectives:

Dominance:	How the customer deals with problems and challenges
Influence:	How the customer relates to people and tries to influence others
Steadiness:	How the customer deals with change and activity
Compliance:	How the customer deals with rules set by others

Each of us is a "blend" of all four types of behavior, as is each customer. The particular blend of each individual tends to have one "primary" behavioral style - one that is most obvious to others.

The DISC theory is very well-researched. It is based on the work of Dr. William Marston, a psychologist from Columbia University in the 1920's. Since that time, the theory has been tested many times.

A style is a consistent pattern of behavior: communications, processing information, relating to others, using logic and making decisions. No one DISC style is "best" for a salesperson - and no one style is predictive of success as a farmer, dealer or distributor. Each style (and remember, each person is a blend of all four) has distinctive characteristics.

Dominance

"Dominance" describes an individual's approach to getting results and solving problems.

High Dominance
A person with a high degree of dominant behavior wants to solve problems quickly and directly. They take an active, assertive approach to most challenges. They are very results-oriented. This is the customer who talks about the "bottom line" all the time. High dominance individuals make decisions quickly, sometimes without all the facts. They can be impatient, but will listen if you can show them a better way quickly. You definitely know where you stand with this person.

Low Dominance
A person with a low degree of dominance tends to solve problems in a more controlled and calculated way. This person has lots of patience with the details. They are deliberate, organized and may occasionally suffer from "paralysis by analysis." However, when the stakes are high, they make solid, well-researched decisions.

Influence

"Influence" describes a person's approach to people and emotions.

High Influence
People who place themselves high on the "influence" scale tend to be outgoing and socially assertive. It may seem like "they've never met a stranger." They are talkative, sometimes impulsive, easy to get to know, and often emotional.

Low Influence

People with a lower degree of "influence" in their behavior are quiet and reserved. They control their emotions and prefer a logical approach. This type of person can seem blunt and critical, if they have both low influence and high dominance.

Steadiness

"Steadiness" describes the preferred pace each person follows in their social and work environment.

High Steadiness

People with a high degree of steadiness prefer a more controlled and predictable environment. They may lie awake at night worrying about changes in their job, their markets, or their family. They value security and appreciate someone who is disciplined, yet genuine. They are often excellent "team players" in their family and community, and can be extremely loyal customers.

Low Steadiness

People with low steadiness behaviors represent the classic "don't fence me in" type. They value freedom of expression, freedom of movement, freedom of pace - anything not to feel confined or tied down. Their great advantage is that they can adapt to change quickly, although they may not have the patience to determine which change is best.

Compliance

"Compliance" describes a person's ability to be comfortable with - and comforted by - standards, procedures and rules.

High Compliance

People with a high level of "compliance" generally have no problem sticking to "the rules" - and they expect others to abide by them as well. They have high standards, for themselves and others. They like things to be done the "right" way, according to the book.

Low Compliance

People who have a low degree of compliance in their behavior like to work independently. Rules are seen as guidelines that can be broken when expedient. Rather than following rules made by others, the "right way is my way." Low compliance people can be very creative in formulating strategies for new circumstances.

The key to using your knowledge of DISC styles is to understand how people with each style operate as they meet new salespeople, consider new product and service options, and form relationships with new suppliers. If you understand what is important to each type or style of customer, you will be able to modify your approach to meet their needs. For example, a "high D" customer usually does not want to see stacks of data, and may not appreciate spending an hour with you to go over every detail. On the other hand, you will have difficulty selling a "high C" customer on a new production strategy or marketing program until they understand both the details of the offer and the logic behind the details.

Ron Pettet
ProAgCo
Sales Representative
Logansport, Indiana

I guess it's also been really important to me to know that I am a relationship person. I am a "High I" on the DISC test. Learning where I fit in that test, early on, has helped me learn to temper my own attitude when I am with the folks with different personality styles. Understanding the DISC analysis has also helped me better know my customers. When I know that this guy is a bottom-line, run-the-show kind of guy, who wants facts in a short span of time, I know that that it is harder for me to work with that type of person than it is for me to work with another relationship or "High I" type person.

But it has also, over the years, helped me modify my approach to fit the needs of the buyer by understanding him well enough to know where he's coming from. Knowing what "style" that person is really has helped out. DISC – I think that's something all salespeople need to learn...about themselves, and about those they work with. Over the years there have been sales that I have lost, just because I didn't approach the person right whereas if I'd applied what I know now about DISC, I would have been able to get and keep that sale.

Table 11.1 summarizes key behaviors and characteristics associated with each style. The behaviors most closely correlated with each style ("High" Dominance, Influencing, etc.) are near the top of the list. Behaviors least associated or negatively correlated to the style appear near the bottom of the list ("Low" Dominance, Influencing, etc.).

Table 11.1
Behavioral Trait Intensity Range

	Dominance	Influencing	Steadiness	Compliance
6	egocentric domineering demanding forceful daring direct	enthusiastic impulsive gregarious self-promoting emotional persuasive	passive serene patient predictable loyal team-person	perfectionist systematic fact-finder conventional accurate diplomatic
5	risk taker adventuresome decisive inquisitive	influential trusting affable sociable	inactive possessive complacent relaxed	high standards conscientious restrained courteous
4	assertive competitive quick self-reliant	confident poised charming generous	consistent deliberate stable steady	analytical sensitive neat tactful
3	calculated risks self-critical unassuming self-effacing	convincing effusive discriminating reflective	mobile outgoing alert eager	own person self-righteous opinionated persistent
2	hesitant weighs pros/cons unobtrusive conservative	factual logical controlled retiring	critical discontented fidgety impetuous	independent rigid firm stubborn
1	peaceful mild quiet unsure dependent modest	suspicious pessimistic aloof withdrawn self-conscious reticent	restless change-oriented fault-finding spontaneous frustrated active	arbitrary rebellious defiant obstinate tactless sarcastic

Getting to Know the Customer – Building Rapport

Let's assume you have the basics down for making a good first impression – how to dress, how to talk, what to talk about, etc., for your particular branch of the industry. You have learned to pay close attention to the customer or prospect upon meeting them. Consciously or unconsciously, you are learning about the customer at this point by paying attention to a list of clues. These clues might include the following behaviors:

- Do they have an "in charge," hurried attitude and speech? Do they seem impatient? Do they ask few questions? They may have High D or dominating behavior.
- Do they talk a lot, often fairly fast? Do they like to talk about people as well as business issues? Do they seem friendly and easy to get to know? They probably have High I or influencing behavior.
- Do they seem polite but somewhat reserved? Do they talk about commitments to current suppliers? Do you see pictures of family, or are they concerned with maintaining their business for future generations? They may have High S or steadiness in their behavior.
- Do they seem very business-like and reserved – a "show me" attitude? Do they seem to have good records and an office or shop where everything is in its place (and some places even have labels)? They may have a lot of compliance in their behavior.

Building rapport means finding a topic of common interest – a "toehold" to use to begin building a relationship with a customer. It may be the first few minutes of the call – or most of the first call, depending on your customer's need to get to know you. Rapport-building serves the function of letting buyer and seller get acquainted. You can use this time to find out what type of person the customer is. The customer, of course, is also "taking your measure" to find out what kind of person you are.

Clearly, building rapport will proceed very differently if your customer is a "High I" than if they are "High C." Your "High I" customer reacts to people and personal issues – this customer wants to get to know you as a person and often looks for topics or common acquaintances to establish a connection with you. On the other hand, your "High C" customer is concerned primarily with the business proposition you will make – and you should make it only after a careful analysis. To the uninitiated, rapport-building looks like innocent, friendly conversation. But to the well-trained, professional salesperson, rapport-building is filled with opportunities to learn about the customer and what makes him/her "tick." Table 11.2 gives you some examples of behaviors and "key words" that work well in building rapport with each type of customer.

Table 11.2
Keys to Building Rapport

Customer's Primary Style	Your Basic Approach	Key Rapport-Building Words
Dominance	business-like respectful of time organized confident	"the best business decision" "bottom line improvements" "competitive edge" "top customers like you" "_____ looks excellent" (crop, livestock, new equipment)
Influence	enthusiastic positive sociable persuasive	"do you know _____?" (common acquaintance) "glad to get to know you" "tell me all about..." "how did you resolve...?" "fantastic! What next?"
Steadiness	quiet not pushy prepared to spend time attentive prepared	"may I ask you about..." "what kinds of service are important to you?" "we'll take as much time as you like" (don't talk too much or too fast)
Compliance	prepared with facts, data reserved and business-like never "cocky" not over-friendly or too personal use logic	"systematic" "process improvements" "accurate" business solutions "collect information to analyze and see fit"

Salespeople often wonder if the adjustments to a customer's style, such as recommended here, really amount to "manipulation." The answer is no. You are not trying to sell the customer something he or she doesn't need or can't afford. You are simply trying to find the easiest way to get him or her talking about needs and priorities. Unless you clearly identify these needs and priorities, you could be in a position later to offer a product or service that did not fit the customer's needs. Using this tool is simply a way of communicating more effectively with the customer – based on the way they want to communicate.

Another important function of rapport-building is to begin development of trust. You are determining whether the customer is the decision maker and how he or she might make that decision. The customer is trying to determine if your interest is sincerely in them, as a person and a business, or just in pushing your latest product. In some small way, you need to show the customer during rapport-building that you are genuinely interested in their business and in making an honest analysis of whether you could help them.

Debra Warman
American Cyanamid
Master Sales Representative
Minnesota Lake, Minnesota

One of my key things is that I just try to get to know the customer and treat them as I would want to be treated if I were a customer. I think this is the key to being successful. You just have to build up that rapport with the customer. It doesn't matter how much or how little experience you have. When you get a new customer, you still have to get to know them and they have to get to know you and trust you. That takes time regardless of how long you have been in selling.

Just be honest and sincere, treating the customer how you would want to be treated. I think regardless of what your product knowledge is, regardless of the number of sales schools you have attended, to have long-term success, that farmer has to respect you and the easiest way to earn their respect is being open and honest with them. Sell products that fit them. You will gain lots of sales.

Don't, however, sell the customer something that is not going to work. Eventually they will realize that it didn't work and you will have lost that trust factor out there.

As common needs and interests are identified, even if the only thing salesperson and customer have in common is the customer's need for profitability, trust can grow. It is not built by any one thing that is said or done, but by a consistent pattern of behavior over time. In a sense, trust can't be developed "consciously" – it happens when you sincerely work for the customer's best interest. And that "best interest" focus begins by adjusting your approach so that the customer is as comfortable as possible.

Above all, remember that the customer should do most of the talking – not you. Many salespeople believe that they should fill in the awkward moments in the first few conversations. As you work with more different types of customers during your career, you will discover that some customers, especially C's (compliance) and S's (steady), may occasionally like a quiet break in the conversation to formulate their next statement or question. If you jump in and talk, you may well miss the opportunity to know what was really on your customer's mind.

Rapport-building is a little like socializing with any new acquaintance, except that it has a specific goal and happens in a specific context – selling. To the casual observer or the untrained, rapport-building looks very much like two people enjoying each other, but in fact, it is a very intentional process designed to learn more about your customer and enhance your relationship. Neither you nor your customer has unlimited time to stand around chatting – no matter how easy the customer is to talk to. If the prospect is especially busy or especially "High D" (dominant) or "High C" (compliant), they may become annoyed that you are wasting their time. After a few minutes of rapport-building, the alert salesperson will look for a bridge over which he or she can direct the conversation toward the purpose of the call. The key? The customer needs to feel that they are in control of these components of the conversation:

- pace;
- content;
- relationship vs. business;
- when to move on.

Make a Smooth Transition

When the customer says what they are looking for

This situation is ideal – and it happens fairly often. If the customer tells you what they need, listen before selling. Ask questions to make sure you understand:

- the specific product, service or business need;
- whether they are considering other solutions;
- why they are considering other solutions;
- budget range, if appropriate;
- delivery/use time frame.

When the customer says they're shopping around

Ask them what they've been looking for, and why. Evaluate the selling challenge – is it price vs. price or can you add value through product performance or service and create some loyalty? Listen before selling.

When the customer says they're "always looking just to see what's new"

Ask the customer what part of the operation they would like to improve, or if there is anything specific they'd like to see or learn more about. As appropriate, offer to walk around the warehouse, or scout a field, or walk through a barn, to see the issues that are important to your customer and begin asking questions that point toward a solution. Again, listen before selling.

When the customer says they're not in the market right now

Ask them what they like about their current products, services and supplier. Look for opportunities to support their management decisions. If appropriate, talk briefly about the philosophy of your business – the emphasis on customer satisfaction, product quality, etc. Use this opportunity to learn all you can about what is important to customers like this.

Sales Call Openers

Sales call "openers" or opening approaches finish the transition from "just talking" – building rapport – to "talking about business" – focusing on the objective of your call. There are several different types of opening approaches, but all have the functions of:

- stimulating the prospect's interest;
- channeling the prospect's attention toward your objective.

Psychologists tell us that the brain can absorb information two to three times faster than a person can speak. Therefore, you have only a short amount of time to fully capture their attention before it wanders.

Standard Approach

One of the most common opening approaches in agricultural selling, the "standard" approach is almost indistinguishable from rapport-building. It involves conversing for a few moments (rapport-building) and then moving on to the business at hand. The standard approach does not grab the attention of the prospect dramatically, but it has several advantages, especially with certain types of customers. First, it is very effective in rural settings and with customers (such as "High S's") who react negatively to a "canned" sales approach or a pushy salesperson. Second, the standard approach meets social expectations in many casual settings, especially if you know the prospect or customer socially. Done properly, the standard approach clearly communicates that you value your customer or prospect as a person, not just an entity to sell to.

The standard approach, however, may not be as easy to execute as it first seems. If you're not sure how to transition to the purpose of your call casually, you may find yourself still engaged in chit-chat 15 minutes later. The masters of this technique are able to subtly steer what appear to be casual questions toward the purpose of the call, until suddenly they are fully engaged in a business conversation. Others have learned to communicate the transition to a call opening *non-verbally* – by leaning forward, taking out a notebook, or changing to a less casual posture. One word of caution – this opening may not be most effective with "High D" and "High C" customers who are far less interested in a social relationship with you, at least in the beginning.

Direct Approach

In the direct opening approach, you simply tell the customer why you are there. The more business-like the customer is, the less "just stopping by" is an acceptable reason. If you have made an appointment (always advisable unless you know differently), you can simply re-state the reason for the call that you shared when you made the appointment. Notice in these examples that this approach also creates an easy bridge to asking about needs.

- *John, as I mentioned on the phone, we have a new 3-step starter feed system that is designed to help multiple-site operations like yours optimize nursery performance....what feeding system are you currently using?*
- *Phil, as I mentioned last week, I wanted to stop by and go over this year's marketing program....did the material I sent ahead make sense to you?*
- *Kathleen, as we agreed when you called Monday with that question about wilt, I wanted to follow up with you right away and take a look at the problem...are you still seeing it? Has it spread at all?*

Remember! The sales objective is not always to sell something on that particular call! Whether you're learning about needs, closing a sale, servicing an account, or handling a complaint, your call should always include a few minutes attention to the *person* and then a transition to the *problem* or *opportunity*.

Some Tried and True Opening Ideas

The following ideas have been used by some very successful salespeople for many years. They can work for you too. Make sure to choose an approach that fits your personal philosophy, the values of your prospect or customer, and their personal style.

Gifts and Trinkets

Take a small gift with you, and take one for each top employee as well. The gift should be useful - tools, gloves, pens, flashlights, etc., all work well. The gesture can help you break the ice, and can build some good will. And, as long as it is used, it will keep your name in front of the customer.

Samples for Demonstration

Product samples serve several purposes. They allow your customer to see the product - consistency, label, packaging, any safety information - and to "imagine" that product in the warehouse or on the shelves. Or, you can show a sample of the result of using your product. For example, compare an ear of corn from your new insect-resistant hybrid to one grown in the same field, but from conventional genetics. Many people in agriculture are experiential learners. It truly helps them remember something they can touch it, hold it, smell it, etc. A tangible product or benefit encourages even "High D" customers to pause for a moment and listen to you or ask a question. Of course, if your customer is a "High C," be ready to say where the corn was grown and how they can be sure comparable ears were collected!

Samples for Trial Use

If you are able to offer a large enough sample to allow trial use, you can use the sample to talk about how the product was developed, how it should be used, and what benefits to watch for and measure as a result of use. Just setting the sample on the customer's desk or table will likely get their attention, and you can share 2-3 key benefits of the product to make sure you have their attention. Then use their attention *first* to determine their needs and only *second* to explain how your product might meet those needs.

Headlines

You can get the attention of your customer or prospect by saying something startling. Say it simply - like a "headline" that describes why you called.

- *We've noticed a serious magnesium deficiency in the area!*
- *Hey, we finally got a local market for our high-oil corn!*
- *Our agronomists are tracking an X insect infestation, and it has reached Dubois, about 200 miles from here....are your farmers ready for it?*

Your "startling statement" must be true, must be relevant to the customer or prospect, and must be of some value to them. Your statement should also have a clear connection to your call - don't open with a "magnesium deficiency" cry of alarm and then spend the call talking about broadleaf weed control.

Come as a Learner

This approach is hard to beat, for almost all types of customers. Ask the customer or prospect about a problem others in the area are having – weed control, micronutrient deficiencies, environmental regulations, or milk quality. The list is endless and depends only on what is happening in your market right now. Ask the customer or prospect their experience with this problem.

- *Have you been seeing more broadleaf problems this year?*
- *Have your customers had any problems tracking this grain market?*
- *Have you seen a lot of re-planting?*
- *How much did that late freeze damage the trees?*

If you <u>genuinely</u> want to learn, most customers will be happy to help you. They know their time will be repaid many times over as you become better and better able to save them money and make them money through your products and services. However, if the customer believes you are "just asking" as a trick, you will have a hard time re-building their trust.

Testimonials and Referrals

In many rural communities, everyone involved in agriculture to any significant degree knows everyone else. It's very effective, especially with "High I" and "High S" accounts, to say that someone referred you and why. However, before you mention another person's name as a referral, make sure that:

- the source of the referral is respected by this prospect or customer;
- the source of the referral has given you permission to use their name;
- the source of the referral will give you and your company a positive recommendation, if your prospect calls them on the phone as soon as you are out the door.

All openers must be worked smoothly into the flow of the call. In the beginning, or with a new prospect, you may want to plan or even practice your call opening as part of your sales call plan. Try a new opening approach from time to time, to stay fresh. Or tag along and watch another salesperson, who uses opening approaches different from yours. Any of these ideas can be implemented with great success. The key is to select the right approach for each specific account and situation.

Summary

Whether you are calling on a new customer or a current customer, the first few minutes of your call are critical. During these first minutes, you have an opportunity to make (or reinforce) a positive impression. Or, you can communicate, without ever saying a word, a negative, careless or arrogant impression. The keys to creating a positive first impression are:

- dress and act in accordance with the "norms" for professionals in your industry;
- adjust your speech and non-verbal communication pace, gestures, posture) to put your customer at ease and to meet his or her highly personal "norms."

One important part of the first impression you make is how you build rapport. Building rapport is a conversational "dance" – a social conversation that you and your customer both use to get acquainted before moving into a discussion of business issues. The behavioral type of the customer (DISC) should be an important consideration in which topics you select to build rapport and the length of time you spend socializing.

After several minutes of rapport-building, you will move on to the purpose of your call. Your customer may trigger the transition to business by suggesting a problem, a dissatisfaction, the need to "shop around," etc. Or, you may move the conversation forward, to business topics. If you choose to move the conversation forward, you can simply begin talking about the issue that brought you to the call, perhaps changing your posture or non-verbally communicating a change of pace. This is called the "standard approach." It's subtle and effective, but it takes a master to execute it well. Or, you can simply state the reason for your visit (the direct approach) or use a variety of more creative opening approaches.

In any case, the first few minutes of the call should communicate your professionalism and your sincere interest in the account. They should establish that you are willing to listen and learn – not do all the talking. They should help you determine the basic style of your account, so that you can make smarter choices in asking questions about needs or selecting evidence of benefits. And finally, the first few minutes of the call should be the first few steps toward a long-term relationship, one built on trust and performance.

Review Questions

1.   Describe some keys to building sound customer relationships. How do first impressions factor into building the salesperson/customer relationship?

2.   List and describe the four perspectives of behavior in the DISC system. Discuss the advantage to the salesperson of using DISC to understand people, particularly customers.

3.   What are a couple of ways you can build rapport with a potential customer on the first visit?

4.   In the case study with Martin Harry in this chapter, what kind of an example does Harry give for building a relationship? How does he accomplish that? Why does it work?

5.   Choose three sales call openers and explain how they differ.

Chapter Twelve

Identify Customer Needs and Values

Learning Objectives:

Upon completion of this chapter, you will be able to:

1. explain how the identification of customer needs and values provides a foundation for a single sale and for a long-term customer relationship;
2. recall five types of customer information needed to sell effectively;
3. identify three types of questions and explain how to use them;
4. describe how a progression of questions can lead the customer toward a sale;
5. recognize effective listening skills and describe common barriers to listening;
6. understand the role of "feelings" in effective selling and how to recognize these "feelings;"
7. recognize four or more common non-verbal "clues" and recall their meaning.

Identification of Customer Needs and Values

The process of selling involves solving problems and uncovering opportunities for the customer. This is true no matter what product is being sold – at least if the salesperson hopes to sell more than one product (or more than one time). Unless a salesperson can uncover customer problems and opportunities, a product cannot be sold on the basis of its benefits. The salesperson will be reduced to selling on the basis of price. Experienced salespeople recognize this fact, and

spend a good portion of their time learning all they can about their customers. New salespeople may feel a little frustrated by this approach. After all, they reason, the product is really good. They know it will help customers. Why not spend what little time the customer has, in talking about the product?

One of the most difficult truths of selling, at least for new salespeople, is that a product's benefits will fall on deaf ears <u>unless</u> the specific needs and wants of the customer have been identified <u>and</u> the product's benefits can be logically connected to those needs and wants. The salesperson can't solve problems through a product or service unless he or she knows what problems the customer is ready to solve. Opportunities for improvement can't be found unless the salesperson knows which parts of the business the customer wants to improve. And, the salesperson can't satisfy the customer – let alone "delight" them – unless the customer's expectations are fully understood. The skills and activities salespeople use to uncover customer needs, values, and expectations are often called "probing" or "needs diagnosis." Probing helps "peel back the layers of your customer's experience with your product and to get into the higher levels of the value hierarchy."[50] What does this mean? It means that probing is the key skill needed to move *beyond* the features (or limitations) of one specific product or service. Probing opens a dialogue about the values and goals of the customer. It allows the salesperson to talk about more than tangible features, such as price or product performance. Probing allows the salesperson to talk about the larger set of needs and intangibles that are important to the customer – reliability, return on investment, service after the sale, and the reputation of the seller's business. Probing, therefore, helps build trust. It helps the salesperson understand the *relative* importance of a feature, an issue or a benefit to the customer.

Effective selling is never a monologue, however entertaining and engaging a salesperson may be. It is a dialogue: a two-way conversation about needs and issues. Customers certainly want their salespeople to *know* everything about their products or services. But credibility—and customer trust don't depend only on what the salesperson knows. The salesperson's credibility as a long-term supplier or partner to the customer's business also depends on what the salesperson is willing to *learn* about:

- the needs the customer has identified;
- the problems the customer wants to solve;
- the goals the customer wants to achieve – profit, growth, etc.;
- the way the customer likes to run their business;
- the way the customer wants salespeople to interact with employees;
- opportunities the customer wants to pursue.

---

[50]Woodruff, R.B. and Gardial, S. F. Know Your Customer: New Approaches to Understanding Customer Satisfaction. Blackwell Publishers, Inc., Cambridge, MA: 1996, p. 186-187.

We've all experienced the *lack* of good probing as a customer. Many people think of car sales when they think of the pushy, obnoxious salesperson who can't stop talking about a great "deal" long enough to listen to the customer's needs. No buyer type is comfortable with this style of selling. Why not? Let's look at how selling <u>without</u> adequate probing "feels" to different types of customers.

High "D" buyers may arrive at the car lot ready to make a decision, but they have a need to <u>tell</u> what is important to them. High "I" buyers simply enjoy a conversation – they want to create a relationship with the seller as a person, and they want the seller to take time to get to know them. High "S" and high "C" buyers don't like being pressured to make a decision under any circumstances. The high "C" buyer is especially unhappy with a high-pressure salesperson, because this buyer has a need for a systematic analysis of the alternatives. He or she can't do a thorough analysis of alternatives when the salesperson is shouting in their ears. In fact, many people will visit a car lot in the evening, when salespeople aren't around at all, just to give themselves time to analyze alternatives. Or, they may say they're "just looking" even when they have a pretty good idea what they want, just because they want some peace and quiet to study the options.

Recognizing the questionable reputation "selling" has in the auto industry, some companies are now training salespeople to behave in the *opposite* way to what we traditionally expect. Saturn, for example, has made "low-pressure" selling a key part of their position, in order to differentiate their company from others. While always available to answer questions, the Saturn salesperson is expected to respect the customer's very individual buying style and pace.

In agriculture, the most successful salespeople stay away from high pressure tactics. But, on the other hand, their approach is also not as "hands off" as a Saturn salesperson. The job of the agricultural seller is to understand business needs as well as personal needs. The goal of the agricultural seller is to create such a strong "partnership" or professional relationship with the customer that they will benefit from working together over the course of many years. In agricultural selling, specific products and services must "fit" the general business management decisions the customer has already made – equipment, tillage practices, business organization, etc. Decisions must result in <u>profit</u>. The stakes are higher than when selling consumer goods. As a result, the skills of probing and listening must be even more sharply honed.

When to Probe

Probing occurs at the beginning, middle, and end of a call. The most effective salespeople <u>never</u> assume that they know enough about the customer's needs and expectations. Even when they have developed a recommendation and have presented it to the customer, they still make a point of asking whether the customer understands the benefits they have presented and sees their "fit" into his or her business. Once the sale is complete, probing doesn't stop. It continues, so that the salesperson can make sure all post-sale service and follow-up expectations of your customer are completely understood.

Most salespeople have been taught that there should be extensive probing at the beginning of the call. They understand they shouldn't sell until they have a full understanding of needs. That is true for almost all types of customers, but there are a few exceptions. When selling to a businessperson with very limited time - such as a veterinarian in a large clinic, or the purchasing manager of an integrated feed operation - it may be necessary to get the attention of the customer *before* beginning to probe. The salesperson, in effect, must justify why this very busy customer should spend precious time discussing a product or service option. This can be done when the appointment is set for the call, or during the first two-three minutes of the call. These special situations involve customers who basically believe they "have no time for salespeople." The salesperson's first challenge is to create a need to consider a new approach to a business problem or opportunity. Once the salesperson has created that need, - and has the customer's full attention, - the customer and salesperson can begin a thorough discussion of needs and product "fit".

- *Doctor, we have developed a new antibiotic specifically to deal with shipping fever. Veterinarians who have used the product feel the results were nothing short of dramatic. Since you have a lot of experience helping cattlemen deal with this problem, I wondered if we could set a time so I can show you some really remarkable performance results from some of the large feedlots in this part of the state.*
- *Ms. Johnson, we have just finished a research study with large farrow-to-finish operations that shows dramatic increases in NBA for sows that receive a diet enriched with Vitamin X. In fact, the increase pays for the cost of the vitamin supplement many times over. Until now, adding this vitamin was a problem due to poor feed mixing characteristics. We've been working on this problem with our customers, and have developed a supplement that mixes easily and still increases NBA, using conventional equipment for mixing and feeding. I wanted you to be aware of this opportunity...what are your NBA goals currently?*

Of course, even when it's necessary to use a few benefits to get the attention of the customer, the salesperson must still probe in several other areas of need and value in order to create a lasting customer relationship. Without this discussion of needs and values, the salesperson may find that the next company with a similar "new or improved" product can easily replace you - and often with a lower price.

How to Probe

Skillful probing uses many different types of spoken questions:
- closed questions, with a factual answer;
- open questions that invite sharing of needs and values;
- confirming and clarifying questions that help salespeople make sure they understand what has been heard; and
- commitment questions that move the call toward a sale.

In later sections of this chapter, we'll explain how to recognize and use each of these types of questions. However, during a sales call, effective salespeople use <u>all</u> of these types of questions! They may use more open questions at the beginning of a call and more closed questions near the end, but they find that some open questions – such as how the customer will measure satisfaction or performance – are very useful even at the tail-end of the call, after the sale has been made. The key is to *never stop listening and learning*. And no one can listen while they're talking.

What A Salesperson Needs to Know

There are six major categories of information that should be collected during the probing or "needs dialogue" in a sales call:

- how the buying decision is made;
- business/production goals;
- relevant business/production practices;
- expectations – how suppliers are evaluated;
- current loyalties and perceived results;
- unmet needs and unmet expectations.

Each of these categories of information strengthens the salesperson's ability to meet the customer's needs, identifies how to add value to products or services, and shows how to satisfy the customer over the long term. Salespeople can plan their probing around these six types of information, developing questions for each category. As a result of this purposeful approach to probing, they find it easier to develop sound recommendations and present them. The key benefits offered to each individual customer must be tailored to that customer's needs and values. Probing in each category ensures that the salesperson gets a full picture of all the customer's needs, and the relative priority of those needs in the customer's eyes.

How the Buying Decision is Made

Selling is a process, not an event. For maximum effectiveness, the selling process should match the customer's buying process. Probing must uncover how this process works – and it will work somewhat differently in each customer business.

- Who makes the buying decision?
- Who influences the decision, even if they don't "sign the check" themselves?
- Is the decision made quickly or only after long analysis?
- What types of things does the customer normally consider when making a decision?

There are two main "clusters" of information to uncover here. The first concerns the decision maker. What "style" buyer are they? A High "D" buyer wants to make decisions quickly, and generally doesn't like being "second-guessed" on decisions already made. A High "S" buyer, on the other hand, makes decision slowly, deliberately and logically. A salesperson needs the flexibility to work with both types of buyers. He or she first needs to recognize which style of buyer he/she is sitting across from! It's helpful to know their personal goals, as well as their business goals.

For example, if a local dealer receives salary increases and/or incentive pay based on sales volume, he or she is looking for products and services that can help accomplish or exceed sales volume goals. If, on the other hand, a dealer is paid incentives based on inventory control, he or she is looking for business partners who will support inventory movement and offer customer discounts that literally "empty the warehouse" before the end of the year. Or, the local dealer might want continuing education so that he/she can be recognized and promoted – either college courses or technical certification. In this situation, the customer is looking for suppliers with an educational/development component to their marketing program, rather than caps, jackets and fishing trips. In these situations, the salesperson must also understand more than the goals of the business. The salesperson must understand the personal/professional goals of the customer.

Business Goals

The business goals of the customer will obviously differ, depending on what type of business the customer has. Row crop farmers think about achieving a maximum return in yield (and marketable output traits). Vegetable, fruit and cotton farmers think about yield and crop quality. Livestock and poultry farmers think about the number and quality of marketable animals. Dairy farmers think about pounds milk produced and the interval between calves. Dealers think about sales volume as well as any other business measures that are used in determining their bonus (such as return on current assets, inventory control, days sales outstanding). Manufacturers and distributors think about the amount of product they can sell, accurate forecasting, and inventory control.

In the final analysis, most businesses find that their goals are clustered into three categories: cash flow, profit, and market share.

- Cash flow describes the movement of cash through the business, from selling products, receiving payment, purchasing new products, paying for these products, using them to generate a marketable crop (or selling them), etc. The objective of cash flow management is to have enough cash in the business at all times to pay current bills and to purchase products and supplies needed to keep the business going.
- Profit can be measured in several ways. Most commonly, it is measured as either operating profit or as a return on investment. Operating profit is the amount of money the business "clears" each year after accounts have been collected (or crops have been sold) and bills have been paid. "Return on investment" measures profit in relationship to the investment necessary to generate that profit.
- Market share refers to the proportion of the total market that a specific business has captured.

Most businesses find that they cannot dramatically improve their cash flow, their profitability and their market share at the same time. Improved cash flow means selling products (and getting paid) sooner rather than later - even if the market might be stronger at a later time. Thus, cash flow strategies also impact profitability. Improving market share in the absence of a new product requires competitive marketing that may either cost more (e.g., promotions, incentives, commissions) or involve lower product margins (e.g., cash discounts, volume discounts). These marketing programs can reduce the profitability of each sale. On the other hand, increasing profitability may mean reducing services, closing less profitable facilities, eliminating an enterprise, or waiting to buy new equipment. These strategies usually also make it difficult to increase market share.

Other types of business goals can also affect the purchase decision. For example, the business owner (farmer, dealer or distributor) will make decisions in a fundamentally different way if he/she is considering retirement or selling the business. Business owners who want to grow look at their opportunities differently than owners who want to stay the same size or simplify. Many salespeople find that business "owners" make decisions very differently from "managers!"

When selling to a business, the salesperson must understand its goals. And, with the exception of hobby farmers, everyone selling in agriculture is selling to a business. An understanding of goals allows the salesperson to see the world "through the eyes" of the customer. Recommendations, product bundles and services can be selected and structured to give each customer maximum momentum toward his or her chosen goals.

Business/Production Practices

Most agricultural businesses – including farms and ranches – have evolved their business and production practices over time. When selling to a farm, ranch, dealer or distributor, it's the responsibility of the salesperson to "fit" new products and services into the customer's current production or business practices.

When the products and services to be sold represent a "new" technology, the salesperson often finds it necessary to "sell" a production practice or business practice as well as a product. Let's assume, for example, that a salesperson is representing a crop protection product useful in efficient conservation tillage. Clearly, the salesperson must determine current tillage practices on the farm before product benefits can be presented most effectively. If the farmer is not currently using conservation tillage, the benefits of minimum tillage vs. conventional tillage (e.g., higher organic matter in the soil, fewer trips across the field) must be explained as well.

The same process holds true in selling to a business such as a distributor or dealer. For example, a company may have an excellent marketing program that rewards the dealer for sales of a specific product line or service line. In order to reward the dealer, however, it is necessary to know how many times the product or service line has been sold. That in turn means the dealer must have a system of sales record-keeping that allows accurate tracking of sales by product or service. Without such a tracking system, the marketing program will be of little use and its benefits will mean little to the dealer customer.

Sometimes the most important business practices are not the most obvious. They are part of the customer's philosophy of doing business. For example, if a feed dealer prides herself on always offering her customers the best possible solution and shares responsibility for that solution's profitability on farm, she will want to be convinced that a new product or new technology is dependable, reliable and profitable. On the other hand, if a feed dealer prides himself on always offering the lowest-cost alternative, he will want to be convinced that a product or service is priced competitively to alternatives on the market. If the salesperson does not uncover these different philosophies, it is very difficult to choose the best set of product/service benefits to present!

Stacy Dunn
AgrEvo USA Company
Sales Representative
Indianapolis, Indiana

As far as real life situations go, you can't sell if you don't probe. I found out the hard way. For instance, my product I was presenting is sprayed post-emergence. To do that, the buyer needs post equipment. I once went into a retailer and gave my whole sales pitch to a retailer who was not even set up to spray corn post-emergence. If I would have effectively probed to uncover that retailer's specific situation, needs and expectations, I would have saved both of us a lot of confusion and struggle.

Coming out of school, probably the biggest realization I've made is that there is so much to learn. In fact, the learning curve takes a sharp upward lunge when you really start selling in the field. Humility helps. A sense of humor helps. You just have to have patience. You have to be willing to learn. Take the time to ask and listen. You have to take your territory as being your own business and make choices wisely.

Expectations – How Suppliers are Evaluated

Long-term, mutually beneficial sales relationships are built on a strong foundation of customer satisfaction. Customers who are not satisfied do <u>not</u> generally tell the salesperson of their disappointment, unless their dissatisfaction is severe. Instead, they choose to shop somewhere else, telling all their friends and neighbors why they are making the switch. Thus, a dissatisfied customer almost always means more than one sale is lost.

Marketing experts have written many books and propounded many theories about customer satisfaction – what it is, how to achieve it, how to measure it, etc. Yet, for a salesperson, the customer satisfaction equation is a very simple one. Customer satisfaction is a function of meeting or exceeding customer expectations. Think of this equation as a mathematical formula:

$$S_x = \frac{A}{B}$$

where: S = customer satisfaction
   A = product, service and seller performance
   B = customer expectations
   x = the customer

As this formula shows, customer satisfaction, to a very large degree, is within the control of the salesperson. To be sure, salespeople don't control product quality. Sometimes they don't control service quality. They do control the quality of their own performance. But the salesperson has a responsibility to <u>know</u> everything possible about product and service quality. Similarly, the salesperson has the responsibility to know everything possible about the customer's expectations. Let's consider two examples, with very different customer satisfaction outcomes.

> *Gerry was in the process of closing a sale for a new combine with one of the largest farmers in the county. His biggest competition had been in-line – a dealer who sold the same products but was located in the next county. This dealer was expanding his territory aggressively and was offering service through a mobile repair truck, so that farmers would experience little-to-no down time during harvest. Gerry was able to convince the customer of the excellent service offered through his dealership, and since Gerry's price was about a thousand dollars lower, he won the sale. Two months later, the farmer experienced a freak breakdown. Gerry's service department offered to take the combine in that same day, and have parts UPS'd overnight to get the farmer back in the field within 48 hours. To Gerry's surprise, the farmer wasn't satisfied – let alone appreciative – of this extra service effort. Somehow he had understood that Gerry's dealership would keep him running, no matter what.*

> *Pete was a salesperson at the same dealership as Gerry. And he had, in fact, encountered a very similar situation. However, as he was closing the sale, he asked the farmer to be precise about his experiences with service responsiveness and his expectations from their dealership. He found that, although the farmer wanted their lower price and wanted to buy in the county, he also expected the dealership to keep him running – no matter what. When this farmer experienced a breakdown a few months later, Pete loaded up a similar combine from the lot, reconditioned and ready to go, and drove it out to the farmer. He picked up the broken combine and took it back on the same truck, returning it repaired in 2-3 days and taking the "loaner" back to the dealership. The result? This farmer can't stop telling everyone how this dealership took care of him.*

A salesperson can only satisfy customers when he or she fully understands the expectations of the customer. Even when the salesperson has explained product performance or service responsiveness in detail, it is dangerous to assume that the customer is thinking along the same lines. Every customer comes complete with a set of "experience baggage" – past sales, past disappointments, past experiences with service excellence. Probing helps the salesperson uncover those experiences and expectations. Once these are known, customer satisfaction is no longer a mystery or something the salesperson must leave to chance. It is predictable, largely controllable, and becomes an important foundation for future business.

Current Loyalties and Perceived Results

Sometimes, probing reveals a need that the customer didn't realize he or she had. This can happen in a variety of ways. Perhaps the customer was not aware of a new product, or a new production practice. Perhaps the customer was not aware of how a marketing program could help them increase profits. Perhaps the customer was not aware of how a new technology could simplify and solve a business problem. Or, perhaps the customer was not aware that one business truly offered a higher level of service than another.

Salespeople often feel that "there is no such thing as loyalty" any more. Nothing could be further from the truth. Very few customers have the time or the temperament to begin each season or each production cycle with a totally "blank slate," evaluating all possible products and suppliers to make a completely fresh set of choices. It is more time-efficient – and often more cost-efficient – for customers to stay where they are, providing the level of price, product, and service quality they are receiving meets most of their expectations most of the time. To be sure, some products have more "loyalty power" than others.

For example, anhydrous ammonia, a common farm fertilizer, is available from most local dealers. It is the same product, no matter where it is purchased, and so may be regarded by the farmer as a "commodity" where price is the key differentiating variable. Of course, it is possible to add value to this product through soil testing, application or availability of application equipment, farm records, etc. But, in general, farmers like to compare price on this product and may buy it from a different local supplier each year. On the other hand, feed is less often considered a commodity. Each feed formulation is the result of research into animal performance and production dynamics. Even though all feeds contain similar ingredients, farmers tend to be much more loyal to a brand of feed that has worked in the past for their farm.

Farmers, dealers and distributors also all have some level of loyalty to the business team they deal with. The salesperson is an important part of that team. In fact, almost every experienced salesperson has been in a situation where his or her price or service package was <u>not</u> the best in the market, and yet the customer chose to stay.

If a salesperson is working with a current customer, it is critical to probe into that customer's loyalty level. What is promoting loyalty – the price, the products, the services, or the relationship with people? Regardless of the results the customer is getting, are they what were expected? Is the customer happy with the business relationship? Whatever the underlying basis for loyalty is for that customer, the salesperson must uncover it so that it can be used to strengthen that customer's loyalty.

If the salesperson is working with a prospect or a "convenience" customer – someone who is buying from the business only when the primary supplier can't deliver – probing is equally important. What is the primary supplier doing to create loyalty? Could your business do it better? What results does the customer believe are reasonable? Could the customer receive better results – beyond current expectations – if they switched to your business? Once you understand why the customer is loyal now to whom and what results he/she perceives, you can uncover opportunities for the customer to benefit more by switching.

Probing into current loyalties and perceived results is important for one additional reason. Sometimes, salespeople get pretty excited about the benefits of their products and services, especially when these involve new technologies. Yet the salesperson must exercise caution. Never tell a customer what they have done "wrong" through their past decisions or loyalties. Every customer makes the best decisions he or she can, using a very unique and individual set of criteria. Every customer wants to learn how to improve, but no one likes being made to feel dense, backward or as if they have been duped by another supplier. Probing into past loyalties and perceived results should always, through every question and comment, convey complete respect for the customer and for past decisions. Whether these decisions were right or wrong, smart or stupid, the customer made them in good faith with the best information available.

Unmet Needs and Unmet Expectations

Probing must also uncover any needs of the customer that are not being met, as well as any expectations that were not fulfilled. This is true whether the salesperson is working with a current customer or trying to sell someone else's customer.

In working with a current customer, the salesperson should always identify expectations and, as far as possible, help shape them so that the customer is satisfied. But, even with the best intentions, sometimes there is an expectation the salesperson didn't uncover. Or, there may be an unusual production situation or business environment that causes a product, service or program to perform differently than everyone expected. In this situation, salespeople sometimes shy away from asking about unmet needs and expectations. They know their product, service, or business hasn't performed as they had hoped, but they seem to believe that the issue is not there if they don't talk about it. This is a very dangerous strategy. Hiding a disappointing result or a missed expectation only allows it to fester in the dark, eating away at the relationship and trust between buyer and seller. Painful as it can be, the salesperson should uncover missed expectations and unmet needs as aggressively as he/she uncovers happier news.

The result of an honest examination of unmet needs will be better service for the customer and a stronger, more loyal relationship.

When calling on a prospect – someone else's customer – probing into unmet needs and unfulfilled expectations has a slightly different goal. Here, the salesperson wants to uncover opportunities to support the customer's business. These may be opportunities the customer already sees, but couldn't capture with a current supplier. Or, there may be opportunities the customer doesn't even see yet. Let's look at an example.

Kathy was recently given a few additional counties to add to her territory as a sales rep for a major chemical company. Her company had some great new products to offer, and they had developed a comprehensive marketing program to encourage dealers to begin selling these products. One of the cornerstones of the new program was a technical training curriculum. Dealer employees could progress through it at their own pace, certifying as they passed each level. The curriculum was constructed so that, when completed, dealer reps would be knowledgeable about the new technology Kathy's company was introducing. But the training also helped dealers "raise the bar" for technical competence in their market, thus strengthening their ties to the best farmers they served.

When Kathy began calling on some of her new dealers, she uncovered a terrific need for more technical support. However, in the past, this support had been offered by tech reps and agronomists from other chemical companies. As technologies changed faster and faster, the best dealers found they couldn't get enough support from these people. Sure, they knew the answers to their question – but they were so overbooked and overworked that they often didn't even return calls for 3-4 days. Top farmer customers wanted an answer faster than that.

Kathy realized that several top dealers had already recognized the opportunity to be technically more "competent" than their competitors. However, these dealers were frustrated that they couldn't capture the opportunity with their current resources. Understanding the opportunity from the dealer's point of view helped Kathy position her marketing/training program as a way for dealers to differentiate their employees and to strengthen their ties with top farmers. For these dealers, "certification" was less important than customer satisfaction. That's OK with Kathy – she is now positioning her new, high-tech products as a way to "deliver results" to top producers, through the best-trained reps in each local market.

In summary, "probing" can be defined as a dialogue that allows the salesperson to diagnose the needs, values, opportunities and goals of the customer as an individual and as owner or manager of a business. That's a tall order! How do salespeople accomplish all this in the short time customers allow them? The best salespeople let customers tell them what's important in their own words, checking for understanding as they go. There are two key skills involved: productive questioning and active listening.

Wes McCoy
Dow AgroSciences
Senior Account Manager, Retired
Minneapolis, Minnesota

When I started out selling, I thought I had a pretty good background having been a County Agent and a little older than the young guys right out of school back then. But I learned the value of listening to learn from my dealers. It helped me be much more successful. By taking the time to listen, both buyer and seller benefit.

Why not ask, then listen to the wisdom they offer? Some of those dealers are gold mines of information you need to or would like to know. They are complimented if you ask for their help and listen actively to what they have to offer. I have had more help and more education from my dealers than I can say. These are people who I was supposed to be helping and they taught me a lot. Most of those dealers have had a lot of experience, a lot of years in the field, in the area, and they have a vast and deep experience. There's so much more to know in agriculture than company/product knowledge. Many of these dealers are good, understanding dealers, and will sort of take you under their wing and tutor you.

Quite a long time ago, our company got into selling anhydrous ammonia, and I felt, having been an old County Agent, that I knew all about that stuff....but, come down to it, I found out just how little I did know about it. And the company at that time, didn't give us a lot of training about the product, they just said, "Sell it!" They gave us an incentive program... "Sell it or your successor will!" So that's what I used...dealer expertise. I asked the first dealer a lot of questions and I listened. The next one, I asked more questions. By the time I got to the third one, I could offer a little input myself. I kept going down the list of dealers that way, and I ended up being the top Dow ammonia salesman in the company.

It was very rewarding, but I have to credit my dealers for showing me the way. If you can take the time and effort to be humble enough to ask, listen and learn, you can always be a more effective salesperson - for both the customer and yourself.

Productive Questioning

There are four basic types of questions:

- open questions;
- closed questions;
- clarifying questions;
- confirming questions.

All of these types of questions should be used in probing. Used effectively, they lead the salesperson to an understanding of what the customer thinks, wants and knows. These questions can also be organized into a flow or questioning process that leads the customer to buy. Let's start by explaining each type of question and how to use it.

Open questions

Somewhere in your career, you may have heard an experienced salesperson say this: *God gave us two ears and one mouth for a reason.* In other words, no one can learn while they're talking. It's only when a person listens that they can truly learn. While this is true for every type of question, it is especially true for open questions. Open questions don't have a yes or no answer. Instead, they ask the customer to give a "slice" of the world as he or she sees it. Right or wrong, this is the world within which they make decisions. To sell to each customer, the salesperson needs to understand that world.

Open questions often start with the following phrases:

- *Tell me about...*
- *What has been your experience with...*
- *What do you think about....*
- *How do you...*
- *Why do you...*

Open questions are often used near the beginning of a call. They serve several purposes here. First, they get the customer talking. Choosing some open questions that are easy to answer set a positive tone for the call:

- *Tell me about that big new warehouse I see out back...*
- *How do you think the weather will affect the grain markets?*
- *What do you think our chances are for winning the championship?*

Not all of these very first open questions need to be directly about the business. Some can simply be a way of building rapport with the customer. Soon, however, the salesperson should begin choosing open questions that help him/her learn more about the business of the customer.

Asking open questions near the beginning of the call helps the salesperson get a "map" of the customer's priorities. Thus, these questions help channel the rest of the call to those topics that are most important to the customer. The salesperson finds that, even though open questions take some time early on, they save time in the long run. They significantly reduce the salesperson's risk of preparing, presenting, and trying to close on products or benefits that the customer doesn't consider critical.

Experienced salespeople find that they use some open questions throughout the call. This type of question can help select products and benefits:

- *There are a lot of benefits of multiple site farrowing and MMEW programs...how do you evaluate programs like this in respect to your new operation's goals?*

Open questions are invaluable when the salesperson meets customer resistance:

- *Why do you think that this process wouldn't work for you?*

And finally, open questions help the salesperson uncover expectations and measure customer satisfaction:

- *How will you measure whether this product (service) has been a good investment for you?*
- *How could we have better met your expectations or provided better service?*

Closed Questions

Closed questions are useful for gathering specific information – facts, figures, trade-offs, and specific problems or issues. Closed questions may have a yes or no answer. The list of closed questions is much like those a reporter would ask:

- *What results did you get?*
- *What products did you use?*
- *Where have you been purchasing X?*
- *Who has been helping you there?*
- *Where do you get technical support?*
- *How many acres (employees, trucks, etc.)?*
- *How much.....?*
- *How fast...?*

Closed questions allow you to gather the factual information you need to make a specific recommendation, position a marketing program, or determine price sensitivity. There are three cautions salespeople should observe when using closed questions.

- Closed questions near the beginning of a call can steer you "off course." A salesperson can only get answers to the questions he/she asks...and near the beginning of a call it's hard to know enough about the customer's business to focus in on the most important issues. As a result, the salesperson may take the "long way round" to get to the most important needs – much like driving from Des Moines to San Francisco using only road signs but no map.
- When salespeople are new (or nervous), they may sometimes ask a closed question and then answer it themselves, before the customer has a chance to think it through. For example, a salesperson may ask a large, High "C" swine producer how many sows he has. The producer may want a moment to think about it, in order to give an accurate answer. A nervous salesperson will chime in "about 600, I'd guess" before the customer has answered. Not only is this rude, but it also tells the customer that the salesperson's standards of accuracy are not as high as his own.
- When time is tight, some salespeople fire off closed questions as if they were holding an interrogation. Remember – the customer doesn't care if she's dealing with Lois Lane, Star Reporter....she wants her salesperson to slow down, match pace to her own, and listen.

One additional note: it's possible to collect massive amounts of important, factual information through closed questions. Customers may give the salesperson this information once willingly, but they don't appreciate being asked the same questions several times. It is the salesperson's responsibility to capture this information accurately. Increasingly, salespeople find that customers don't mind the salesperson taking notes, especially if they are asked permission:

- *Bob, I'd like to get some of this information down so that I don't need to ask you about it again...would you mind if I jotted down a few notes?*
- *Leona, I'm getting a really good feel for the problems you've been having in the greenhouse, but I'd like to just jot down some of those reduction figures to make sure I remember them accurately – is that OK with you?*

Clarifying Questions

Effective clarifying questions represent two skill sets: the ability to ask a good question and the ability to listen. Clarifying questions "play back"[51] what the salesperson has heard and ask the customer to clarify or explain a little more. Clarifying questions have three very important functions.

- They show the customer that the salesperson has been listening.
- They help the salesperson check the *implications* of what he/she has heard.
- They encourage customer's to give additional, important detail as they correct misunderstandings or explain what they've said.

Let's look at some examples.

Customer:	*I buy the seed and fertilizer. Of course, Dad likes to stay active on the marketing side.*
Salesperson:	*Then if I understand you correctly, you make the input decisions and your Dad makes the marketing arrangements?*
Customer:	*Well, actually, Hank and I split the input decisions – for anything about soybeans, you'd have to talk to him. But basically, yeah, you're right – I do corn inputs, and Hank, Dad and I all together decide the marketing.*
Customer:	*If you want to work in this county, you're pretty much going to have to work with me.*
Salesperson:	*So you make decisions pretty independently in terms of which distributor you source products from?*
Customer:	*Well, actually the sourcing of products is pretty much set by the regional office. But the marketing programs are all administered here, and I set the sales goals for this location together with my manager.*

As you can see from these examples, clarifying questions are very important. They offer the salesperson a "gentler" way to ask about some really tough issues. Rather than asking: *Exactly what do you have the authority to decide here,* the clarifying questions allows the salesperson to use one piece of information from the customer to learn more.

---

[51]Daley, K.R.. and Wolfe, E. Socratic Selling: How to Ask the Questions that Get the Sale. Irwin Professional Publishing. Chicago IL: 1996.

Confirming Questions

Confirming questions allow the salesperson to "check for understanding." Unlike the clarifying questions, the confirming question is not really asking for more information, however quietly. The confirming questions simply help the salesperson check their facts, perceptions and understanding. A few examples follow:

- *Have I got that right?*
- *That was 30,000 finished cattle a year?*
- *The rolling herd average is around 22,000 lbs., you said?*
- *That was four employees now, but you usually have five?*
- *Most of your tech support comes from your reps, then?*

Building a Question Flow

As salespeople become more proficient using different types of questions for different purposes in a call, they often find they are using questions to "drive" the call toward a close. That "close" may be a sale, or it may be some other type of customer commitment. Although their process of asking questions may have evolved with experience, the process can also be taught and learned by new salespeople. This process has been described several ways by different authors. A good description was developed by Neil Rackham in *Spin Selling*.[52]

1. Begin by exploring the situation.
2. Uncover any problems or obvious opportunities for improvement.
3. Investigate the implications of those problems/opportunities on the business.
4. Develop a "need payoff" - what it would be worth to solve the problem - and ask for agreement on it.

This process allows the salesperson to work through the entire sales process - opening the call, probing for needs, presenting benefits and closing - using questions rather than high-pressure presentations. It is an excellent approach for agricultural selling, and works very well with current customers as well as new customers. Let's look at some examples.

---

[52]Rackham, N. Spin Selling. McGraw-Hill, New York, New York: 1988.

Figure 12.1
Question Flow – An Example

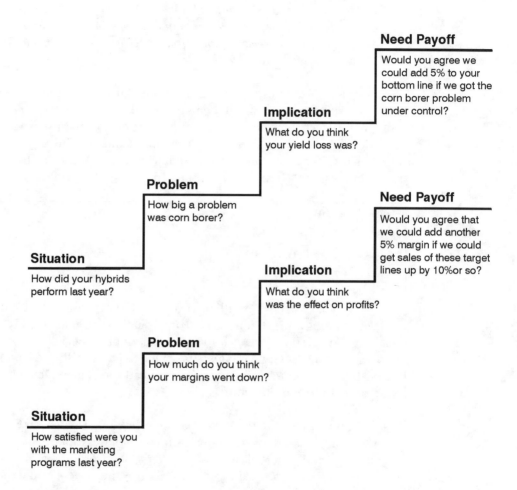

Productive Listening

In general, human beings are rather inefficient listeners. For example, research shows[53] that, immediately after listening to a 10-minute lecture, the average person can only understand, evaluate and retain about half of what was said. Within 48 hours, the amount retained falls to 25% of that which was communicated.

---

[53] Steil, L.K. Your Personal Listening Profile. Sperry Corporation, Great Neck, NY: 1980.

Yet listening is probably the single most important selling skill.

> *You must let the prospect speak about himself or herself; the information you'll receive as a result is invaluable. Ram-rodding your points through, and merely overpowering the person rather than showing how much you can help, is a sure way for you to descend into the stereotypical "hard sell" that no one likes. Such behavior is a great way to lose sales.*[5]

Listening is ironically also the communication skill we "use" the most – more than reading, writing or speaking.[6] It seems to be well-accepted that most people don't listen well. In fact, some believe that the average person may listen with full attention for only about *15 seconds* before "tuning out" to think up the next question to ask or the next intelligent remark to make. According to Schiffman,[7] not listening is the "Number Two mistake" made by salespeople.

Rob Vincent
American Cyanamid
Sales Representative
Iowa City, Iowa

Something I have struggled with since day one is that I always want to tell, tell, tell instead of asking and listening to find out what the customer really is looking for. Asking good questions is truly important. But for me, especially when I was starting out, solid listening was just something that was really difficult for me. I had all this new product information in my head and I knew it inside and out. I was ready to tell them everything.

Listening remains one of the key areas I have developed which has really improved my interaction and ultimate outcome (better rapport, better relationships and better sales) with customers. Good, productive listening for me means I have to slow down and get them talking – then listen to find their hot buttons. The more I can learn from listening to them the better I'm ready to trigger the sale of our product.

Why is attentive listening so difficult? How can salespeople improve their listening skills?

---

[54] Schiffman, S. The 25 Most Common Sales Mistakes and How To Avoid Them. Adams Publishing. Holbrook, MA: 1995.
[55] Marx, R. Personal Selling: An Interactive Approach. Allyn and Beacon, A Division of Simon and Schuster. Needham Heights, MA: 1994.
[56] Schiffman, p. 22-23.

Why Listening is Difficult

Salespeople are like all people – it's difficult to listen when you are distracted, tired, or bored. Five common reasons salespeople don't listen well are:

- they are bored;
- they don't really care about the speaker or his/her opinions;
- they think they already know what the customer is telling them;
- they can't focus on someone else for very long;
- they are nervous and are preparing the next thing they want to say.

These poor listening habits aren't confined to sales situations. They happen to everyone in daily life as well. Spouses, friends, children and parents routinely remind each of us that we ought to be listening better. In a sales situation, however, the stakes are higher. The customer will rarely remind a salesperson that he/she should be listening more closely...instead the customer simply stops giving information and finds another salesperson or supplier who <u>will</u> listen.

How to Listen More Effectively

Effective listening is active listening. It affects what the salesperson is thinking, how the salesperson stands and moves, whether or not he/she takes notes, and above all what clarifying and confirming questions are asked. Daley and Wolfe[57]

call this type of focused listening "full-value listening." Others call it "active listening." In active listening or "full-value" listening, the salesperson cannot move through a question "script." Instead, the flow of the call is directed by the customer, as he/she explains what is important. As Daley and Wolfe remind us, "Giving full value means you take into account everything the customer says."

Not only is it important to listen to everything the customer says. It is critical to listen for the *way* the customer says it, and to carefully observe all non-verbal communication. Think of it this way: you must listen for three types of information:

- facts;
- feelings;
- non-verbal cues.

---

[57] Daley, K. And Wolfe, E, p. 78.

Listening for Facts

Listening for facts sounds easy. All the salesperson has to do is ask a question and then stop talking long enough to hear the answer. However, communication is never 100% reliable. The salesperson may not completely understand what the customer says. The customer may not tell 100% of the story. Or, the customer may tell 100% of the story and the salesperson may listen, but they may not have the same meaning for the same words. For example, what does "on-time delivery" mean? Within two hours? Within 24 hours? Within 48 hours?

Listening for facts should always be "active listening."

- Use clarifying questions to help make sure you understand the implications of what the customer is saying.
- "Sub-verbally" support the customer and encourage them to keep talking. Some of the most effective active listening happens when you reinforce your customer with "oh?" "Yes," "I see," "Uh-huh," or simply a raised eye-brow or a nod of the head.[58]
- Use confirming questions or re-phrase what was heard to make sure the customer's intent and standards are clear.
- Take notes, draw diagrams of fields or sites, draw organizational diagrams. Use any written tool to make sure structure, decision making and facts about the business are clearly remembered.
- Prepare for the call by reading background on any technologies, organizational structures or industry specifics that will help clarify what the customer is explaining.
- Never answer your own question, just because the customer is taking awhile to think it over.
- Never stop listening before the customer has finished answering the question.
- Never get "side-tracked" by interruptions such as the phone, beepers, other employees, Email, etc.

Listen for Feelings

Feelings are just as important as facts when a customer is making a major purchase. In today's agricultural selling environment, there are many good products and many alternative solutions to almost any problem at almost any level of the business. The customer knows this. The customer also knows that the value of any product or service is intimately tied to the integrity of the salesperson and his/her willingness to "go the extra mile" and make sure promises are kept.

---

[58] Alessandra, A.J., Wexler, P. S. and Deen, Jerry D. *Non-Manipulative Selling*. Reston Publishing Co. Reston, VA: 1979.

How can a salesperson listen for feelings? It helps to remember that a selling relationship is first a sound human relationship, and only secondly a business relationship. Experienced salespeople have learned to "listen" for the following cues.

- How fast is the customer talking? While High "Ds" and High "Is" tend to talk faster in every situation, talking fast can be a cue for:
  - excitement about a problem or opportunity;
  - nervousness about an issue;
  - eagerness to move toward a result.

- How much information does the customer share? High "Is" and some High "Ss" tend to share information more freely, but in general customers share information when:
  - they are comfortable with the salesperson;
  - they believe the salesperson might be able to help them solve a problem;
  - they have a complaint;
  - they feel their expectations are high and want to communicate them.

- What do they talk about? Customers who talk about people and experiences:
  - may be High "I" or High "S";
  - need to have a personal relationship with salespeople and consultants.

- Customers who talk about facts and figures:
  - may be high "D" or High "C";
  - haven't yet had cause to "trust" the salesperson's experience or expertise.

Watching for Non-verbal Cues

Sociologists tell us that most of our communication occurs through non-verbal messages, rather than words. Again, anyone with even rudimentary experience in human relationships knows this is true. Let's look at a simple example.

The minute Lee walked in the apartment, she knew something was wrong. It was quiet, the blinds were still drawn, and Pip was sitting in the kitchen, head in hands. "What's wrong?" Lee asked. "Oh...nothing," Pip replied softly.

In this example, what would most people believe - the spoken word, or their combined life experience that tells them "nothing wrong" is probably not true? Most people trust their *nonverbal* "listening" or processing over any verbal messages. In fact, about 55% of our communication occurs through non-verbal messages. An additional 38% occurs through tone of voice. Only 7% occurs through the words themselves.[59]

Non-verbal communication includes actions, gestures, body posture, facial expressions, nerve responses (such as a flinch) and even pheromones. These non-verbal cues are powerful communicators, for both the salesperson and the customer. Communication is always a two-way street – the customer is "reading" the salesperson just as the salesperson is "reading" the customer. If a salesperson says all the "right" words, but appears listless, disheveled, irritable, impatient and bored, the customer will remember the 93% of the sales interaction – boredom, impatience, etc. – not the 7% that was nice words.

Experienced salespeople have learned to watch for some common "clues" to the customer's state of mind through observing their non-verbal behavior:

- leaning away can be a sign of discomfort – a literal "distancing" from the topic;
- leaning forward is a sign of interest and involvement;
- leaning back, arms behind head, or standing with one foot on a bumper or fencepost is an "alpha" posture – it means the customer is in charge and is very comfortable in that position;
- crossed arms may indicate defensiveness or "holding in" of feelings;
- furrowed brow may mean a need to slow down and allow the customer more time to ask questions and process information;
- pursed lips may indicate impatience or anger;
- nervous leg-shaking or pencil-tapping may indicate anxiety or a need to move the call along; and
- looking at a watch or clock means the salesperson is out of time.

The most expert salespeople not only "read" their customers' non-verbal communication. They also are able to control their own. They may do this in several ways.

It is possible to "re-direct" a customer's feelings by modifying non-verbal responses. For example, if a customer is angry, maintaining an open, friendly, non-threatening posture helps calm the situation down. Crossing arms, leaning away, or frowning only aggravate the situation.

It is also possible – and actually very natural – to "mirror" the body language of the customer. Most people do this unconsciously, at least to some extent. Author Michael McCaskey, in his book, *The Executive Challenge: Managing Change and*

---

[59] Mehrabian, A. Silent Message. Wadsworth Publishing Co. Belmont, CA: 1971.

Ambiguity, discusses numerous key patterns of non-verbal communication that can offer important insight to the communication occuring between two individuals. Especially in moments of great rapport between individuals, human behaviorists note that remarkable patterns of non-verbal communication can develop. The two people may "mirror" each other's movements – sweep the brow with a hand, shift folded arms or cross their legs at exactly the same time. Often this "mirroring" takes place so quickly that without a "video instant replay," it is unlikely to be noticed.

Again, many salespeople do not realize that they are "mirroring" the non-verbal communication of their customers. It happens naturally – without conscious thought. Nevertheless, once salespeople recognize this mirroring phenomenon, they can also notice when mirroring stops, or becomes especially intense. This should be a clue to the salesperson that the call is in trouble – or is progressing exceptionally well.

Keeping Track of What Is Learned

It is hard work to listen actively and attentively, to ask the "best" questions at each point in a call, and to watch for non-verbal cues. But it is not enough. The customer will judge a salesperson not only by what he or she has understood, but also by what happens as a result. Few people are able to remember all the information, feelings and nuances that happen in each call with each customer even for a few days, let alone for the month or two until they have time to visit this customer again.

The salesperson is responsible for learning – not just collecting – important information about each customer. It's impossible to "learn" enough to avoid mistakes or missed promises without some form of organization for all the information collected. It is less important whether information is collected and stored in sophisticated sales record-keeping databases, in customer files in an office, or on 3x5 cards in a box on the back seat of the salesperson's car. It is important that there is a system for organizing, categorizing and updating customer information on a regular basis, and that salespeople use this information to prepare for each call on the customer. What information do you need to record? Include:

- information about the decision maker – name, all phone numbers including mobile phone, Email and FAX, names of key employees, secretary's/bookkeeper's name, potentially names of key family members;
- information about business goals and critical success factors for the customer's business;

- facts about the business – size, number of employees, current products and services, current suppliers, age of facilities/equipment, how profit is calculated, business/value philosophy, etc.;
- how suppliers are evaluated;
- current satisfaction with current suppliers and any opportunities for improved results;
- any unmet needs or unmet expectations.

In short, the salesperson must collect and organize all the information needed to make the sale and then ensure that the customer is satisfied for the long term.

Making the Transition to a Recommendation

Clearly, the salesperson can't make a good recommendation without some understanding of the customer's needs, values and priorities. Just as clearly, some types of probing – asking questions and discussing alternatives – continues throughout every sales call. However, for most salespeople and customers, a moment comes in the call where the customer expects the salesperson to *process* what he/she has heard and begin sharing some ideas. This transitional period is sometimes called *arousing interest.* It is a bridge between uncovering basic needs and values of the customer and sharing some alternative solutions.

There are several possible ways to "manage" this transition. Sometimes, it happens naturally. The customer may ask about a specific product or benefit. Perhaps the salesperson mentioned this benefit when calling for an appointment. Perhaps the customer knows about it from talking with another manager or with a neighbor. In any case, the transition may go something like this:

Customer: *...and so we finish about 12,000 pigs a year, most years.*

Salesperson: *And did I understand correctly that that's been a pretty steady production number for you?*

Customer: *Yes, it has... but that's not to say we wouldn't like it to be higher. As I said, I'd like to see better performance in the nursery. We're losing too many there, still. So tell me about this new program you guys have been working on...*

Sometimes, the customer "waits" for the salesperson to make the transition, once he/she feels enough information has been collected to make a reasonable recommendation. In this case, the salesperson can use one of the following transition tactics.

- "Unpack" a technical feature or system that might be useful, given what has been learned about the business.
  - ➢ *Bob, our technical folks have developed an improved yield monitoring system that will hook right in to your GPS information...may I explain how it works?*
  - ➢ *Terry, we have a computer support system that will help you track pounds on the ground so that you are assured of getting accurate rebate payments...can I show you on my computer what it looks like?*

- Arouse curiosity in potential results – begin "customizing" a product and service bundle that fits this particular customer's needs.
  - ➢ *Jim, this medicated feeding program gets each calf off to a good start and may be able to help you improve your throughput, especially combined with some of the other improvements you're making...can we see what the difference might be?*
  - ➢ *Stacey, our technical training program may be able to help you grow the expertise you need with your own employees, instead of hiring someone special...let's see if we can figure out how to get sales up to a level that allows you free access to the program.*

- Use a testimonial – a "witness" from a customer who had a similar problem and is benefiting from the solution. Of course, the salesperson must make sure the customer respects the person whose "testimony" is being quoted, and that permission has been given to share any information.
  - ➢ *Fred, Dick Reed over in Atlantic has a very similar set-up to yours here. We've worked together for about 2 years now and we've been able to improve his yields by over 10%...could we think through how to get a similar return for you?*
  - ➢ *Jill, you may know Steve Thurman over in Faribault...he's been using some of our software for about 3 months now and just loves it...would you like to see what he's been using?*

- Show a personal analysis. This is particularly expected on the second or third call, when the salesperson has had time to collect information and analyze it thoroughly.
  - ➢ *Petra, I've roughed out some numbers here that incorporate some of the things you mentioned needing as well as a few ideas from our veterinarian...*
  - ➢ *Jon, we discussed a variety of needs and types of facilities. I've taken the liberty of asking our engineer about your concerns, and he has some preliminary ideas, pending a more thorough review of the site itself...*

- Set up a hypothetical "what if?" This builds a future situation that illustrates how your product might meet the customer's needs.
  - ➤ *Myna, what if we could get the rolling herd average up by 2-3,000 pounds within the next complete lactation cycle....we have some ideas for you to consider that might help you do that.*

Summary

Probing is a process of diagnostic questioning, listening, and capturing of what was learned. It is a critical skill for selling in agriculture. With the small (and shrinking) number of farm producers, dealers and distributors, no salesperson can afford to ignore, neglect, under-service or mis-sell a customer. There just aren't a lot more customers out there to replace the ones a salesperson loses. Gaining and keeping customers happens when the salesperson truly understands their personal and professional needs, their values, their business, and their past experiences and expectations.

Probing involves several types of questions – open, closed, clarifying and confirming. Each type of question plays a special role in understanding the needs of the customer. Probing also occurs throughout each call, not just at the beginning. In fact, it is possible to open, probe, present, close and follow-up on a sales call using questions alone.

Along with good questioning skills, salespeople must practice their listening skills. Listening is loosely defined as hearing and confirming spoken information through active listening, as well as listening for feelings and observing non-verbal behavior. All three of these forms of listening are important to "read" a customer and understand his or her priorities and concerns.

Finally, although probing continues throughout the call, at some point the customer "expects" that the salesperson will begin offering information about products, services and benefits. Obviously, the salesperson must be able to remember or reference all information collected up to this point, and use that information to select a reasonable recommendation for the customer. There are a variety of ways to transition from collecting information to sharing features and benefits. The best way depends on the customer and the situation. In the next chapter, we'll delve more deeply into selection and presentation of a customer-specific solution.

Review Questions

1. Since early in this book, customer needs and values have been explored at ever greater lengths. Describe how those customer needs and values are gathered in probing. What specifically does probing allow the salesperson to accomplish?

2. What are the six major categories of information that the salesperson should collect while probing? Choose two of those categories and explain why they are important for the salesperson to explore.

3. What is the customer satisfaction equation? What does the equation effectively illustrate?

4. Good questioning skills are essential for good salesmanship. Describe the four basic types of questions and give examples of each.

5. What are listening skills? Why are they important? How and why do they contribute to the probing effort?

Chapter Thirteen

Presenting Your Value

Learning Objectives:

Upon completion of this chapter, you should be able to:

1. organize customer needs, customer style and product/service benefits into a sales presentation;
2. understand and apply the concept of a "total product" or value bundle;
3. translate product and service features to customer-specific benefits;
4. plan, develop and practice a sales presentation.

Elements of a Successful Sales Presentation

Consider the last time you bought something with the help of a salesperson. What comes to mind? You may remember their helpfulness, or their patience. You may remember the way they explained the benefits of one product over another. You may even remember a cost/benefit analysis they did for you, depending on the purchase. When considering the elements of a successful sales presentation, it's natural to focus on the presentation itself and the communication or interpersonal skills of the salesperson.

Yet a successful sales presentation doesn't begin when the customer walks in the door, or when the salesperson arrives at the farm to make a sale. In order to present a product or service to a customer, the salesperson must have a thorough knowledge of:

- the customer's business needs;
- the customer's values;
- the customer's style (how they evaluate products and make decisions);
- the features and potential benefits of the product or service;
- the "total product" that best meets the customer's needs;

- the competitive options to the product or service;
- the process of presenting – confirming needs, discussing alternatives, etc.

The majority of the chapters in this book have been devoted to helping a salesperson prepare for this moment – the presentation. That's no accident. The presentation – that moment when you are actually ready to present your solutions to help the customer – is a window of opportunity for you and your company. The presentation is the Olympic event, the "big game," the day of the election. And, like these other activities, skills and strategies for the big event are necessary for success. However, they are not likely to be sufficient if you are not prepared properly. Months of preparation are necessary for an Olympic athlete to win. Months of research and relationship-building are necessary for a team to win whether it's a homecoming game or a state election. When you make a sales presentation to an agricultural retailer or distributor, or to a commercial farmer, months of preparation and relationship-building are also necessary. The good news is that every salesperson has it within their power to adequately prepare for the presentation.

Let's briefly review what it takes to be "ready" for a successful sales presentation.

Know Your Customer's Needs

Your customer's needs are the place to begin. In order to make a successful presentation and close the sale, it's not necessary to talk through *all* the benefits associated with a product or service. In fact, it's not advisable to do so. Instead, the customer expects a competent sales person to be able to pick and choose from among all possible features and benefits and present those that address the customer's *specific* needs. It is a mistake to bore a prospect with lots of information they can't use or are not interested in – no matter how impressive those points.

Most understand that they must ask the customer about needs. But it is important to know more than a list of needs. You need to know which needs are most important to this particular customer. You need to identify which needs of the customer are "nice to haves" and which are "have to haves." Understanding the difference between "nice to haves" and "have to haves" means understanding the customer's value system. In the end, you must understand not only the need, but what a solution is worth to the customer, and how you can make sure your solution is worth more than competitive solutions. This is what creating the "best value" is all about. Creating the best overall value gets the sale every time.

Bob Woods
Penn Jersey Products, Inc.
Sales Supervisor
New Holland, Pennsylvania

I remember the first year that I started in the Harvestore business. I thought I
knew a lot about agriculture, corn and cows. Maybe I did, but I didn't know how to
sell the product. But one of the things that helped me the most was when I was
told to go down and help someone sell that Harvestore. I got down there and
those two farmers ate me up. I remember standing there and the guys were
saying, "What about this and what about that? How much money?" Just a million
questions a minute. I didn't know what to say, how to act, or what to do. I made up
my mind at that time, that would never happen again. I was going to get my ducks
in a row. They were like wild men. I got them settled down and about 2 hours later
we sold them a Harvestore.

They were satisfied, but it taught me a valuable lesson: know your customer, what
they need, why they need it, how they can use it, what can they expect to gain
from it, what kind of return can they expect. Do your homework before you get
there. Talk about what they can expect to achieve when they make that
investment. That first experience of not being prepared to present the sale was
one of my worst experiences. That wasn't presentation. That was persecution –
my own, and it wasn't anybody's fault but my own. It could have been avoided if
I'd done some homework before presenting them the sale.

To know your customer's needs, you must know:

- specific production or profitability problems;
- opportunities the customer understands and wants to pursue;
- the priority of needs in the customer's mind;
- which high-priority needs your solution will address better than
  competitors.

Experienced salespeople listen to the whole set of needs, even if their product or
service only addresses a portion of the total need. Then they know enough about
the customer's needs that they can express those needs in the customer's own
words. This level of understanding allows them to present their product or
service as the "best fit" to the customer's goals and to the customer's business or
production systems. The sales presentation, for these highly successful
salespeople, is more like a summary of key needs and alternatives – not a listing of
product features.

Bill Brockett (owner and president of Virginia Beef Corporation) summarizes this approach to customer needs very well:

> *A lot of times a customer, even though he might know what he wants, might not get it expressed well in one sentence. It is imperative that a salesperson be able to talk and communicate very, very well with that potential customer so they really, really understand what that customer needs. Not what the customer thinks he needs, not what the salesman thinks he needs, but what he <u>really</u> needs... You can't just sit down in a minute's time and understand what a customer wants unless he's buying windows for a 1967 car...something very specific. If he's dealing with anything that has any ambiguity to it, which I think most things do, he really has to get into that customer's business, inside their head, and really understand them all the way so they really, really have an absolutely clear thought as to what he wants.*

For more information about questioning and listening skills that will help uncover customer needs, see Chapter 12.

Know Your Customer's Style

The customer's "style" is a description of how they act – how they evaluate products and services, what type of information they want, how much information they want and from what sources, and generally what they expect from the salespeople who work with them. In Chapter 11, *Opening The Call To Build A Customer Relationship*, four different communication "styles" of customer were introduced:

- D or Dominant – like to make decisions, like to be right, like to be first, little tolerance for lengthy explanations or excuses;
- I or Influencing – like to be around people, like to persuade and be persuaded, like to talk, like personal relationships, sometimes make decisions impulsively;
- S or Steady – like things to stay the same if possible, dislike change for change's sake, often heavily involved in family, church and community activities, often very loyal;
- C or Compliant – have rules to follow and expects others to also; like data and analysis based on facts, dislike overly friendly approaches, don't readily share a lot of information.

In other sections of the book, three styles of buying were introduced:

- relationship buyers – buy on the basis of personal trust, like to buy from people they know or who know people they know;

- economic buyers – often buy based on the relative cost of a solution or service; like "deals" and special considerations;
- business buyers – buy based on an analysis of profitability.

The communication style of a customer generally holds true for most aspects of their life also. If a farmer is data-oriented and wants to see performance tests when buying new equipment from you, he or she probably carries a copy of <u>Consumer Reports</u> into the local discount store to buy a new dishwasher. The buying style may be stronger or weaker. Sometimes it holds true for everything the customer buys, but it nearly always holds true for items that are critical to the customer's business. For example, a dairy farmer may be a business buyer when it comes to feed – he or she wants the feed that will produce the most pounds milk per cow. This same customer may be an economic buyer when it comes to seed corn for silage – his results are less obvious and he may assume most hybrids are about the same. Or, a retailer may buy a "clone" computer to save a few hundred dollars, figuring they all do about the same thing, but agonize for weeks over the software package that will give the best results for the business.

In order to be most effective in a sales presentation, the salesperson needs to understand the communication style and the buying style for the particular product or service being sold. Sometimes this is easy: a high I (Influencing) customer is fairly friendly, curious about his neighbors' choices, generally loyal to suppliers and requires a high level of "relationship" trust when he/she buys. However, theoretically any communication style could be associated with any buying style. In the following table, we suggest some of the ways to recognize and sell each style combination. Of course, these are only suggestions – your own knowledge of the customer is what is most important.

Table 13.1
Recognizing and Selling by Style

	Relationship	Economic	Business
Dominant	"Old boy" network; wants to be treated with respect; time for people he likes, not for "salespeople"	Pushes hard on price; feels she deserves the "best" price; not afraid to go direct	Knows what he/she wants; expects a concise analysis of benefits; wants to make the decision himself/herself
Influencing	Buys from people who are trusted; likes to like the salesperson; can help new salespeople build contacts	Likes a "good price" especially as a favor; status needs must be met	Keeps one eye on the bottom line, but picks and chooses services/products from people he/she likes
Steady	Loyal; likes to buy from people he/she knows; expects seller to respect the relationship and "take care" of him/her	Loyalty to family/farm business drives economic decisions; worries and talks about effect of rising prices; will sacrifice quality to avert change	With time and trust, will allow a "partnership" with seller to develop; looks for advice and expects profits
Compliant	Rare combination - may seem to depend on relationship but watches performance on promises very carefully	Fairly conservative in trying new products; risk-averse; would rater have a product that works than a more expensive one that promises better	Very data-oriented; may not share much information, but expects seller to provide data analysis anyway; tracks profitability to a plan or budget

What do you do when you have identified the communication and buying styles of a customer or prospect? You adjust your approach and presentation to meet them on "common ground." Let's look at two examples.

Kevin worked for a swine genetics company that had a wide range of products, most oriented toward producing lean-gain pigs. He had two producers on his customer list that were outwardly very similar: both were established farmers, successful businessmen, and both had recently expanded their hog operation to about 2000 sows. Yet calling on them, Kevin noticed some big differences.

- *Fred Hutchins was on the State NPPC board, consulted with one of the leading swine practitioners in the state about his new facility, and had the reputation of being tough to sell and tough to please. Kevin figured he was a*

High D (Dominant), with a business mindset when it came to the expansion of the hog operation.

- *Doug Fairmount was a quieter guy – didn't have all the best equipment, but what he had, he made full use of. He was reserved, and had the reputation of being slow to make a decision and then really a stickler for service. More than once, Doug had been heard to say "I won't do business with X again – they're just too sloppy."*

For Fred, the High D business-oriented buyer, Kevin's presentation will be very well-prepared. He will have selected a few key facts and will have supporting data to leave if Fred wants. He probably won't go through it, but he has it organized so if he's asked a question he won't fumble, looking for the answer. He knows he will have to justify his price, based on the value (profit and service) he can offer. He knows he can expect a decision within a few days – if not on the spot. On the other hand, when selling genetics to Doug, he expects to get pressured hard on price, and to have to match or exceed any "deals" Doug is getting from his current suppliers. He knows his product will have to be cost-effective to buy – not just the best at producing profit. He has prepared a 3-4 page "report" or "bid," with data to back up his claims. And he knows he'll need to carefully define what service he can offer at the low price that is demanded, because this customer will keep track of his performance after the sale.

Features, Advantages and Benefits

There is one basic expectation that is common to all customers – they expect salespeople to know all the features of their products and services. Not only should they "know" these features, they should understand how they apply to specific production situation or business situations. For example, it's not enough to know the features of a herbicide's weed spectrum, formulation, and cost. It's also necessary to know how it fits with a farmer's crop rotation plans, how it is to be applied, whether buffer strips are required, whether it requires special application equipment, etc. Similarly, it's not enough for a manufacturer sales representative to know the facts about a marketing program – he or she needs to also know how to fit the program into the retailer's business plans and customer base.

When a salesperson begins to "fit" a product or service into the customer's business, she is translating features into advantages and benefits. How do features, advantages and benefits fit together?

- Features are the facts about product performance, service delivery, distribution, people, etc.

- Advantages explain to the customer how a product or service will "fit" into the business.
- Benefits explain why that "fit" is a good one - the problems that are solved or the opportunities that are uncovered.

Features

Features are measurable. They can often be proven with performance data or worksheets. They are usually very tangible: they can be seen, demonstrated, touched and smelled. Salespeople often think in terms of features because they are technically oriented and find it easy to concentrate on factual information. The salesperson may be new, and not familiar with the needs of customers in his territory. Or, the salesperson may be asking about needs and "shopping" for someone that fits the features their product offers.

Customers are often interested in features. They provide a factual basis of comparison between products. For example, horsepower, 4-wheel drive, fuel consumption, gear ratios and optional cab equipment are all features of equipment that can easily be compared from one brand to another. In fact, some customers may approach the salesperson with a list of features in mind. They may simply want to know if your product or service has these features, and how much they cost.

Even when a customer approaches you with a list of features to compare with the competitor, your presentation must be much more than responding to the features list. The customer may have needs he/she doesn't know can be met by your product. Or, you may have services that are new or different from the competition - services that could allow the customer to capture more opportunity than he or she could imagine. Again, you can't make a successful presentation until you understand the full range of customer needs, and what features of your product or service "fit" with those needs.

Advantages

Eventually, the customer begins to ask: *What's in it for me?* The best product or service in the world has no value unless it fits into the customer's business plans or current systems. *Advantages* describe this fit. Explaining the advantages of a product or service is an intermediate step between listing features and talking about results customers can expect through those features. The advantage translates a feature into "action" - it helps the customer see how a feature could "go to work" in the operation. Let's look at some examples.

- *Because this herbicide can be used pre or post (feature), you'll have a longer window of opportunity to apply the herbicide (advantage).*
- *Because this new records system keeps track of all inputs on a field by field basis (feature), you'll be able to compare herbicide and fertility programs over a given time period (advantage).*
- *Because this product is injected subcutaneously (feature), you won't have as much muscle damage as with intramuscular injections (advantage).*

The advantage spells out what will happen when the product is used.

Benefits

The final benefit is the results of using the product. The benefit is often stated as a direct business result.

- *You will save trips across the field...*
- *You will be able to farm more acres...*
- *You will be able to attract commercial farm customers to the business...*
- *You will be able to store records in less time...*
- *You will be able to make better decisions on inputs.*

In some markets and for some products, the benefit may be stated as an indirect business result or as the solution of a long-standing problem.

- *You will have more satisfied customers and clients...*
- *You will be able to plan more effectively...*
- *You will be able to take advantage of a shift in the market...*

The Features - Advantages - Benefits Statement

Part of your preparation should be the development of as many features-advantages-benefits "strings" as you may need in your marketplace. When you're starting out, the following phrasing will be helpful:

Because of (feature),
  You will be able to... (advantage),
    Which means... (benefit).

Let's look at several examples.

- *Because this herbicide can be used pre or post (feature), you'll have a longer period when you can do your application and still do some good (advantage). That weed control means higher yields with less risk (benefit).*

- *Because our new record system keeps field by field records* (feature), *you'll be able to compare herbicide and fertility programs over time* (advantage). *That means you will be able to increase the return on your input dollars by doing more of what works best here on the farm* (benefit).
- *Because this product is injected subcutaneously* (feature), *you won't have as much muscle damage as with intramuscular injections* (advantage). *That means less cut-out at slaughter and better carcass yield* (benefit).
- *Because this marketing program is so flexible* (feature), *it allows every retailer to customize it to a specific business and market* (advantage). *That means you can continue to meet a variety of customer needs and still optimize your program payment dollars* (benefits).
- *Because this injectable product has a non-stinging carrier* (feature), *it will not cause pets so much discomfort when you administer it* (advantage). *That means higher pet owner satisfaction – and more return visits* (benefit).

Selling The Total Product

Customers almost always buy more than a physical product when they decide to do business with your company. They may also buy peace of mind. They believe the product will work or the service will be delivered as promised. The package may include services that are part of the product – seed delivery, or calibration of equipment, for example. They may expect to be able to access expertise from your staff or your company in return for doing business with you. Or, in the best case, they buy all of these things – a total product that delivers a total solution to their needs so that it creates real value for your customer.

These four levels of product can be illustrated as ever-expanding circles of satisfaction – like ripples in a pond:

Figure 13.1
The Total Product[60]

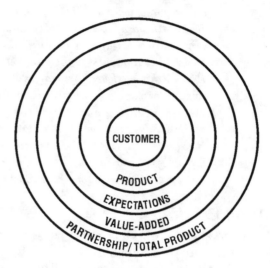

The *basic product* is at the center of the circle. This is what the customer came in to buy - or what you went out to sell. The basic product is the physical product, plus any basic expectations about performance. For example, a herbicide should perform as labeled. A software program shouldn't crash or lose data. A seed product should have dependable germination, little foreign matter or weed seed, and an accurate count per bag.

The *expectations* ring includes the set of services or features that make your product a little better than the ordinary - features and benefits that raise your product "onto the radar screen" or "into the consideration set" of the customer. For example, commercial farmers want equipment that is fully assembled, is supported by a class in equipment operation, has current manuals (even if it is used), and is dependable and fuel-efficient. In the herbicide market, most retailers expect the manufacturer to support the product with a competitive marketing program, product education, complaint handling, etc. Many activities that are now "expected" were developed to add value. However, when many companies offer similar services and "perks," customers come to expect these from anyone they do business with. Thus, these services don't really add value in

---

[60] The "total product concept" is presented in G. Manning and B. Reece, Selling Today, An Extension of the Marketing Concept, Allyn and Bacon, Boston: 1992. It is an adaptation of a model described in "Marketing Success Through Differentiation - of Anything." Harvard Business Review, Jan-Feb 1980.

a meaningful way anymore. They have become a prerequisite for being considered as an alternative source of supply.

Value-added activities, services and features can take your product beyond what the customer expects and differentiate it from the competition. When companies plan to "add value" to a product or service, they try to develop a service or benefit that cannot easily be imitated by others. They want to create a position that is "head and shoulders" above the competition. For example, a seed company might place highly qualified agronomists in the field, and make them available to key accounts for consultation on a variety of crop planning and agronomic troubleshooting issues. A crop protection company might hire interns to calibrate planters for a soil insecticide. A farm management company might offer a tax service. Or a manufacturer might offer training in management to independent retailers. When a value-added service works well and can be imitated by competitors, it quickly becomes offered by every company in the market. Over time, the "value-added" service may become just one more "expectation."

The *potential product or partnership* is the total set of results possible. It describes results considerably beyond the product alone. These results emerge through a strong buyer-seller relationship, a "partnership" of efforts and resources. For example, a manufacturer may provide equipment, financing and expertise to help an independent retailer comply with EPA guidelines. A feed company may pay for an agricultural engineer to evaluate facilities prior to expansion. The "total product" is as a value bundle – many benefits assembled in such a way that they build the customer's business in ways he or she could not do alone. The value bundle or total product is unique to each customer, because it is built around that specific customer's current facilities, people, business goals and needs. You should know what the "preferred total product" or preferred value bundle looks like for your top 10 customers, if you want to keep them!

Competitive Options

Let's assume you know your product, your customer's needs, and you have a variety of services you can use to add value. Will you get the sale? Not necessarily. Your competition is also preparing to sell this customer – and they may be doing many of the same things you are. No one likes to get to the end of a sales presentation, just to hear: *But your competitor says he can do the same thing for about 10% less...* How can a salesperson prepare for competition?

1. Know their products as well as you know your own. You may be asked to compare them – feature by feature. Know where you are relatively strong and weak and be ready to demonstrate off-setting benefits where you are not as strong.

2. Have a good general idea of the prices and services your competitor is offering. (Some salespeople even call competitors to compare prices.) Remember, you are selling a "value bundle" that contains more than product – you should compare the total value bundle, not product alone.

3. Be honest about differences in products, services, programs and prices. If your competitor has a lower price offer, don't deny it. But look for other ways to add value so that your total attribute set becomes the best value. Always be scrupulously accurate about anything you promise to do, any price deals, any extra services...it is never worth it to get a customer one year and lose him for life because you couldn't live up to the promises you made.

4. Never speak poorly of the competition. Sometimes badmouthing a competitor puts the prospect on the defensive as they try to justify a previous relationship. Some customers may try get you to say something negative about the competition. They may try to draw you out. Don't fall for it – it doesn't reflect well on you or your company. Besides, with the pace of consolidation, one day you might be working for them.

The Process of Presenting

The process of presenting benefits of your product or service is very much like the process used in uncovering needs. In fact, the word "presentation" is probably not an accurate description of what the most effective salespeople do. Remember, your goal is to create a "partnership" based on the total product – the combination of all the products, services and value-added elements you can provide to help this specific customer meet business and personal goals.

You can't build a partnership when only one side is talking.

It is *critical* that your customer stay involved in the conversation during a presentation. Their involvement communicates many things that are essential to a healthy long-term relationship – and to making the sale.

- It reinforces that the decision is theirs. This is particularly important for High D's (Dominants) and High C's (Compliants), who need to feel that they control the sales process. However, all customers need to understand that they make the decision, they own the results, and you are not "talking them into" anything inappropriate.
- It reinforces the sales process as a problem-solving process. Remember that the bulk of your communication is non-verbal and tone of voice - not information. Thus how you act and how you share

benefits will set a "tone" for your relationship with the customer more effectively than what you say.

- It allows you to uncover objections and misunderstandings as you go. No salesperson wants to come to the end of a brilliant presentation, only to find out that the customer knew all along he/she couldn't afford the product or service, or didn't have the facilities or equipment to implement the solution you suggest.

The most effective salespeople can "present" product and service benefits through a questioning process. New salespeople may find they have to practice that a bit - especially how to transition to closing the sale - but the basic process is worth learning and practicing.

Donna Berry Hines
Pfizer Animal Health
Swine Industry Representative
Quincy, Michigan

Preparation and then preparation again is really important to me. That was especially important early in my sales career. Still, after all the preparation is done, it is more important to be ready or able to drop all those facts and figures in "canned" order and be personable and flexible in presenting yourself and your products to the customer.

For instance, I get invited to a lot of organization or company meetings to present my company pitch. Sometimes you may prepare a 45 minute speech and then be informed that you only have 15 minutes. You have to be flexible and intuitive enough to give then the pertinent information in those 15 minutes. Also vice-versa. Being flexible and comfortable with that flexibility makes the customer feel at ease with you and what you represent.

I would like to think that I usually can make people pretty comfortable with me. Still, I think that it is important that you are sincere. You have to be a real person. You have to not get ruffled because sometimes people do things to throw you off track just to see how you will react. Some people really enjoy that. You have to learn to be flexible and roll with the punches. People respect this a lot more than losing it - getting upset, confused, angry about someone giving you a hard time or an unusual situation.

Process Steps

1. Confirm the primary needs of the customer and the current satisfaction level. This is the first step – did you hear all the needs? Do you understand which ones have the highest priority for the customer? Is the customer satisfied with current solution to those needs – the person he/she is buying from, the company and the products or services? This step is critical because it confirms which benefits to emphasize and how difficult the sale will be. Closed and confirming questions work well here. If you can get the customer to agree with your summary statements, it logically and naturally leads you to the next steps – and demonstrates that you have been paying attention and really understand them. It also builds trust. If you find you were not completely on target, you will need to back up, get some more information and move back to this point again.

2. Ask for any additional needed information
This should be an open question: *Is there anything else I need to know about your operation? Is there anything else that would be helpful in making a decision?* This step reinforces that you want to sell a total product – a total solution – not just a specific product or service. It takes you out of the realm of product sellers, who only want to push their product into as many businesses as possible, and into the realm of customer-needs selling. This step is also useful in uncovering resistance to your solution early in the presentation, before it becomes the "make or break" issue determining the sale.

3. Offer more than one alternative.
This may seem like strange advice: after all, haven't all your efforts been directed at uncovering the "best" solution? Certainly you want to have one preferred solution to offer your customer. However, the customer always has alternatives – including not to buy your product or service. By offering more than one alternative, you allow the customer to choose a less costly solution, or a different solution. You offer the customer a choice between solutions, rather than the "all or nothing" choice of buying your "best" solution or buying from another company.

4. Fully develop benefits and results for the chosen alternative.
This is where your preparation really pays off. You can use your knowledge of the product and your knowledge of the customer's needs to describe the results the customer can expect when he does business with you. Depending on your product, you may need to be flexible at this point. In essence, you must be prepared to discuss the results that can be expected from any of the alternatives you offered. Don't let poor preparation put you in the position of saying: *Gosh...that's what you want to*

do? I'll have to go back and work up some numbers on that one... after you have come this far.

In Table 13.2 you will find some typical examples of this presentation flow for various products and services.

Table 13.2
Presentation Process Examples

	Selling a crop protection product to a retailer	Selling a field information system to a farmer	Selling feed to a large swine operation	Selling financing for an expansion
1. Confirm needs and satisfaction	Then your key need is to attract the largest farmers by offering them products that cut down on time in the field?	Then what you need now is a system that tracks all inputs - including drainage and soil amendments? And your current system is not quite powerful enough to do that?	So the key needs for you are to improve the weight gain and reduce mortality for nursery pigs? And you feel, given your facilities, that feed is the next best place to make an adjustment?	Let me see if I fully understand your goals here, John...you'd like to add this additional 250 acres, farm it in corn and beans now, and maybe eventually create a livestock facility there? And you thought you'd look beyond your current bank for a loan of this size?
2. Ask for additional information	Are there any other business goals that could be impacted by which product line you emphasize?	In the long term, what other elements of the business would you like to track?	Is there anything else that would be helpful in building a nursery feed program for you? Are you considering any changes in the facility or medication program?	Are there any other expansion plans on your plate right now? Have you worked up a preliminary cash flow on the new farm?
3. Offer more than one alternative	We could work together on a volume discount, that you could pass on to large farmers... or we could arrange a rebate for applied product, to strengthen your application business...which sounds better to you?	We could set up a system that downloads information from your harvest monitoring system - you would still have to enter other inputs by hand. Or, we can develop a "handshake" between our GIS application systems and your software, and pick up an additional set of information that way.	We could start with a complete 3-phase nursery feed program, to make sure we control the entire nursery nutrition... or we could add a 4th late-phase start feed to that to ensure a good transition to the grower barn...which might work best for you, given your experience with the pigs when they leave the nursery?	It seems to me like we have a couple of alternatives. You could take a shorter term financing on the land, if you think you can cash flow it, and ten have more equity when you want t expand the livestock operation. Or, you could take a longer term loan on the new farm, and finance the livestock expansion against another part of your farm, where you currently own land.
4. Develop benefits for the chosen alternative	I agree, the $1.00/acre rebate for applied product is good for your customers and helps build your application business...could we walk through the numbers...?	Ok, then, it looks like the best place to start is with a system where you still enter some of the information? That's fine...it will allow you to continue using your own spray equipment, which means...	Well, it sounds like the primary problem is really in the nursery. These start feeds complement the developing digestive system of the pig and can also be medicated... that means less scouring, better weight gain, and fewer days in the nursery.	I agree, Fritz, the conservative approach is probably the best one...let's take a look at how a shorter term loan would cash flow...

Selecting Evidence

Some customers like to see a full analysis of how your product or service will benefit them: spreadsheets or worksheets, examples of similar situations, data on product performance, etc. Others may only ask for your word that a product or service will bring them the results they need and expect. The evidence you choose should reflect your understanding of how the customer wants to communicate, as well as which benefits are most important to him. For example, economic buyers are very concerned about price...business buyers are also concerned about output or profit. In every situation, however, you should be prepared to offer <u>some</u> evidence that your product or service will perform as described. This evidence can take many forms.

Testimonials

Testimonials are the experiences of other customers with the benefits of your products or services – their "testimony" to your value. Testimonials are especially useful for relationship-oriented buyers, as well as for High "I" (Influencing) and High "S" (Steady) buyers. These buyers like to know that a product or service is working for people they know and trust. High "D" (Dominant) and High "C" (Compliant) buyers may be more interested in factual information than in neighbors' experience. If you want to use a testimonial:

- make sure that you have the permission of the person whose experiences you are sharing;
- make sure that this person is a "respected source" for the customer you are selling;
- never divulge any confidential information (i.e., <u>never</u> start out a testimonial with: *You wouldn't believe how screwed up his program was...*

Calculations of Cost/Benefit

Commercial farmers and retailers increasingly want to know what a new product or service will do "for them", not just what it will do on a test plot or in a test facility. This approach is also very effective when presenting or "forecasting" the results of participation in a marketing program – how many units must be sold to trigger different levels of program dollars or points. Cost/benefit calculations work especially well for customers who want to "control" the decision process and decide what is best for themselves, rather than taking your word. High "D" (Dominant) and High "C" (Compliant) customers both like this approach, although the High "D" may not have much patience with a lengthy analysis. You can calculate the cost/benefit of your products and services in a variety of ways. In each case, <u>preparation is essential</u>; you don't want to spend 30 minutes of your sales call calculating cost/benefit, only to find out that your product or service is not the best solution for the customer. It is always better to use the customer's own assumptions and numbers to demonstrate the cost/benefits of a solution. But that is not always feasible. Some options include:

- show a prepared worksheet giving typical use levels and typical results for your area;
- prepare a spreadsheet with several options – different levels of use or product combinations – and corresponding costs and results;
- prepare a "blank" worksheet or spreadsheet and walk through it with the customer as a decision aid, allowing them to enter their own typical costs for your solution and alternative solutions.

Controlled Trials

For many products and services, there is still a place for data from controlled trials. These trials may be completed by an objective third party, such as a university, or by the company itself. For example, a new animal health product or crop protection product must pass many regulatory hurdles before being registered for sale. Much of the same data used in the registration process can be useful in demonstrating the product's efficacy to potential customers. Of course, trial results and field results are not always the same, because by their very nature trials control many of the confounding variables that a producer must deal with daily. Trials should also be discussed with the customer within the context of other problems in the business. For example, a vaccination, however effective in controlled trials, will not be effective in a livestock operation if the animals have already been exposed to the disease. Controlled trials are also useful for other products...for example, fuel use trials for equipment, engine wear and tear for oil products, or even savings in input expenses from a more targeted GIS approach to farming.

Demonstration Trials

Demonstration trials are different from controlled trials because they take place in the local community, or close by. Demonstration trials go by a variety of names, depending on which branch of the industry conducts them. For example, the seed industry holds "field days" where farmers and potential dealers can come and see, touch, and sometimes observe the harvesting of new hybrids. The equipment industry may also have a type of field day (often at farm shows), where farmers can try out new equipment, or they may send around a "road show" of selected equipment, allowing farmers in many different parts of the country an opportunity for a first-hand and up-close look at new equipment. Trials in the feed industry and animal health industry are somewhat different, because of the biosecurity issues involved when strangers enter a facility. Trials may be completed in a "typical" operation and then written up and published. While some of these trials may be provided by your company, it is quite common and often highly effective for the local sales rep to establish some of these trials, tailored to local conditions.

On-Farm /In-Business Trials

These trials are the ultimate tool to convince some farmers and retailers of a product or service benefit. In farm trials, support is offered to the farmer to make sure that the trial is fair and objective. For example, a seed company will ask the dealer to help the farmer plant "side-by-side" trials with similar field conditions, and enough of each product to get a fair comparison. In feed trials, the producer is also given support to make sure that all other production parameters are the same for both groups, and the performance of the feed can be fairly "isolated" from other variables in the operation. When selling products, programs and services to a retailer, the "trial" may consist of a specified sample use period, followed by an evaluation between the salesperson and the manager. For example, a new product might be displayed for a limited time to get a feeling for its power to attract customers. Or, a piece of software might be offered with a limited number of features, to help the retailer judge whether the full version would be helpful in the business. Usually, product that is "on trial" in a business or farm is offered to the customer at a sharply reduced cost or at no cost.

Photographs

There is still a role for photographs for many products...a picture still speaks a thousand words. Photographs and their high-tech cousin, computer-based sales presentations, allow the customer to see and judge a product's performance. Photographs and computer-based presentations are particularly useful in several situations:

- setting product performance expectations – for example, whether an herbicide will kill a product in 2, 10 or 20 days can be most easily shown by a time-lapse series of pictures that show the farmer and retailer what to expect from the product;
- showing product features – for example, the construction of a tool or facility, or the satellite pictures from a GIS precision farming product;
- demonstrating product mode of action – for example, the mode of action of a new antimicrobial can be simulated and animated and easily understood, whereas the scientific explanation of mode of action could be confusing and even counterproductive to people with no veterinary training.

Many types of evidence are available in most companies. Sometimes, evidence or "proof" statements are beautifully packaged in promotional literature or computer-based decision aids and presentations. In other companies, "proof" rests primarily with satisfied users, and the salesperson may have to take action to pull evidence of benefits together in a way that appeals to other potential customers. When demonstration trials and on-farm trials are planned, the salesperson should always be involved, and should not be shy about asking for help from agronomists, software experts, on-staff veterinarians, etc., to make sure the trial is organized and executed properly.

Summary

A sales presentation may sometimes feel like an event - the time to really explain the benefits of your product or services. However, in the best situations, a sales presentation is a continuation of an ongoing discussion between a salesperson and a customer. It is one more step in finding and implementing the best possible solution for the customer, and in creating a satisfied customer for life.

The most effective presentations are totally focused around a specific customer and that customer's needs, values, style and goals. They include the customer - not just by summarizing needs and offering solutions, but by letting the customer re-state needs, add any additional considerations, ask questions and make choices. If you find yourself doing all the talking in a presentation, you will find it harder to close the sale.

The other element that is essential for a successful presentation is preparation. In a recent NBA tournament, the coach of a championship team was asked about the percentage of baskets vs. shots taken from the free throw line. He mentioned casually: *We practice free throws every day...hundreds of times.* When your customer agrees to spend time with you hearing about the benefits and results from your product or service, he has invited you to "the tournament." Your competition may not be there to play face-to-face, but they were there the day before or they will be there the next day. Preparation and practice don't guarantee that you'll win this customer's business - but a lack of preparation ensures that you will lose. This preparation should include:

- understanding the full set of customer needs;
- planning to match or complement the customer's style (how they evaluate products and make decisions);
- a thorough knowledge of the features and potential benefits of your product or service *for this customer;*
- the "total product" that best meets the customer's needs;
- the competitive options to the product or service and how they compare to your offer;

- a plan for your presentation discussion confirming needs, asking for additional information, suggesting more than one alternative, and benefits (and evidence) for the chosen alternative.

Review Questions

1. Presenting the sale represents "the neck of the funnel" of information you've developed toward making the sale. What are at least four components the salesperson must know of before presenting a solution to the customer for the first time?

2. Define features, advantages and benefits.

3. Let's say you are selling protein pellets to hog farmers. Develop a list of features, advantages and benefits you might use to "sell" your hypothetical product.

4. Review the basic process steps of presenting the sale as illustrated in Table 13.2. Explain why each step is important toward filling the customer's needs and values.

5. What are four common types of evidence? When is each most appropriate?

Chapter Fourteen

Dealing with Resistance

Learning Objectives:
Upon completion of this chapter, you will be able to:
1. define objections and explain how they differ from questions or excuses;
2. identify four types of objection and what they mean to the probability of sale;
3. describe a four-step process for handling sales resistance;
4. recall at least three specific techniques for handling spoken objections and apply these techniques appropriately.

What is "Resistance?"

Ray McLaughlin
Blue SEAL Feeds
Dairy Product Manager
Dairy Manager at Bow, New Hampshire Facility
Londonderry, New Hampshire

You have to get over customer resistance – which isn't really the objection at all. You've got to tend to separate the wheat from the chaff very quickly. If you can do that you tend to get more results than a salesperson who gets hung up on all the little stones that the farmer or the prospect is throwing out to you, which are merely part of the game. And you have to be able to see beyond that.

Resistance is an opportunity to answer a need or a question – a desire for more information or more reasons to buy. You can't miss the real point that this is kind of a dance that you have to go through in the selling process. Another way to look at objections is to consider them as a list of final reasons for the customer to buy. They mean you are or can be close to getting the sale if you manage the objections with reason and integrity.

When new salespeople think about encountering resistance in a sales presentation, they imagine the objections they might hear—and how to overcome them. Resistance to purchase, however, actually comes in two varieties: passive resistance and active resistance. Left un-addressed, either one is sufficient to stop the sale.

Active Resistance

Active resistance takes the form of objections. The most simple definition of an objection is a reason not to buy. However, excuses and questions sometimes sound like objections, even though they are not and should therefore be handled differently than objections.

Objections

Objections are <u>valid</u> reasons not to buy — at least in the mind of the customer. When a customer states an objection, he or she is stating a disagreement or misunderstanding about the value of a benefit or of the total product/service bundle. Objections are often presented as a negative reaction: what the product *cannot* do; why the price is *not* a good value; or why the services promised will *probably not* be delivered. There are three common reasons for objections:

- misunderstanding;
- misinformation;
- lack of information.

<u>Misunderstanding</u> happens frequently, especially with new products and services or when working with a new customer. For example, the feedlot customer may not understand the need for multiple vaccination with an inactive biological, and may therefore believe that past vaccinations from the same company "don't work." The distributor customer may not fully understand the marketing program presented by a manufacturer sales representative, and thus may not feel it is as profitable as last year's program. Or, a row crop farmer may misunderstand a volume discount program or a fee-for-service program and feel that he or she is not getting the best "deal." Misunderstandings can be greatly reduced if the salesperson has organized the benefits presentation around questions and if "full-value" listening is used. Experienced salespeople constantly check for agreement and understanding as they present benefits — especially when dealing with new products, services or technologies:

- *Does that make sense to you, John?*
- *You did say you wanted to improve NBA, right Megan?*
- *Am I right that you're more interested in your breeding program than in sourcing cheaper genetics right now, Sam?*

<u>Misinformation</u> is another common cause of objections. The customer may have heard something about your product, your services or your company that is simply not true:

- *I heard you guys couldn't service all the acres you contracted last year.*
- *I talked to my neighbor and he doesn't think he saved anything with this new system.*
- *I heard about this new program from another manager — you guys are really sticking it to us this year, aren't you?*

When a salesperson encounters misinformation, it must be handled gently but firmly. The person who shared the information originally may be a friend, a neighbor or a relative. Of course, it could also be a competitive salesperson. No matter where the bad information came from, attacking the source is not a solution. Instead, give the correct information and, if necessary, any supporting evidence.

Lack of Information

Sometimes, an objection arises because the customer doesn't have enough information. He or she may only know part of the story about a new product or service. Perhaps the customer used a similar product in the past and didn't see the promised results because of a lack of knowledge or skill in proper product use. Or, the customer may not be able to accurately estimate the value of your product or service because of a lack of information within their own business.

For example, in order for a farmer to be fully convinced that your high oil corn will bring additional profit, he has to be able to market it at a premium sufficient to cover the cost of production. In order for a veterinarian to know that your "puppy package" of immunization programs will generate additional office calls and income, she has to know how many office calls per puppy she is generating now. In order for a retailer to know that your product will increase application income, he has to know the profitability of current application services. Increasingly, the salesperson is asked to help a customer generate, organize or find the information needed to make a sound economic decision. Many sales reps now use spreadsheets, electronic worksheets in computer-based decision aid programs, or sample profitability worksheets from similar businesses to help the customer understand value when they do not have the data necessary for a valid comparison.

Excuses

Excuses often sound just like objections: "Your prices are just too high!" They are given by the customer as a reason not to buy. However, an excuse is different from an objection because it is less based on any benefit you have presented and more based on some other circumstance, a situation beyond the performance of the product or your business. Excuses are "smoke screens" often designed to hide the real reason for not buying. Because excuses are often based on circumstances beyond your control, they are difficult to deal with. And, in fact, some experienced salespeople recognize the excuse for what it is and don't try to convince the customer otherwise.

Why would a person make an excuse not to buy? There can be many reasons:

- they are not the final decision-maker — but don't want to admit it;
- they may not have enough money to buy the program you suggest;
- they may not have enough management skill to implement the changes you have recommended, or the goals you have set together.

There are three "dead giveaways" that you are dealing with an excuse. First, it usually comes out of left field. If a potential customer has been working with you over several calls to put together a package that will meet their needs — and you have qualified them as a buyer who can afford your package — suddenly hearing that you are "too high" or that the customer is "just not ready" to make a decision means you are probably hearing an excuse. The second characteristic of excuses is that they are almost impossible to handle — they effectively stop the presentation and the sale. If a customer says he or she wants to "think about it" or "look around," it's hard to think of how you could persuade them to make a decision now. If a customer says your price is too high, but really doesn't want to talk about how you could work out payment or a less expensive option, they've pretty much stopped you — unless you know how to deal with it. The third characteristic of excuses is the *nonverbal* message from the customer. These cues are less dependable, but still very useful. When giving an excuse, customers often look away — or even walk away.

Occasionally, the customer will become unnaturally aggressive — as if you had been pushing them into something. In both cases, the customer is signaling that something is bothering them. This barrier will keep you from going further until you deal with it.

When a customer stops your presentation with excuses, what can you do? Of course, one option is simply to pack up your things and call it a day. But that often isn't the best course — not only did you not sell to this customer today, but you don't really know what the issue underneath the excuse was. Until you do, you may not be able to *ever* sell to this customer. When you feel you have not heard the "real" objection, don't leave. Meet the customer's need to "stop" the sales presentation and go back to probing.

One method is to take the blame yourself for any misunderstanding, and gently ask for the root cause:

- *You're the boss here, John...have I somehow misunderstood your needs*
- *I sure don't want you to move on this until you're really ready, but I am a little curious...what cooled your interest in trying this new program?*

Tom Giese
Cenex/Land O'Lakes
Livestock Production Specialist
Canby, Minnesota

You've *got* to be open to listening to customer objections. If there's a failure or something that goes wrong I want to know why. Let's learn from this thing. I think that's where I have been successful.

I just had a particular instance where we had a dairy farm I was trying to sell. The guy was trying our product out. He was unhappy with a current feed supplier. He agreed to test out our feed...kind of a trial before agreeing to a sale. I came back after a couple weeks and he says, "We put your feed in and the cows wouldn't eat the feed." The problem there was simply salt. He had some musty corn and when we went in there and ran the rations and gave the recommendations, I had salt in there. Well, he had put block salt in the box and nothing in the grain mix. Then he had pulled the molasses away - different from what we had calculated. He had been putting molasses in the corn which was covering up the musty smell.

I got to the farm and I got my tailed chewed, no doubt about it, but I didn't back down either. I said, "Wait a second. Cattle always eat grain. You say it's our product causing the problem? Well let's figure this out." By the time I left the farm, about and hour and a half later, we had resolved the situation to the point we left on good terms and he's going to buy.

If you're wrong you admit it and take care of it, but if something goes wrong, I guess the thing to tell a newer salesperson is, don't walk out frustrated, find out why and learn from that. I use objections as an opportunity. I think, "Wait a second, I want your business." The objection may make me mad. But I don't want to be driving off the place with the customer saying bad things about me and my company and our products. Now it's time to work through it and figure out the missing piece of the puzzle to making your product fill his needs. When some of these customers raise an objection, they're really just asking for — "OK, help me understand this better. Help me get it." Some, on the other hand, just strongly object to change.

To somebody starting out in the field, there is a big difference between getting hit with an objection, turning tail and running versus, "Okay let's manage this and keep a cool head." Then, go back and review everything to keep the customer happy. That's really what it's all about.

Questions

Questions are sometimes confused with objections, especially if they are stated in negative terms or by a customer with a more aggressive personal communication style:

- *Why <u>wouldn't</u> I stay with my current supplier?*
- *These products seem to do the same thing...why should I go with your program?*
- *So how much is this new approach going to cost me?*

Questions should always be answered honestly. And, when answering a question that requires a complex explanation, it's always a good idea to check for understanding:

- *Did I answer your question?*

Passive Resistance

Passive resistance takes a variety of forms, some of which are almost invisible to new salespeople. The sales process seems to be working; the customer seems to be agreeing to the value of the benefits you are presenting. Yet somehow, it seems impossible to close. There is always one more person to talk to, one more comparison to make, one more delay before a decision.

Experienced salespeople have learned to watch for the signs of passive resistance. It can block a sale just as effectively as stated objections. The only difference is that you never hear the objection and thus can't deal effectively with it. When passive resistance occurs, the salesperson must often be the one to break the stalemate — to *ask* for objections and get them out into the open, where they can be addressed.

- *Dan, it sounds like this product will meet your needs and your budget...am I missing something here, or are you ready to get started?*
- *Pete, you have a good understanding of the program...yet you seem unsure at what level you want to participate. Is there anything holding you back?*
- *Sarah, we've met several times on this...is there any additional information or issues to resolve before you make a decision?*

When you sense that the customer is "putting you off," it's wise to find out why. This is particularly true for manufacturer reps who are "selling" a marketing program. If the retailer *acquiesces* but does not *buy* the program, it is unlikely that the goals you set together will be met. Near the end of a call, some salespeople simply try a closing tactic — a trial close — to uncover these silent objections. We'll explain the trial close tactic more fully in the next chapter, but its function here is to stimulate the customer to tell you why he or she is holding back. Are they seriously interested? Or have they simply been too polite to tell you that they have already decided on someone else? If the decision has already been made — or if they are unwilling to make any decision at this time — it's better to know, so that you can invest your time with a customer who is still willing to buy.

Is Resistance a Positive or Negative Sign?

Many salespeople fear resistance. They seem to feel that the sales presentation is their "final exam" and resistance from the customer is a sign that they might fail the test. Not so.

The only "bad" objection is the one you don't hear. That's why passive resistance is so dangerous. When a customer states an objection, it shows that they are actively considering the product or service and how it might work in their business. It's helpful to think of objections as "trying on" your solution. The customer is imagining what their business would be like, living with your products, services and solutions. When the customer states an objection, he or she is openly testing the viability of your benefits against their current production or business practices, their assumptions about what works and what doesn't, their loyalty to current suppliers, and their understanding.

Larry Barmann
American Cyanamid
Marketing Specialist, IMI - Corn
Red Oak, Iowa

When people start giving objections, I think that's actually good. They are interested and they want to know more. The person who is well prepared knows the products, the features and benefits will do very well in handling objections. Feature/benefits are, I think, what the customer looks to hear in their mind, but they are also searching for that transition statement that means, "here's what that statement means to you." Here's a feature of a product. The benefit will further define that to the customer you are working with. I think they are looking for the key phrases of what it does, but then, the transition to <u>what it does for them</u>. So, feature, benefit, and the result that it brings to you often can resolve the objection.

The big advantage of the stated objection is that you get to participate in this "testing" process — to show your knowledge, skills and an attitude of customer focus. They allow you to show that you respect your customer — whether you agree or not. When you accept an objection as valid, if only in the mind of this one customer, you take it seriously, answer it conscientiously, and thereby show the customer that you take <u>him</u> seriously, or that you will always be conscientious with <u>her</u> concerns. It allows you to demonstrate a level of responsiveness and customer focus that you otherwise would not get to show until after the sale.

Four Types of Objections

Earlier in the chapter, we said that most objections arise from misunderstanding, misinformation or lack of information. Think of these as the "root sources" of the objection or of passive resistance. Whatever the "source," the stated objection tends to fall in one of the following categories.

I Don't Need Your Product

This objection occurs when the customer honestly believes they don't need your product — whether they actually need it or not. The source may be a misunderstanding about the product's benefits, misinformation or a lack of information. You may not have done enough to make them understand the costs involved with their current program, with allowing the problem to continue, or with not taking advantage of increased profit opportunities. You have some catching up to do! In some cases, of course, the customer may be correct. They really don't need your product or program — that is, your alternative is not a significant improvement over what they are currently doing. In this situation, you have not done an adequate job of qualifying the customer, determining their primary needs, and making a good needs/benefits match.

I Guess I Need It — But Not Now

This is a classic example of passive resistance. In some cases, it is perfectly true — the customer does not need to make a switch right now. Again, unless you are dealing with someone who is trying to stall you, you must re-assess your original needs/benefits match. What would be the benefits of buying now vs. later? What are the costs of waiting, whether in poor business performance, reduced yields, or higher costs? Have you adequately explained the cost/benefit value of your solution? When can the customer expect to see improved results? What is the ROI on the investment you want the customer to make? Answering this objection calls for a solid knowledge of the product or service value, *as well* as a solid knowledge of the customer's business.

I Don't Want It

There is a wonderful old story that illustrates this point very well, and you may hear it several times during your sales career. As the story goes, there was once a national sales meeting for a dog food company. The nutritionist stood up and explained the unique advantages of the dog food's formula and presented the results of several research trials. The marketing people stood up and explained how they had lowered the price to generate demand. They showed several cute ads that had been placed that year, and talked about all the money that had been spent on marketing. They mentioned their distributor program, and showed the new packaging designs that had been introduced the year before. Finally, the president of the company stood up. His point was simple — why hadn't the sales force been able to sell more product, given all the support they were getting? The room was silent for a few seconds, until one old salesman from the back called out: "Dogs don't like it."

Every salesperson has had moments when the "dogs don't like it" story seems all too appropriate. Sometimes, even though the customer agrees with and accepts your benefits and truly needs the product, he or she just "doesn't like it" and doesn't want to buy. There are two primary reasons this occurs.

- The customer is simply not motivated to buy. This situation is similar to the "I need it but not right now" objection, except that "not now" might last a lifetime. The customer may object to the product's mode of action, or to buying a service he or she could perform themselves. Or, they simply do not have enough energy to make a switch. Occasionally, the customer may object to a product on principle. For example, when bovine somatotropins (products that increase the amount of milk a cow will produce to the genetic potential of the cow) were first introduced, objections to them were highly political. In some areas, farmers feared that this type of product would accelerate the advantages of larger producers, and thus accelerate the death of the small family dairy farm. Producers were able to understand the economic benefits of the product — but deciding to use it was a political as well as a production decision. Some farmers put profit before politics, and began using the product. Others realized it could benefit them, but decided not to buy.

- In the second situation, the customer may understand that they need the product but they may be unsure if they can manage it. Or, they may need the product and be unsure if they can realize a return from it, in their unique time frame. For example, a farmer may understand the benefits of precision farming and may know that he/she needs better information and more targeted inputs. Yet, if the farmer is going to retire in 4-5 years, he or she may not be motivated to buy grid mapping, software and monitoring hardware because their span of management is almost over.

This objection is very difficult to overcome. If, in fact, the customer cannot realize a return, either because of management skill or management tenure, you should have uncovered this fact during prospecting and qualifying. If the customer simply "doesn't want" the product — for personal, social or political reasons — you probably did not uncover key buying motivations during probing. While the benefits are there, and are believed, they are not strong enough to "tip the scales" toward a purchase. The best way to handle the objection is to accept it as valid, for this customer, and re-explore the customer's needs and business goals with an eye to a new solution.

I Can't Afford It

If the customer indeed cannot afford your product, again you probably have not done a good job of qualifying. Often, however, customers may believe they cannot afford a product or service because they don't adequately understand the potential profits it could bring. Or, for capital purchases such as buildings and equipment, they may not understand the life of the product and how the purchase price will actually be spread over many years of use. Finally, customers sometimes offer this objection because they are not aware of your financing programs. If you have done a good job of qualifying and you are fairly sure this customer <u>can</u> afford your product or service, ask them about their feelings and try to find a mutually agreeable solution.

When to Quit

Some objections are simply misunderstandings. These are relatively easy to clarify, although the salesperson must always allow the customer to save pride in the process of learning new information. Other objections are quite valid. Your feed price may indeed be higher than some competitors. Your software may indeed not be compatible with all operating systems. Your equipment may not have the highest resale value.

Of course, to the customer, *all* objections are valid until proven otherwise. When handling objections in a sales call, the salesperson's goal is to remove as many obstacles as possible to the sale, and to reinforce benefits of the product or service as well as the benefit of working with the company. If the benefits outweigh the objections, a sale is made.

Experienced salespeople also know when to quit. The customer may have problems that prevent buying your product — problems they don't wish to reveal to you. Pushing too hard in these situations only alienates the customer. Or, occasionally, despite excellent prospecting, qualifying and probing, you find a customer who really <u>doesn't</u> need your product as badly as you supposed. If this happens, accept it gracefully. If you have honestly uncovered all the needs and shared all pertinent information, if you have made the best possible "match" and it isn't good enough — thank the customer and leave. If you have been honest and sensitive to their needs, you'll have another chance at a later time.

Can a Salesperson Prepare for Objections?

As a salesperson calls on more and more customers, the same objections will be heard again and again. In fact, many salespeople say that there are four or five objections that account for 80% of all the objections they hear. This is particularly true if the salesperson has segmented the market, i.e., has prioritized and focused on a few groups of customers with similar needs and similar patterns of purchase. To be sure, every customer is unique, and not all objections are exactly the same (or even of the same importance) from customer to customer. Yet the objections themselves recur. And because they recur, it is possible to prepare for them in some very specific ways, not just by "boning up" on product knowledge or competitive offers. There is just no excuse for a salesperson not to have a plan or strategy in mind for handling all of the common objections they hear.

Guidelines for Handling Objections

There are three general rules to follow for handling all objections.

1. Handle the objection when it comes up. Putting it off may signal to the customer that you don't have an answer. And if the objection is on their mind, they are likely to be distracted and miss other important points you are making. The only exception is price. You should recognize the price objection when it comes up, but handle it once you have had a chance to demonstrate value.

    Terry, our price is a little higher than last year...the package is much stronger however, and I'd like a chance to explain it to you. I'd like to come back to the issue of price after I have had the opportunity to explain some of the exciting new parts of our program.

2. Always accept the objection as valid in the customer's mind, and treat it seriously. The customer always has a reason for an objection and it is logical in his/her own mind...an experience, some information, some lack of understanding that causes a concern to arise.

3. Avoid arguments — even if you win, you lose. You may be right and the customer may be wrong, but no one is standing in the wings giving out an A+ for the "right" answer. Your objective is not to prove the customer wrong. It is to help them meet their needs by finding a solution that will work, and that they believe is the best possible choice. Experienced salespeople use one or more of the

following tactics to avoid an argument. These work most of the time — even with the most argumentative customers.

- Accept blame for a misunderstanding.
  - ➤ *I'm sorry, I didn't explain that very well...*
  - ➤ *That's my fault, Julie, I should have asked you about that...*

- Help the customer save face.
  - ➤ *Many people ask about that...*
  - ➤ *That's a complex process, isn't it...*

- Blame the situation.
  - ➤ *These disease outbreaks often happen in damp weather...*
  - ➤ *Isolating the performance of one product is always difficult...*

- Anticipate and answer common objections in your presentation.
  - ➤ *You may have heard we're not working with the same satellite communications vendor any more...*
  - ➤ *People often ask about what kind of profit record our farm management company has...*

Best Practices for Handling Objections

There is also a generally-accepted "best practice" for handling most objections that arise during a call. This process has four steps:

1. Listen.
2. Restate.
3. Ask for more information.
4. Handle.

Listen

Whenever a customer states an objection, there is a tendency to react quickly — to anticipate their needs and to answer them as completely as possible. However, the best thing to do when an objection is stated is simply to listen. Listening carefully to the customer's concern indicates you are paying attention and taking him or her seriously. And it gives you a few moments to determine the best response.

How the objection is stated is as important as the *content* of the objection. Concern, doubt, lack of trust, or past bad experiences are all expressed in the tone of voice — or in a worried facial expression. Listen for the concern — but also listen to how important this concern is to the customer. Allowing your customer an uninterrupted chance to tell you about concerns also communicates your respect and your willingness to work with the customer as a consultant — not just a seller.

Restate the objection

Restating what you *think* you heard is always a good idea. It's one of the critical components of active listening. When a customer states an objection, restating is even more important. Putting the objection into your own words gives it validity. Initially, salespeople think that "validity" is not a good idea — after all, the objection may be based on a misunderstanding or bad information. However, restating the objection in your own words tells the customer that you have heard the concern and are prepared to take it seriously. If you did not understand the objection correctly, it gives the customer a chance to state it again and helps you avoid wasting time dealing with the wrong issue. When you restate an objection, you may want to "cushion" it slightly. Try to remove the emotion from the issue and state it calmly, as a problem to be solved together, not as a chance to prove that you're right and the customer is wrong (or vice versa).

Let's look at several examples.

Customer A: *You suppliers are all alike — you set up delivery schedules that are good for you, no matter what else I have going on...*

Salesperson A: *Getting delivery at the right time is pretty important, so I can understand your concern, Bob. How often do you need delivery with your set-up? What are the best times of day?*

Customer B: *I've seen enough marketing programs to last a lifetime. They're all alike in one respect...the goals are so high we never seem to be able to achieve them, and so we never get all those great rebates and other benefits you keep talking about.*

Salesperson B: *So what I hear you saying is that the goals from some of your manufacturers in the past have been unrealistic? How did you go about setting them — were they given to you, or did you have a chance to set them with the rep like we are now?*

Customer C: *You know, I don't think that motor has enough horsepower to do the job.*

Salesperson C: *You're concerned that the motor on this model will not get the job done, right? Is your concern more about pulling enough weight or that the motor will be under too much stress at peak periods?*

As the examples above show, the first part of cushioning an objection is to restate it in more neutral terms. This allows you to agree with the customer — they have a concern and you have heard it — without agreeing to the objection itself. The second part of cushioning an objection is to ask a question or two to get at the "real issue," an issue you can solve together.

Ask for more information

This step is crucial to successfully handling an objection. After all, if you had all the information necessary to meet the customer's needs and find a customized solution, you probably wouldn't have heard an objection in the first place. Asking for more information accomplishes several goals:

- it continues the discussion as a *dialogue* — a collaboration on solutions;
- it de-fuses any anger or emotion the customer is feeling;
- it helps you understand the basis for the customer's concern, so you can deal with it more effectively.

Handle the objection

Once a salesperson has truly understood an objection and the experiences that caused it to arise, he or she is in a much stronger position to handle it effectively. There are a variety of techniques for handling objections. The "best" technique in any given situation depends on the salesperson, the customer, the type of objection, and the level of relationship between the salesperson and customer. Making the "best" choice is a skill that comes with experience and with a sound knowledge of your customer.

Specific Techniques for Handling Objections

There is no one "best" way to handle every objection, any more than there is one "best" medicine for all diseases or one "best" solution to every problem. The "best" way to handle objections is to master all of the major techniques, and then choose the one that is most effective with each customer and each objection.

Feel, Felt, Found

This is an effective technique to respond to an emotionally-based objection. It works especially well with High I (Influencer) and High S (Steady) customers, because they want your solution to be based on your knowledge of them as *people* — not just as business problems. Listen to the customer's feelings as well as the content of their objection. Then respond with a "feel, felt, found" sequence that shows your empathy with their situation and also your command of the facts.[61]

Customer A: *I really don't think I will ever be able to learn how to operate one of those digital satellite communications computer things.*

Salesperson A: *I understand how you feel, Mike. Many of our customers felt the same way, until they started using our JMJ330 unit...to their surprise, they found it easy — even fun to operate.*

Customer B: *You guys talk a good line, but when it comes to actually working your program, it was so confusing last year we just gave up and sold what our customers asked for first.*

Salesperson B: *I understand how you feel, Mavis. I know other dealers felt that way about last year's program — you're not alone. But we listened, and dealers have found that this year's program is a lot easier to understand and use.*

The objection behind the objection

Sometimes an objection is not clearly stated. You know the customer is concerned — maybe even angry or defensive. But you can't really understand the specific problem. In this situation, you need to find out the "objection behind the objection." Sometimes, the customer is telling you about symptoms, rather than a cause. For example, the symptoms may be that software doesn't perform consistently or dependably. The problems may be various and seem irregular to the customer. The root cause may not be the software, but an incompatibility in the operating system. You need to find out the root cause before you can address the problem. Or, the customer may be concerned that your company doesn't offer responsive technical support...the root cause may be that he/she doesn't have the right sources to call, or that they misunderstand what level of technical support is offered.

Clarifying an objection to get at the root cause can take some time. Don't be afraid to ask the question, though. Objections never go away because they are ignored, they only "go underground" where they can effectively block the sale. If you think this discussion will take awhile, it's wise to ask the customer how much time they have, or if they would like to discuss their concern in more depth. If the

---

[61] Manning, G.L and Reece, B.L. Selling Today: An Extension of the Marketing Concept. Allyn and Bacon, Needham Heights, MA: 1992.

answer is "yes," pursue it. In other situations, you may surprised to find out the customer was only "letting off steam" and wanted to make sure they had your full attention. Let's look at some examples of questions you can use to get at the "objection behind the objection."

- *You seem to have had a bad experience with that...can you explain what happened?*
- *You seem to be surprised that we can deliver parts in 24-48 hours from our warehouse...what has been your experience?*
- *You've said a couple times that you are just not a (company name) type of seed customer...can you explain what you mean?*
- *You seem really concerned about our ability to meet your needs...I'd really like you to tell me some specific concerns or issues, if you would...*

Another technique to draw out the customer's underlying objections is the "echo" technique.[62] This technique works exactly as you might imagine — you "echo" the key point in your customer's objection as a way to get them to further explain or give you an example.

Customer: *I carried your products a few years ago, and they just sat here.*

Salesperson *Sat here?*

Customer: *That's right. They didn't move because the price was just too high.*

Salesperson: *Too high?*

Customer: *Yeah... your competitors had a really aggressive couponing program. They ran ads in the paper offering money off each purchase.*

Turn the Objection into a Selling Point

In this technique, you agree with the "facts" the customer has stated, but use logical explanation to show why this "fact" is a benefit — not a disadvantage. Obviously, this technique doesn't work for every objection. However, when it is appropriate it works very well. Let's look at some examples.

Customer A: *Your jug product is more expensive.*

Salesperson A: *You're right — the jug product is priced a little higher than bulk product. We have a container return program on those jugs to help you*

---

[62] Marks, R. B. Personal Selling: An Interactive Approach. Allyn and Bacon, Needham Heights, MA: 1994.

> *pay for safe container disposal from your customers. The bulk product saves us about 3%, and we gladly pass that along to the customer.*

Customer B: *Your shop isn't as big as the dealer I was working with — I don't see how you'll be able to take care of everyone's needs at busy times.*

Salesperson B: *You're right — our shop is not as big as the MegaFarm dealership over in Knightstown. Instead, we have two mobile service trucks, fully equipped with what's needed for all but the most major repairs. Our customers like it that we come to them during busy times, instead of asking them to stop work and bring equipment in to us.*

Counter with a question

Restating an objection and following up with a question is very useful to uncover "real" or underlying objections. Sometimes, however, a question can be a good way to counter the objection itself. It allows you to state a fact, clear up a misconception, or flatly disagree with the customer without being confrontational. Think of the statement you would like to make — and convert it to a question. Make sure your tone of voice and non-verbal communication is also that of a learner — relaxed and open, not aggressive. You are simply asking the customer to consider another possibility. You'll find your "rebuttal" much easier to accept.

Customer A: *You promised me higher yields with this new drought-resistant seed, but my yields last year were only 150 bushels — that's 10% lower than my five-year average.*

Salesperson A: *150 bushels? Gee, did you realize that was 20% <u>above</u> the country average?*

Customer B: *I don't really think the brand of feed makes all that much difference...I've tried three or four in the nursery, but I'm still seeing too much scouring.*

Salesperson B: *What made you think it was the feed, Jim? Is it possible that these consistent problems could be due to a low-level infection in the nursery pigs?*

Agree when appropriate

Sometimes, the objection of a customer is not a misunderstanding, or lack of information, or misperception — it's the statement of fact. The reality is that almost all products or services have advantages and disadvantages. When your customer recognizes something that is a clear disadvantage to him or her, recognize it. Agree with the objection. If there is a good reason why things are that way, you may state it. Your agreement shows the customer that you are honest, and that you understand your product or service is not "perfect." Follow up on agreement by reinforcing your willingness to work with the customer until you have both agreed on the best solution — or demonstrate how the benefits outweigh the disadvantages.

Customer: *Fertilizer is fertilizer, and your prices are a couple dollars a ton higher than everyone else!*

Salesperson: *You're right — our prices are a little higher. And, while we do try to get a clean product with relatively less dust, its analysis is probably about the same as other places. I guess the difference with us is that we've geared the business to the commercial producer (the agronomist on our staff is on call, for instance, and watches for insect and disease problems in the cotton all season, so we can help you avoid problems. Some of our prices are little more....I guess it depends on what you want from a supplier.*

Customer: *I don't think I need yield insurance...I could use that $14,000 somewhere else, believe me, and besides, my yields are generally as good as or better than most of my neighbors.*

Salesperson: *You're right — you don't have to have yield insurance. It really only protects you when yields are down around the county, due to bad growing conditions. On the other hand, if you consistently do <u>better</u> than your neighbors, it could pay out for you in a bad year when your yield might still be OK. It all has to do with how much risk you want to take.*

Deny the objection when appropriate

Sometimes a customer will state an objection that is simply not true. He may have heard a rumor. She may have been misinformed. When you hear something that is just plain wrong, *don't abandon the basic process.* You should still listen, restate, and ask for clarification before you handle the objection. Perhaps <u>you</u> misunderstood something!

When you have to deny what the customer thinks is true, be ready to back up your denial with evidence. If you don't have evidence with you, send it later — don't forget, because the customer will be waiting! When you have to deny an objection, do so firmly but tactfully. Help the customer "save face" and not be embarrassed by their mistake. If a rumor is the cause of the objection, see if you can track down its source.

Customer A: *I heard you guys had to recall a big batch of vaccines last month.*

Salesperson B: *Several people have asked me about that. The fact is, there was no product recall — at any time. You're not alone in thinking there was...that rumor is going around right now. Where did you hear it — I'd like to check its source.*

Customer B: *Your credit policy is tougher than anyone else's...must be because you guys about went bankrupt after that last set of mergers, huh...*

Salesperson B: *Bankrupt? I don't know how that rumor got started but you're the second person this week to tell me that... in fact, our stock has gone up a couple of bucks just in the last month...the tighter credit policy is just a function of our working with fewer, larger businesses — like yours — where we are exposed to more risk...a tight credit policy keeps costs down and an even playing field for everybody.*

The Irrational Objection (He Said <u>What?</u>)

Most of the objections salespeople hear are fairly common. In fact, because objections re-occur so frequently, the best salespeople are usually prepared to answer them, right down to having the evidence to back their claims in the back seat of their car. Every once in awhile, however, a salesperson will run into a customer or prospect who is <u>not</u> thinking logically. When customers let emotions get the better of them, their objections don't always make sense — nor are they particularly willing to listen to a logical response.

Every beginning salesperson dreads being in a situation where the customer throws out objections faster than they can be answered. Every experienced salesperson knows there are situations where the customer just needs to let off some steam. The best thing you can do is listen empathetically until they have wound down or to talk to them at another time, and to not even try to handle every objection until the customer is calmer and the true issue emerges. What are the signs of an "irrational" objection? What is behind them? Nirenberg[63] identifies five signs of irrational objections.

1. *Vehemence.* When a person opposes an idea with more intensity than it deserves, it often means they are not completely comfortable with the position they have taken on the issue. To paraphrase Shakespeare, when the customer "doth protest too much," it may mean he or she would really like to adopt the very idea they are opposing. To overcome the inclination to say yes, the customer overreacts.

2. *Unresponsiveness.* When a person clings to a fixed position by not responding to the salesperson's questions or offering any explanation, they often have a need to hold the position for reasons they don't wish to reveal. They have a private need to hold back — perhaps out of embarrassment about the price or their lack of understanding, or out of loyalty to a current supplier. In either case, the underlying issue is one they aren't ready to share — so they stop talking altogether.

3. *Irrelevance.* The introduction of irrelevant arguments to prop up a position usually means that relevant arguments can't be found. This happens so frequently in family relationships that it has become the subject of comedy routines. If a relevant argument were available, it would be used...accept the objection and try to focus the discussion on solutions the customer <u>wants</u> to pursue.

4. *Rationalizing.* Sometimes the customer seems to be inventing logic as they go, trying to "invent" an explanation. This is often an attempt at concealing the "real" reason for resisting. For example, the customer may exaggerate the importance of a fairly minor disagreement, or may use guesses and wishes as if they were facts. Again, focus on what the customer wants to achieve in his/her business.

5. *Objection-hopping.* When the customer jumps from objection to objection without waiting for answers or absorbing them, the objections may not relate to the real reason for resisting. In fact sometimes, they don't relate to the product or service at all — they may just be a way to discharge feelings that have "spilled over" from another area of the customer's life. Let the customer talk it out, and then choose one or two fairly simple ways you could work together to improve things. If they can focus on your discussion, you may be able to salvage the call.

---

[63]Nirenberg, J.S. Getting Through to People. Prentice-Hall, Englewood Cliffs, NJ: 1989.

Summary

Objections are a natural part of selling. For many salespeople — even the most seasoned professional — they evoke a feeling of defeat or, worse, combat. The first impulse is to retreat and come back another day, or find someone else to call on. The second impulse is to fight — to smother them with all the reasons you are right and they are wrong. Both of these "natural" reactions arise from a misunderstanding of the nature of an objection. And both can be fatal to a successful sales call and a successful, open relationship with the customer.

Many customers don't like objections any better than their salespeople. With a few exceptions (such as High D or Dominant people), no one likes to argue or disagree, especially with someone who might know more than they do. When a customer shares an honest objection with you, they are sharing a need that hasn't yet been met or discussed — at least as far as they understand. If you think of it this way, objections are actually offering you a chance to prove the trust of the customer.

On balance, then, objections are a positive sign. If you don't hear any objections, you don't know if you will make the sale. And if you do make the sale, you don't know if the customer has appropriate expectations about your product, your services, or your company. When you hear objections, you have a chance to see the concerns and priorities of the customer. By understanding their expectations, their past disappointments and their priorities, you are in the best possible position to meet or exceed their expectations.

When you encounter an objection, the first thing you should do is listen. Make sure you understand the objection by restating it in your own words, and asking questions to clarify it. Then and only then should you handle it, using whichever technique is most appropriate. An objection handled well is a strong timber in the bridge you are building between yourself and your customer. An objection that is ignored or handled combatively may be seen by customers as a "preview" of what will happen when they have a problem or question in the future. In short, the only "bad" objection is the one you don't hear. Once you know what concerns your customer, you can apply your technical knowledge and problem-solving skills to a solution. And finding solutions are what selling is all about.

Review Questions

1. What are objections? How do they differ from questions or excuses?

2. Distinguish between active and passive resistance. Give examples of each.

3. Explain the four types of objections and suggest a means of dealing with each.

4. Give an example of a conversation between salesperson and customer where the salesperson uses feel, felt, found techniques to respond to an emotionally-based objection.

5. What is an irrational objection? How do you determine if an objection is irrational? What techniques might you use to manage this situation?

Chapter Fifteen

Closing the Sale

Learning Objectives:
Upon completion of this chapter, you will be able to:
1. identify several incremental "closes" that should take place during the selling process;
2. understand why closing is difficult for many salespeople and why they need to overcome their discomfort;
3. explain the process for a "trial close" and in which situations it should be used;
4. recall five techniques to close the sale and identify situations where they should be used;
5. recall the basic steps to setting customer expectations for what will happen after the sale.

What is the "Close?"

Close   1.   (adv) near; close by
2. (adj) bringing or having proximity in space or time; similar in degree, action, etc., near in kind or relationship
3. (v) to unite; to reach an agreement[64]

---

[64] Adapted from *Random House Webster's Dictionary*, 2nd edition. Ballentine Books, NY: 1996.

Perhaps there is nothing more frustrating to a salesperson than to be *close* to a sale – and yet to not be able to *close* the sale. The "close" is the moment when the customer says "yes." It is when the customer makes a commitment to work with you, your company and your products or services. The close is also when the time, energy and creativity you have invested in finding a solution for a customer must return results.

The close does <u>not</u> always mean getting the sale. There may be many "closes" in the course of your relationship and your search for solutions with a customer. However, there is one hallmark of a close, no matter when it occurs in the call or the selling process – it is when you ask for commitment from the customer. You might be asking for the sale on a $200,000 combine, or for permission to set up a 20-acre trial plot, or for use of your nursery feed in one barn for a six-month period. You may even simply be asking for the information you need to work on a more detailed, customized solution for this customer. In all these cases, the close is when you ask the customer to begin working *with* you – to make an investment of time, money or information in a solution that involves your products and services.

There are many techniques to closing a call and closing the sale, but there are only two guidelines that should always be followed:

- closing always means asking for a commitment from the customer;
- every call should have a close.

When each call has a close, i.e., it ends with a request for some commitment from the customer, each call builds toward the sale and also builds the relationship between buyer and seller. The sales relationship is like any other, in that it can't exist for long if one side is doing all the "relating" and the other side is simply listening. In order to meet your overall objective as an agricultural salesperson, you need to develop and explain solutions that will help your customer. You need to create a win-win solution. That's pretty difficult if you never ask you customer to participate in the development of the solution.

Why Does "Closing" Seem so Difficult?

Many salespeople shy away from closing. They may feel that the close is when they will be accepted – or rejected – as a person. Or, they may feel that the close is a "test" of their knowledge, selling skill and credibility, and they are afraid of failing. Like a student going to class, they come to the customer many times, learning about their business, and then wait to ask for the sale when they are sure they understand everything, much like a student letting his or her entire grade rest on the final exam. And, because we all have been students at some time in our lives, we have been taught not to work collaboratively – to do our best and not show our work and "take the test" to measure how good we are.

In agricultural selling, it's critical to erase these old "tapes" from school. The close is not a final exam. Asking for commitment should happen as a natural part of each call. Each time the salesperson asks for commitment, collaboration increases. The point of agricultural selling is not to develop a solution *for* the customer – which they can then accept or reject – but to develop a solution *with* the customer.

The ease with which a salesperson can ask for commitment is therefore directly related to the quality of the discussion that has gone on up to the point of the close. If you have asked good questions, considered the customer's answers thoughtfully, and worked with the customer to honestly evaluate the "fit" of your products or services, your customer expects you to ask for commitment to take the next step. In fact, the customer would be surprised if you *didn't* ask. Let's look at an example.

> *One afternoon last Spring, Mike and his two boys walked into the showroom of Heartland Equipment. They told Bob, the salesperson, that they were looking for a dependable mower at a good price. Well, thought Bob, I have a lot of those...which one would be the best for this customer? Instead of presenting the features and benefits of each mower (starting with one in the mid-price range), Bob began to ask Mike some questions. Was the mower for the house? Who would be using it? How heavy would the use be? What types of situations (hills, large lots, etc.) would the mower encounter? As they talked, Bob learned that the boys were starting a mowing service on their subdivision. Mike wanted them to have a dependable mower, because they were too young to have much mechanical knowledge and Mike himself traveled a good bit. As they talked further and began to look at various mowers, Mike realized that the mower's safety was at least as important as its durability. His boys would be working unsupervised and, while they were careful kids, he wanted to take any action he could to make sure they were well-protected. Once Bob and Mike had agreed that durability and an extra measure of safety were most important, they agreed on the mower that offered the best combination of both. It wasn't the cheapest – but it was the best solution for their needs. In fact, all Bob had to do to close the sale was ask: "So this model with the extra safety features will be the best for the boys?"*

Let's look at what happened in this sale. Of course, when selling lawn and garden equipment, the salesperson may only have one chance to discuss needs with the customer. He/she may never have seen the customer before and may not see them again for a long time. In some ways, this is a much more challenging sales environment than working with a customer over a period of years, getting to know their business, and building each sale on a past relationship. But the basic process is the same.

In the example, the salesperson actually "closed" three times. Each close brought *incremental progress* toward the final sale. These three "closes" take place in most calls. If the salesperson skips the first and the second, the final close - asking for the sale - is a lot more difficult.

> Close #1:. <u>The salesperson asked for and got the customer's commitment to discuss needs and find a solution together.</u> Bob opened the call by asking Mike about his needs. He demonstrated concern for his needs as a customer and as a father—his product needs and his emotional needs. By letting Mike talk about his needs and helping Mike uncover some needs he hadn't thought about before, he convinced Mike that it was worth his time to talk to Bob.

> Close #2: <u>The salesperson asked for and got the customer's permission to collaboratively evaluate the features and benefits of the product that would best fit.</u> When Mike came in, he wanted to evaluate mower dependability for the price. As he and Bob talked, he realized that safety was also a need. Bob got Mike's commitment to consider safety as well as dependability in their collaborative evaluation of the mowers available.

> Close #3: <u>The salesperson asked for a commitment to purchase.</u> Once the needs were clear and Bob had Mike's commitment to evaluate products based on safety and dependability, they could make a good decision together, using Bob's knowledge of the mowers. The final close - asking for the sale - was a natural conclusion to the conversation.

Effective salespeople close *many times* during the sales process, by asking for incremental commitment. The first commitment is to the salesperson—that it is worth the time of the customer to discuss needs and solutions. The second commitment is to collaboratively pursue a solution—including time or information the customer must contribute to making that solution as "smart" as possible. The third and final commitment is to ask for the sale. Let's look at another example, this time from production agriculture.

> *Megan believed in talking to all her seed customers in July or August. She felt that, even though this year's crop wasn't harvested, she could learn a lot about their needs and their current satisfaction. And besides, in the Summer, most of her customers had more time to spend with her.*

> *A few weeks ago, she made an appointment to call on Jim Whithers, a large farmer with about 800 acres of corn. Jim had bought seed from Megan's company*

in the past, and had planted about 60% of his acres to it again this year. When Megan called on Jim, she spent the first few minutes introducing herself and explaining that she wanted to learn about Jim's needs, why he had bought their seed in the past, and how they could improve his satisfaction with their products. The salesperson asked for and got the customer's commitment to spend a few minutes discussing satisfaction/needs.

As they discussed this year's hybrids, Jim seemed pretty satisfied. The crop looked good. He had heard that corn borer was in the Southern part of the state, but he hadn't seen much evidence of it yet in his fields. He hoped he wouldn't have to spray. Megan asked Jim why he wasn't planting ECB-resistant hybrids. Turned out, he didn't think it was a good investment, since corn borer infestations requiring chemical control usually happened only every 5-7 years. Megan asked Jim if they could walk his fields and take a count of corn borers, and then evaluate the level of economic damage – if any – they could be causing, with an eye to making the best possible seed decision next year. Jim was impressed that she would take the time and readily agreed. The salesperson asked for and got the customer's commitment to collaborate on a "best" solution.

Megan came out a week later and they spent an afternoon in the field. They found a low-level infestation of corn borers—not enough to spray, perhaps, but enough to reduce yield by 5-10%, according to some university data Megan had on infestation level and economic loss. Megan asked Jim to re-consider his decision on ECB-resistant hybrids, and he agreed to try one large field (80 acres) next year. The salesperson asked for and got the commitment to buy.

When you find yourself dreading that final call when you will ask for the sale, remind yourself the many times this customer or prospect has already said yes – has already made a commitment to work with you toward a solution:

- Has the customer agreed to spend time talking with you? Have they followed up on that commitment by giving you some of their time?
- Has the customer agreed to work with you to find a "best" solution? Have they given you information, access to fields or barns or employees, or talked with you about their satisfaction with past solutions?

Remember, the customer wants to find the best solution, too. If a customer doesn't believe that solution might be you, your products, your services, and your company, they are usually unwilling to waste their time and energy talking to you.

What if They Say No?

Sometimes, even though you have done everything you can, the customer still says no. He may have found a similar solution at a lower price. She may find that she can't change other aspects of her business to take full advantage of the solution you have planned together. Any way you cut it, it's very disappointing. And disappointment can easily turn to resentment if you have invested a lot of time together to plan a "better way" and then the customer "shops" your solution and chooses a lower-priced supplier.

- Did you clearly understand their budget? No matter how great a Mercedes is, you can't sell it to someone with a Chevy budget.
- Did you accurately identify the most important needs? If someone is interested in new products but is more interested in a steady and dependable income flow from their business, selling "newness" may have been counterproductive.
- Did you undersell yourself? Many salespeople are quite modest, and don't focus enough on the value they personally bring to the customer. The same product may be available for less somewhere else—but only you can offer a unique level of service and support.
- Did you have the commitment of the customer that a "new solution" was even seriously being considered? Most business people like to hear about new products and new ideas...many fewer are ready to switch now.

Above all, don't take a "no" as personal rejection. If you have been selling through questions and have based your solutions on needs, you have been working collaboratively. Selling must be a win-win proposition. If the solution is best for the customer, great! If it is not, analyze why not. Learn from the situation—your customer may be surprised that you ask, but most farmers, ranchers and business managers are glad to help their salespeople improve. Ask for one final commitment. Can you come back and continue to visit, bringing new ideas and solutions? The answer is almost always yes.

Bill Stuever
Consolidated Nutrition, L.C.
Regional Director of Operations
Springfield, Missouri

Closing the sale is something many people never learn to do and because of this they never succeed in sales! Using proper closing techniques helps bring to a conclusion what is being presented or discussed.

By using closing skills, the sales person can get a better understanding of (1) what the main objections are the prospect has for not buying, (2) another appointment, or (3) better yet, the actual sale. But, if you never learn to use closing techniques in a conversational manner, you really give up an important tool in the selling process.

In my past experiences, when a sales person asked for the order and the answer was NO, I have been amazed at how many times the salesperson just quit. They don't ask the most obvious question at that time, "Oh, well, why is that?" or "Why not?" You must ask these open-ended questions in order to find out what the objection is that the prospect has or you may end up leaving without a clue. If you don't make the sale, never leave until you know exactly why, so that you can return with the right answer or information to answer their concerns!

Another common mistake many salespeople make is once they have asked for the order, they don't shut up! When you have asked for the order or next appointment, or even when trying to clarify an objection, be quiet until the prospect talks. Never talk until they talk! For example, "We both agree that you could use my product to lower your cost and improve performance in your cow herd. Can we deliver the feed tomorrow at 8 a.m. or is 3 p.m. better for you?" This is a clear request to buy. Just be quiet until they say yes or no, and if the answer is no, then ask why not and handle the objection and close again. Remember, after you have successfully received the order, thank the prospect and leave. Do not hang around talking and let them change their mind. Learn to close using proper techniques, but use them in a conversational style that fits your personality. If you learn to properly close a sale you will be very successful!

When to Close

When is the best time to close, or ask for commitment? Whenever it is appropriate. You may have set aside an hour to discuss a complex new marketing program and encourage a retailer to increase his product sales goals. If that dealer is ready to make a commitment to you after 20 minutes, ask for it! Many salespeople, especially those with great technical knowledge, feel compelled to tell "the whole story" before asking for the close. In so doing, they test the patience of some buyers and can actually talk themselves right out of a sale. If you could be a "fly on the wall," you might be amazed at what you would hear.

Customer: *I've been thinking, and I like this idea...*

Salesperson: *But wait, I haven't told you about...*
Well, let's take a look at this worksheet I prepared first...
Great, but let me show you this special feature...
But don't you want to know about the financing program...
Well, I thought you might want to try a small plot first...

The time to close the sale is when the customer is willing. If you are asking for commitment to develop a solution, that will be when the customer is thinking through his or her options—in the Summer/Fall for farm seed, in the Fall/Winter for farm chemicals, in the Fall for retailer orders, in the Summer for combine sales, etc. If you are asking for a final sale, the time to close is when you have explored needs and solutions, collaborated on a "best" solution, and get some "buying signals" that tell you the customer is ready to make a decision.

Verbal Buying Signals

Remember, a sales presentation is less a "lecture" on features and benefits and more a collaborative discussion about solutions. Since it is a discussion, the customer should be doing almost as much of the talking as the salesperson. By carefully listening to the customer, the salesperson can identify the "right" time to ask for the sale:

- after getting agreement on a key benefit;
- after handling an important objection well;
- when the customer asks about financing options;
- when the customer talks freely, giving confidential information or imagining with you how your solution would improve their business or their own professional success;
- when the customer asks about delivery;
- when the customer asks about the warrantee;
- when the prospect wants to plan with you how to service the business;
- when the customer asks how soon he/she and/or employees could be trained.

The type of verbal buying signal a customer gives may depend somewhat on their general communication style. For example, a High D (Dominant) buyer doesn't want to spend too long talking about anything. They are eager to move to closure. In fact, this buyer often doesn't ask as many questions as he/she should. Once they are convinced something will work, they want you to close, handle all the paperwork, and let them get on to something else. On the other hand, a High I (Influence) buyer may want you to convince them that you believe it will work and that "leading" farmers or retailers are using your solution. They may ask "So who else is using this? " or "So you think this would be good for me?" A High S or High C buyer is more cautious by nature. They may want to know everything – from financing to delivery – before weighing their alternatives and making a decision.

The type of question also varies somewhat by the dominant buying motivation of the buyer. For example, economic buyers often ask about price or deals as a way to signal they are ready to make a decision. A relationship buyer may ask for re-assurances, how often you would follow up, or what support they would have from you personally. A business buyer wants to know about price and support, but his/her "buying signal" questions usually revolve around performance – documented yield, documented re-sale or reliability, acceptance of your profitability worksheet on a marketing program or cropping system, etc.

Non-Verbal Buying Signals

Non-verbal signals are at least as important as verbal statements. Remember, over half of what we understand in a conversation comes to us through *non-verbal* communication, and another third or so comes through tone of voice. As the salesperson, your non-verbal communication should be positive, upbeat, confident and helpful. Your tone of voice should be calm but with good energy – a good rule of thumb is to adjust your volume and speed of speech to your customer's. Body language and tone of voice are wonderful indicators of how people feel – all the more so because, with the exception of a few Norwegian bachelor farmers, most people don't even try to control their non-verbal  communications. They just happen naturally – and honestly. The following table contains some common body language you may encounter in a sales call, with suggested interpretations.

Table 15.1
Non-Verbal Cues

Posture	Cue
Sits upright, leans toward you	Positive - actively collaborating
Leans back, pushes back from desk or table	Negative - not ready to make a decision or ready to make a negative decision
Face	
Avoids eye contact	Negative
Looks past you	Negative (or thoughtful)
Shuffles papers on desk	Negative - sign that you should finish up - have you asked for commitment?
Makes frequent eye contact	Positive; willing to see what you can do
Smiles	Positive
Allows lips to be relaxed, open	Positive
Rests chin on hands	Positive, patient; listening
Arms and Hands	
Folds hands	Defensive; trying to be patient
Presses fingertips together	Lecturing you - pay close attention, maybe even take notes
Makes fists	Angry and defensive - don't close now
Holds arms relaxed and open, palms toward you	Positive
Rubs hands together	Positive
Handles, studies your materials	Positive
Puts finger to lips	Thinking; may like to interrupt you
Makes calculations	Positive; ready to make evaluation
Reaches for price or order book	Positive - let him/her write in it

How does this work in the "real world/" Salespeople rarely if ever have the opportunity to wait until they get all the verbal buying signals, or all the non-verbal cues for that matter. In most cases, the salesperson gets *enough* cues to indicate the customer is willing to commit. Learning what "enough" feels like comes with experience. Let's look at an example.

> *Evelyn was a sales representative for a major feed company. She was calling on Ted Williams, manager of a large feed and animal health retail business today – her third call in the last six months. During her first two calls, she had spent a considerable amount of time learning about Ted's business. After the first call, he had agreed to go out with her and talk with some customers who were using her company's feed, to learn about the sales challenges Ted and his staff faced. Today her sales objective was to develop sales goals with Ted for the next year's business. She had prepared three options: a preferred customer agreement with high sales goals and maximum technical support from her company; a "master customer"*

agreement with slightly increased goals; and a set of goals that simply asked Ted to sell about what he had sold last year.

Evelyn started off by reviewing the challenges she had learned about and the ways to potentially overcome them, as Ted had expressed these in her earlier conversations with him. She asked if Ted had had any more thoughts about these challenges – he hadn't. She then explained to Ted that she had three options to present to him, and that she wanted to discuss the Preferred Customer Option first because she thought it provided more of what Ted needed to grow his business. As they discussed the technical training, the Point of Sale materials, the farm trial program and the volume incentives associated with the Preferred Customer Agreement, Evelyn asked Ted to react to each point. The more she explained, the more excited he got. Without ever actually saying "yes," he came around the desk, leaned forward, took hold of one side of the proposal she was reading from, and began adding up the required sales volume for participation in the program. When they had finished talking about the Preferred Customer Agreement, Ted sat back with a look of anticipation. Evelyn took a "mental deep breath" and asked: "Well, Ted – do I even need to talk through the other options, or is this what you want to do?" Ted's response was "yes" – as long as Evelyn could provide support to help him reach the sales volume thresholds of the program. She asked him to pull his records from last year, and after a cup of coffee they happily went to work figuring out how Ted could make the program work for his business.

The Trial Close

Sometimes, even though you listen carefully and watch for non-verbal cues, you simply can't tell whether your customer is ready to make a commitment or not. A "trial close" helps the salesperson evaluate where the customer is in the decision process. For customers who carefully "guard" their verbal or non-verbal communication, a trial close can be invaluable.

In a trial close, the salesperson asks for commitment in a low-key, low-pressure way about three-fourths of the way through the call. Usually, the salesperson has not yet explained all the benefits of the product, service, or program, but the customer is not giving enough information to guide the salesperson in choosing the most important selling points. The customer may have an objection that hasn't been stated, but that he/she believes is a "deal-breaker." So the customer listens patiently until the salesperson "runs down," and then politely says "no." Or, the customer may be ready to buy, having already made their own analysis, and is simply waiting for an opportune moment to say "yes." In either case, the trial close will help. If the customer has an objection, the trial close helps uncover it so you can deal with it. If the customer is ready to buy, the trial close allows them a chance to say yes.

A trial close is also very useful when you have been describing how something works in theory, and you need to make the transition to how it will work for the customer in front of you. It determines the customer's "mental preparedness" to buy now.

The trial close usually takes the form of a question. It often is phrased in the subjunctive mood – "how *would* you" rather than "how *will* you" handle delivery, financing, etc.

- Ask for general agreement:
  - ➤ *Would something like this work out for you?*
  - ➤ *Does this solution make sense to you?*
  - ➤ *Are these sales volume goals about what you expected?*

- Ask about how the product/service would be used:
  - ➤ *How often would you want to contact an agronomist under this service?*
  - ➤ *What percent of your use would need the four-wheel drive option?*
  - ➤ *How often would you generally need delivery?*
  - ➤ *What application rate should I use in calculating your per acre cost?*

- Ask for information that helps the customer "imagine" the sale:
  - ➤ *Would you want to use our financing or your bank's?*
  - ➤ *I need to run this past my manager – will you be around next week?*
  - ➤ *Would you want to redeem your incentives in training or in trips?*

If the trial close gets a positive response, treat it like a very strong buying signal. Ask for commitment. If the trial close uncovers an objection, handle it. The trial close may also result in a customer saying "I'm not ready for that question" or "You haven't shown me yet why we should do business together." If this happens, don't get discouraged. <u>DO</u> take a step backwards and make sure you fully understand the customer's needs and what they value. This situation can be disconcerting, but it's not fatal. When the trial close results in "I'm not ready," it is functioning like a safety net for the salesperson – you fell, but no bones were broken and there's still time to reach the summit.

Bill Brockett
Virginia Beef Corporation
Owner and President
Haymarket, Virginia

People are afraid to ask people to sign on the line. They want to get the sale, but they don't want to push the guy so hard when he won't make his mind up that he'll say no. Nobody wants to hear no, so they're afraid to push it. There's a fine line there between pushing enough to having him say yes and sign the line, and pushing so hard he says, "No, I don't want it." Then you're out the door...and you've got to work your way back in and that's a harder thing to do.

How to Close

When you ask for commitment from the customer, it's time to show confidence in the solution worked out together and confidence in your company's ability to support the implementation of that solution. While the smart salesperson never makes assumptions about the "obvious value" of a product or service, he or she also should be comfortable asking for commitment. There are a variety of ways to ask for commitment - closing techniques. Before introducing these, let's take a moment to review how <u>not</u> to close.

How <u>Not</u> to Close a Sale

Some salespeople are so intimidated by a particular customer or by the whole idea of asking for commitment that they "apologize" their way into a close. In so doing, they dig a hole they have to climb out of later. If you have done a good job of identifying needs and creatively thinking through solutions, you have nothing to apologize for. It is both your right and your responsibility to ask for the sale. So - if you ever hear yourself starting off a close with one of the following statements, mentally slap your hand and promise to never let these words cross your lips again.

- *I know you really like your current supplier, but...*
- *You probably don't want to buy any X today, but...*
- *I know we're higher priced, but would you consider...*
- *I don't know if we've talked about everything that's important to you, but...*
- *I'm not sure that this will do what you want, but...*

Techniques to Close the Sale

There is no "one best technique" to close the sale or to get commitment from the customer. The "best" technique depends on the type of customer, the skills of the seller, the degree of competition and the size or complexity of the purchase. When you fully understand the needs, values and buying style of the customer, you can choose the technique that works best for each individual customer. Over time, you should develop flexibility to use a variety of closing methods. Used as part of a selling dialog, *none* of these techniques will feel "pushy" to the customer. There are five commonly-used techniques:

1. the direct close;
2. the summary close;
3. the choice close;
4. the assume close; and
5. the special features close.

1. The Direct Close

In the direct close, the salesperson simply asks the customer for their business.

Gloria, we'd like to do business with you. How about giving us a chance to show what we can do?

In this technique, the salesperson asks the customer whether it is all right to take an order for products or services. This technique works well when the sales relationship is open and positive, the customer has been able to state their objections, and the salesperson has been able to answer them. It also works well when the salesperson has just handled a difficult objection.

It seems clear from your numbers that this would be a more cost-effective system for you. Even though the initial price is a little higher, the output gains are much higher. Can I go ahead and write up an order?

This technique also works well when the salesperson and customer have a long-standing relationship. By formally asking for the sale, the salesperson shows the customer that he/she is not being "taken for granted." That's important to many customers, who are being courted by competitive companies.

2. The Summary Close

In this technique, the salesperson briefly summarizes all the major points made in the presentation, including benefits to the customer but also including the customer's concerns. This technique usually involves the following steps.

- List the customer's concerns and key needs.
- Ask the customer if there are any other issues.
- List the positive results of the proposed solution, including financial, performance and "peace of mind" benefits. Be sure the last benefit is one the customer highly values.
- Review the list. The positives should outweigh the negatives.
- Ask for a favorable decision.

This technique works well with complex purchases or when the salesperson is proposing a solution to a complex problem. It works particularly well when the customer will have to make other adjustments in his/her business to take advantage of the solution, because it shows the salesperson's understanding of these business issues and the willingness to help resolve them. For example, this would be appropriate when selling a farmer on the use of crop chemicals that allow effective weed control in conservation tillage systems. The conservation tillage itself has additional benefits (reduced compaction, better soil moisture, better soil condition), but also added costs in equipment for a conversion from traditional tillage to a conservation tillage system. Another example would be selling a new accounting package or PC platform, which would offer considerably more speed and power but would also require a changeover from the current system.

The summary technique works better with some types of customers than others. Customers who enjoy analysis and a deliberate, logical approach like this method (High "C's" or Compliance customers like it - especially if they are also business buyers). This type of buyer may even like to see the analysis on paper, as a spreadsheet or a formal proposal. On the other hand, this technique takes some time and patience, and may not be appropriate for some High "D" (Dominant) or High "I" (Infleuncer) customers, who like to make a quick decision.

3. The Choice Close

The choice close offers the customer a small choice - an easy choice - but <u>not</u> the choice between buying and not buying. Some consumer goods salespeople use this technique almost exclusively:

- *Would you like the standard or the deluxe model?*

However, these salespeople are also often not as successful as they would like because the choices they offer have little or nothing to do with the needs the customer has expressed. In agricultural selling, the choices the salesperson offers should be drawn from information the customer has shared:

- *Will you want to deliver this contracted grain to the elevator yourself, as in the past, or use our trucks to pick it up?*
- *Will you want to pull samples for our feed assay service yourself? Or would you like me to pull them?*
- *Will you want us to deliver bulk product in the Fall, or would you rather we wait until early Spring?*
- *Do you want us to set this up as a single account, or do you want to keep the landlord portions separate?*

In the choice close, the salesperson essentially sets up a choice between buying and buying – whatever the choice, it is a commitment.

The choice close is a very strong technique. It expresses confidence that the customer will buy. It works well when the buyer and the salesperson know each other well – it appears then simply as another way to make life easier for the customer. For this reason, Relationship Buyers like it and respond well to it. If buyer and salesperson don't know each other well, or haven't taken the time to fully explore needs and evaluate solutions, the choice close can feel <u>too</u> aggressive.

4. The Assume Close

When a customer is as excited about a solution as the salesperson, there may be no need to formally ask for the order. The salesperson can simply assume the customer is ready to buy and they can begin planning together. This method works well with current, satisfied customers. There are several types of assume closes, but there are two guidelines that apply to all of them:

- Always test your assumption in some way – make sure the customer knows that you are assuming a "yes." For example, make the assumption, begin planning – but get a signed order before you leave.
- Be particularly alert to resistance (verbal or non-verbal) as you begin planning together. If the customer steps back, stops talking, or begins raising objections, you may have assumed they were closer to a commitment than they were. Treat it as a trial close, and go back and re-establish value before trying to close again.

There are four types of assume closes.

- Routine Assumption – begin planning.
  - ➤ *Great! I'll stop by next week to pull some soil samples and we can get started!*

> ➢ *OK – I'll talk to our credit people and send you all the forms you'll need to fill out!*
> ➢ *Super – I'll talk with the field manager about getting those 500 acres grid-mapped.*

- Command Assumption – state the customer's need for the product forcefully.
  > ➢ *Sounds like you need to get started as soon as possible. I'll check schedules and see if the nutritionist can get out this week still.*
  > ➢ *Sounds like you may need a different set of nozzles but otherwise you're ready to go...I'll ask the delivery guy to bring some along.*
  > ➢ *Sounds like we better get this paperwork signed as soon as possible, so we can get a farm management plan back to you within the next few weeks.*

- Dramatized Assumption – paint a positive picture of the future solution.
  > ➢ *You're going to be amazed at how much easier this insurance paperwork is than what you've been dealing with.*
  > ➢ *You won't believe how much faster you'll be able to access the Internet.*
  > ➢ *You're going to love not having to stop and unload as often.*

- Action Assumption – Say nothing – begin sketching field patterns, filling in marketing goals, or finalizing paperwork for their signature before you leave.

5. Special Features Close

The "special features" close has several uses. Basically, in this close you add something extra – a small discount, an extra service – right when you ask for the sale. With some customers, especially those who pride themselves on being good negotiators, this can "tip the scales" and make the sale. The other situation where this technique works well is with loyal, long-standing customers. These customers often want (and increasingly expect) that you will contact them with any special deals or offers that would help them. After all, they reason, if you are truly interested in their business success, you will "watch out" for them and bring them any special services or discounts. For example, farmers often state that they would like their primary fertilizer supplier to call them in the Fall, if fertilizer prices are lower than anticipated Spring prices, so they can buy at a good price. Veterinarians often appreciate notice of product specials, so they can "buy smart." When you let a long-standing customer know about a special deal that will benefit them, you can often close the sale on the spot.

There are two cautions if you like to use the "special features" close. First, with some customers – especially new customers – use of this close may "train" the customer to always expect a "special deal" from you. In fact, although they are ready to buy in every other way, they may put off making a decision next time until you come through with their "special deal." This selling process isn't healthy for anyone. The customer is making the decision based on what he/she can get – rather than what he/she needs. The salesperson is reduced to selling on the basis of price discounts, deals and incentives rather than solutions. And of course, every year the customer wants <u>at least</u> the deal they had before – preferably more. Second, some types of buyers (such as some Business buyers and almost all High C buyers) may resent this approach. They feel that you should honestly represent your product and what it can do – and not offer different prices to the "squeaky wheels" among their peers. They may also feel that a "limited time offer" or "limited availability" approach is merely a ploy to manipulate them.

Setting Expectations for Satisfaction

In the next chapter, you will find a system to plan for, achieve and measure customer satisfaction. However, the first and perhaps most important steps to customer satisfaction should be taken right when you close the sale. There are two major steps.

- Reinforce why the choice to buy was the right choice.
- Discuss expectations about post-sale service and follow-up.

Reinforce The Customer's Choice

Immediately after saying "yes," many customers experience second thoughts. It's natural. It doesn't mean the salesperson has done anything wrong, or that the sale should have been handled a different way. You can notice this behavior in yourself. If you make a major purchase, you may suddenly see the object you have purchased more often. You will notice their advertisements in the newspaper, in magazines, on billboards or on the TV. The formal term for this phenomenon is *post-purchase dissonance*, but many salespeople know it by the more common term of *buyer's remorse*. Buyer's remorse takes many forms, but usually the customer begins to ask himself/herself one or more of the following questions.

- *Did I really need that product or service? Could I have gotten along without it?*
- *Did I need to buy it now – should I have waited?*
- *Did I pay too much – could I have gotten a better deal somewhere else?*
- *Will this product really meet my needs?*

Buyer's remorse happens after you have left the customer. In that sense, there is little you can do about it except to give the customer a call a few days after any major sale and ask if they have any additional questions. The contact from you at this time, while they're having second thoughts, is probably as important to increasing their comfort as any specific questions that you answer.

You can also help customers avoid a severe attack of buyer's remorse by reinforcing with them, at the close of the call, why they made the right decision.

- Restate the benefits that they will receive.
- Restate why this is the best solution overall.
- Ask for any questions about the product or service, how it works, when or how to use it, etc.

Set Expectations and Next Steps

The second step effective salespeople always take at the close is to set expectations. It's important to set expectations in three areas:

- what the product will do and how to measure performance;
- what you will do to follow up;
- what the customer should expect from your company.

Satisfaction is no more (and no less) than meeting or exceeding the customer's expectations. It is a relative concept, not an absolute measure. It makes sense, then, that the salesperson would want to set expectations throughout the call that he/she knows the product can meet or exceed. Reviewing these expectations at the close gives both buyer and seller an "extra margin of safety" for satisfaction.

Product Expectations

Some years ago, a new herbicide was introduced. As a systemic non-selective herbicide, it was extremely effective at controlling a wide variety of perennial and annual weeds. However, because it was a systemic herbicide, it didn't have an immediate and visible effect on weeds. In fact, a day or two after spraying, weeds didn't seem to be suffering at all (although 20 days later they were dead as could be). In order to have satisfied customers, the company selling this product had to educate customers to the mode of action of the product and to not expect to see an immediate kill. Once the customer knew what to look for, they could see the herbicide working in a few days and were content to wait for it to do its job.

While this may be an extreme example, *every* product has a set of performance expectations attached to it. It's critical to review these expectations, and thereby to avoid customer dissatisfaction. For example, ranchers buy a respiratory antibacterial because they believe it will effectively treat respiratory disease in their cattle. The drug does work and will work for them – but it may not work in cattle that are immunocomprimised or cattle that are suffering from a respiratory disease complex with viral or mycoplasmal origins. Or, software may function perfectly under most circumstances – but may experience some problems if used on an older or newer operating system than that for which it was designed. Customers understand that it isn't a perfect world. But they also expect that you know enough about your product, in a variety of use situations, to help them determine whether it is performing as it should.

In order to make sure product performance expectations are understood, many salespeople do one or more of the following follow-up activities.

- They provide the customer with printed use information and make sure the customer understands it.
- If the customer will not use the product or service for a few months, the salesperson follows up close to the time of first use to review instructions, help calibrate equipment, etc.
- The customer receives a "1-800" number to call, with any questions or for additional information. Many salespeople also make sure the customer knows how to reach them personally.
- For new products and new technologies, many salespeople arrange local or regional "training days" or "clinics" to demonstrate product use and review expectations.

Salesperson Expectations

One of the pet peeves of many customers is the salesperson who won't leave them alone until they say yes – and then is never heard from again, or at least never shows up until it's time to buy something else. If you have executed the selling process well, you have communicated to your customer that you truly care about finding good solutions to his/her business needs. The sudden disappearance of the salesperson makes the customer feel manipulated, rather than satisfied.

Of course, your job is to sell. That means constantly cultivating new business, rather than spending all your time with the customers you have already sold. However, most customers really don't expect all that much from you, given the investment they have made. In fact, most customers would be ecstatic if they had the following post-sale contact:

- a brief telephone call 1-2 weeks after the sale to ask for any questions or additional needs;

- a brief telephone call to confirm timely delivery, if the salesperson did not deliver product or services personally;
- a face-to-face visit sometime during peak product use periods, to confirm that the product is performing as expected and to begin evaluating whether the solution needs to be fine-tuned for next year;
- a thank-you card some time around the holidays;
- an appointment for a face-to-face visit to plan for the next cycle of product purchase.

Of course, some customers want more contact. Others want no contact, unless they originate it themselves. The most successful salespeople include a discussion of on-going contact in their "expectations" conversation as they close, and then develop a completely individualized contact plan for each major account. The key? Make sure _you_ understand what your customer expects. If you can't meet the customer's preferences (i.e., you can't be there every week), make sure to negotiate expectations that you _can_ meet. And of course, deliver on what you promise. Always.

Company Expectations

In many situations, the salesperson cannot personally deliver all the services that he or she has sold. There may simply not be enough time. Or, the salesperson may not have the expertise of others in the company. And finally, there are policies geared toward customer satisfaction that every customer should be aware of.

When your customer has a question or a problem that you cannot personally resolve, you will turn to your manager, your company experts and your company policies for solutions. In some cases, such as replant policies, product warrantees, or expert assistance, your company probably has a policy they would like to see implemented consistently across all salespeople and all customers. While your customer doesn't need to know everything about company policy (that's why they have you), there may be a few key policies that you want to share as a way of setting expectations.

For example, in seed, most companies state their replant policy – what % of the crop can be replanted with free seed if it is destroyed by weather. Equipment companies have specific warrantees on new and used equipment. Animal health and crop protection companies have policies for investigating and resolving and product performance inquiries. Depending on the concerns your customer has raised with you during the selling process, you may wish to share specific policies of your company. The key – avoid unpleasant surprises should problems occur, and give them a basic process to follow when they do.

Summary

Closing means asking for commitment. In a collaborative selling process, the salesperson asks for commitment many times. Specifically, most salespeople ask for:

- the commitment to spend time with the salesperson - agreeing that they may have something worthwhile to contribute;
- the commitment to work collaboratively toward a solution - including the investment by the customer of some time, information and resources to help determine the "best" solution;
- the commitment to purchase the product or service.

The best time to close, or ask for commitment, is when the customer is demonstrating high interest and an eagerness to see the product at work in his or her business. If the salesperson doesn't see many of these "buying signals" from the customer, or receives conflicting signals, a trial close may help uncover hidden objections and give a more accurate assessment of the customer's willingness to buy.

There are five different techniques for closing a sale. All of them are enhanced by a positive attitude and confident approach. None of them guarantee success - that is guaranteed only by a call that that has diligently uncovered needs and collaboratively mapped out solutions up to the point of asking for the sale. The five closing techniques are:

- the routine close;
- the summary close;
- the choice close;
- the assume close;
- the special features close.

Once the sale has been made and the customer has said yes, there is still one more critical activity: setting expectations for satisfaction. At the very least, the salesperson should reinforce the benefits the customer will see from a purchase, to help minimize buyer's remorse. The most effective salespeople undertake a structured approach to follow-up after the sale, including education about product performance and personal contact.

It is tempting to think of the closing as the "end" of the sale. But in agriculture, the close of this sale must be seen as a step in building an even stronger, more productive relationship over time. In many communities, it is not uncommon for a salesperson to work with the same farm for years - sometimes more than a generation. At the manufacturer level, such relationships are less common but also occur. Agriculture is a business where this year's decisions always impact next year's potential. Agricultural selling is part of that environment. And thus closing a sale now is not an end at all – it's the beginning of the next step customers and salespeople can take together.

Review Questions

1. Give two reasons why closing the sale is difficult for some salespeople. What should the salesperson know to help diffuse that "fear?"

2. What signals might a customer give that they are ready to be asked for the sale? Give three examples.

3. What does a trial close accomplish? How is it different than asking for a close?

4. The case study with Bill Stuever in this chapter points out a couple of common closing mistakes salespeople make. What are they? Why and how do they inhibit or preclude the sale from occurring?

5. Five techniques for closing a sale are identified in the chapter. Choose two and compare and contrast them.

Chapter Sixteen

Creating Customer Satisfaction

Learning Objectives:

Upon completion of this chapter, you will be able to:
1. define customer satisfaction relative to expectations;
2. describe the four levels of customer satisfaction;
3. identify ways to ensure satisfaction for each level;
4. develop appropriate activities to ensure satisfaction at each level;
5. integrate customer satisfaction efforts with sales efforts into a call cycle.

Defining "Customer Satisfaction"

Customer satisfaction is a relative concept. Customers define it according to their own expectations and their concept of value. For this reason, it is critical to understand each customer's expectations and to meet or exceed expectations, in order to satisfy customers.

How is customer satisfaction achieved? In theory, the answer is obvious - the job of the salesperson is to develop solutions that will benefit the customer and to offer them at a fair price. If the solution benefits the customer, sh or he will be satisfied. If the customer is satisfied with the solution and the benefits, she or he will buy again.

In practice, however, satisfying customers may not be as straightforward. That is because the expectations a customer has are fluid. They are always changing as needs change and as the competitive solutions offered in the marketplace change. Salespeople don't control the type of solutions - product and service value bundles - offered by competitors (although, as a participant in the marketplace, they influence them). Salespeople <u>do</u> influence and even control the expectations that each of their individual customers has about their particular level of personal service, their company's approach, and their product's performance. Let's look at each of these sources of expectation briefly.

Marketplace-driven Expectations

Every supplier, at every level and in every buying cycle, tries to add as much value as possible to its products and services, within the company's overall philosophy and strategy. Each company is looking for a *differential advantage* relative to its competitors - a reason why customers should buy from them, rather than someone else. In the search for a differential advantage, new services and product features are added each year by one supplier or another. The marketplace watches carefully, to see which extra services or product features had the most success in "adding value" and securing a differential advantage. The most successful strategies for adding value are then often imitated the following year by a few companies, the next year by a few more companies, and so forth until these special features and services that once added value have simply become expected - a part of doing business.

The market for agricultural salespeople is extremely competitive. There are many "good" solutions that compete with yours. Therefore, it is critical to understand the *general* level of service and feature expectations in the marketplace. You must meet these expectations (or offer a better alternative) to meet the minimum level of customer expectations. Let's look at an example.

> *Veronica was excited about her new job - selling agronomic consulting services in a key tree-nut-vine market in upper New York State. As she began to develop a territory strategy, she thought of how she could differentiate her services from the "unofficial" consulting currently being done by several experienced salespeople at local agricultural chemical/fertilizer businesses. She decided that she could develop a database of crops and applications of chemicals or fertilizers by field; help farmers understand the profitability of specific inputs; scout crops for early signs of infestation by insects or disease; leave scouting reports at the farm after every visit; and help farmers plan their crop management program. This was a lot to undertake for someone with so little experience, but she felt she could do a good job and that these services should add enough value to the basic crop management consulting that she could clearly differentiate her company.*

> *When Veronica began calling on farm customers, her results weren't what she had hoped. In fact, she found that several of the companies working in her territory were already providing many of the services she would charge for as a part of*

"doing business," at least for their larger customers. Sure, some of them charged extra for scouting. But most of them offered the input advice, the record-keeping and the profitability analysis to their top customers at no additional charge. Added to the fact that these businesses had worked with her top farm prospects for years, her job was going to be a little tougher than even she had imagined.

The salesperson cannot meet and exceed expectations created by competitors unless he or she knows what they are. Once these expectations are identified, the second step is to understand their perceived value. For instance, in the example above, Veronica may know that the records she could keep with her specialized software are far superior to the records kept by local fertilizer/chemical dealers. In fact, her records may be more "valuable" – but until she has educated farmers to the difference, they are not "worth" more than the records they are currently getting for free. So, while Veronica may not agree with her customer's expectations ("It's just not fair!" she often remarks), she has to deal with these expectations in order to succeed in this marketplace.

A variety of services and features that added value at one time have now become widely accepted as "standard" for leading companies. While this list varies somewhat by product or branch of the industry, many of the following services are now expected:

- a quality product, free of defects, that will perform as promised under a wide variety of use conditions;
- consultation on the best cropping program or specific product selection (e.g., the best hybrid, the best feed, the best antibacterial), given the customer's unique situation;
- delivery of the product on-farm;
- customer education on product use, whether informal (one-on-one explanations) or through formal workshops such as combine clinics;
- answers to most common questions and product performance concerns at the local retailer level;
- additional technical support beyond the local level, whether through a manufacturer sales rep or a toll-free technical support number;
- some type of product guarantee or responsiveness to product failure, especially for equipment, chemical products and seed products;
- purchase incentives for large-volume sales.

Even though these expectations may be generally held by most customers in your marketplace, they should always be clearly stated during the sales process. There are two reasons for this.

First, assumptions are very dangerous. Even though you may have done a thorough job of identifying what most of your competitors are offering, you may have missed something – particularly if you are selling a new product, technology or you are in a new territory. Many of your services will be stated in the course of sales calls. However, it is always wise to ask about additional expectations the customer may have. Usually, you can meet these expectations – but it's hard to meet expectations you haven't identified!

The second reason to explore expectations in detail is that you may be able to offer something different or more, even in an area of expectation that is very well established. For example, many retailers keep records of every product they apply by field. They may even include these records as they invoice customers. But not all retailers sit down with customer and analyze their records field by field, comparing the crop management program to yields and profits. Or, as another example, most companies have a service that delivers products to customers for free or for a nominal fee. However, perhaps you can offer a more responsive delivery – such as within 4-6 hours for crop chemicals from a local retailer to the farm, or sending equipment replacement parts to a local dealer within 24 hours or less via common carrier. Because there is no "perfect" way to deliver product, or use records, or make technical expertise available, there is always room to improve and offer your top customers an improved service that has clearly recognized worth.

Sales-driven Expectations

In the course of selling a top account, salespeople may make many promises. Satisfaction demands that those promises be kept. You must clearly spell out to your customer what you are willing to do, after the sale, to *continue* supporting his or her business success. Like all elements of selling, this should be a dialogue – not your monologue. If you discuss support expectations with your customer, you will find tremendous differences. These differences often mirror the different behavioral styles of customers. For example, a High D (Dominant) customer has little time for small talk and visiting and a great need to be in control. He or she may not want regular visits, but rather will call you when they need something. On the other hand, a High S (Steady) customer may want to see you often, especially if they are beginning to implement a new technology. They need and appreciate your support, and may measure their satisfaction by salesperson support as much as product performance.

Many effective salespeople think of themselves as "solution brokers." They identify the need for a solution and customize the solution to fit a specific customer's needs. They take care of initial financial arrangements, such as agreeing on a price and getting any financing started. Post sale, they work as an advocate for the customer inside their company, channelling to the customer the resources and information needed to get the most value from implementation of the solution.

Remember – in agricultural selling, your success demands that you sell many times, over many years, to the <u>same</u> customers. The satisfaction of the customer depends only in part on the job you do, when you make the sale. Satisfaction is much more dependent on the service you provide post-sale and the ability of the customer to implement the solution you planned together.

Jim Jackson
Land O'Lakes, Inc.
Swine Program Manager
Indianapolis, Indiana

Alignment, risk sharing, partnering. These are what our particular customer is after. This is what they value. Customer satisfaction comes from an alliance they have with our company. Most of these operations are looking to grow their operation and are involved with some kind of financial institution. The security that is offered to the customer through their financial institution when a company like ours is involved really means a lot to them. For us it involves some risk, adds some contingent liability, but it also means long term business commitment from the customer. In addition, we bring the customer a whole toolbox of services and packages that help alleviate additional risks. Satisfying the customers and exceeding their expectations means loyalty. Loyalty from the customer means success to our company.

Four Levels of Satisfaction

Over the last 20-30 years, a variety of customer satisfaction models have been created. Many of these measure the total satisfaction of the customer with a company's products and services. The salesperson, as stated above, does not control all of these elements. However, there are some elements only the salesperson controls – the quality of the sales call, the common understanding of customer expectations, contact and services after the sale, etc. If we consider those elements of satisfaction over which the salesperson has the most control, we can identify four levels or types of satisfaction.

- Level I: Quality of the sales call – process and skills
- Level II: Customer value added through the sales process
- Level III: Implementation of a collaboratively-developed solution
- Level IV: Benefits to the customer's business – increased profit, reduced cost, etc.

Levels I (sales call process quality) and II (value for the customer) apply during the sales process, even if a sale is not made. Level III (implementation) and Level IV (business results) can be measured after the sale.

Level I: Sales Call Process

Every call should have an objective and plan, and should build the relationship a little more. Every call should move "trust" one notch further. Each call should build a picture in the mind of the customer: what would it be like working with you? Would you be dependable? Honest? Organized? Fair? Even-tempered?

The most successful salespeople regularly debrief each major call – especially with key accounts. If their manager or a technical support person was on the call with them, they eagerly ask that person to debrief the call with them. But what if there isn't anyone there to share your "post-mortem?" What if, like most salespeople, you call on customers day after day by yourself and rarely have the luxury of an observer or a coach? Can you still debrief your sales calls and identify areas for improvement?

Yes, you can debrief your own calls – and you must. The following process is one used by many experienced salespeople. It requires only three ingredients – all of which you have.

1. Take the time. If you drive to see your customers, pull off the road after your next few calls and evaluate yourself. If you are a telemarketer, go get a cup of coffee and sit somewhere quiet for a few minutes.
2. Be honest with yourself. If all your customers seem "out to get you," it could be your company's fault...but it could also be your own attitude or the fact that you consistently promise more than you can deliver.
3. Develop a "standard set" of questions that you always use to debrief each call (Table 16.1).

Table 16.1
Sales Process Debrief – Questions

1. How do you feel about the call? What's your dominant emotion and why?
2. How close did you come to achieving your objectives?
3. How well did you plan for the call?
4. How well did you implement the strategy you had planned?
5. What went "right?"
6. What could you do differently next time?
7. What is your next step? Is it in your calendar?

Level II: Customer Value through the Sales Process

Of course, after each sales call, you want your customer to respect and trust you – if not like you. In addition, every call should leave the customer with something that has worth to them. This "something" is not a hat or a keychain – it is information, data, a referral, or an answer to a question. It is something the customer can learn from you that will help him or her improve business results. Think of this as "the sale before the sale." Before a customer will buy your product or service, he/she must be convinced that you – and your company – understand the business, its goals, and will work on its behalf.

For major purchases or complex products and services, it is not unusual for the sales process to require four, five or six or more sales calls before closing a sale. It may take several calls to really understand the business and to identify a "better" solution for the customer. You may need to research special data, or figure out financing, or prepare a comparative spreadsheet illustrating your products and services. Each call must build trust and credibility in your ability to find a good solution. Thus each call should also provide the customer with some evidence of the value that will come from working with your company and with you.

Isn't it enough to leave a little something – popcorn, a pocket knife, a small tool – with the customer? Most customers still will take such small gifts and thank you. Many simply expect them. But no customer believes that a pocket knife or a keychain is adequate compensation for the time they spend with you. Think of it this way – today's large farmer routinely has gross sales of over $500,000. Today's larger retailer routinely has sales of $50 million or more. What is the half day they spent with you worth to them? If you expect to have a second half day, and a third, and maybe a fourth, you need to recognize the investment the customer is making in working with you. That investment is much faster repaid through valuable information or services than trinkets.

How do you know if you are satisfying your customer's expectations that you will add value *before* the sale? The following questions will help. These questions will also help you estimate if you are ready to ask for the sale. (Table 16.2).

Table 16.2
The Sale Before the Sale Debrief – Questions

1. Is your customer convinced that there might be a "better way" or "better supplier" than used in the past?
2. What has the customer <u>said</u> or <u>done</u> to show this?
3. Does the customer understand – dollars and cents – how your product or service would benefit the business?
4. Have you answered all questions the customer has asked to date?
5. What information or advice *apart from* the product have you shared that this customer can or will use?
6. If you asked the customer to describe the product to a friend, what would they say?

Many experienced salespeople routinely complete this "satisfaction" step without even realizing it. They start off each sales call in a series of calls by asking:

- *OK, what have we established so far?*

This allows the customer to summarize, and gives the salesperson a clear idea of what the customer has learned, what they will use, and what they do not yet understand. While the first satisfaction step – the call debrief – is hard to do with the customer, this satisfaction step is not hard at all. The customer usually *wants* to tell the salesperson if they are offering information that is worthwhile. Remember, they want the most return possible on their investment of time with a salesperson.

Level III: Implementation Satisfaction

This measure of satisfaction happens after the sale. Here, you are looking for how the solution you developed with your customer is being implemented.

Services

If you are selling a service, such as grid mapping, farm management or consulting, you are primarily responsible for implementing the service itself. However, the customer is the one who decides if the service was worthwhile. As a result, your work isn't done when the service has been delivered. Often, additional support is needed to make sure that the service is producing the results for the customer that were promised.

John was an experienced agronomist. Last year, he decided to leave the basic manufacturer for whom he had worked the last eight years and strike out on his own as an independent consultant. Over his career as a staff agronomist, he had seen many situations where trouble could have been averted or increased profits could have been realized, if only the customer had an expert consultant at his side to advise him. He knew he could help improve profitability and he was eager to get started.

One year later, John took a critical look at his consulting business. He had worked with about a dozen large clients, and he had carefully worked out a program with each of them that would guarantee improved profits or reduced costs equal to or greater than his consulting fees. Yet, when he went back to these clients to sign them up for another year, he learned with a shock that several of them were not going to re-sign. Due to a variety of circumstances, including their own unwillingness to implement the suggestions John had made, they had <u>not</u> realized the savings and profits that were promised. What's more, they had told their neighbors about their experience (leaving out the part about not following John's suggestions), and John found it very challenging to get new clients for the coming year. Maybe consulting wasn't such a hot idea after all – why take the time to work up a special program for a client if they weren't going to follow it anyway?

When services are sold, they must be delivered as promised. But when the service involves asking a customer to make changes - in their cropping program, their business management processes, or their past relationships - the customer is also responsible for the success of the implementation. Thus, when selling services, regular monitoring of implementation is critical to salesperson success and customer satisfaction. This follow-up should answer the following questions on a regular basis - monthly for many types of services.

Table 16.3
Service Implementation Debrief – Questions

1. Does the customer understand what he/she needs to do to implement this service?
2. Does the customer have the equipment and trained staff necessary to implement?
3. Does the customer understand the consequences of late or slipshod implementation?
4. Is the customer completing implementation tasks on time and with acceptable quality? If not, why not?
5. What additional services may be necessary to make sure the customer gets full value from the service they have purchased?

Products

Customer satisfaction for product sales, at the most basic level, happens when products perform as promised. Excellent product performance, in turn, happens when:

- the right product is chosen for the situation;
- the customer understands the product's limitations as well as its benefits;
- the customer uses the product as recommended;
- unforeseen variables don't undermine the product's performance.

As a salesperson, you have worked hard to find the right "fit" for the product you have selected with each customer. When the customer begins using the product, you need to continue to follow up and support them, making sure that the customer knows how the product works and how to work it into current management practices. The following activities are often undertaken to help customers learn the best use of a product:

- in-business demonstrations (whether it's a new combine design or a new sequence to mix a chemical with water-soluble packaging);
- initial set-up (such as calibrating a planter or validating the mixer at a feed plant);
- in-service quality expectations (normal oil use or wear rates for equipment; normal control level and speed for a herbicide or insecticide, or for an antibiotic);
- spot-checks on operating efficiency and/or concerns (phone or visits);
- periodic "audits" of satisfaction (in-use, post-use).

When the performance of the product will be affected by other, non-product variables, special actions may be necessary. For example:

- feed antibiotics must be thoroughly and evenly mixed with the feed before it goes to the animals; feed assays and mixer validation tests may be provided to ensure the antibiotic is delivered as planned;
- harvesting efficiency of a combine depends on adjustment to local weather and field conditions; during severe or highly unusual conditions, customers may appreciate a review of typical adjustments via direct mail;
- point-of-sales software requires training of all staff in use of the product at the retail register and training of managers in use of the resulting financial information.

The following questions will help salespeople assess customer satisfaction with the use or implementation of the their product (Table 16.4).

Table 16.4
Product Use Satisfaction - Debrief Questions

1. Was the product used as intended? If not, why not?
2. Did the customer have any problems using the product?
3. Did the product perform as intended? If not, why not?
4. What could you do differently to ensure better use?

Level IV   Business Benefits

For many customers, this level of satisfaction is the most important. Manufacturers, distributors and retailers have business goals. Increasingly, farms and ranches are run like any other business, with business plans, cash flow projections and financial goals. If the sales call process (Level I), the "sale before the sale" where you began delivering valuable information and support (Level II), and the product use (Level III) all were satisfactory, you have sold a product or service that will meet the business needs of the customer.

How can you evaluate whether you have met business needs? In some situations – such as manufacturers placing product and "selling" sales goals through a marketing program, the measure is very clear – sales results and rebate payments. In fact, whenever possible, the salesperson should choose a measure for "business success" that is easy to use because the customer is already collecting information on it. The best way to determine if you are meeting business needs and satisfying business expectations of your customer is to ASK. Are customers satisfied with the increased yield, increased efficiency or decreased cost you promised? ASK! Are customers satisfied that working with you was the best possible business decision? ASK!

Bill Brockett
Virginia Beef Corporation
Owner and President
Haymarket, Virginia

In the sales process, the number one way I think I can help bring value as a salesperson to both my customer and my company is by satisfying that customer. The best advertising you have, the best tribute to your company's reputation and to you as a salesperson is the very, very best satisfied customer. Probably, there's no way to get better advertising than word of mouth from an existing customer. So, if one customer says to another customer, "These guys are great. You can't beat these guys." There's no way you could pay for advertising that good. No way at all. So you have got to take care of each customer from beginning to end and then some.

And you build your whole base when you start out with one customer. You try very, very hard to please that one. Then you try very hard to please the next one and you try very, very hard. And then, you build on that one. And then the next one...and it's like building blocks. You build one on top of the other. You don't want to make a mistake – you don't want to stumble because one bad customer will tear you up for a bunch of others. You don't know how many other potential customers he's going to talk to.

The other thing we like to get in our written advertisement is the permission of the exiting customer after we have done whatever we say we're going to do for them – after they've gotten their calves back and we talk to them and they're really happy, we like to get them to allow us to use their name in our advertisement. The only thing we're doing in the advertisement is thanking them for their business. If you say "Thank you for your business," and their name is in there, it implies immediately that they were satisfied customers. So when another person reads it and says, "Oh, if xyz company or that seedstock producer used them and was happy, they must be all right." And if they know xyz company or that other producer, they're going to pick up the telephone and say "How did you make out over there."

So, using that name association type thing, we get a tremendous amount out of our advertising. We do the same thing in our sod business. It is dramatic. It feels the same way...one customer leads to another. Satisfaction is mutually gratifying for the customer, salesperson and company.

Integrate Satisfaction into the Call Cycle

The sales cycle doesn't stop once you have closed a sale with a customer. Indeed, it is only starting. You will continue to work with your customer over the next months and years, teaching them, learning from them, supporting them and selling to them. Regularly asking about satisfaction is an important part of this cycle.

- As you approach closing a sale, evaluate yourself on Level I (sales process) and Level II (customer value). Do you make the grade? Can you improve?
- After you have closed the sale, continue working with your customer to fine-tune product use, application, integration in the business, and results.

Summary

Your customer is someone else's prospect. The more satisfied your customers are, the less vulnerable they are to your competitor. The less satisfied they are, the more likely they are to buy somewhere else next year, or the year after that. What's more, dissatisfied customers complain to their friends and neighbors for a long time before they will complain face-to-face to you. In fact, a couple of dissatisfied opinion leaders can "sour" an entire local market.

Customer satisfaction is often as much the responsibility of the customer as the salesperson – for example when a product must be used correctly, or a service must be implemented appropriately. Nevertheless, one of the customer's expectations is that you are responsible for satisfaction. Since you can't control all its elements, you should find out what the current level of satisfaction is. In many cases, that means talking to your customers. In some cases (such as Level I call quality) you may only need to have an objective heart-to-heart conversation with yourself.

The wonderful thing about customer satisfaction is that people like being asked about it, as long as you ask at a convenient time and don't ask for more detail than they want to give. Some studies show, in fact, that satisfaction increases just because people are asked if they are satisfied – it's that positive!

Integrate satisfaction measures into your regular call cycle. Try to measure all four levels of satisfaction regularly – it helps you see the "big picture," but also what actions you could take to improve it. When in doubt, ask your customer.

Then sit back and listen. They will almost always have something to say. And most of it will almost always be good news.

Review Questions

1. Customer satisfaction, like value, is a relative concept. Explain how customer satisfaction can be defined relative to marketplace-driven expectations and sales-driven expectations.

2. Define the four levels of customer satisfaction.

3. Consider again the four levels of customer satisfaction. Of the four levels, what level do customers often consider the most important?

4. How can the salesperson best determine whether or not they have satisfied the customer?

5. What function do debrief questions serve in determining customer satisfaction? When and how should a salesperson debrief relative to the sales call?

6. In the case studies in this chapter, Jackson and Brockett talk about a couple of ways to develop customer satisfaction and use it to build a customer base. What are they? Describe how or what you might do to build or develop greater satisfaction with a customer.

Code of Ethics

Code of Ethics - Professionalism in Agri Selling

When we speak of a code of ethics, several things come to mind – a set of rules, moral principles, code of conduct, and business rules superimposed over manners and decency. In this Appendix, a code of ethics for agri selling is outlined. The key to successful, long-term selling relationships is trust. The key to trust is simple, honest and ethical behavior 100% of the time.

Professionalism

Professionalism. In one word, so many factors critical to your career are held. Without exception, each of those interviewed for case studies in this book spoke the word. Professionalism. It is a manner, an attitude, a state of being. It reflects on the little things you do, and the big things you plan. Without it, you may have a job – for the time being. With it, you may have a rewarding career that effectively serves you and your family, your customers, and the company you work for, as well as the agricultural industry itself.

"Professional" is not a title to take lightly. A professional has copious responsibilities to customers, company and self. Maintaining and constantly improving one's professionalism requires unceasing discipline. Read, know, and review your responsibilities several times a year. Understand where you are. Honest evaluation and reflection on these responsibilities can help you grow as a professional at each juncture in your sales career.

One element of a sales career that makes it so appealing to many is the independent nature of the daily schedule. Still, that means that you and you alone are responsible for the daily assessment and improvement of yourself as a professional. It is, quite honestly, a choice you make as an individual. Choose professionalism.

Responsibilities to Customers

Serve Customers' Best Interest

Find ways that you, your company, and your products/services can fill each customer's economic needs, or fill social/individual needs. Let customers decide what is best for them, but make sure they understand the facts. You have no obligation to point out competitive alternatives.

Never Misrepresent or Mislead the Customer

Don't build false expectations intentionally, or unintentionally, as they hurt long-term relationships and violate basic ethics and common decency. The customer wants to believe in you. You may have to "unsell" on occasion to avoid misrepresentation of product or service.

Protect Confidences, Avoid Unauthorized Incentives

In sales, as relationships develop, confidences are shared. Trust is imperative to long-lasting sales relationships. A broken confidence ultimately results in broken trust. Protecting the customer's best interest often involves discretion and careful consideration on your part. Remember that innocent comments can embarrass you or worse, the customer. Kickbacks are illegal. Even small special favors become addictive. They are not in the customer's best interest.

Responsibilities to Your Company

Remain Loyal

Relationships with customers sometimes become strong and make it difficult to be loyal to your company. Don't wane. Practice "we," not "they." You don't have to like or agree at all times with your company policies. However, you must support them. If you can't, resign.

Support the Total Marketing Effort

Remember, selling is only one part of marketing, but an important part. Recognize the importance of the following:

- market intelligence;
- forecasts;
- inventories;
- special reports;
- office work;
- electronic correspondence.

Responsibilities to the Public

Do Not Downgrade the Competition

Downgrading the competition makes you look bad and may also make your customer look bad. Be knowledgeable about the competition, but avoid negative selling. Sell your positive benefits.

Be Informed and Uphold Regulations

Legal regulations must be upheld - even if you disagree. Remember this simple equation: personal risk = company risk. Company policies usually have a purpose. Question regulations with company staff - not customers. Professionals have the obligation to be informed.

Responsibilities to Yourself

Constantly Upgrade Self

To a professional, growth is never ending. It may be difficult, but remember, you don't *make* time for personal improvement, you *take* the time. Critically and honestly evaluate yourself and your performance in the areas of technical ability, selling skills, and "people skills."

Separate Personal and Professional Life

Do not let personal matters interfere with professional life or your professionalism. Recognize that personal and professional lives cannot become completely separate. Engage the support of spouse and/or family (those who are the center of your personal life) to make it happen.

Constantly Strive to Represent Yourself and Your Company in a Professional Manner

You are the company. You are a sales and service representative. Are you a professional?

Code of Ethics of Professional Agricultural Salespeople

- I will continually work to serve the best interest of my customers, seeking to find ways my organization's goods and services can help fill their needs.

- I will never knowingly misrepresent my product or mislead my customers in its use.

- I will not reveal confidences shared by my clients and will neither offer nor accept any unauthorized compensation, financial or otherwise, for the product or service being sold.

- I will not intentionally downgrade a competitor or a competitor's product in order to benefit myself.

- I will work cooperatively to execute the total marketing plan of my organization and do my best to conduct my field activities in a profitable manner.

- I will stay informed about and vigorously uphold all legal restrictions and regulations pertaining to my area of responsibility.

- I will make a continual and concentrated effort to upgrade my professional selling skills and my technical ability so as to perform my duties effectively and efficiently.

- I will maintain my personal life so as to avoid any situations that would jeopardize my effectiveness in carrying out my professional responsibilities.

- I will constantly strive to represent myself and my organization in a manner which will enhance the stature of the agricultural selling profession.

- I will strive for professionalism in agriselling, continually improving, always and in all ways representing my company, my customers, and myself to the best of my ability.

Working at Farm/Trade Shows

Farm shows or trade shows can be viewed as the opportunity to enhance or tarnish an agribusiness' reputation. It is at the farm show, whether it be a giant national exhibition or a local fair, that images are on display.

Opinions are varied as to whether or not the money and time spent at farm shows is worth the expense. Most will agree, however, that to remain competitive, they must participate. Even if they do not see a tangible increase in sales, exhibiting keeps the company's name and employees in the public eye and establishes a company's credibility as a member of the agricultural community. Sometimes, your absence may be more noticeable than your company's presence in a farm or trade show.

Once the decision to participate is made, many hours of work lie ahead to ensure the time spent is profitable. If it is worth doing, it is worth doing well. Two lounge chairs sunk in the mud behind a poorly constructed display with a few old brochures and matchbooks convey a clear message, but not a positive one. On the other hand, a sparkling booth with friendly staffers and sufficient information says, "We want to be here and we'll make good use of your time and ours."

That kind of successful attitude will result only if proper planning takes place. The following tips will help prepare you for participation in most farm/trade show situations.

Physical Arrangements

Companies spend money on everything from tables with standup displays to carpeted areas with live music. More expensive does not always mean more effective. You will do well to have an exhibit that represents your company accurately.

If your company does not have an attractive display, it may benefit you to enlist the help of a professional. Firms that deal in displays can help design an exhibit that will stress company philosophy and portray an appropriate image.

Location makes a difference in which type of display you utilize. Outdoor locations may mean watching the weather to avoid soggy literature, or may preclude certain audio, visual or electronic displays. Indoor locations may stifle equipment demonstrations. Know the physical details and limitations of the show location in advance and plan accordingly.

Have appropriate company literature on hand, even if the primary reason for exhibiting is to display products. You can refer to it as you demonstrate products and send it home with show-goers as a reminder of your interaction and your company.

Attention Grabbing

To be recognized as the company with something more, you'll have to grab the attention of the passerby. Countless gimmicks have been used – give-aways, games, prizes, etc. Gimmicks can, however, also detract. The trick is to use the attention-getters as a means to an end – to draw the customer's interest to the product itself. For example, a prize for identifying weed types that can be eliminated by your company's product will put the focus right where you want it. Enticing people to your display area is not an easy task. If you have too many staffers, passersby may feel overwhelmed. Staffers who spend their time talking among themselves may alienate would-be visitors to the area. The key is moderation. Realize there will be peak times during the show and increase the staff assigned to work during those periods.

Visitor Relations

Don't sip lemonade in the shade and wonder why people are passing you by. You'll have to draw people out with a friendly smile or handshake. Initiate discussions that will lead to your product or service and if necessary, prepare a short presentation that highlights product benefits.

Make the customer comfortable. Go out of your way to see that regular customers feel recognized and valued and potential ones get a positive first impression.

Designate a "special situation area." Whether you have a hot prospect or an irate customer on your hands, you'll need a spot away from the crowds in which to conduct business. The "special situation area" affords exhibit staff a mechanism to separate "high potential" prospects from the show crowd.

Show Follow-up

After the show has ended and the truck has been packed up, the tendency is to wipe the show out of your mind. The most important work may still remain. Following up on new leads and taking care of information requests and complaints is the payback for all the time and effort at the show. Without follow-up, it is difficult to justify your presence at such a show.

In order for the follow-up contact to be most effective, pre-show planning and preparation should take follow-up mechanics into account. An efficient system of obtaining, classifying and recording leads, particularly those with seemingly higher potential, is essential. Prepare and mobilize dealers, distributors and the appropriate company salespeople to handle the process well in advance. Involvement on all fronts tends to encourage individual recognition of the value of the farm show and follow-up.

Make follow-up contacts promptly. Whether it is a phone call, sending information or a personal call from the local dealer or distributor, follow-up activities are most valuable when the prospect still has a recollection of the exhibit and company.

Again, if it is worth doing, it is worth doing well. A well-planned and attractive exhibit staffed by courteous, knowledgeable personnel and backed with a systematic follow-up will accumulate in more than just another off-season activity. It can be an integral part of your organization's overall marketing strategy.

Summary

- Most companies exhibit at farm or trade shows because attendance gives them exposure as part of the competitive agricultural community.
- Expensive displays do not necessarily equate a successful exhibit; creating a positive, accurate portrayal of the company is more important.
- Making your presence valuable at a show means getting the attention of passersby. Only then will they be receptive to you and your product information. Most people have to be encouraged. Making them feel special will pay off in good public relations.
- The work is not over at show closing time. Correct follow-up in disseminating further information and arranging for calls is crucial.

Handling Customer Complaints/Conflicts

The customer may not always be right, but if you lose a sale - present or future - or precipitate a messy lawsuit, you're the one who loses. There are worse things than a customer voicing complaints - such as complaints that are never heard, only to show up later as the customer refuses to deal with your company. This is particularly damaging if the customer tells others about their displeasing experience.

We live in an age of consumer awareness, spurred in part by government regulation, court rulings and media attention to consumer issues. The average farmer has become more willing to exercise what they see as their basic right to challenge or question a product or service. When the salesperson neglects to resolve a complaint, they risk losing the customer and/or perhaps winding up in court.

Agricultural supply and marketing firms are particularly susceptible to this kind of action. Therefore, it becomes critical for the salesperson to recognize the potential of any complaint. While legal action against agricultural suppliers is not widespread, it is increasingly common and consequently a consideration in customer relations.

Because complaints are frequently unpleasant for a salesperson, and because they have the potential for damaging future sales or spurring legal action, it's easy to see the negative side. But there's a brighter side as well. Successful salespeople always recognize the need to turn a disadvantage into a plus whenever possible - and complaints may offer just that opportunity.

Tips for Managing Customer Complaints

- Most customers consider it their right to complain if a product or service does not deliver what they expected. Therefore, complaints are sometimes a matter of emotion or unrealistic expectations rather than logic.
- It is the salesperson's responsibility to judge the validity of a complaint and choose appropriate action. Complaints may be

viewed as opportunities because, if handled in a tactful, correct way, they may allow the salesperson to increase credibility with their customers.

- Preparation is an important component of handling a complaint. A salesperson should have background information on the person who issued the complaint, along with facts about the farming operation. Knowledge about company restitution policies prevents the promising of unrealistic compensation.

- Salespeople handling complaints need to maintain calm and tact and react with interest and respect to a customer's charges. They must also properly maintain their status within the company in order not to shift blame from themselves to their firms.

- Many complaints can be prevented before they ever arise by carefully monitoring the customer and their operation. An alert salesperson will sense potential problems and help alleviate them before they occur.

Tips for Managing Conflict

- Listen to the person's emotion. Don't just wait until they are done speaking – be able to discuss what they say.
- Be empathetic in your listening – be understanding and professional.
- Explore the emotion before getting to factual discussion – don't dismiss it.
- Use phrases that reflect the emotion but don't belittle it:
- *So, what you heard upset you, because…*
- *I can understand that feeling based on what you've said…*
- *Others have felt that way, and they discovered…*
- *I hear what you are saying – that's a tough situation to be in…*
- *That makes sense – I can see why you would respond that way…*
- *That must be frustrating…*
- Don't be defensive – whether the customer is right or wrong in your eyes, the emotions are still real and need to be acknowledged before you can move on.
- Remember: an emotional response is a gift – a chance to listen, empathize, and solve the situation.
- If you need to, buy time – remember, your specific response at this point is less important than your promise that you will respond:
- If you need to gather more information, say so.
- If you'd just like to think about it more, ask permission to do so.
- Give no excuse, but promise to get back to them at a specific time and keep your promise.

The time-honored advice of "counting to ten" applies here. Once you've thought about the matter, you'll be able to <u>act</u> constructively instead of <u>reacting</u> in a way that's likely to produce a lose-lose outcome.

Summary

You can create opportunity from complaints/conflict every day:

- when your mother says you don't visit her enough, you have an opportunity;
- when you bump into another car in a public parking lot, you have an opportunity.

This is not a skill unique to sales or even to customer relationships. It does, however, recognize a universal truth about how people want to be treated: people want their opinions to be respected.

As you know, turning conflict into opportunity is an art, not a science. Sometimes it takes more than one try to get past the emotion and see the benefits. Other times, dealing with the emotion is enough; the customer just wants to have their opinion known. And in some cases, the customer will use conflict as a tool to get their way - free seed, money settlement, or extra attention. In any situation, it is up to you to figure out what the conflict is, why it is there, and how best to find the opportunity for your customer relationship so the relationship lasts a lifetime.

> When disputes arise, don't take things personally. Don't let concerns over who's right stifle open discussion and problem solving. Pursue mutually acceptable settlements…Look for win-win solutions.
> - EEO Home Page

Collecting Accounts

"The sale isn't complete until the money is collected" is as accurate a rule today as ever. Collecting overdue accounts is one of the most unpleasant functions of sales – but it is a job that is often assigned to the salesperson. It's uncomfortable and sometimes embarrassing to have to ask a customer for money. And there is always the worry that, unless the situation is handled very tactfully, it could result in a lost customer. On the other hand, a customer who doesn't pay in a timely manner may not be a desirable customer.

Part of the problem is that there's a good deal of emotion tied to money. People learn early that money is not a subject for discussion with strangers. Collection is associated with villains in black capes and handlebar mustaches who prey on honest, hard working people. It seems personal matters aren't appropriate topics of discussion for moral agriculturalists – and that's where the problem starts.

Collecting money is an essential part of the selling process. And when problems arise, the logical candidate for making the collection call is the person who knows the account best - the one who made the sale. Still, most salespeople approach the collection call with fear and trepidation.

Having some responsibility for collection makes salespeople more cautious in encouraging accounts that have questionable payment records. Salespeople with some responsibility for making sure accounts are collected are usually more cooperative with the credit department of their company.

One big reason for the focus on collecting accounts in a timely manner is that, the older the account balance, the less it's worth to the business. This is because, when your business is carrying an account, is ties up your firm's cash. Your company will have to either borrow money to cover the account while it is unpaid, or, even if it doesn't have to borrow, it can't use that money for other things. Either way, it is a very real cost to the business. Whether the cost is a real cost or an opportunity cost it must be considered in measuring the profitability of that customer. The longer the account is not paid, the greater the cost. And the longer the account goes without being paid, the greater the likelihood that it will never be paid. These two factors together cause the value of the account to decline over time. It's as though the money the customer owes you actually shrinks the longer it goes unpaid. An Iowa State University Extension publication, *Credit Management For Business Firms*, reports overdue accounts rapidly decline in as illustrated below:

Table D.1:
Declining Account Value

Account Status	Value
Current	100¢ on the dollar
2 mos. past due	90¢ on the dollar
6 mos. past due	67¢ on the dollar
1 yr. past due	45¢ on the dollar
2 yrs. past due	23¢ on the dollar
3 yrs. past due	15¢ on the dollar
5 yrs. past due	1¢ on the dollar

Why Customers Don't Pay

There are many reasons why customers don't pay on time. While excuses are never acceptable reasons, understanding them offers a clue to dealing with them.

1. Don't Understand Credit Terms

Credit terms can be complicated – especially on highly seasonal agricultural products. Manufacturers and distributors of fertilizer and chemicals, for example, offer early-order discounts and credit terms to encourage customers to buy earlier and to spread their sales and shipments over a longer season. The result is complex credit terms that vary widely from company to company.

A farmer or dealer exposed to several different "simple" plans may easily get confused or just misunderstand.

2. Poor Managers

They're habitually slow and often busy with the physical operation that they let financial matters slide. They don't intend to pay late, it's just not a high priority.

3. Cash-flow Problems

They just can't pay when the bill's due. It's not as bad if the customer at least notifies the salesperson or company that he can't pay on time. But when she/he lets it go, it becomes a problem for everyone. These customers are not intentionally dishonest, they just have a tendency to avoid reality – believing that if ignored, the problem will go away. A farmer or dealer in financial difficulty may not think logically.

4. "Push the Supplier to the Limit"

They know what they're doing. They pay late intentionally, banking on their importance to the supplier that nothing serious will come of it. This customer operates on such a "float" regularly. Once he/she learns a supplier will not take action until a couple of weeks past the due date, he or she will commonly pay late.

5. Dishonesty

Fortunately, dishonest customers are few. But occasionally, a customer will openly attempt to delay payment for a variety of "manufactured" reasons – designed as excuses to withhold payment as long as possible or even permanently.

Collecting Begins With Communication

The most critical part of collection begins before the sale is completed. The customer must thoroughly understand the total payment process – including any cash discounts that may be applicable to the purchase. A clear understanding is critical to smooth financial relationships with customers. This will draw upon the salesperson's communication expertise.

Question the farmer or dealer about his or her understanding of the terms of the sale – assume nothing. Remember, if a misunderstanding occurs, the customer almost always blames the salesperson. This is only reasonable, since it's the salesperson's job to create understanding. If something does go wrong, there's a good chance it will affect the customer's perception of the product and the salesperson's competency – hurting future business.

Educate the Customer

The customer must be educated about the real cost of credit and value of any discount policy. Help analyze available credit plans and select the one best suited. Steer the customer to other sources of credit available from banks, PCAs etc., that offer a cheaper source of cash. Often the salesperson can add additional value through a more favorable payment schedule that will actually save the customer money.

This not only builds credibility with the customer, but saves the company unnecessary grief. Most manufacturers, suppliers, dealers and distributors do not want to be in the credit business. It's costly, even with high annual interest rates. Carrying charges of 1-1.5% a month cannot cover the cost of extending credit in most ag firms. Only a few firms, especially at the retail or distributor level, ever make profit through their credit programs.

Maintain Sales/Credit Relationships

Salespeople should work closely with the credit manager in obtaining complete financial information and credit applications from customers. For many salespeople, this is a real nuisance, because they do not see it as part of their jobs. Sometimes there's a tendency to be sloppy or the salesperson is so anxious to work with his or her customer that he or she forgets who they are working <u>for</u>.

Sometimes, in the eyes of salespeople, the credit manager's primary objective seems to be to prevent salespeople from meeting their sales goals. And it is also true that some credit people tend to view salespeople as irresponsible extroverts who promise anything in order to make a sale. This conflict often leads to credit problems in the field.

Both departments should meet regularly to discuss each other's problems and keep the lines of communication open. Each has an important role to play in the successful use of credit as a marketing tool.

Provide Help With Credit

Sometimes it makes sense to help the customer obtain credit somewhere else. In fact, some sharp salespeople work with their customers in preparing cash-flow projections and even accompany them to the local lender to assist in arranging financing and helping them take advantage of cash discounts. After all, commercial lending institutions are in the business of lending money – they want the business. But if the local bank or Farm Credit Cooperative won't extend credit to the customer, watch out.

This effort is time-consuming, but pays off in present and future transactions. Salespeople should familiarize themselves with how credit can be arranged. Get to know local bank loan officers and Farm Credit Association managers. Take them to lunch occasionally. Once they trust and respect you, they can be a source of good leads, as well as a help in arranging customer credit.

Collecting Overdue Accounts

An account is usually considered overdue when its due date has passed. Most companies have established policies and procedures to follow. Normally, the credit department issues several impersonal reminders to the customer - each a little stronger than the one before. It often only takes one reminder to complete the collection.

It's important that the salesperson be kept advised of the collection process, as the subject may come up during routine sales calls. Or, more embarrassing, the salesperson may continue to sell the customer - compounding an already sticky situation.

Sometime during this process, the salesperson may be called upon to visit the customer about their unpaid bill. The salesperson must be familiar with the situation and all applicable company policies. Take care not to make promises, threats or imply judgments to complicate the problem further.

The call should be handled tactfully, but firmly. If there has been a misunderstanding, it can be cleared up and some procedure for satisfying the established account. If the problem persists, it is likely a company supervisor will accompany the salesperson on a call to the customer. It's up to the salesperson to arrange this if necessary. Eventually, a legal suit may be filed by company lawyers. However, this is an expensive last resort.

The collection process need not be distasteful, if approached fairly and firmly. In fact, many ag customers report dissatisfaction with suppliers who do not enforce stated credit policies. Inconsistent treatment is unfair to those who manage their financial affairs well. They are well aware of their share of the cost of credit over-extended to others. Such inconsistent treatment has legal implications for the company as well.

Credit as a Tool

Credit can be an effective sales tool when used wisely and responsibly. Most ag companies provide credit because it's an accepted means of doing business. In fact, it can be highly effective value-added marketing tool.

It's up to the sales force, in tandem with credit personnel, to use it properly. By accepting this responsibility, salespeople can turn credit from a nightmare into a positive tool for working with customers.

Summary

Salespeople may share the responsibility for collecting overdue accounts because of their close ties to the customer. Customers don't pay bills for a variety of reasons: they misunderstand credit terms, are poor managers, have cash flow problems, know they can get away with late payment, or may be dishonest.

The salesperson can help alleviate some problems before they occur by communication, education, good sales/credit department relationships and by assisting the efforts of customers to procure credit.

Planning and Preparing for Customer Meetings

Conducting Farmer Meetings

Every winter, the average agribusiness salesperson arranges, or rushes to and from, farmer meetings, dealer meetings, sales meetings, customer appreciation dinners and technical meetings. Each is heralded as a potential boon to sales. And, each meeting may potentially enhance or tarnish the firm's reputation. The key to an interesting, productive customer meeting is proper planning, preparation and attention to detail – combined, ideally, with a wealth of experience.

Developing Objectives

Developing objectives is the single most important factor in planning customer meetings, yet many firms virtually ignore this factor when formulating their plans.

Customer meetings, like good sales calls, require well-defined goals. What do you hope to accomplish with the customers who attend? How will you measure your degree of success in reaching these goals? Even an intangible goal such as "building goodwill" requires some standard of measurement. It might be the percentage of attendees who mention the meeting favorably during subsequent sales calls. What about the number of requests for new product presentations? The choice is yours, based on the objectives you have chosen.

The Written Plan

Once you have decided on your objectives, commit them to paper along with the yardstick you have chosen for measuring results. This helps to solidify the objectives in the minds of everyone involved and avoid potential misunderstandings.

Never assume key employees know about the meeting. Such people can contribute significant key input and support to the effort if they are included in the planning. Talk to them about the meeting and solicit their ideas.

The set of written objectives doesn't need to be formal. It might read as follows:

1. To establish or maintain contact with key customers.
2. To provide farmers with the most recent findings concerning use of a key product.
3. To enhance an image of professionalism among customers.

Your measurement of the first objective's success could be the number of customers who attend. The second objective would be met through an informative presentation. The third and least tangible objective might involve oral and written customer evaluations.

Tying a Theme to Objectives

Your meeting will be more cohesive if you tie a theme to one of your main objectives. If the theme is "Acme Fertilizer – Safety First," you might consider focusing customer attention on the objective of safety through tasteful banners, table decorations and gifts (e.g., safety goggles). This lends visual impact to your verbal message.

Handling Details

Once overall objectives have been established, shift your attention to the many details that make a meeting effective. This may mean keeping a checklist that outlines the steps to finalizing the meeting. Several of the checklist items are of special importance and should be considered separately.

Location Counts

One particular aspect of the meeting communicates a great deal about your firm – the location you have chosen. The key word here is *appropriate.* Fried chicken at the local community hall may work if the meeting is intended to communicate technical information but it will not create the same impression as steak at a first-rate hotel. On the other hand, if the firm goes overboard and sponsors an elaborate affair, the customer may worry that he has paid for such excesses in higher-than-necessary prices for the firm's products.

Meetings for key customers are usually first class, befitting the customer's status with the firm. Everything else is a matter of judgment and taste.

Basic Checklist

No matter what kind of accommodations you choose, check that all the basics are in order. The place should be clean, well-equipped, roomy and comfortable with adequate lighting and ventilation. Confirm your reservation *in writing* and check that every item you need is available before committing yourself to rent the facility.

Room Size

The chances of a room being precisely the right size for the number of people you intend to host are slim. It's better to have too much space than not enough. You can always eliminate unnecessary chairs and direct your audience into one small area. Never crowd people; they should feel comfortable enough to be receptive to your message. At the same time, never allow them to scatter over a large space. This tends to make individuals feel isolated, which hampers communication.

Media Considerations

Nothing can kill a sales or informational presentation *and* throw off your confidence faster than poor, inadequate, or non-functioning audio/visual equipment. It is of utmost importance that you become comfortable with the equipment itself and with using it in presenting *before* the meeting.

PA Systems and Audio

The room size must be evaluated: is the Public Address (PA) system you are using sufficient for the job? A meeting in which individuals can't hear sufficiently is wasted time. You must be heard before you are appreciated or considered effective. Often, restaurants provide audio equipment and may assure you that all is in order. Still, it is critical that you know how it works, where the volume control is, where "off" and "on" are located on the microphones and amplifiers. Cordless microphones may come equipped with battery packs. Make sure you know how to add fresh batteries to them and have the appropriate size available.

If audio is required for additional presentation materials such as video, slide/audio presentations, etc., check before the meeting to ensure you don't get feedback from the microphone system when playing the audio. If feedback is an issue, ensure that microphones are disengaged or turned off prior to playing the audio. If the microphone system is used to broadcast the additional audio, ensure that sound is amplified well enough to be clearly understood.

Speaker Considerations

Your speakers may have special A/V needs as well. Be sure to identify what materials or equipment they will need for presenting before the meeting. The speaker who shows up needing a projection unit for computer-generated display materials, when only an overhead projector is available, is at a loss. So are the customers who won't be able to view the information this speaker has prepared. Know ahead of time what speakers' needs are and have the equipment available to them. Ask if they can come to the meeting a little early so you can familiarize them with the unit they will be using and to ensure all is compatible.

Additional Media and Equipment Considerations

There are many media available to help reinforce your messages to your audience. In planning and preparing for your meeting, it may be beneficial to use a checklist to ensure you have the bases covered.

* Flip Charts - Do you have sturdy easels available? Is there a place to post pages? Do you need pins or tape to post pages? Do you have enough flip charts? Consider having individuals on opposite sides of the room simultaneously writing on the flip charts to ensure all participants can see well and become involved in what you are doing. Do you have enough markers for writing on the flip charts? Do you have individuals with good handwriting selected to help?

* Slides - If you are providing a slide projector for a speaker, be sure to clarify if the slides are in a cube or in a carousel. Have a screen available of an appropriate size for all meeting attendees to see. Run through the slides once to ensure you have no flipped images (upside down, sideways, or backwards). Do you need to consider how you will darken the room? Slide images are often darker than overheads and require lights dimmed or shades drawn. Make sure this is possible. Daytime meetings often prevent adequate room darkening and may obscure effective use of slides. Does the projector have a remote? Does it work well? Does the unit have the remote on a cord connected to the machine itself? Does it reach the speaker at the podium?

* Overhead Projection - Do you have an extra bulb? Do you know how to quickly change the bulb? Do you have adequate transparencies prepared? A rule of thumb on transparencies is to have no more than six words across or six lines per overhead transparency. Do you have an appropriately sized screen? Does the unit project adequately? Watch out for an obscured, or trapezoid effect of the presented material when the projection unit is poorly spaced from the screen. Distorted overhead transparency images are

often unreadable or distracting to the audience. Do you have visual markers for you or a speaker to use for illustrating points on transparencies?

- <u>Video</u> - Do you have a VCR and (TV) monitor that work and are compatible with the tape you hope to show? Do you need more than one monitor, given the size of group you are hosting? Are monitors dispersed well enough that all participants can see and hear the tape well enough?

- <u>Accessories</u> - Do you have or need electrical extension cords and or adapters? Do you know where the outlets are located? Do you know if there is an individual at the meeting site who is knowledgeable and capable with the equipment? Again, do you have additional bulbs, markers, pencils and/or paper if necessary? Do you have or need scissors, tape, pins/tacks? Is a pointer necessary – laser, pen light, or good old fashioned wooden stick?

The time and effort you put into preparing media can make or break the delivery of the information.

Seating Arrangements

People are sometimes intimidated by the "schoolroom" style of seating in which they wind up looking at the back of each other's heads, while someone in the front of the room speaks. A roundtable seating plan enhances the group feeling, even when meals are not served. Since the traditional "breaking of bread" together has connotations of sharing in rural America, coffee at the beginning or middle of the programs often serves as a harmonious icebreaker. Tables arranged in a horse shoe shape or in a "V" arrangement offer additional possibilities in mixing the crowd comfortably.

To avoid the pall that cliques can bring to a well-planned meeting, conduct an activity to break the ice and encourage mixing at the meeting's onset. Provide explicit instructions, as most people are more comfortable when they know precisely what they are to accomplish. For example: ask each group to total the number of children those seated at the table have, the number of people who prefer beef or pork, or total acres of corn or cotton, etc. To avoid the impression that such activities are contrived or juvenile, link them somehow to the objectives of the meeting. The psychological strategy of early participant involvement will pay off with a more cohesive meeting.

The MC (Master of Ceremonies') Role

The chairman or "MC" has a critical role in the success of a meeting, because he/she sets the tone and keeps the proverbial ball rolling. Customers will feel more important if the person chosen for the job is perceived as having an important position. The MC need not be the top person in the organization, although the VIP should be heard from at some point, if only to welcome the participants to the meeting and introduce the MC.

Strive to keep the program fast-paced. When it comes to joke telling, the best idea is to avoid it unless the MC is capable of a top-notch professional delivery. Humor is appropriate, but avoid inside jokes understood by only part of the audience as well as any religious, gender, ethnic, political or vulgar jokes that may be offensive.

Focus on Personnel

Customers often like to see the person with whom they've been doing business "all cleaned up" and on display, so introduce company personnel along with brief bits of information about each. Don't embarrass anyone. In the interest of keeping the program moving, be sure to request that applause be held until all the introductions have been completed.

The Beverage Question

The question of whether to serve alcoholic beverages can best be answered by consulting local traditions and customs. In some areas, customers may find it offensive, particularly at husband/wife dinners, while in others it will be expected. If you decide to serve such beverages, do it as a gesture only. Offer soft drinks also. See that customers are not given enough to cause embarrassment to themselves, their peers or the sponsors of the meeting, or to endanger their driving skills.

Choosing Speakers

Entertainment is appropriate in some instances, such as appreciation dinners, but can be a very tricky thing to coordinate. Scout the entertainment personally before you contract for it. Be on the lookout for possibilities months in advance of an anticipated meeting. Seldom is a meeting made successful by entertainment alone, but it definitely can be hurt by entertainment that is poor.

Speakers - such as extension personnel, supplier representatives or outside experts - are usually a welcome addition to a meeting, but they must be carefully selected. The speaker's contribution is as much the responsibility of the sponsor as the meal arrangement, since both reflect on the sponsor. Work closely with the speaker on content, length and style of presentation, particularly if he or she is not a professional.

Time Considerations

You will do yourself a favor – not to mention the speaker – if you set a time limit, anticipate any problems with visual aids and leave ample time after the meeting for questions.

You may choose to have a clock or watch subtly fastened to the podium for speakers and MC to see while they are presenting. Often, when there is a series of speakers, or if there are numerous overheads or projections and the room is darkened to accommodate them, speakers may not be accurately watching the clock. To ensure the time limit is followed, have a member of your staff stand in the back of the room and signal each speaker <u>two minutes before</u> their time is up. This is a tactful way to accomplish the objective of keeping the program moving, while not embarrassing anyone.

MCs have been known to resort to the use of an oven timer to "police" several speakers. This device sounds off impartially with each passing of scheduled time. All are treated equally. The more firmly and consistently you treat time limitations, the happier your audience will be.

Even a poor speaker can make a good impression if you plan carefully. If such a person can field questions well, allot 10 minutes for the formal speech and 20 minutes for the question-and-answer period afterwards. For added assurance, "plant" a few questions in the audience, in case the discussion does not begin immediately.

When a large group is anticipated, meet with the speaker in advance and plan 10 questions for participants to ask that will coincide with the speaker's major points. Directing the discussion will often make an otherwise dry subject more appealing, since the question-and-answer format focuses attention on the issues.

Length of Program

The best way to ensure that the customer is enjoying the program is to look at it from the customer's point of view. How long should each part run? What if something starts to go wrong? Allow time for the mechanical things – like the clearing of the dishes after the meal – and add a few minutes onto each time estimate, in case things start to go wrong. Make contingency plans, including a determination of which things can be best shortened, cut out or lengthened, if other parts of the program don't go as scheduled. Give the customer a starting and ending time for the entire program only. This way you and only you will worry if the program starts to lag behind schedule.

Since audience discontent is fired primarily by expectations, wrap the program up five minutes early rather than five minutes late. As they say in show business, "leave 'em wanting more."

It's natural for some parts of your program to be more interesting than others. All this means is you will have to pace it, so that everything flows smoothly. Don't start with a speaker who brings down the house and end with one who puts them to sleep. Not only will you make the latter look bad, but you'll leave a bad image of the meeting in customers' minds.

Remember, too, that the mind can only absorb what the seat can endure. A stretch break before an important speaker will pay off in dividends of attentiveness. Restroom breaks are often in order, particularly if drinks have been served and/or the audience has been shifting in their seats for a couple of hours.

Follow Up

It's bad enough to make a host of mistakes but there is no excuse for repeating the same ones year after year. Try to step back and see your meeting objectively after it's all over. Above all, learn from your mistakes.

A short evaluation on the back of the program may help you to see things the customer's way. Or invite a representative panel of customers to lunch - perhaps a week after the meeting - and invite their ideas, suggestions and complaints. But be sure to get responses promptly, as time has a way of coloring people's memories. Not only will the customers' responses help you to plan future meetings more effectively, but they will demonstrate to the customer in a concrete way that you care what he/she thinks.

Summary

Developing objectives and proper planning are keys to successful farmer meetings. Meticulous attention to details results in a smooth meeting and lasting professional image.

Facility, space and media considerations must all be carefully planned. A good meeting location, a well-arranged room and audio/visual equipment that functions properly and is well seen/heard means the message will be delivered to the customers attending.

An important planning factor is the time element. The audience shouldn't be forced to sit through a tedious program. Boredom can be prevented by a strict schedule and quick-moving agenda.

Speakers should be chosen with care. A less-polished speaker may appear more at ease and be more enjoyable if the time is spent answering audience questions instead of straight speaking.

The audience can give vital input on the success of the meeting through either a written evaluation or during a follow up meeting.

List of Figures and Tables

CHAPTER 6

CHAPTER 7

CHAPTER 8

CHAPTER 9

CHAPTER 10

Glossary

A/V

Audio Visual

**Adopters,
Early**

Farmers who accept and implement technology earlier than most farmers, although they are not the very first in their communities to do so.

Adoption Diffusion Curve

A normal distribution of farmers on a bell curve, according to the speed with which they adopt new ideas.

Adoption Process

The process by which new technologies or ideas are embraced, accepted and implemented by the customer.

**Agency, Environmental
  Protection (EPA)**

United States government agency whose mission is to protect human health and to safeguard the natural environment.

Anhydrous Ammonia

Ammonia that is not in an aqueous solution (ammonia gas).

Aquaculture

The cultivation or farming of food or feed products in water (as of fish or shellfish).

Basic Product

The hard good or core product that is the central item featured by a manufacturer. The basic product may be surrounded by complementary goods and services.

Benefits
(of a product or service)

The positive results experienced by a customer when a product or service is purchased and used.

Benefits Statement,
Features - Advantages

A statement about a product or service which demonstrates that because of **F** (feature), the customer will gain **A** (advantages) and therefore **B** (benefit) will result.

Bio-Engineered Seed

Seed that contains modified genetic material, to add specific input traits (e.g., insect resistance) or output traits (e.g., high-oil corn).

Biosecurity

The practice of managing the health status of an animal herd by limiting exposure to pathogens such as might be carried on the clothing of workers or visitors.

Body Language,
Mirroring

A pattern of nonverbal communication in which one party subconsciously mimics the movements of the other. Examples of mirroring behavior would be to cross legs at the same time or sweep the brow.

Bovine Somatotropins
(BST)

A naturally occurring substance that can be reproduced through bio-engineering and injected in lactating cows to increase the amount of milk a cow will produce relative to genetic potential.

Bulk Product

Products such as pesticides that are delivered in large quantities and stored in large tanks at the retailer or on a farm until used.

Buyer's Remorse

A common name for cognitive dissonance, or "second thoughts" the buyer has after making a purchase.

Buying Signals

Verbal and non-verbal signals that the customer is ready to buy.

Buying Signals, Non-Verbal

Gestures, posture or facial expressions that indicate the customer is ready to buy.

CCA Certification

Certified Crop Advisor Certification is administered by the American Society of Agronomy with state affiliates. The CCA encompasses a set of international and state standards, certification and an examination that requires working professionals to be proficient in nutrient management, water and soil management, integrated pest management, and crop management. A specific number of Continuing Education Units (CEUs) must be accumulated every two years to remain certified.

CCPC Certification

Canadian Crop Protection Certification, a national certification standard for product support for agricultural professionals launched by the Crop Protection Institute of Canada. To receive certification, course participants must complete a series of training modules in all aspects of pesticide application including application technology, legislation and regulations and pesticide and environmental safety.

Calibrating

Adjusting machinery to make sure that it emits the right amount of product (i.e. herbicide, insecticide).

Calibrating a Planter

Adjusting a planter to make sure that the proper amount of seeds per acre or hectare are being planted.

Cash Flow

The movement of cash through the business, from selling products, receiving payment, purchasing new products, paying for those products, using them to generate a marketable crop or selling them.

Certification, Pest Control Advisor

A program of advanced post-graduate study and examinations required by certain states for all employees or consultants making crop protection and/or fertility recommendations.

Close (the call)

The point at which the salesperson asks for a commitment and sets up the steps that will occur next.

Closing

Asking the customer for commitment.

Code of Ethics

A set of guidelines or rules followed by professional salespeople to ensure consistent quality of service and integrity.

Cold Calling

Calling on a potential customer who hasn't been met before and/or for whom there is no reference or "lead".

Commissions

Salesperson compensation based on the level of sales attained rather than salaries.

Commitment, Incremental

Increasing commitment by a customer, culminating in the commitment to purchase.

Commodities

Products produced and sold, or publicly traded, in large quantities (such as corn), for which prices are easily compared; increasingly used to refer to agricultural inputs when they are sold in large quantities and/or without services at a basic price.

Common Carrier

A transportation company that delivers packages for the general public, e.g., UPS, Federal Express, DHL.

Compaction

Soils that do not contain sufficient air space, thereby causing poor plant growth.

Competency

An integrated description of knowledge, skill and attitude in the work environment which is measurable and describes human behavior in the work environment.

Competitive Strategies

A business plan designed to maintain or increase a company's position in the market relative to competing suppliers.

Concentration Goals

Goals relating to the proportion of each customer's business that is captured by a company or product.

Consideration Set

A mental "short" list of companies and suppliers that a grower will consider as viable suppliers, based on needs and values.

Contracted Grain

Grain produced under a contract between producer and buyer.

Conversion

In livestock production, refers to the ratio of pounds of feed to pounds of meat or milk.

Cooperative Distributors

Farmer owned cooperatives that act as regional distributors, buying from the basic manufacturers and selling to cooperative retailers who in turn sell to farmers.

Counter Selling

Selling in a retail or farm store environment as opposed to on-farm selling.

County Extension

A government-supported source of information for agriculturalists, horticulturalists etc., bringing information from universities to the public.

Credit Terms

The guidelines agreed to when a company offers to finance the sale of a product and allow payment later or over time.

Cross-Sell

A product strategy that encourages the purchase of a second product or service when a first is bought.

Customer Settlements

Money or free product offered to customers to compensate for documented non-performance of a product or damage caused by that product.

Customer Turnover Goals

Goals relating to the number of customers retained or lost in a given time period.

Database (customer)

A system for organizing, categorizing and updating customer records and information on a regular basis.

Demographics

Information about people that can be observed, collected and measured, such as age, income level, education, or employment.

Demographic Segments

Groups of people recognized according to common demographic criteria, such as "all producers over the age of 50."

Dialogue

A two-way conversation between the customer and the salesperson about needs and issues.

Differential Advantage

A benefit or service that makes a product or company unique and worth paying more.

DISC

A personal work style analysis which divides behavior into four categories: Dominance, Influence, Steadiness, and Compliance. DISC Style Analysis is used to help individuals develop the best strategies to meet the demands of their work environment, co-workers and customers.

Discounts, cash

A pricing discount for goods or services purchased when cash is paid.

Discounts, Volume

A pricing discount for products or services when they are purchased in a large quantity.

Dissonance

In sales, the lack of confidence or doubt that customers sometimes feel after the sale, when they question whether they made a good decision.

Distribution	The process by which a product moves from the manufacturer to the farmer or end-user.
Distribution Channel	A specific path a product takes from manufacture to use; may also refer to companies that distribute product.
Distributors	Also known as wholesalers, these companies buy products from manufacturers and re-sell or "distribute" them to local retail businesses and large producer customers.
ECB	European Corn Borer; a type of worm which gets into the corn ear as the ear nears maturity and eats the kernels and the cob.
E. coli	*E. coli* is the abbreviated name of the bacterium *Escherichia* (Genus) *coli* (Species). This bacterium is responsible for a variety of diseases, usually of the intestine.
Early Majority	Early majority farmers comprise the approximately 34 percent of the farmer population willing to try a new idea or technology as the "second wave" of adopters.
Economic Exchange Model	A model in which customers are assured to give sellers money, services, or goods equal to (or less than) the value they receive for a purchased product.
Environmental Protection Agency (EPA)	SEE Agency, Environmental Protection

External Analysis	External factors to consider in developing the market plan, factors which affect everyone in the marketplace, such as the current economic environment, political climate, cropping or livestock numbers, technology, the regulatory climate etc.
Farm Credit Cooperative	An organization that is owned by farmers and offers financing to farmers and/or rural businesses.
Farm Services Agency	This agency of the U.S. Department of Agriculture oversees the administration of farm commodity programs; farm ownership, operating and emergency loans; conservation and environmental programs; emergency and disaster assistance; domestic and international food assistance; and international export credit programs.
FDA Guidelines	The Food and Drug Administration oversees production and labeling of food, cosmetics, medicines and medical devices, and radiation-emitting products in the U.S. such as microwave ovens. Feed and drugs for pets and farm animals come under FDA scrutiny.
Features	The concrete, measurable, or technical characteristics of a product.
Features - Advantages- Benefits Statement	SEE Benefits Statement, Features - Advantages.
Federal Agency, Guidelines	Any United States regulatory agency's interpretation of a Congressional law.

Feed Assay

Analyzing animal feed for nutritional value and/or the proper level of feed additives such as vitamins or anti-microbial products.

Field Trials

Product tests done in a natural environment to determine the effectiveness and/or environmental fate of products.

Floriculture

The cultivation and management of ornamental and especially flowering plants.

Forecasting

In sales, predicting the amount of a product that will be sold in a specific time in a specific geography.

Generic

A product that is not branded, but may be sold under a variety of names.

Genetics

1. A branch of biology that deals with the heredity and variation of organisms. 2. The genetic makeup and phenomena of an organism, type, group, or condition.

Genetics Company

Any company that alters the genetic code, whether through traditional breeding or biotechnology to achieve desired results in plants and/or animals with a view to developing healthier organisms.

Germination

When a seed starts to develop into a plant. Specifically, germination refers to the time when a growing seed penetrates the soil surface.

Going-Rate Pricing

Competition-oriented pricing where a company tries to keep its price at the average level charged by the industry.

Grid Soil Mapping

Soil sampling method in which a field is divided into square sections (grids) of one or more acres/hectares. Samples are taken randomly from within the grid. They are then analyzed and the results are used to generate maps of soil fertility.

Gross Margin Dollars

Sales $ - Cost of Goods $ = Gross Margin $.

Gross Margin Target Pricing

SEE: Pricing, Gross Margin Target

High C

Preferred style of work in which Compliance is the predominant trait. High C's approach their work with adherence to established standards, procedures or expectations.

High D

Preferred style of work in which Dominance is the predominant trait. High D's like obtaining results and problem solving.

High I

Preferred style of work in which Influence is the predominant trait. High I's approach their work by interacting with people and emotions. High I's meet new people in an outgoing, gregarious, assertive manner.

High S

Preferred style of work in which Steadiness is the predominant trait. High S's approach their work, with a controlled vs. flexible pace.

Horticulture

The science and art of growing fruits, vegetables, flowers, or ornamental plants.

Ileitis, swine

Inflammation of the ileum, the part of the small intestine that connects with the large intestine.

Immunocompromised

Having the immune system impaired or weakened (as by drugs or illness).

Innovators

The first 2.5% of farmers anxious to try a new brand or idea. Innovators keep abreast of industry developments, use a scientific approach to problem solving and have an ability to deal with abstract ideas.

Internal Analysis

A careful evaluation of a company's capabilities – processes, procedures, resources, expertise, flexibility – to compete in the marketplace. Usually completed as part of the market planning process.

Internet

A global communications network in which PC modem connections and software programs allow individual access to vast quantities of information from a variety of sources.

Kickbacks

A return of a part of the price received for purchase; may result from a confidential agreement or from coercion.

Laggards

The last 16% of farmers to adopt a new idea. These farmers are the least progressive, are averse to taking risks, are less educated and afraid of debt.

Late Majority

The 34 percent of the farmer community that adopts innovation more slowly than average. They are often skeptical about new ideas and tend towards a "wait-and-see" attitude.

Leads

Referrals from a current customer or peer, identifying a potential customer.

Lean Gain

In livestock production, weight gained as muscle rather than fat.

"Linked" Distributor/ Retail Organizations

An organization typically owned by a corporate entity with multiple outlets, where retail stores buy all product from their own corporate distribution business.

MEW

Medicated Early Weaning, a practice by which piglets are weaned from their mothers early and placed on a carefully controlled regimen of nutrition and disease control.

Margin

The difference between purchase price and cost of product.

Market Intelligence

Knowledge about an existing market and the trends in that marketplace; may come from formal research or informal sources.

Market Penetration

Increasing the number of customers who buy a product.

Market Share

A percentage of a market that is controlled by a company, business, or individual: *PENETRATION x CONCENTRATION = SHARE.*

Market Strategy

The planning process that analyses the market, identifies opportunities and develops tactical approaches to achieving goals.

Marketing Mix

The complete set of activities involved in marketing: **P**roduct, **P**rice, **P**lace (distribution), **P**romotion and **P**eople as they relate to a specific product or service.

Marketing

Anticipating the needs and wants of target customers and meeting those needs profitably.

Mark-Up Pricing

A cost-oriented pricing scheme: *COST + % + PRICE.* For example, a 20% mark-up of an item that cost $1.00 is $1.20.

Mission Statement

An official statement of purpose by a company that represents the beliefs, values and goals of the company.

Mode of Action

The biological or chemical activity of a product that results in its performance or efficacy.

Mycoplasmal

Any of a genus *(Mycoplasma)* of microbes that are intermediate in some respects between viruses and bacteria, and cause a variety of animal diseases.

NAFTA

North American Free Trade Agreement.

Need Payoff
A strategic method of closing a sales call wherein the salesperson asks the customer what it would be worth to solve the problem, proposes a solution and asks for agreement on it.

Nematodes
Plant nematodes are microscopic parasitic worms which feed on bacteria, fungi and other soil organisms and may cause yield losses.

New Task Buying
A purchase where the customer has very little experience or knowledge of a product or service.

Non-Selective Herbicide
A herbicide that kills almost every plant species except hybrids or varieties specifically developed to be tolerant to the herbicide's mode of action.

Objections
Statements or questions the customer asks that show doubt, disagreement, or disbelief of stated product benefits.

Open
The beginning of a sales call in which the salesperson establishes rapport with a potential customer in order to establish a firm, profitable, and consistent business relationship.

Opinion Leaders
A customer (or potential customer) who is respected by his or her peers for business success.

Orientation
Training offered to new employees or on new procedures; gives basic familiarity and information.

Overhead Projector
A machine that sends light through a transparency, enlarging and projecting the image onto a screen.

PA System	Public Address System: an apparatus including a microphone and loudspeakers used for broadcasting to a large audience in an auditorium or outdoors.
PC Network	Two or more computers and associated devices that are connected by communication facilities in order to share information and applications.
Parity	Same or similar performance.
Partnership, Potential Product	The total set of results possible beyond the product alone. These results emerge from a strong buyer-seller relationship or "partnership" of efforts and resources.
Penetration Goals	A numerical target that denotes the proportion of all customers a particular product or company expects to sell as a percentage of all customers. *PENETRATION x CONCENTRATION = SHARE.*
Pheromones	A chemical substance produced by an animal as a stimulus to other individuals of the same species.
Point of Sale Materials	Promotional displays, advertisements, flyers, etc., located on or near the sales counter or in other highly visible store locations.
Post Purchase Dissonance	When a customer fears that their expectations of a product or service will not be met after the sale.

Pricing, Gross Margin Target

Pricing products to result in a specific gross margin. For example, a gross margin of 20% on a product with a cost of $1.00 would be $1.25 (20% of the price).

Probing

A method of uncovering customer needs, opportunities and values; asking open-ended, closed-ended, confirming and clarifying questions to assess what the customer wants or thinks they need.

Problems, Non-Performance

Failure of a product to perform as advertised or as promised.

Product Goals

A sales volume or a unit volume target set by a supplier or manufacturer within a defined market.

Product Inquiry

Term used by some companies for customer questions or concerns regarding product performance.

Product Label

The legal statement of a product's formulation, accepted uses, rates and cautions.

Product Usage Segments

Groups of customers who have the same technical need or product use pattern, such as farmers who have problems with morning glory weeds.

Profit Margin Pricing

Refer to gross margin pricing.

Profit

The money remaining from a sale after cost of a product and operating expenses have been paid.

Promotion (Strategies)

Activities that communicate a company's value to the customer.

Prospect

A "prospect" or "prospective account" is an account with whom you are not doing any business yet, or with whom you are doing business only occasionally.

Prospecting

Prospecting describes activities the salesperson undertakes to identify potential new accounts.

Psychographic Segments

Psychographic segments are groups of customers who value similar things or make decisions in similar ways.

Psychographics

Psychographics describe how customers think, or in marketing, how they buy.

Pull

A method of promotion focused on creating end-user demand.

Push

A method of promotion focused on placing product in the distribution channel, making re-sale of the product attractive in the form of incentives, marketing programs, discounts, etc.

Questions, Clarifying

Questions to help the salesperson understand what has been said and heard.

Questions, Closed

Questions that have a factual answer.

Questions, Commitment

Questions asked in a manner that moves the call towards a sale.

Questions, Confirming

Questions that re-state the customer's ideas, issues or values.

Questions, Open

Questions without a right or wrong answer; they encourage the customer to share his or her needs and values.

ROI

Return On Investment. Many measures are possible. The simplest is Profit ÷ Investment.

Rebuy, Straight

Purchase of a standard item from the same vendor on a regular basis.

Rebuy, Modified

When a customer considers making changes in an existing product order or service, price or supplier.

Replant Policies

Guidelines for providing seed to farmers when the first planting is lost due to weather or adverse conditions; "50% replant" means seed is provided at 50% of the normal cost.

Resistance, Active

A form of objection that often involves clearly stating a reason not to buy.

Resistance, Passive

A form of objection that involves no clearly stated reasons, but rather a series of delaying or avoidance tactics.

Respiratory Disease Complex

Acute respiratory disease caused by a combination of stress, viral infection and invasion of the lungs by certain bacteria.

Retention

Maintaining a customer from one year to the next.

Rolling Herd Average (Production)

Rolling herd average is the average amount of milk produced per cow in a dairy herd in a year.

Salary, Plus Commission	A compensation package that includes a set annual salary and in addition, an agreed-upon commission dependent on sales.
Salary, Straight	Compensation as a guaranteed, predictable, salary.
Sales Presentation	A formal or informal sharing of key benefits of a product or service, organized around the needs of the customer.
Sales Volume Goals	The amount of sales in units or dollars that must be reached within a given time increment, such as quarterly or annual sales.
Segmentation	The process of dividing your market into segments or sub-markets in order to maintain or increase and improve efficiency.
Segments	A group of customers or prospects with similar needs and/or buying processes.
Selling Responsibilities, Direct	How the salesperson implements the sales process and works when face-to-face with the customer.
Selling Responsibilities, Indirect	Tasks the salesperson must carry out to prepare themselves to sell, satisfy the customers they have sold, and to create a fertile climate for continued selling efforts.
Selling Strategy	A plan to get and keep the business of an account.

Sensitivity Test

A diagnostic procedure that evaluates whether a given pathogen is vulnerable to a specific antimicrobial substance.

Situation Analysis

A pre-planning phase in the development of marketing strategy or plan in which a company examines all the factors affecting the market, such as customer needs, competition, and capabilities.

Software, Contact Management

Software programs that allow the salesperson to manage daily account contacts and keep a record of important account information that can be retrieved quickly and accurately.

Status Quo

The way things are now.

Strategy

A strategy is a plan to assemble all available resources such as skills, knowledge, energy, time and people in order to decide the best way to organize and use them to achieve objectives.

Subverbal (Subtext)

Conversation or dialogue which happens below the surface level; subverbal conversation is a conversation which is ostensibly about one topic but there is a secondary message.

SWOT Analysis

A step in market analysis, based on a company's **S**trengths, **W**eaknesses, **O**pportunities and **T**hreats.

Telemarketing	The use of phone representatives to contact clients or potential clients to sell them a product or service, or to support past sales.
Territory	The geographical area or group of customers from which a salesperson is expected to generate sales.
Testimonials	Statements of witness from customers who have positive experience with a product, service or organization.
Tillage, Conservation	Preparing the soil for planting and avoiding excess cultivation in such a way so that 30 % + residue remains on the soil.
Tillage, Traditional	Plowing the soil and cultivating or disking plowed ground so that less than 30% crop residue cover (stalks, etc. left after harvest) remains on the soil surface.
Trade-In	Redemption of a used item or product as partial credit toward purchase of a newer item.
Training, In-House	Training which occurs on-site within the company.
Training, Ongoing	Regular, periodic, formal training offered by a company to assist the sales force in keeping up to date with developments in the field.
Transgenic Products	Genetically-engineered products created by inserting a foreign gene or genes into the genetic makeup of an organism.

Transparencies — Clear plastic squares upon which text or a picture is placed (as on film) and viewed by light shining through it or by projection.

Trials, Controlled — Research tests of a new product's safety and/or efficacy under strict experimental protocols.

Trials, Demonstration — Sample use of a product or service to allow a potential customer and/or others to view the product under normal use conditions.

USDA — United States Department of Agriculture.

Validating the Mixer (at a feed plant) — To test or "assay" the finished feed from a mixer to ensure accurate amounts and even distribution of all feed ingredients.

VCR — Video cassette recorder: a videotape recorder that uses videocassettes.

VIP — Very Important Person. A person of great influence or prestige; especially a high official with special privileges.

Value Bundle — The total combination of proposed goods and services suggested by the agriseller to the customer.

Value, Intangible — Any value or result that is not quantifiable but is based on the perception of value by the customer, e.g., a salesperson's rapport with the customer.

Value, Tangible

Any value or result that is quantifiable via testing, use, or sales.

Value-Added Activities

An incidental or deliberate extension or expansion of a contracted service that increases the worth of the product or service to the customer.

WTO

World Trade Organization.

Water-Soluble Packaging

A container used for pesticides that allows the product to be dropped directly into an agitating spray tank where the package dissolves, resulting in significantly lower mixer exposure and less time spent mixing chemicals.

Wholesale

The sale of commodities in quantity for resale (as by a retail merchant)

Index